I NEED TO KNOW:

The Lost Music Interviews

Bill DeYoung

ST. PETERSBURG
PRESS

Dedicated to the memories of

Dave Hunter
Diane Chun

CONTENTS

An Introduction   i

1   Tom Petty: Everything is done with a southern accent   1

2   Neil Young: Get back to the country   11

3   Tom Petty: Rednecks in space   18

4   Tom Petty: The talk on the street says you might go solo   27

5   Seals and Crofts: We may never pass this way again   38

6   Mary Hopkin: 'She's a Joan Baez type, but we'll soon alter that'   52

7   George Martin: 'These are my boys, the greatest in the world'   63

8   Tom Petty: Just the hits   72

9   Emmylou Harris: Sweetheart of the rodeo   79

10   Linda Ronstadt: An act of Dolly   109

11   Dave Mason: We just disagree   114

12   Guy Clark: Step inside my house   136

13   Neil Young: 'The World does not need another awards show'   144

14   Rodney Crowell: The Houston kid   151

15   Rosanne Cash: Love hurts   183

16   Merle Haggard: Pride in what I am   187

17   Stephen Stills: As I come of age   209

18   The Bangles: Girls keep swinging   221

19   Bo Diddley: 'The day is coming, and that's a guarantee'   248

20   Jethro Tull: Living with the past   259

21   Linda Ronstadt: 'I grew up thinking I was a boy soprano'   271

22   *Something Extra: A conversation with Robert Duvall*   282

23   *Something Extra: A conversation with Gregory Peck*   291

An Introduction

"Lost" is a subjective word. About half of the interviews collected in this book were conducted for some newspaper, magazine or other. I transcribed what I needed and tossed the cassette tapes into a box, with the vague idea that they might be useful someday. Life intervened, as it does, and they were largely forgotten. Now, many years after the fact, they've been fully transcribed – in effect, the raw, recorded Q&As were "lost."

I also wrote a dozen or so cover stories for the record collecting magazine *Goldmine*. These involved several hours of taped interviews with the artists. Included in *I Need to Know* are some of the best of these. The actual tapes have long since vanished, but I think they're pretty good stories on their own. And since they were published exactly once, in a niche periodical, they too fall into the "lost" category.

Music has always been an important part of my life. In 1976, when I was 17 years old, I wrote my first story for the hometown newspaper, the *St. Petersburg Times*. It was a concert review, although I don't remember the performer. It was thrilling to see my name in the paper, it made my parents proud, and after I'd done three or four more of them I began to think I could get used to this. I enjoyed the attention and I loved the idea that I was communicating with lots and lots of people.

Then I began writing feature stories about music and musicians. I interviewed them. Getting paid to talk about something I was already passionate about seemed just about perfect; if I could be a professional writer, maybe I'd never have to get a real job. That was the prevailing logic.

Journalism, of course, is a very real job, and a pretty difficult one, whether you're an investigative reporter, a news writer, a columnist, a sports analyst, a proofreader or a page designer. Or an arts writer and editor, which is what I became. You have to learn a little about everything in the newsroom, and you have to understand your beat – what you're writing about, every day, and how it works in your community – because if you don't, you won't last long. Newspaper journalism, which was my life for 35 years, is all-consuming.

It wasn't always easy, and it wasn't always fun, but I wouldn't trade the training I got, the experiences I had or the friendships I made during those years.

There were other newspapers, and other music periodicals, and in the 2000s I started getting hired as a liner-note writer for CD reissues. At the end of that decade I began working on *Skyway*, my first book, and there have been life and job changes aplenty – lots of water under the bridge, as it were – since.

The artists' lives and careers moved on too, of course. Think of these interviews as snapshots. Ghosts in the flashbulb pop. We were all so much older then. We're younger than that now.

Bill DeYoung
June, 2019

BILL DEYOUNG

Rest in Peace Tom Petty, George Martin, Merle Haggard, Bo Diddley, Guy Clark, Susanna Clark, Bonnie Owens, Fuzzy Owen, Rick Jaeger, Tommy LiPuma and Gregory Peck.

John Siebenthaler/Siebenthaler Creative

1. Tom Petty (1985)
Everything is done with a southern accent

Tom Petty loved the Don CeSar, the garish luxury hotel on the south end of St. Petersburg Beach. Built in the 1920s, the opulent Don was a favorite of Jazz Age socialites, celebrities and muckety-mucks; its cobbled Moorish-meets-Mediterranean design looked like nothing else along Florida's west coast, and because the façade was painted pink, it stood out like a sand castle carved out of cotton candy. The rock star and his family were partial to the 8th-floor suite, with its enormous, open-air patio overlooking the Gulf of Mexico, and when Tom Petty & the Heartbreakers' tour itinerary included a week's worth of dates in Florida, the Don acted as home base. They'd fly out of the airport in Tampa, play the show, fly back and overnight in the sweet embrace of the "Pink Lady."

In April 1985, Petty and company spent three days camped at the Don, trailed by an MTV film crew making a 30-minute documentary about the new album, Southern Accents. *Petty conducted phone and in-person interviews with the global music press while he was there, too.*

Because I was the guy from the band's hometown newspaper, the Gainesville Sun, *I was invited down to chat. And my visit happened to coincide with filming the big finale of the MTV special, a hastily-arranged concert on the Astroturf, out there on Petty's patio. I was one of just a handful of outsiders allowed to watch. He and the band played for 45 minutes as the cameras rolled. When it was all over, he put his guitar down, walked over and shook my hand - taking a moment to show me the scars from his recent hand surgery - and we went inside to talk about* Southern Accents, *and how he got from there to here.*

You left Gainesville in 1974. Was there a feeling in your mind that "I don't care if I never come back here?"

No, I don't think so, no more than anyone else who leaves home. Most people get bored with their hometown. One thing I've noticed from traveling is everybody's saying, whatever town you're in, "There's nothing going on here." Whenever you ask, they always say "This place is dead." And so we always wonder where it isn't dead.

But no, I never had anything against it. I just wanted to make records. The other thing was, we were young and we wanted to go out and do things, make records and be on TV. And play places other than we'd played a dozen times. Or more. It was as simple as that.

Then once we were in California, it's a much easier place to work. For a while I thought about coming down to the South to make the record, and then I thought no, because I need technicians, and I need this and that, and there I can pick up the phone and get it. And here, it's not orientated toward recording.

Even before we went to California we went to Macon. There was a record company up there, and they weren't interested because it didn't sound like Marshall Tucker or whatever. And we went "Well, it's L.A. or New York. And New York's gonna be a cold place to starve." So we went to California. Which is a pleasant place to be hungry.

One record company after another turned Mudcrutch down when you went to L.A. Why?

Well, we were pretty different from what was going on at the time. What was going on at the time was sort of extended guitar solos. It was the '70s, say no more. It was the mid '70s, and the stuff we were doing, if you hear those first albums, was pretty crude. Snappy. I remember they used to say "The songs are so short!" and "They're too short!" They didn't understand.

And I'm jumping ahead, but it was really not until the Heartbreakers went to England, where the first album was a hit and we were already headlining. And we were still playing bars in L.A. We were still playing the Whiskey and opening for Blondie or whoever.

Short, punchy songs were cool in England.

It was happening there, and we'd seen the punk thing come down. We'd already seen it before America really got a look at it. When we came back to Hollywood, we were playing the Whiskey and all of a sudden there started to be a little club scene again. And people started coming in from there. It just slowly built.

What are you real proud of – songs, moments, lyrics?

I don't know, I'd have to think. Today we were doing some old songs, like "American Girl" I hadn't heard in a long time. I sang that today and I thought "Now, this isn't a bad song." And "Southern Accents," the song, I was pretty proud of that. I thought I really got one there. Got a big bass in the boat there, I knew. "Rebels," when I wrote that I knew it was good.

When did you start writing lyrics? Were you a poetry guy in high school?

I never read poetry. I've been reading some poetry for the first time. I've been reading some Dylan Thomas. But I never cared for poetry too much. I never saw it as poetry until I started reading the reviews. Sometimes we'll pick it up and go "Look – we wrote a book!"

What's your earliest song that got on a Heartbreakers album?

Probably the first track we did on the first album – maybe "Strangered in the Night"?

What about the first song you ever wrote, do you remember? Was it like "Runaway," A minor, G …

Yeah, that's as much as I can remember. It was kinda A minor, D minor … probably had a G in there. And it just grew from that, slowly. There was point with Mudcrutch, around '71 or so, around there we made a commitment to "Let's really try to make our own music." And it got very hard to work at that point, and make a living. We didn't want to cover other people's songs. We wanted to be doing our own songs, and find an audience for it. And it made things difficult. It made the gigs a lot more selective.

It's the same way now, with clubs and bands.

Yeah, I think it's a shame. In England, it's not like that at all. People accept what the band's gonna play. Here, they almost want them to have those big collars that come up to the shoulders, and play the hits. Really quietly. We couldn't take that.

Mudcrutch was actually a real good group. It was just way too far ahead of its time. To coin a phrase. It reminds me of groups like R.E.M. and stuff. It was a lot like that – we might play country, or we might play heavy metal. There were a lot of different styles of music contained within the group. Which might have been its downfall, really. Because it could never settle into any one particular direction.

You still go through that now, though, don't you? I understand you cut different versions of the songs on Southern Accents.

Well, it's really just like a craft, sort of – there's a craft side where if you know how to do that, then you have the luxury of finding the best version of the song. What really comes across as the most believable version.

When you talk about it all, it sounds a lot more planned than it really is. It's really just going on; there's no one really thinking it out too far. I love records to have a lot of textures throughout the album. I hate an album that's just the one deal all the way through.

Is it still fun to make records? I know you said you could live in the studio.

That was before this album! I do live in the studio, lately. But yes, there's nothing like it. It's great. It can also be living hell at times. This project was hell, you know, it was one of the worst times in my life.

Why?

It's just, you put a lot of pressure on yourself. I tend to push myself pretty hard, and get really frustrated with myself. And when you're that frustrated, and it's with yourself, you can really get pretty miserable. If you're waiting for magic to happen, and it won't happen, there's nothing you can do but wait for it. And that can get strenuous.

There were huge ups when something went right, and then there were a lot of times when things got really difficult.

With this album, the question is, why now? The fact that you're from the South isn't something you'd talked about a lot in your music. So why now?

Well, I think everyone knows where we're from. We were just dealing with the present most of the time, and we were in California. When I was down here on the last tour, whenever that was, I started realizing there was a lot of material down here. We were staying here (at the Don CeSar), and we were flying on a private jet, going to Atlanta and coming back, going to Miami or Gainesville and back. We were spending a pretty good amount of time in the South. We saw a lot of people we hadn't seen in a long time, and I don't know how it came to me: 'This is interesting to me.' That going along with the fact that there's so much good music, rock and R&B and even jazz and stuff, from the South that I thought it might be interesting to try to tinge it with these musics and write something.

So I started writing the album a good two and a half years ago, maybe more. The first things written were "Rebels" and "Trailer," and a few more, and I eventually wrote about 20 or 30 songs before the album was begun. During this year we had off. It was a lot easier album to write than to record.

Why was that?

Beats me! Because I did a lot more experimenting than I usually do. I wanted to do something different. Sometimes a song would be cut in three different arrangements. We'd do one and then I'd write three more verses, and that would dictate a whole 'nother approach. I wanted to make an album different from what we'd been doing. If you're going to be a group for nine years, then there's not a lot of point in doing it unless the music's growing and it's going somewhere. That and the fact that I was completely bored with what I was hearing on the radio and stuff. Pretty passé for me, for the most part.

If you look at anybody that's been around very long, they've had a few drastic changes. There are too many people these days, especially in American rock, that are just really content to keep making the same record over and over. We weren't trying to make a hit record; we were just trying to make one that we liked.

Yet it's at No. 10 in its third week on the chart.

Yeah, it's selling a lot of records. That pleasantly surprises me a slight bit, because it's so different from what we'd been doing. I have this theory that if you have a good song, the whole game's over. Once you have a good song, the rest of it is just making a record. Not really hard for us to do.

The hardest thing about this record was agreeing - we were dealing with 48 tracks. Some of those songs, I mixed for more than a month at a time. One song at a time. It was very meticulous work, moreso than I want to do again for a while, I think.

Could these songs have come at an earlier time? Could Long After Dark have been the album where you were thinking about the South?

You can only do things when they come up, you know? I think there were times the South has come up – even with "American Girl," where it mentions 441. But this is the most sort of thematic album we've ever attempted. It was a little bit ambitious, really. I didn't expect it to take quite as long. At first, it was intended to be a double album, so I knew that was going to really take a long time. That's why I built the studio and everything 'cause I knew that this was going to be too long to just block-book a studio and sit there.

So you cut 30 songs. With regard to sequencing, how meticulous are you? 'This fits in with what we want to say, but this doesn't …'

Pretty meticulous, I'd say (laughing). This one was really sort of my baby, this album. I went out on a limb with everyone around me, even the band. There were those days when they thought I might be nuts, you know? All I could hope for was to finish it and like it myself. That's all I can really ever do.

You acknowledge, certainly, the people around and their reaction to it – but as I'm making it, I can hear it in my head. Sort of, and until it did what I wanted it to do, I wasn't happy. So that is what took a great deal of time. I was real choosy. And there was a lot of songs that didn't get on; after 20 minutes on a side, you start to lose the sound. So song selection was a couple months, just deciding what was gonna go out and what was gonna go in.

I got the sense that you were a little bit down after the last tour.

I was tired of touring. I didn't want to tour any more. It had been a lot of years of touring, then going back in, and 10 love songs and here we are! And then back. I just hit a point at the end of that tour – though it was a very enjoyable your, musically, I just was ready to stop. I wanted to stop everything for a year and try to resume living.

Because it was dawning on me that it's impossible to write about things if you're not out there living a fairly normal life. If you're in a plane and a car and a room for years on end, things to write about leave you. This album was written really quickly, in a couple of different phases. It wasn't hard at all to write the songs. It had to do with waking up at a certain time every day, or things as regimented as that. Going in a store and buying things. Just having the time to hang around, you know? I went over to England and did nothing for a while. I took trips. Me and Stan would go to Las Vegas and hang around, and it was real good. It was very relaxing.

Was that new for you?

It was, because there had never been time, for years, to do anything at all. Because even if there's a break, there's something hanging over your head: "In a week, we've got to be in England," or "We've got to be here, and then there's going to be three more months of this," and it just to be where I quit. I didn't want to do it any more.

The band all got involved in lots of others things – 'cause they'd play the rest of their lives, I think – so while they were out doing that, it was the first time I ever had that much time to write without any pressure, and it was fantastic. You can't sit down and write under pressure. It's awful for me, anyway. So I was just doing it for something to occupy my time.

How far down the line do you think things out?

Not far any more! I got pretty tired of doing that. Well, you know, there's a lot of people planning all the time. Right now I think I'm planned up through the end of the summer. That's the shortest period of time in a long time.

Two years ago, Mike was telling me that you were in the process of doing the final mixes on a live album. What happened?

I did that album and finished it. Double album, cut the acetates, then I went home and played it. And I never went back in and played it for a few weeks. And then I thought "Why ain't I listening to this?" I just got hung up. I wanted to do something new. It just sounded like more of the same to me. It's real good; it'll probably come out at some point. The timing felt weird to me. It had a lot to do with how long we were away, because when I said I was gonna take a year off I thought I was gonna put the live album out. I just ex-ed it for the time being.

Even in *Long After Dark* I was wanting to do something much more experimental, but was kind of committed to finish what was started. So the live album, I did finish it, and I hope it comes out, 'cause it's good.

It was made up of tours from '76 to the last tour. There was 22, twenty-something songs on it.

I imagine it's nice to not put pressure on yourself, and have to book specific time in a studio and have it done by a certain release date …

Yeah, I couldn't have made this album in a commercial studio, because it was much too erratic. When it's gonna happen, it's gonna happen. We're not the sort of group that can …

it's not like we can say "Tuesday at 8" if you want to do it right now. And the other thing was, I didn't want to spend a few million dollars in studio time to make an album. And I've always wanted a studio at home, anyway, because I don't like doing demos. I'd rather just do it. We never beat the demo; it's always like "Why does the demo feel better than the one we're doing?"

I heard that "Rebels" was partly the demo, and that "Don't Come Around Here No More" was your demo, embellished.

That's the only time I sang that song. Never sang it a second time. I think all the vocals are on the album are the first time I did it. I don't think I did any vocal overdubs.

A lot of those things were real immediate. Like "Don't Come Around Here No More," the basic track was done in an hour. I worked with it for another six months after that.

Did you intend for that to be a single, to make people jump at how different it is?

I think David and I wrote that song in about 30 minutes of meeting each other. Once it was like "Let's write this song," I remember David saying "Let's make a single. Because if we're going to work together and do this, we may as well do something really good. And if it's not really good, let's just erase it when we're done." It was that attitude.

You can do that when you have a studio in your house.

"It Ain't Nothing to Me," I think we had like two verses done when we started cutting the track. 'Cause we were writing it up in the bedroom – then it was just "OK, something's happening, downstairs here we come."

What is that song saying? I can't find the southern point of view there.

I think it's a cynical song, in some respects. We were watching the TV news, and writing real fast while we were watching the TV news. And it also has a sense of humor, more than anything. I just think it's funny that a lot of times issues that seem so important in the media, when you actually get down to the guy they're talking about, it's completely irrelevant beyond "I wanna be rich. And not work."

That's my theory. If the bomb comes down, it's not going to matter anyway.

I know! And everyone'll be out disco dancing. It won't matter. And that's all that's about. I thought that was a pretty southern song. The whole idea was, it was some riff we'd heard in a New Orleans jazz record. We were trying to make a New Orleans-y kind of dance track, horn thing going on.

"Mary's New Car" is the one that seems almost out of place on the album. After all this experimentation, it's a pretty straightforward Heartbreakers-sounding track.

The Heartbreakers never used horns. Psychedelic. Saxes. And that echo on the voice is pretty different. I don't know, I just thought that it was a good cruise.

Was it always going to be in the album sequence? Was it always there in your mind?

It was always there, yeah. It was one of the first things we did. There's three or four, usually, that are moveable. We did a sequence I think the day before the album was mastered. We never even did a sequence. And we were always a little bit nervous, saying "Boy, I hope this stuff works together." Because I knew it was gonna start with "Rebels" and end with "The Best of Everything," but beyond that it was "I hope this stuff blends." That was the first sequence I did, the one that came out. I sequenced it once and then played it, and went "Wow. It works."

Let's talk about "The Best of Everything." You'd been playing that one live as far back as '79.

Robbie Robertson wanted to use a song in this movie he was doing. And I said "Yeah, well, you can have this." We edited a verse out that used to be there, to make it a little more concise. Then Robbie said "I've got a great idea for some horns." And he did. And when I heard it, I said "Boy, that's a whole new dimension to the thing that I hadn't heard in my head." And then it dawned on me that we could use some input. Because we'd been such a tight little ship for long, not allowing anyone to be around. I said "I think on this album we should use our friends and let them give us input. And if it don't work, it don't work. But if it does, even if it kicks us in a different direction, it's gonna make this project more interesting."

So Robbie was the first one that came into my mind, like boy, there's a lot more we can do than just guitars and drums.

The song then sat for another two years.

There was never a place for it. I didn't think it'd fit into *Long After Dark*. On that tour, I played Nick Lowe that mix that Robbie had done. I was already working on the southern album. Nick didn't know that, though. He said "Boy, this is really southern." He loved it. He kept playing it. And I was thinking "Yeah … I got a great slot for this!" I'm glad I waited instead of just slotting it in someplace. It seems to sum up the whole thing nicely.

Like "Don't Do Me Like That," "The Best of Everything" was an older song that turned up on a later album. Ron Blair - who left the band quite a while ago - is playing bass. Do you have tracks lying around that suddenly appeal to you later: "Let's put this one out now"?

Oh, yeah. There's quite an extensive tape library of all the stuff left over, because I tend to work a long time in the studio. I spend probably an inordinate amount of time in there. So yeah, there're a lot of stuff lying around. Just from this album alone, I know there's another 20 tracks. There's probably six that I completely finished, mixing them, that I didn't know till the last minute. Maybe six songs left over. And then if you really went through … I mean, you could fill that kitchen with the tape.

Ron also plays bass on "Between Two Worlds," on Long After Dark, which was Howie's first record with the band …

Actually, it was the first sessions for that album. I think he played on maybe one or two sessions before he was gone. Ron keeps poppin' up, doesn't he?

Was that the real story, that he quit because he didn't want to go on the road any more?

As far as I know, yeah. That wasn't a manufactured story. I didn't go up and say "Ron, I hate you. Leave." It was more gradual than that. He was just slowly and slowly fading away, it seemed like. Fading far away from us. We're all pretty close, and when we didn't see him socially, ever, and in a lot of sessions he just wasn't there ... Mike would play the bass, or Duck Dunn played a lot of bass for a while. I don't really know what it was, just he was just disillusioned, I think. I think he was tired of ... Big Business rolls into the picture. And I think Ron was just a pretty casual person.

And it wasn't like we were sad to see him go, either. Because it's no fun having somebody in the group who isn't really into it, you know? He was very nice when he called me and just said "I really don't ever want to get on the bus again. I can't take it." And I understand.

Was "Trailer" supposed to be on the album?

It was gonna be in the album, and then there just wasn't time, and I had to make a decision. I said "Look, let's just put it on the single, and that way people can have the single and they have a supplement if they want." I've got a jukebox in my house, and when I stuck it on there, it sounded great.

It's so much more fun getting an extra track. It always looks a little bit lazy when it's just another track from the album. I like it when there's an extra track on the back of the single.

Right now, on the next single, they're asking me what's gonna be on the back? And I don't know, because none of that stuff's been mixed down. And I've got to find a day to get I and mix the stuff. I'm gonna really try hard to put something on the back.

The Beatles used to do that.

Yeah, and in those days, they didn't always put the single on the album, which just isn't done any more. There were times over the last couple of years when I'd say "Can I put out a single?" And they'd say "No, because we won't have an album to go with it." The way the big machine works is they don't want to put their power behind a record until they have an album to work.

Give me an example. In your mind, what would have been a great one-off single, no LP?

I thought "Don't Come Around Here No More" was a single. It was made like, say, "Good Vibrations" was a single. We wanted to make something that was very different, that was gonna come on the radio and sound really exciting and different. I never worked so intensely on a record, on the production of a record, so hard. And I would've liked to just send it out as a single. Eventually I did get it out about a month before the album.

And I'm still really jazzed at the way it's doing. I love it when I hear it on the radio, still — it's just wow, listen to that, you know? It comes on after Michael Jackson, and "A Night in

Bangkok," and then all of a sudden there's this "Byow bing bing…" Cracks me up.

It's Number 15 this week. It is, in all honesty, an unlikely candidate for a hit single.

It's funny, there were two camps when I played it for people. There were people would go completely religious about it, like just have to hear it all night. And then there was the people that just sort of looked at me like I'd lost my mind. Which in a way encouraged me; I'd think "Well, if it's getting that drastic a reaction it's definitely something worth putting out here." If it's shaking people up, it's usually pretty good.

Because I wasn't getting like "Oh, that's disgusting," I was getting "What IS that?" "What is on your mind?"

Bugs, my roadie, says that that song could be a Time-Life book series, the making of that song was such an extreme experience. It was very layered. Dave Stewart really likes layers. The first thing to get used to, when I was working with him, was that sometimes Dave is thinking six layers and I was used to always thinking "The song is like *this*." I'd say, but there's a huge hole here, and he goes "Yes, but I hear this, this, this and this." Ah, OK. But the musicians would be really confused – "you want me to what?" I just want you to play, you know.

The hardest thing about that one was that there was 48 tracks of instruments and voices, and when it came time to mix it the arrangement could go a million ways, depending on what batch of faders were up or down. So I had to mix it for at least a month, off and on in seven-day stretches. I think four different times. And then finally I got the version that came out.

Ebet Roberts

2. Neil Young (1985)
Get back to the country

Sept. 16, 1985. The very first Farm Aid concert, in Champaign, Illinois, was six days away. Young had just put out Old Ways, *a pure country music album, and was on tour with a band of Nashville cats called the International Harvesters. The album, and the show (which stopped in Gainesville this night) were as far away from rock 'n' roll as he'd ever ventured. And despite his insistence in the interview that he was tired of his old songs, and his declaration that "I'm more concerned now with family, and with songs about growing up and growing old, and surviving," he wound up abandoning the country music thing almost as quickly as he'd adopted it. He was doing something completely different in 1986. Very Neil.*

What he never let go of was his activism on behalf of the American family farm. At this writing (2019), he, Willie Nelson and John Mellencamp have headlined a Farm Aid benefit every single year since this first one. In this conversation (which took place on his tour bus, in the venue parking lot after the show) he is determined to explain why farm reform is so important, and why he'd written and paid for an open letter to then-president Ronald Reagan urging him to take action.

He reads the letter, which would be published four days later in USA Today, *out loud to me as I'm sitting there, 26 years old and stunned that I'm sitting alone in a tiny room with one of my biggest musical heroes. I tried to act cool, and I'm sure I failed.*

Another snapshot of another moment in time.

How did you get involved with Farm Aid?

Well, I got involved in it through Willie, and Bob Dylan. Bob said what he said at Live Aid: It's too bad we couldn't give some of this money to our own farmers who are in so much trouble. And that started it. Willie said "Do you think he really meant that?" And I said, if he said it, be believes it. I told Willie I saw Bob after the show, and we were talking. He wasn't just blowing air. He feels it. He's into it. He wants to help the farmer.

But he didn't know what he said was gonna start this. Willie said "Well, maybe we can get something going like Live Aid and help the farmer." It was Willie who came up with the idea from Bob's inspiration. And I just happened to be there right at the time when Willie was having the idea. And I backed him up on it all the way, you know.

He's the perfect man to do it, and I'm the perfect man to help him do it.

It's something I can relate to, I understand the problem, so I immediately took it upon myself … first of all, I gave myself a position … I became the fact-finder, basically. I interviewed all of the organizations before Willie got there to Champaign. I had the sheets of paper, and all that they stood for, and whether they were salaried and everything. And what they wanted. And then we had the meeting, and when somebody's get up and start talking, I'd have all the backup paper and show it to Willie …

I love Willie. He's just a wonderful man. And there couldn't be anybody better. He's like the President of Music. And I'm one of his helpers. And I feel very lucky to be around him.

I saw you on a TV talk show, which I know you don't do. Which led me to believe that you must really believe in this.

Oh, yeah, I wouldn't be doing it to sell my album or anything like that. I have to have a reason, because if my music doesn't sell my records, nothing will. So I don't want to get out there and promote it that way.

The main thing we found out while we were there was that they (the farmers' organizations) don't care about the money. They don't want a handout. They don't want us to bail them out of their loans. They want farm reform. They want a policy change. After I got all my facts together and everything, I realized there was this consistent thing running through all the organizations.

So that's my thing. I've already been to Washington, I've met with the Senators that are backing his bill, I've met with Congressmen who support it. I've had a lot of meetings. I talked with Senator Harkin, who wrote the bill, two or three times a day. Keeping on top of what the developments are, putting together the advertising campaign for it. Which is basically me, and different Senators.

I volunteered myself as kind of a rock 'n' roll representative, on the political side. Nothing could be more obvious; this is a very political issue and I'm right in the middle of it.

Why has no other issue taken your fancy so strongly over the years – why did this particular thing go right to your heart?

Because it's basically an American problem of unbelievable proportions. And it's so subtle that if someone doesn't enlarge upon it no one will understand it. And that's what I can do. I have a grip on what it is.

I've written an open letter, that I've paid for – I bought a page in *USA Today*. And it's gonna be in on Friday coming up. So it'll be in all of Farm Aid weekend. And then next week after the is the vote on the bill.

I just feel that this issue is so important because it's the family – it's not just the family farmer, it's the family business in America which is threatened. People don't really understand that if the administration continues on its present course, the family farmer in this country is finished.

That's not a catch-all phrase to get attention, it's the truth. There won't be any more family farmers. Little farmhouses along the freeways, there's not going to be any families living in them. It's gonna be over.

So I think it's a time to make a point that America stands behind its own. We can't let this happen. Because what kind of signal does that send to the family business throughout the United States?

We don't care enough about own families to support them? Is this what we're really saying?

I'll just read you this letter. If I had a copy of it, I'd give it to you, 'cause it makes the point. This is an open letter to the President of the United States and all American people. I stayed up all night last night writing this letter. I had already written the letter and sent it to *USA Today*, and I was reading it and decided it was a piece of shit. That I hadn't done a good job. So I had to write it over again:

"An open letter.

His great-grampa worked this farm, his grampa and his daddy worked it. He's 30 years old. His wife and children at his side, he stands in the window of the old farmhouse. A car comes up the driveway. A man in a suit is behind the wheel, his briefcase at his

side. Today is the last day for this family farm. Tomorrow is foreclosure day.

President Reagan, in many ways you have been a great leader. Today, as you read this, your advisors are telling you that America must be strong. America must compete in the world food market. They advise you to keep prices way down, lower than ever. You know that this is killing the family farm, and that only the large conglomerate farm units will survive.

Mr. President, you have a decision to make. Will the farmer be replaced by the farm operator? Will the family farm in America die as a result of your administration? Will the family system in America be dealt a fatal blow right at the core, sending a tremor of fear through every small business in America? What will this do to the American spirit?

Pictures of your family are neatly framed in the Oval Office, showing your love and reminding you why you took on the great task of making America strong again. At the end of the day, your wife looks in your eyes and tells you she believes in you. All over America, farmers' wives do the same. But sleep does not come easily for you tonight, nor does it for them.

As we sell our low-priced food products to the world market, we undercut the family farmers in those countries, forcing them out of business. They turn to cash crops such as textiles and other non-food related products, in an effort to earn money to buy American food. Must we destroy their native food chain, and their family farmers along with it?

What happens if we have a drought, or some other act of God that ruins our crops here at home? Then we have to raise our world food prices. What will our world food market customers do with no native food, and not enough money to buy ours? Consider the consequences for America, and for the families of the world.

Senator Tom Harkin has a bill, the Harkin Farm Policy Reform Act of 1985. Farm Aid, and the family farmers of America, consider this to be the only way to save the American family farm. It does not increase the deficit, and it passes on only a 3.5 percent cost increase to the American consumer. It raises the price of a loaf of bread by only one penny. It costs the taxpayer less than any other policy idea presented at this time.

We urge you to stand beside us and save the family farm. The Harkin Farm Reform Act of 1985 comes to a vote in Congress three days after the Farm Aid concert. All Americans interested in preserving our family system should call their Congressmen by Tuesday, September 24, 1985 in support of this bill.

To the American people and the President of the United States, we say: Save the family farm. God bless you all, Neil Young from Farm Aid."

That's beautiful – do you think it'll have an impact?

Yeah. I think it'll have some impact. We'll find out. It's had a great impact on everyone who's heard it in Washington, because it comes from such a different place.

In layman's terms – for someone like me – what does this act actually do?

Well, it re-structures the loans without taking money and subsidizing the farmers. It just re-structures their debts so that they can pay them off. And by giving them a 30 percent cost increase and parity – parity is a reference of our prices to the world food market – it gives them 30 percent more profit than they're making today. And re-structures their loans. All at a cost of 3.5 percent to the consumer.

We're not gonna sit back and let this happen without making a lot of noise. And we think we can change it

The suicide rate among the American farmer is up by 25 percent this year. It's amazing how important this is. See, if we sell the family farmer down the river for conglomerate farms, and change the structure in America, then every small business I this country will be petrified. I mean, if we sell the family farmer down the river, who gives a shit about anybody else?

There is absolutely no doubt, in anyone's mind, that the family farm will die in this country.

It's amazing, the strength of a musician and a politician side by side. It's something that no one has seen before. It is awesome and it attracts an incredible amount of attention. This is a cause that calls for us to be side by side.

And we're all older. I'm older now that I was at Woodstock. I have a family, and we pass food around the table.

I noticed during tonight's show that you only played two songs from the new album. Are you drifting away from it already?

Not really. There were a lot of songs that are from the next album. And there's a lot of country in those songs.

I can't go on singing the same songs forever. I have to turn it over. All those songs on the record, I sang for two and a half years on the road. While I was being sued for making a county record, and they stopped me from making my record. So I just went out and sang the songs. I've done two tours supporting this record already, where I sang all the songs. So I'm finished with it. I gotta move on to the next one. I'll be putting out another album within six months. Basically a country record. It'll be a little harder. I'll play a little more electric guitar on it.

I'm bringing rock 'n' roll and country a little more together on the next album.

The material on Old Ways is different from your earlier roadhouse country kind of music. There's a very different flavor to it; It's … smooth. I wondered why you did that?

It's just the way it came out. It was recorded the same way, it's all live. It's not an overdubbed, smooth record. The musicians are all older, more accomplished players. If you listen to it, it's real music; we're all singing and playing all at once.

Why did you swing into country this time?

It's always been there. And I just feel more comfortable with country people, and with country music. I'm not gonna stop playing rock 'n' roll – you heard some of the new stuff we did tonight. "Grey Riders" is just a Neil Young song. But there's a fiddle in it, a steel guitar in it. But that's nothing new. I've been doing that for a long time. None of this is really anything new.

I think during *Reactor, Trans* and *Everybody's Rockin'* I was sort of searching for something. I don't feel at home with mainstream rock 'n' roll today at all. I don't associate myself with it.

Because you can't?

Just because I don't. I just don't like it. Some of it's good – I think Springsteen's got some really good songs, and his delivery's real good and he's sincere, and it's good rock 'n' roll. And I think there's good groups out there.

But you know, I've been doing it for 20 years, and there's something about my music that's … I'm just more at home with country music. At least country players, and those kind of people. I'm just more at home with them. I just feel better.

Why was that? After 20 years, why is it "Get Back to the Country"?

Maybe rock 'n' roll, to me, I look at it and it looks like a dead end street. How long can I go on singing songs like the ones that I've sung in the past? When I was younger, I wrote these songs and they were really rock 'n' roll and everything, and it all was natural.

But there came a point where it wasn't so natural for me. It's not that it's not natural for me to play my guitar, play rock 'n' roll guitar and have a great time, and play loud and be rowdy. I still do that. But where I'm comin' from is a different thing. It's not so much of a style – it's just I'm more concerned now with family. And with songs about growing up and growing old, and surviving. Because that's what I'm doing.

"Misfits" on the album is interesting. It stands out. The reviews are saying "This is the Neil Young song, as opposed to the country stuff" … Was that song always part of the thematic thing for this record, or was it an afterthought?

I'd written it about the same time as I wrote a lot of the other ones, but I didn't record it until all the other stuff was recorded. It was the last thing we cut. I looked at everything I had, and I said "Well, this is all really great, and I really love it. But it has nothing to oppose it." There was nothing there to put it in its place. There was nothing there for people to grab onto that's over in another area. So that's why I put it in there. And it makes perfect sense to me, lyrically, with the rest of the record. It's just abstract, that's the only difference. Instead of being right in the middle, it's abstract.

All the songs relate – "Bound for Glory," and the Indian ridin' his pickup truck down the Needles Highway, they're all the same. All the same pictures.

You've made no bones about your distaste for making a commercial record – of course you can do it, and you have done it, and for me and a lot of other people some of your best stuff is your least commercial. If you think that there's something the public wants of you, would you bother to give it to them?

I don't think I'd bother to give it to them. After I'm finished, then I know what I'm doing. After I've finished the record. And I don't know I've finished the record until I know that the songs are there. I recorded 30 songs for *Old Ways*. Keep singing, keep writing, keep recording. And I keep all the information in the back of my head, everything I'm doing. And then one morning, I wake up and I'm finished.

It's not a conscious thing where I write it all down and sat "This is gonna work great." I just keep going. Just the way it happens. And the way it comes out is enough. I've always done it that way. It's a waste of time to try to contrive a concept.

This is the year that you turn 40 …

I wrote a song about that! It's called "Leaving the Top 40 Behind." (laughs)

Watching you sing "Sugar Mountain" tonight, I was thinking about how it was about being 19 and turning 20. Now you're 39 turning 40. I wonder if you thought about that, or if it's just a song that you do now?

It's just a song that I do because I do so many new songs in the set – tonight I think I did five or six unrecorded songs, which is a large percentage for a normal concert. But I've always tried to do that.

So you have to balance that out. You give people songs from the different periods of my life, I do that and then I sprinkle in all the new ones, and try to make it so that it all holds together…

Well, I wondered whether "Sugar Mountain" held a special place in your heart …

It makes it for me. The older I get, the more sense it makes. You see people out there, they close their eyes and just drift away when I sing that song. I don't know why, there's more reaction to that song than there ever was before. More reaction to "Heart of Gold" than I've ever had before.

Growing old and trying to preserve tradition, family life, all of these things, they're very important to me now. Much more important than creating a trendy synthesizer-based rock 'n' roll record. I mean, I could do that if I wanted to. But it bores the shit out of me.

I mean, I have all of the equipment. I got synclaviers, and digital tape recorders and all that stuff. It just bores me, so I don't want to do that any more. I may do it again someday.

Photo by Bill DeYoung

3. Tom Petty (1986)
Rednecks in space

To set the stage: This freewheeling, slightly intoxicated interview was conducted around midnight July 16, 1986 in Tom Petty's suite at the Omni Berkshire Place in New York City, after the first show in a three-night stand at Madison Square Garden, which New York Times reviewer Jon Pareles would describe as "oddly paced and willful." Bob Dylan with Tom Petty & the Heartbreakers were playing three-hour concerts that summer, with no intermission. This was, Petty gleefully told me as he strummed an unplugged Fender Telecaster, the only interview he'd agreed to do on the entire tour.

So what have you been up to?

Since I've seen you, I did the *Southern Accents* tour, I did a film of that tour, then I mixed the double live album. I did Farm Aid with Bob, then a trip to Australia, New Zealand and Japan with Bob. Mixed the HBO thing. Did a double album in four weeks. I did a single for Bob in Australia, called "Band of the Hand." What else did I do? I did a part in a movie called *Made in Heaven*. I did that and flew right back to the studio and got the ol' double LP done. It was cut between the Australian and the American tour. I produced two songs for Bob on his album, and we wrote some songs together that are gonna be great, that we ain't got around to doing yet. And then I jumped on the bus for this.

So you're going to make this a double album?

I think I have to. You always hear "there's a bulk of material," but there really is a bulk of good material. Real rock 'n' roll stuff. I think just one slow song on a double album. It's real barrel-out stuff.

Why did that happen?

I don't know! I'm still mystified by it.

(Mike Campbell enters)

Ladies and gentlemen, Mike Campbell. Mike, you got anything to say to the newspapers?

Campbell: You want to write some songs tonight?

Petty: You never know, man. I'm a songwritin' machine!

So, this new stuff is full-steam rock 'n' roll?

Campbell: Is that what you called it, Tom? Full-steam rock 'n' roll?

Petty: Well, full steam hasn't really come out. It sounds kinda like a redneck bar band, or a garage band. It's real light stuff ...

Campbell: With a little bit of a cosmic edge to it.

Stan (Lynch) says it sounds like the first album.

Petty: It sounds better than the first album. It's a lot more raucous than the first album. You know how they always say "God, I wish he'd make a rock 'n' roll record like he used to"? Well, this is a lot better than the rock 'n' roll records we used to make. This just happened, in the studio. I'd say – (*he plays the opening chords to 'Can't Get Her Out'*) – and the band would start playing. Then I'd start singin' a little thing, you know? And then it's done.

Why hadn't that happened for years? What got in the way?

You gotta be kind of good to do that, and you gotta have a band of a certain mentality to do it. We've been fuckin' around together 10, 15 years.

We just felt like playing. We weren't even meant to be there. We went there because I'd booked the time for Bob, and he wasn't ready to go in. So we just jumped in there to try out some songs me and Mike had written. We went in with about four tunes and left with 35. We're gonna put a number of them out.

You've cut "Got My Mind Made Up"?

Yeah, there's a Heartbreakers version and a Bob version. We wrote that together, and there's a lot more verses. So I think in our version there'll be a lot of the extra verses that didn't get on Bob's.

Campbell: Bob wrote the verse about Libya.

Petty: I wrote the verse about Libya.

Campbell: You did?

Petty: I did. Well, if the truth must be known ... Bob says "Let's write a song about Florida!" And I said no. He goes (singing) "I'm going to Tallahassee .." and I said no, "I'm going to Libya." And he sings "There's a guy I gotta see/He's been living there three years now/In an oil refinery …" Great! And then we did another one.

Writing with Bob is great, because if you throw one line he comes back with three great lines.

Could you tell him if he came up with a lousy line?

Oh yeah, sure. No, no, no, you don't want no lousy lines.

Well, Dylan has written some bad songs too …

Petty: What great man hasn't?

You've written some bad songs. Both of you have.

Campbell: I've never written a bad song in my life!

Petty: Well, so has everyone. I think Ludwig Van had a few clinkers. Lennon, certainly.

You can't be great if you don't show your ass now and then. Or you're not trying to do anything. I mean, Bryan Adams might not ever write one that you notice is bad, because they'll polish that turd to a high chrome!

Come on. This is the only band in America who doesn't know who's gonna take the solo. Fuck 'em! The name of my album's called *Let Me Up I've Had Enough.*

You're gonna call it that?

Petty: That's right, because I've had enough. It's called *Let Me Up I've Had Enough,* written by me and Brother Campbell.

You've got a song called "Let Me Up" and another one called "I've Had Enough"?

Campbell: No, they're one song, in two parts. A "Let Me Up" part, and then an "I've Had Enough" part.

Petty: It's heavy art! (laughter)

How can you guys stand each other after so long?

Petty: Oh, we hate each other. We can't fuckin' deal with each other. I don't know how the fuck I put up with you after all these years!

Campbell: It must be 'cause I'm so good-looking!

Petty: Looks is a good part of it.

There's a lot of talk right now about Jagger and Richards not writing together any more. And you guys have been working together for a while ....

Petty: Since 1970, if we must reveal it …

Campbell: See, the thing is, we don't write together. We write apart, and …

Petty: Not till we're in the studio do we look eye to eye and try to bang it out. Unless I'm doing something and I can't think of a bridge, Mike'll think of a bridge.

I'm curious about this new stuff. It sounds like it's "The Heartbreakers, Mach II."

Campbell (to Petty): What does he mean by that? Mark 2?

Petty: "Mach." Mach II. It's another era. "No more funny glasses and backward tapes," is what he means. I see people in New York wearin' them glasses now.

So we're back to playing live in the studio, without overdubbing?

Petty: There's hardly any overdubbing. But we never did that much overdubbing anyway, really. We tried a lot but it never got on the record most times.

Do you think Dylan's slash-and-burn approach – "go in and do it" – has rubbed off on you?

Petty: It's too early to tell. I could tell you in a year, maybe. We've been running around with Bob for about a year now. I think we rub off on him more than he rubs off on us. You know, you can slash and burn but it's still gotta come out good.

I think it's just a real good band, you know? This band keeps getting better. Another thing was, me and Mike are producing this record, and there was never a producer there to sort of like throw a wrench in the works, or suggest another idea. Or make it feel like you were making a record. We didn't ever talk about making a record!

If you hear the tapes, I'm calling the chords. Some of them we only ever played maybe once or twice. And that was the writing and the playing of the song. So when I hear them, they're still real fresh to me.

Campbell: In Bob's defense, that was something we learned from him.

Petty: We probably did learn that from Bob. We learned the joy of throwing some chaos in any time things … Bob will never let things get too settled. When all of a sudden you feel like "I got this thing down," he's gonna change it. And that may sink, but if it really happens it REALLY happens. You can't fake it then, buddy. You really got to do it.

I'd rather hear somebody try, and sink, than turn on their fuckin' computer and just drift by. I'm not into that. That shit's gonna die. People are gonna catch on to that.

You have these raw tapes now. If you sit on them, will you start thinking "Ah, I could do this better," or do you want to get them out fast before you start to think?

Campbell: You don't want to think. If you start thinking, you're in bad trouble.

Petty: There's no thinking involved. If you're thinking, there's something wrong. We've done some of those intellectual albums. *Southern Accents* was a real production piece. Two years of production.

And we're not in the mood to do that. Not that we won't do it again, no promises, but this is what we're doing now. We're "Rednecks in Space," you know? It's a garage band, but a good one.

It's very kamikaze. You cut all these tracks in such a short period of time. It's unlike you guys.

Petty: Well, I'm sure it'll come out that Bob Dylan did that. Maybe he did do that.

Campbell: And we might throw all those tracks out and start all over again.

Petty: You never know … we might go back and do something else. But I think we won't, because I really like this album so much. I really do. I ought to play you some of it … but I don't know, it might scare Michael.

How is your relationship with MCA?

It's great. I've known Irving Azoff for years and years. I don't do a lot of record business any more, but I know Irving and he's somebody I can call up and talk straight with. All he asks of me is to bring him a record. He never rushes me. He didn't rush me for two years. He'd come down and listen and say "When it's right …" He knew what I was doing.

So you're going to try to get this album out this year?

You betcha!

Will Irving let you do another double, after the live album?

I never asked him. I just assume he will. Why wouldn't he? Irving's a reasonable man. (laughter)

Irving must've been the guy who decided to make "Needles and Pins," a four-year-old track, the single from the live album?

I don't know. I don't pick the singles. I thought they should have put out "So You Want to Be a Rock 'n' Roll Star." I just thought it was such a great record. And you know what they said? They thought it was too rock 'n' roll for the radio. And at that point I said well, guys, we really don't have anything to talk about. At the time, it was the Number One Airplay song in the country. And they wouldn't release it as a single because it was "too rock 'n' roll." That's … you know, let me up, I've had enough. (laughter)

What was the inspiration for "American Girl"? There's always been a story that connects it to Gainesville …

Petty: Naw, that's myth …

Campbell: It's got 441 in it …

Petty: … and it's probably got a southern setting. A lot of songs are based around there. I've written a lot of songs with a southern setting. "Magnolia" could be that area. There's a lot of magnolias there.

I'm trying to remember writing "American Girl." I think I wrote it in an apartment in Encino, California in '76 or '75.

Campbell: It was the Fourth of July, wasn't it?

Petty: Fourth of July. And it came quickly. It was written very quickly. Instantly.

It's a song about suicide …

Campbell: Naw. BULL-shit!

Well, the story goes that the girl jumped from Beatty Towers in Gainesville …

Petty: No, the line is "If she had to *die trying* …"

Campbell: Love is dead, that's what it was about. It's a figure of speech! "If she had to die trying …"

Petty: "If she had to die trying." She didn't have to DIE. "It was one little promise she was going to keep."

Well, it's desperate …

Petty: Yeah, it's very desperate. Well, maybe that's why they thought she just lept off the balcony. I always pictured her as a much more stable bitch than that.

That was back in the period where all the songs were two minutes, 25 seconds.

Petty: Yeah, we just figured "Let's get in, get out," you know? We were highly criticized at the time for that. I kinda miss that, you know? Verse, verse, chorus, solo, verse, chorus, get out. A good rock 'n' roll song doesn't need to be more than a few minutes long anyway.

We got songs on this record now that are nine minutes long. There's one song that's probably a whole side. I don't know, Campbell will probably edit it.

We just play. We record everything played in the session. If one guy's playing, it's recorded. And there's always somebody out there playing. It's not the kind of band that can learn a song and do, say, 10 takes any more. We're too impatient. We'll go on to something else. Because we just want to hit a feel and play it. If we know it too good, we can never record it.

Is the live stuff as much fun now as it was when you first started playing with Bob last year?

I like playing with Bob. Bob's all right. He's just a good friend to play music with. And God, he sure has done a lot for us. We're allowed to do whatever we want. It's kind of like having another band. We got another singer who writes, you know? We treat it like a group. That's the way Bob's arranged it. I respect him for that.

It's kind of like jamming for three hours. You don't really know what you're gonna play, or what rhythm it's gonna be.

You're hanging back a lot in these shows.

I like hanging back. I sing a lot in this show, man. I must sing 15 songs in this show. I got at least five songs to sing with Bob, and what'd we do tonight? Eight. That's a lot of singing.

Still, where's the ego fit in, when you're playing a supporting role?

What ego? What are you talking about? Listen, man, if you're in a rock group and you're even dealing with ego, you're not going anywhere. You can't deal with that and do anything!

That's not what I heard.

Well, there's a lot of things you hear that ain't true. I've done this a long time. I'm much too smart to get into ego. I want to make Bob good, and Bob wants to make me good. And that's why we get along, because we're way above that.

It's a matter of feeling, this music. It's all about feel. To send out something and make somebody feel good. It's not any deeper than that. And if you can learn that, then you're gonna be around more than a record or two.

Bob was out there tonight pulling these Jesus songs out of the hat …

And rightfully so!

Right after your second set, after Ronnie Wood came out for "Rainy Day Women," then there was a Jesus song. I could feel the momentum dive.

Yeah, but see, you're still talking about it. You know what, the Beach Boys wouldn't-a done that. They've have probably just steamrollered that baby to the end like Bruce Springsteen. But that's not what we're doing. That's not what this is about. He had something to say at that point.

This ain't show business, man. This ain't show business. That's Bob Dylan. He had something to say at that point. He had something to say about Jesus right then. He sang "Like a Rolling Stone," right? He'd already done that.

Listen, man, you gotta dig that there's a lot of great songs about Jesus. David Lee Roth might not want to do that. But I admire a man that's confident enough in himself to do that. And I tell you what, nobody left.

Campbell: He does that on purpose. I know what you mean by momentum. It builds up and it's boogie till you puke. Bob doesn't want to boogie till he pukes.

Petty: I respect a man that can bring it down and still hold 'em. This is not boogie till you puke. We're not there to do that. We're there to offer an alternative. To expose people to an alternative.

A lot of times we don't know who's taking the solo or what's gonna happen. This is the only band left like that. And it's a shame. Except for some of the younger bands that nobody wants to give the time of day to. And I'm real concerned about that.

A rock show's gotten to be such an organized, routine thing. I don't know when's the last one I went to, because they're so fuckin' predictable. You know what's gonna happen. You know they're gonna play an encore. You know they're gonna do another encore. Da, da, da, the big lights are gonna come on …

Fuck it! It's like you may as well watch Johnny Carson. Bob did a great show, and he didn't concede to anything. And that's an artist. That's when you start calling this shit art. (laughter). If you must!

A lot of these guys are great performers and entertainers, but they're not taking the medium anywhere as far as I'm concerned.

But is Bob's intention, with those kind of songs, to get people to follow him?

They're never gonna follow you. Did they ever? If they'd ever followed him, I mean, there wouldn't have been a war. They'll follow you to the record store. They'll follow you to the concert hall. And they might have a great time, but very few retain a sense of "following," as far as taking the lyrics … but you can inspire them. You can inspire them to think for themselves, which is the greatest thing you can do for them. You can inspire them; you don't want them to follow you.

Campbell: Even the Jesus songs, they're not pro-Jesus. They're just sort of calling attention to it.

Petty: You have to ask Bob those questions, because I don't really know how to interpret that. But I respect it. And I don't think he's ramming anything down anybody's throat. And he certainly offered a wide variety of his material tonight. Bob's done 35 albums; if he played one song from each of his albums, that's the show.

MCA Records

4. Tom Petty (1989)
The talk on the street says you might go solo

Petty is in a chatty mood during this interview, conducted over the phone – he's in California, I'm in Florida – to generate goodwill and good ink for his first solo album, Full Moon Fever, *which was about to come out and would in due course become the biggest-selling record of his career. He'd put the recording sessions on ice for a while to make* Traveling Wilburys, Vol. I *with George Harrison, Bob Dylan, Roy Orbison - and Jeff Lynne, the studio wizard behind the Electric Light Orchestra who co-produce*d Full Moon Fever *along with Petty and Mike Campbell.*

(The reference to tire manufacturer B.F. Goodrich concerns the company's use of a Petty sound-alike for a TV commercial. He sued and won.)

It's a fascinating conversation because it catches the moment when he is about to transition from a scrappy southern guy out in front of a great rock 'n' roll band into an a-list superstar. Nothing, after this, was ever the same.

I think everybody assumed that the album you were making with Jeff would sound like ELO – those loping rhythms and synthesizers. The smooth Jeff Lynne sound. But that's not what happened.

Well, I think there's a lot more to Jeff than ELO. I feel sorry for Jeff in some ways just because that's all anyone seems to associate him with, you know? But that's been 10 years ago or something. Good artists usually keep growing, and I think there's a pretty wide spectrum to his work. ELO was one phase of his work, and *Cloud Nine* was another. And the Wilburys was another! And this is … another (laughs). On and on. He's a very talented man. He's really one of the most talented people I've ever encountered in the studio. And that alone …

If I didn't work with him, he'd still be my good pal and everything. But I haven't ever run across anyone with quite that much talent at making records.

I always think of Americans and Brits as different animals. I couldn't have guessed Tom Petty and Jeff Lynne.

That's sort of what I like about it, really. (laughs) Really, we're very similar in what we like musically. Brits aren't so bad! I met him at the end of '87, in England. We got to know each other there. I really wasn't thinking about working with Jeff, though I admired his work quite a bit. Always have, really.

Then we ran into each other out here and started hanging around, did a couple of things and it was so much fun we just kept doing it.

Was the chemistry like what you had with Dave Stewart?

I think in a different way. In this case, Jeff was more of an equal partner, where Dave would just kind of come and …. Naw, I guess it was about the same, really. It seems that I just spent more time with Jeff than I did with Dave.

How did all this come about?

It was a situation where we were hanging around, over the Christmas holidays in '87. And we spent some time together. At the time, I didn't live very far from him. He has a house here as well, and we were kinda neighbors. Not around the corner, but not far away. Most people were out of town then, and we were just hanging around. I had written the song "Yer So Bad." We were playing the guitars one day and I showed him the song. He said "Yeah, that's great!

What if you put an E minor here?" I said oh, let me try that, I did it and said oh, that's good … show me something else! And he said "It's OK, really, it doesn't need anything else." And God, that really changed it.

I've never had anybody around that would say "Yeah, but if you just try a C and a D right there, it'll really be a lot better." And he has that knack of just knowing what's needed, and then not really fiddling with it much more. We wrote a couple songs, and I thought "It'd be great to put these on tape or something."

Because I was under the impression that Jeff was leaving any day. We went over to Mike's house, and went in his studio – I just called up and said "Me and Jeff are coming over." And we came over, and we started working, and at the end of the day we'd done the record. And in two days, we'd done two. I said "God, this is good" – I didn't picture it as the Heartbreakers because they weren't around.

Was it ever going to be "Tom and Jeff's record"?

No, Jeff didn't want that. I had to constantly deal with Jeff wanting to stay in the background. He was very sensitive to it; he didn't feel it'd be right if he appeared too much on the record. So I'm still laughing about when people talk about the "Jeff Lynne background vocals," because a lot of the time it's just me. It's not Jeff at all. But they get that stigma in their head and think "oh, that's Jeff." But it isn't always.

There's a really nice close harmony on the song "Depending on You."

That's just me and me. I learned a lot about singing harmony from Jeff. He's a brilliant harmony singer. It was just a real pleasure to make the record, really. There was never a day where it was tense, or pressured or anything. It was just us out in the garage, hanging out and having fun.

Do you remember a point where the intent became more serious: "I am now making an album"?

Let me try to remember. We'd done a couple. We'd used Phil Jones on the drums, and I said to Mike "It ain't the band, is it?" And he said "No it ain't." I said, well, I don't want to cut these again, and try to bring the band in and have them do this. So I'm going to call everyone up and tell them I'm going to make a solo record." It was at a period of time when I don't think the Heartbreakers were planning to work anyway. So that's what I did.

I'd say to Jeff aw, come on, let's do one more. He'd say "I've got to go back." I'd say, just one more. Like that, through the whole album, really. Oh, come on, you can do two more, can't ya?" And it just kept going on like that.

Were you consciously trying to make a record that didn't sound like the Heartbreakers?

Well, that was just taken for granted that they weren't there. So I never considered that I was. I wasn't really hung up on what kind of record I was making. I was just enjoying what I was doing. It was really incredibly easy with Jeff there. He has this amazing knack for arrangement. He showed us tons of things we'd never come across – and by the same token, I think he learned a bit from us. I think that's why it was such a pleasurable experience, because it was all new – new guys hanging out together and stuff.

In "A Mind with a Heart of its Own," you mention the towns Micanopy and Brooker, which are near Gainesville. So the area's still in your thoughts?

Oh yeah, sure it is. I think it'd be a stretch of the imagination to think I'd ever get it out. Because shit, I spent a long time there. I love it there. I think it's a very nice place.

Do you still think about Gainesville and the old days?

I think I remember only the fond parts. With time, you get where you don't remember all the awful parts. I think it was a great place to grow up, and a wonderful place to grow up playing music. I don't know if they still have music there?

Well, the environment's changed a bit. A lot of original music bands these days – which, of course, can make it difficult to get work in clubs. Kind of the same problem you had!

You know what we used to do? We'd say "Here's one by Santana," and just play one we wrote. We used to just call out whoever was popular at the time.

And nobody knew the difference?

Naw, they don't know fuck out there. And the club owners don't know. People would go "Oh, I dig Santana," and they'd hit the dance floor.

The legend lives on about the Mudcrutch Farm. What was it, sort of a hippie commune thing?

Sort of! It wasn't a commune. It was just an old shitty house. Officially it was Mike's and Randall's but everybody else just kind of moved in. It had a big field, and woods around it – the kind of thing you'd probably pay two million dollars for now. A wonderful time, really.

We'd have these shows there, sort of like pop festivals I guess, where we'd just start calling all the bands we knew. And we'd have nine or 10 bands, and two days of fun and music.

They still talk about that here.

Of course they do, it really rocked the town at the time. It was a major mess. We had no planning, other than us just saying "OK, we'll book these guys and everybody'll play for free. We'll make some posters and put 'em around." And then it turned out like, 13th Street was backed up, and cops were out, and "you can't do this, son." People were sleeping in people's yards, and they were getting pissed off … it was that kind of thing, where it got bigger than we ever dreamt. And they finally kicked Randall and Mike out of the place as a result.

So had you ever thought of a solo record before?

I think I'd thought of it, but I'd never really taken it seriously. I probably won't do one again, I don't think. It was more or less something that was happening before there was time to really think about it. So once it had happened, I was having too much fun, well, 13 years, I think I can make a record on my own if I want.

Was there ever a time when you missed the Heartbreakers in the sessions – where you could look at Stan, and think "he knows what to do there"?

No, because by that point I had got it in my mind that I was doing something different. And so I didn't really want it to be like the Heartbreakers.

How did you and Jeff write together?

I wrote most of the lyrics, I think. Jeff might put in a line here or there, but he never really tried to write much lyrics. Most of the time, Jeff just sat there and played with me. A very natural collaboration, with just two acoustics sitting nose-to-nose.

Acoustic guitar is very prominent on the record.

Well, that's how we wrote them. We got real good, the two of us, at playing together on the acoustics. With the drums, we'd just put down the acoustic rhythms. And don't forget, Mike was there. Mike was very much involved in everything. Maybe not the writing. He engineered the record. So he was always involved when decisions were made. He had a good deal of input.

But it was just one of those things where we were enjoying doing it. We wanted to get all we could drag out of Jeff, really. We wanted to do something kind of fresh, you know?

On the more rocking songs, "Runnin' Down a Dream" and "A Mind With a Heart of its Own," it's like the bass is different, or there's no bass ... it doesn't sound like a Heartbreakers record.

Not at all. It was a completely different approach.

You mentioned "Yer So Bad." The first thing I thought was that it sounds like George Harrison's sense of humor. Or maybe Ray Davies. It doesn't sound like Tom Petty.

Well, it's nothing like a lot of the work I've done. I've always had a sense of humor, I just don't always use it in the songs. But I think I've hit a point in my life where I'd rather have a laugh, you know? I think it still has plenty to say, that song. I think it has quite a lot to say. But sometimes I think you can make the point maybe even stronger with a little bit of humor.

And I'm so bored with all these pompous people in music, anyway. I don't like it when it's overtly serious.

And "Zombie Zoo," of course, is a great big slab o'humor.

Yes, but that song is also grimly serious in a way. A lot of these songs are like "I've got to laugh, or I'll cry."

"I Won't Back Down." Is that just a line, or are you thinking about something there?

Well I hope I'm thinking about something with all of 'em. I think that one's real self-explanatory, from the classic cookie cutter of TP (laughs). It's just one of those songs, y'know, it's very self-explanatory. It is what it is, and I meant it and all that. It's embarrassing to talk about it very much because it's so bold.

Somebody suggested you were saying "I won't back down from B.F. Goodrich."

Nah, I don't really see B.F. Goodrich as a major enemy in my life! I'm more concerned with how I'm gonna breathe the next year, if there's going to be any ozone layer. Or if we're gonna just fuckin' die so we can have hamburgers. Things like that. There's a lot of things, I won't back down. You better not back down from banning automatic weapons. Schoolyards of kids are being mowed down. It's pretty horrific if you go around the world, it's really scary, man. You better have a laugh while you can.

Is "All Right for Now" for your daughters, or your wife …?

It's for all the girls. I don't know if I really zeroed in on who it was for. I wrote it late at night, when I was just about to fall asleep. It was one of those where you get lucky, you're playing your guitar and this song comes in. I put it on the cassette deck, and I got up in the morning and took it to the studio. And I was really surprised that I'd written a whole song. Because I thought I was going to take it to the studio and start working on it. I got it out, and I was 'Hmm, this is fine. I like all of this.'

"Free Fallin'" is one of my favorites. It's a story about someone. It's funny cos' it's got that exhilarating vocal jump in it, but when you really listen to the story, it's kind of depressing.

Could be. I'm just realizing that myself, that he's not really a cool guy. It's just a character. I think the San Fernando Valley has more to do with that song than anything. There's one side of the valley that's all hills and country, and beautiful, and if you cross this imaginary dividing line that's Ventura Boulevard, the other side is just everything that's wrong with the world, on display. I think I kinda got caught up in that, and that's where the characters came from, people that live in Reseda.

"Runnin' Down a Dream" sounds like a car song. Did it come to you while you were driving? It has that feeling.

That's what I imagined in my mind as I was writing it. I was trying to use a car as a metaphor for trying to run away. And of course, you can't really run away.

Why did you do the Byrds cover – and why such a faithful arrangement?

Well, why not, you know? Jeff and I went out to see them one night – they had this reunion concert out here. And they're pals of mine, for a long time now, the Byrds. And they did that number, and I said "I like that number, I might record that." We didn't take it very seriously. It wasn't even a scheduled session when we did it. We were at Mike's house, and we were telling Mike about the concert. We just started playing the song, and we just did it. Really, it's so faithful because I couldn't find any other way that the song sounded right to me! I guess that's probably from playing it all my life. Mike knew the solo by heart. We didn't even have to get the record out.

I played it to McGuinn the other day, and he loved it. He said "Is that us?" And I said hell, no, that ain't you. (laughs)

When I heard it, I thought you must have had a hoot doing it. It's like that Todd Rundgren album Faithful. It's perfect.

Yeah, it is, and there's no good excuse for behavior like that! I just said "Well, it's my solo record, I'll do whatever I want." I don't think I could've got away with doing that with the Heartbreakers. My daughter thought I wrote it, for weeks.

You used Phil Jones, who's been hovering around the band for years, on drums. Was that a conscious choice?

Well, we needed a drummer that day, and he's always been one of our favorite pals and players and everything. We called him up and he was good enough to come over. I wish Phil was famous and more people knew about him; since those sessions, Jeff's used him on just about every record he's done. Because he's just brilliant.

Last year, Billboard Magazine said the album was going to be called Songs From the Garage. Tony Dimitriades played four songs for the writer.

Songs from the Garage was the first title I came up with, 'cause we were working in the garage at the time. That's when Tony played them those songs; that was all I'd done. I changed that later because I thought it might give the impression that it was like garage rock or something. Which it wasn't at all, even though it was us in the garage! But you know what I mean, it wasn't like the Standells or something. I didn't think that was gonna hold up, and I changed it.

And the long delay was because it wasn't done, and you put it aside for a while to do the Wilburys?

Yeah, it was the first record we started and the last one we finished. When I started the Wilburys, I had nine done, which wasn't quite enough.

Was "Last Night" ever intended for your solo record?

Oh, no. All the Wilburys songs, people want to think that we wrote 'em individually, but we didn't. I think Dylan wrote most of "Last Night." We'd sit on the floor, the five of us, and literally wrote all those songs.

That whole thing was unplanned and spontaneous?

Yeah, it's even hard for us to believe, really.

Were you surprised by how good it came out?

Well, it was an unusual thing in that when we started that record, another thing that people don't really understand, is we had been hanging around for a while. Quite a while, really. All of us, except Roy. Even when I started the Wilburys, Roy had already been hanging around our sessions. I think he'd sung on one of mine, and then we'd written a couple for Roy – in the same sessions as my album we did "You Got It" and another one. And maybe another one!

We'd stop one day and say "OK, Randy Newman's coming today – we're going to do one for Randy Newman." And we'd do that. Then, we'll do one for Roy today. This would be the same band: Phil Jones and me and Mike and Jeff. And George'd be there a lot of times. That was the basic band that was around.

So the only addition was Bob, who I already knew pretty well, for years, really. And George did. And Jeff had already even worked with Bob. So it wasn't like we were all getting together for the first time. It was just the whole bunch there at once for the first time.

What was it, 10 days start to finish?

Well, it was 10 days to write them, if you don't count "Handle With Care," which was done first. So it was 10 days to write nine more. We did the basic tracks and then we went to England for another month and finished it up.

I can imagine the feeling, getting more excited with every new thing you did.

Yeah, we were like little kids, leaping on each other's backs. We were so thrilled. When you could finally put it up and hear it going by, that's when I started to think "Hey … this is a pretty good album." We didn't think about it much until then because we were so busy. It was a frantic pace we were keeping.

Was there a definite point where somebody said "OK, we're not just messing around here, we're actually making an album"?

Well, we set out to make it a great album. We didn't want to do it if it wasn't going to be real good. And we knew we'd get a bunch of shit if it wasn't real good.

From our standpoint, it was a real innocent thing. 'Cause we were gonna be hanging around together anyway, and we might as well make a record. Well, that's a little bit of an exaggeration, but we were digging each other's company to a great extent and we knew it had to be real good or there wasn't any point in putting it out. That's a tall order sometimes.

But on the other hand, we still talk about it and don't know how we did it. It just was one of those magical times - you just got rolling and everything just seemed to fall into place.

I know what a tremendous Beatles fan you've always been. Was it uncomfortable at first, working with George?

Oh, no. We've become real good pals. I don't think of them in that light, really. You know, I'd met George years ago, I think before I was in the Heartbreakers. And when we got to really know each other was over in England, at the same time I met Jeff.

You know like people that you meet and you just get along real well with? And I don't think the Beatles have ever really entered into what we'd got going.

Of course, I don't want to be glib; I was real pleased to be playing with all those guys. But I think the Beatles is something that happened a long time ago, and they're just people, you know? Now. I don't really see 'em as Beatles.

Well, for those of us who aren't you, it was cool when you were touring with Dylan. But … the Beatles? I would've been on the floor.

Yeah, I know what you're saying. I probably was. But you can't get any work done sitting around admiring each other. You can only say "God, I love ya, and it's wonderful to know ya and to be your pal."

They don't want to be treated that way. And I wouldn't want to be treated that way.

We just did a video in London where we had Ringo play the drums, and George, and Jeff. And Mike and me.

For "I Won't Back Down"?

Yeah. And that was a thrill. I'd look around sometimes and there they'd be, and I'd think "That's really wild," you know? But I'd just tell them, "Boy, you guys are wild."

But you can remember boppin' down to Woolworth's and buying Beatles '65 when you were in short pants …

Yeah, but in the Wilburys it was all balanced, 'cause George could remember boppin' down and getting his Roy Orbison records. It was all relative to each other.

I think all those guys, Bob, George and Roy were just as equally pleased to be playing with me and Jeff and to get input from us. I don't think we could've become friends if we were all just in awe of each other too much.

Did you ever feel like you were the "young" member of that ensemble? The junior partner?

Well, I was never treated that way. I was the youngest by many years, yeah …

Even including Jeff, who was making records while you were still kicking around Gainesville.

Was he? I guess he was. Gee … it was never … I always had as much say as anybody else. And they were so kind and sweet to me, I never felt that way, no.

What was it like to work with Roy?

Oh, it was a pleasure. I miss him.

You know Bill, looking at it now, I'm just glad that I knew him. I feel honored, really, that I got to spend that much time with him and work with him.

The thing with the Wilburys was that all those guys … I would've loved them all if they didn't play an instrument, or if they'd never been in a band. And that's the charm of all those people – to me, they've all been friends far beyond music or anything to do with it. They've just been my pals, and I'm glad to just have them in my life.

I bet Roy must have been pretty happy when the record was so successful.

He was just ecstatic. I think the last conversation we had, a few days before he died, he was just over the moon about it. He was really happy about his album (*Mystery Girl*) because they'd just finished that. Roy had a good idea, I believe, that things were about to really go his way. We all wish that he could've seen the great success he's had because boy, he would've loved that.

But Roy was a real happy guy. He wasn't an unhappy person or a lonely guy. And he seemed to me to each day be aware that "I'm living for today, and let's really enjoy it." I miss his laugh more than anything. He used to laugh, and it'd just make us all start laughin.'

It was an awful thing. We weren't prepared for it, none of us; he wasn't ill or anything. God bless him is all I can say now.

And … the status of the Heartbreakers is what? The heart still beating, as it were?

I believe so. We worked for about three days trying to get another album together, and right now they're off finishing the commitments they've made to other people over the last year. They're busy boys. To get 'em all together takes a little bit of planning.

But there is still a band?

Yeah, definitely, and there always was. The record'll get done; first of all, they're all working on different records, which is a slight problem … it's not a *problem*, but we just can't start right now.

And I haven't had a break since *Southern Accents*, I don't think. I've worked steadily through all that. So the plan now is look, we'll go on tour, and that should be some sort of bonding for us, I hope. I hope that we can all just be the Heartbreakers again and get back to that. But I never had any intention of quitting, or leaving the group.

But is there any kind of alienation there – "Tom and Mike are doing this … and then there's the rest of us"?

Alienation, I don't think so. No more than you would expect. I'm sure that they weren't real happy about all that, in the beginning. They were almost nasty about it at some point. But in an understandable way. I think they were pretty big about it in one sense, too. But I was always up front with them. I said "I'm not quitting, there's just something I want to do. And I can't live my life if I can't do what I want."

When you've been in a band this long, you've gotta protect it in some ways. And if you're just always doing it and you don't know why, that gets dangerous, I think.

I think in a way it'll be good for us when we go back together and start. I don't want to do it if it's not gonna get better, or if it's not gonna be different.

I don't want to make the same record over and over like most of these groups do. I just can't understand that. I don't want to make records like "Refugee."

Warner Bros. Records

5. Seals and Crofts
We may never pass this way again

In the pre-Internet days, out of curiosity I used to go out of my way to write in-depth biographical stories about artists that I liked; in the case of Seals and Crofts, who'd been huge in the '70s but had subsequently been all but forgotten, I found precious little that talked about more than the duo's early successes with songs like "Summer Breeze" and "Diamond Girl." I had loved so many of their deep album tracks. I'd seen them live and stuck around for the after-show "fireside," about their deeply-held Baha'i beliefs. I also remembered the career-stalling "Unborn Child" controversy, and their regrettable disco record, and … well, I wanted to hear what they had to say – about all of it – in retrospect. So I called them up. This story appeared in Goldmine *in 1992.*

When the 1960s turned into the 70s, and the flood of longhaired, acoustic guitar carrying singer-songwriters began, sensitive and poetic and wearing their hearts on their sleeves, Jimmy Seals and Dash Crofts had already been through the star-making machinery. With the Champs, the pair jumped on the pop music merry-go-round, grabbed the brass ring and, not thinking too much of the experience, got off again.

But as Seals and Crofts, they forged a career their own way, playing by their rules and making records that said exactly what they were feeling inside. What set them apart from the other early turn–of–the–decade pop folkies was their commitment to God and their deep religious beliefs, which dominated and ultimately illuminated their songwriting. Over the course of a 10-year recording career, Seals and Crofts never wavered in their pledge to declare and advance the Baha'i faith through their music.

Even so, they wound up with a bunch of hits.

Jimmy Seals was born October 17, 1941 in Sidney, a dusty Central Texas oil town where the family picked up musical instruments to amuse itself, simply because there wasn't much else to do. Jimmy's father Wayland Seals was a driller who played guitar in a local swing group called the Tom Cats.

One day, Jimmy recalls, his dad's musician friends came home for supper – young Jimmy was about 6 – and the bunch of them wound up entertaining the family in the living room. Jimmy was enthralled by the violin player, who could turn a mean western rag, and that night he asked his parents for an instrument of his own.

Eventually, he got one, and by the time he was nine, Jimmy Seals was good enough to complete in the Texas State Fiddle Championship. He remembers that he played "Sally Good'n" and "Listen To The Mockingbird," and that when he won the state contest he beat out fiddlers from all age groups, including grown-up musicians with many years' experience under their worn rawhide belts.

About 25 miles to the northwest of Sidney, in slightly larger Cisco, Texas, Dash Crofts was waffling between a future in music and a future in baseball. Four years older than Seals, he'd begun playing piano at the age of five, and had some lessons, before switching to drums at 10 or 11. When they met, Seals was in the eighth grade and just learning the saxophone, and Crofts was a high school senior drumming in a moderately popular local swing and country dance band, having given up his dreams of the ballpark.

(Crofts' given first name is Darrell; he has a twin sister, Dorothy, and when they were tots, their mother entered them in a "beautiful baby" contest in Cisco, thinking they'd be ever so cute as Dot and Dash. The nicknames stuck.)

Teenaged Seals had joined Dean Beard and the Crew Cuts, a swing band that was working its way into rock 'n' roll, courtesy of Seals' honking tenor sax and Beard's boogie-woogie piano. When the Crew Cuts lost their drummer, Seals suggested his Cisco buddy Dash Crofts, and the group carried on.

Beard and his band were managed by Slim Willet, an entrepreneur and early Texas TV star who'd written and recorded the hit "Don't Let The Stars Get In Your Eyes" in 1952.

Willet led the Crew Cuts through their paces at West Texas teen dances and the occasional nightclub, but only on weekends so the 13–year old Seals could be home for school on Monday mornings. Through Willet, Jimmy Seals cut a pair of instrumental singles in 1958 on the Winston label.

Beard, who bragged he "knew Elvis" and believed he was himself destined for stardom, had hit moderately with a couple of singles for Edmore and Atlantic, and he and his group had backed a number of performers cutting demos in Texas studios, among them Charlie Walker and LaVern Baker.

And this is where the story of Seals and Crofts really begins. The Champs, from Los Angeles, three months into their chart–busting success with "Tequila," were on the road when a dispute began over ownership of the group name – did it belong to guitarist Dave Burgess or saxophonist Chuck Rio?

When the smoke cleared, Rio and drummer Gene Alden were back in Los Angeles, and Burgess and company were in the middle of a tour with only half a band. "Dave Burgess called somehow and got a hold of Slim Willet," recalls Jimmy Seals. "They said they were looking for a saxophone player and a drummer. They were looking for somebody who wasn't married, who could be kind of groomed for the part."

"Jimmy said to me, 'Would you like to tour through Texas and be *Big Time?*'" Crofts says with a laugh. "So I went with them."

Seals: "They settled on me and Dash, but Slim told them the only way they could have us was if they took Dean, because Dean had a record out on his own."

Says Crofts, "They said, 'We don't need a piano player,' and then he said, 'Well, then you can't have 'em.' We didn't know anything about this." But the Champs took Dean Beard anyway. "They found out later that he was stealing from them," Crofts recall, "so they fired him and kept us." The three erstwhile Crew Cuts joined the Champs tour in Baton Rouge, the fans none the wiser for the sudden change. The musicians had their clothes torn off at the very first gig. Someone called in a bomb scare too.

Seals, who was by then 14, was having trouble at home. His parents had divorced, younger brother Danny going off to live with mom while Jimmy stayed in Sidney with Wayland. When Burgess invited Seals and Crofts to move to Los Angeles to record as full–time Champs, Jimmy had no trouble saying yes.

"I said, 'Look there's nothing out here in West Texas at this time but tumbleweeds and jackrabbits," he remembers. "If I'm gonna do music, I've got to go where it's being done.'" So the teenage Texans moved to California, where they spent the next six years recording and touring with the Champs (Crofts was drafted in 1962 and spent two years with the Army in Fort Bragg, North Carolina; he was replaced, and his replacement was in turn fired upon Crofts' discharge from the service).

Because "Tequila" was an instrumental record, the Champs were an instrumental group, which Seals and Crofts began to find increasingly claustrophobic. They loved to sing, and so did Dave Burgess, but Champs records were just not vocal records. That was that.

"For me, it was very frustrating," Seals recalls. "We were starting to write songs and when we'd come back from touring we'd beg them to do some records vocally. They never really got into it. We formed another group with Dave Burgess, called the Chimes. The three of us did a couple of records with that group on the side; they just didn't want to put the Champs' name out there with it." (The Challenge Records discography lists the artists on these 1962 records, "Desire" and "Peg O' My Heart," as the Trophies. Both Seals and Crofts say they were recorded as the Chimes, and they'd always thought they were released under that name, but Burgess most likely changed the moniker at the last minute.)

Crofts remembers the Chimes only too well. "Dave Burgess wrote a couple of songs and wanted us to sing background on them. We'd go: 'Bong…BING…Bong…' That was our big debut as vocalists, and we said, 'This is not happening too much. We'd like to get into something a little more creative.'"

Challenge Records continued to refuse, even though Champs guitarist Glen Campbell wanted to sing on records too. Of Burgess, Crofts says, "We found out later that he owned the name the Champs. So he brought in all the dough and gave us salary. He was making money hand over foot. Then he decided that he would stay home and run the record company and send us out on the road, like work horses. And that's what he did."

Still, they were turning a profit. "It was a pretty good salary for those days, $500–$600 a week," Crofts says "Pretty good for us, because we were irresponsible teenagers. We'd buy shirts and throw them away and buy others instead of taking them to the cleaners."

"Too Much Tequila" in 1960 had been the Champs' last Top 30 single; still they slogged on. In 1965, after nearly seven years as a Champ (he'd had four singles released under his own name on Challenge, too, and they all bombed), Jimmy Seals had had enough. When the band was booked for a tour of the Orient, with dates in Korea, Japan and Hong Kong, Seals announced he would not be going.

Crofts recalls that Seals was terrified of getting drafted, and thought that he ought to stay low, staying off international airplanes and out of the newspapers. And – according to Crofts – Seals married a woman he didn't really love, simply to reduce the risk of being called up. The two actually argued their way into a fistfight, and Crofts, hurt by what he saw as abandonment by his old friend, left for the Far East with a chip on his shoulder.

When the Champs returned, he too, resigned. His heart was no longer in it. The band dissolved for good soon afterward. Both Seals and Crofts spent the next year or two as Los Angeles session musicians, and eventually they patched up the friendship.

Seals, who'd started messing around with the guitar and was writing songs prodigiously, was particularly affected by the end of the Champs. "To live through the decline of the group was very depressing," he says, "although the group was progressing musically to where we were doing Blood, Sweat and Tears or Chicago–type material at the end of the run."

Crofts went back to Texas, while Seals "collected pop bottles" in California, taking session work when he could get it. In 1966, Seals hooked up with guitarist Louie Shelton and bassist Joe Bogan to form a cover band dubbed, among other things, the Mushrooms (Seals says they changed the name regularly to get re–booked into places that otherwise wouldn't invite them back). Crofts was persuaded to return west and take the drummer's chair. The Mushrooms played rock 'n' roll, jazz, country, any kind of music that was needed to bring in jobs, Crofts says.

One night, the group was playing at a Los Angeles bowling alley, the Hollywood Bowl, when they were approached by three sisters; Billie, Donnie and Lana Day. The Day sisters, who were quite taken with the young musicians, introduced themselves as singers.

Right away, the gears started turning. "We thought 'We'll gang up together, go up to Vegas and make some big bucks,'" Crofts recalls. "We were making a living, but figured that if we added three girls and went to Vegas, we could make a bigger salary."

The new group was dubbed the Dawnbreakers. The girls' mother, Marcia Day, was an agent for a couple of Hollywood actors, and she lived in a gray, three–story house on Sunset Boulevard with her family and sometimes dozens of "friends." Day became the Dawnbreakers' manager, and it was she who got them a "fill–in gig" in Las Vegas, fitting them out with matching stage suits. Back in L.A., Dash Crofts started dating Billie Lee Day, and the boys in the band were invited to move into what was affectionately known as Marcia's Place. Soon, Seals, Crofts, Shelton and Bogan started regularly attending the Friday night meetings, or "firesides," Day held in her home to discuss with many friends her belief in the Baha'i religion, based around the teachings of the 19th Century Persian prophet Baha'u'llah. During his subsequent imprisonment he wrote hundreds of letters and books that became the principal Scriptures of the faith.

Seals and Crofts, dissatisfied with many things in their lives, began to listen. "It gave us a lot of food for thought," says Crofts. "Our priorities began to change. When you get into music, your goal is to become as famous and rich as you can become. It's an ego trip. When we came across the Baha'i faith, it talked about things like oneness of god, the oneness of mankind, the oneness of religion, equality of men and women, elimination of prejudices of all kinds. And we thought, 'Wow, this is really lofty stuff.'

"Probably too lofty for us, but it interested us. And so, we started looking into it." Crofts, because he was romantically involved with Billie Lee Day, was the first to convert to the Baha'i. Seals considered himself at a spiritual dead end. His marriage was over and his career was going nowhere fast. Still, he resisted at first. "Because we were working together, they didn't want to make me feel like they were pushing religion or anything on me," Seals relates. "So what it boiled down to was, no one really told me directly what the faith was all about. Finally, one day Dash started trying to tell me about it. We were driving down Hollywood Boulevard, and he got so frustrated because he just wasn't getting through to me. He pulled over to the side of the road, slammed the brakes, and told me what Baha'u'llah's claim was, that he was the promised one of all ages."

In the Baha'i Scriptures, Seals found answers to the questions he'd been asking all his life. When you stripped away the conventions of each of the major religions, all the prophets were saying essentially the same thing: love one another. The basic tenets of the Baha'i faith – love, tolerance, absolute equality of all sex or race and worldwide unity – appealed to the young Texan.

"From that point on, I just started ripping books apart," he says, adding that the words of Bah'u'llah "became the foundation for the writing that we did with Seals and Crofts." ("I've been trying to find a loophole now for 26 years," says Crofts, who married Billie Lee Day in 1969. "And I haven't found it yet. I was really skeptical.")

Shelton and Bogan married the other two Day sisters, and Seals became involved with Ruby Jean Anderson, another "friend" who'd stopped by to sit in on the Friday night firesides at Marcia's Place and stayed a while. One night when no one else was home, Seals and Anderson were thrown together, helping a young woman who'd overdosed on drugs on the Day doorstep, then tending to the victims of a car crash down the block. They wound up sitting over coffee and talking all night, excitedly sharing their feelings about life, love and spirituality. They were married in 1970.

The Dawnbreakers actually cut a couple of sides for Dunhill in 1968, produced by Richard Perry. However, Crofts says with a laugh, Perry crossed paths with Tiny Tim during this period and "we got dropped like a hot potato." Perry hit the top with "Tiptoe Thru The Tulips" and the Dawnbreakers' wax never materialized.

Meanwhile, Louie Shelton, who was making tons of dough as a session player while starving with the Dawnbreakers, decided to leave the group to work as a session guitarist and producer. Bogan went with him.

"Louie started moving into producing and Joey started moving into engineering … it just kind of naturally broke up, but we were all still together, in an indirect way," recalls Crofts. After all, he says, "Three marriages came out of that group."

But he and Seals had already done some hard thinking about something new. "In the Champs and the Mushrooms, and in the Dawnbreakers, we were playing a harder kind of music," Crofts says, "and we were kind of sick of that. So for therapy we would go into a room and write these little, pleasant soft songs, like wandering troubadour kind of music. And we didn't play it for anybody. We'd just go play it for ourselves, just a therapy. And then we got to where we thought we'd try it out in between sets — at the breaks, when everybody took a break, Jimmy and I would sit there and play these little tunes. And we saw that people liked them."

Crofts wanted an instrument to complement Seals' acoustic guitar; drums simply wouldn't do. So he borrowed a cheap mandolin from his brother — who kept it on the walls as an ornament — and taught himself to play. "I just plunked it and it sounded really good," he remembers. (Eventually, Crofts wandered into Barney Kessel's Music Store in Los Angeles and bought a vintage Gibson mandolin for $125, an incredible price even in 1969. He played the instrument on "Summer Breeze," "Diamond Girl," all the big Seals and Crofts records, and he still has it.)

Seals: "We worked out counterparts on the mandolin and guitar, and also on the vocals, and then we tried to work it out sometimes where we would sing two parts, and play the other two harmony parts on the instruments. Being from a small band, we were trying to make it sound as big as we could."

Seals and Crofts played their first show as a duo at the Ice House in Pasadena,

California, in 1969. Next, they signed on to perform at the legendary Hoot Night at Los Angeles' Troubadour club. Seals recalls that he had to borrow the $2 the club required as a guarantee they'd show up.

"We went on between two hard rock bands," he says. "And we only had four songs. We played those, and the whole house stood up and just went crazy. So we sat down and played them again. And we told them, 'We're sorry, we'll have to come back when we write more.'"

And so the teenage prodigies from Texas abandoned rock 'n' roll and the big beat more or less forever, and found their "true calling" in folksy, acoustic music, dedicating their work – as they did their lives – to the teachings of a Persian religious leader who had been dead for almost 100 years.

Day got them a record contract in 1970, with Talent Associates (TA), a low–budget subsidiary of Bell. Two albums were released that year, *Seals and Crofts* and *Down Home*, both largely self–written collections of "wandering troubadour music." They were sweet, simple and folksy, and despite the release of two singles from each album, there were no sales to speak of.

Still, Seals and Crofts' performance following grew progressively larger, and in early 1971 they were signed to Warner Brothers Records, then on a roll with James Taylor and on the lookout for more introspective singer–songwriters to bankroll.
Seals and Crofts' sound, a vaguely medieval blend of acoustic guitar and mandolin, was mannered and polite, courtly even, and their lyrics – almost always penned by Seals alone – were radiant and positive, talking of a kind of love that could have been about the opposite sex or about God, depending on how you read them. The songs were full of love, faith, peace and talk of "the truth." And that, not to put too fine a point on it, was the sort of thing that was selling in 1971.

To produce their first Warners album, Seals and Crofts brought in their old Dawnbreaker chum Louis Shelton (suddenly they could afford him). To further keep it in the family, Joe Bogan became their engineer. Crofts, Shelton and Bogan were at the time happily married to the three Day sisters. "We had been drawing 3,500 to 4,000 people a night for like two years without a record," Seals recalls. "So we felt like, if we ever got a record that would appeal to the masses, we would be able to draw more people and have a career."
Year Of Sunday was released on Warner Brothers in the waning days of 1971. A vast improvement, sonically, over the TA albums, it also featured sharper and more pointed songwriting. One particular ballad, "Antoinette," was an exquisite blend of harmony vocal, acoustic guitar and mandolin soloing.

The Baha'i influences were everywhere if you looked. "When I Meet Them," the first single, was a plea for universal brotherhood, as was the R&B–flavored "Sudan Village." The title track, in fact was based around the Baha'i belief in "progressive revelation," that is, the teachings of the prophets, in succession, forming a sort of map for mankind to follow. "We all live in a year of Sunday," then, meant that every day was like a church day, with something to be learned. Heady stuff was for the pop charts, to be sure, but expertly put across. Despite a massive promotional push by the label, however, *Year Of Sunday* did not light the world on fire.

Those were the days when record companies actually believed in their artists, and instead of getting the hook for their poor sales showing, Seals and Crofts were encouraged to try again. "This was all an experiment," Seals says. "We never dreamed we'd be heard on the air. Some of it sounds like shopping cart music. Nobody knew what they were doing."

In the summer of 1972, the duo signed on as opening act on a national tour by the supergroup Chicago. The exposure was priceless, as their second Warner Bros. album *Summer Breeze* was to be released in July. *Summer Breeze* is, arguably, the definitive Seals and Crofts album. All the elements were in place, including top–notch songs and deft performances by the twosome and a band of friends and studio acquaintances (bassist Bobby Lichtig, who played with Seals and Crofts for most of the '70s, made his debut here, and the widely–seen Chicago tour featured just him backing Seals and Crofts). Here, they found the ideal commercial formula.

Again, Seals wrote most of the lyrics, and he and Crofts collaborated on the melodies. On *Summer Breeze*, they came up with mystical–sounding ballads ("East of Ginger Trees" and "Hummingbird," both of which included verbatim quotes from the Baha'i Scriptures), a finger–snapping, bluesy acoustic ballad that was literally about faith ("The Euphrates"), a couple of socially relevant "pop" songs ("Funny Little Man," "Yellow Dirt"), a beautiful if obtuse folk ballad ("Advance Guards") and an excuse for Seals to take his hoedown violin out of mothballs ("Fiddle In The Sky"). He played a little sax on "The Euphrates," too.

Then there was the title song, a simple celebration of home and hearth. With its catchy chorus ("Summer Breeze makes me feel fine/Blowin' through the jasmine in my mind") and unforgettable signature "riff" (played in unison on Crofts' mandolin and Lichtig's bass), "Summer Breeze" became a classic "soft rock" single overnight.

The single reached No. 6 in September, and the album went gold, spending 100 weeks on the *Billboard* chart. Seals and Crofts appeared on every television show that showed an interest, and began a touring schedule that would hardly abate for eight years.

"We were ready to be disc jockeys, roadies, sound mixers or whatever, just so we could be in and around music," Seals explains. "Because that was all we had known. We didn't have any grand delusions about what might happen; we just took the next step when it came. If the door opened, we went."

"Hummingbird," the second single, made it to No. 21 in January 1973. By then, Seals and Crofts were almost finished with their fifth album, the one that would ultimately prove to be their biggest seller, and, as each of them would come to realize years later, the beginning of the end. The album was *Diamond Girl*, and it too went gold soon after its release in May. The title song – jazzy, with some complex changes – was released as a single, and like "Summer Breeze," climbed to No. 6.

There were no simple acoustic duets on the album – Seals and Crofts had acquired a band. A rather large band. Seals: "After *Summer Breeze* hit, somewhere in between there and the recording of *Diamond Girl*, we realized that we could not progress any further… we were very limited as to the kind of music we could play. But there was no way that we could play anything any harder. If you're playing with a band, all of a sudden you're in competition with

10,000 other bands. The band has got to really cook; and it's got to have an identity. And for the crowd that we were playing, it had to be hard rock. I feel like we lost a little bit of uniqueness in what we were doing, because we started leaning more and more on the band."

Once again, the words and teaching of Baha'u'llah were prominently displayed, in such songs as "Intone My Servant" ("Intone my servant/the verses of your Lord") and "Nine Houses," a symphonic "suite" that paid homage to the nine major organized religions of the world. Then there was "We May Never Pass This Way (Again)," which retold the story of the fabled "year of Sunday": learn all you can in this lifetime; it may be your only chance. This was the second *Diamond Girl* single, released in September and slightly edited from the album version. It climbed to 21 on the charts.

Seals honked his tenor sax on the jazzy instrumental track "Wisdom," and the duo tossed out a humorous cowboy song, "Dust On My Saddle," that would become an in-concert staple.

Another highlight of the album was "Ruby Jean and Billie Lee," which Seals and Crofts wrote together as a love letter to their wives. "We kept it a total secret at the time we were doing it," Crofts says. "We wanted to give them a gift that would last for a while. So Jimmy started writing the song about Ruby, and I said, 'You can't write one for her without me!' So we decided you write a verse, I'll write a verse, and we'll put the kids in the middle. We had one kid apiece, Joshua and Lua. The funny part about it was, they'd show up at the studio and we'd start calling it 'R&B Waltz,' instead of 'Ruby Jean and Billy Lee,' so they wouldn't know what it was. That was the code name."

Seals and Crofts put perhaps the best signing of their careers on this one recording. "Finally, the day came for us to spring it on them. They came down to the studio, and there was like four or five Warner Brothers executives there with big cigars in their mouths and all that; we started playing it for them and they started crying, and then the executives started crying, big tears in their eyes. It turned out to be really neat. We said, 'This is specifically for you guys. We're not even going to release it as a single, we're just gonna give it to you, and you can have it.'" It never was released as a single, but it was included on the duo's *Greatest Hits* album two years later.

By now, Seals and Crofts were a major touring act, a top grosser, with a private plane for Seals and Crofts themselves, another for the band, and another for the crew. Still burning with the fervor of the newly–converted, they devised a way to "tell" their fans about their Baha'i beliefs without, they hoped, coming off like pushy religious zealots. After each concert – about 20 minutes after the house lights had gone up – the duo would return to the stage and chat, sans microphones, with anyone in the crowd who wanted to hear about it. These little post–concert rap sessions, announced at the beginning of each show, were called firesides, just as they had been on those long–ago Friday nights at Marcia's Place.

"We tried to take our art and use it toward something that would further civilization in some way," Crofts says. "Yeah, we were successful and we got hit records and we started making bigger money, but what we did was hire more people and try to make it a better show. But we decided at the same time to put in our contract that every place we have the alternative to talk about the Baha'i faith. We never incorporated it into the show itself. We always said that they came to hear music, and that's what they're gonna hear. And afterwards, if somebody wants to hear about the Baha'i faith, we'll come back and tell them about it. We're not evangelists."

Seals put a lot of stock in these discussions. "It was something we felt was like a great responsibility, because you don't want to be like parrots out on the street, telling everybody that comes along this, that and the other," he says. "And the other thing is, you're having to try to live it. You can call yourself whatever you want, but how you live your life is your religion.

"It was at a time when it was very important that the faith become known in this country, because there wasn't enough Baha'i at that time, and because they can't take donations from outside, and they can't proselytize, the only way you can do it is through an interview, or if you have firesides.

"You also can't have people come listen to music and then force religion on them. So it was a strange setup. If people know that you're gonna talk about something that is religious, or that's your faith, if they're attracted to that and want to stay and listen to it, I don't think you can hurt yourself."

The year was 1973. Richard Nixon was looking at another 12 months in the White House, tops, the Vietnam War was raging away … and Roe vs. Wade, the landmark Supreme Court decision legalizing abortion in the United States, had just been handed down.
"I think you can ruin your career, as we almost did, by taking a concept and trying to put it into a record," Seals says, "where it becomes sucked into the political scheme of things."
Lana Day Bogan, wife of the group's recording engineer and longtime crony Joe Bogan, had seen a television documentary on abortion and were moved to write a poem, from the point of view of the unborn child.

Seals, at Lana's suggestion, put it to music.

"Oh, little baby, if you only knew.

Just what your momma was planning to do…"

This was "Unborn Child," Seals and Crofts' follow–up to the sweet and singable pop hits "We May Never Pass This Way (Again)" and "Diamond Girl." The album likewise, was called *Unborn Child*.

Crofts: "Warner Brothers warned us against it. They said, 'This is a highly controversial subject, we advise that you don't do this.' And we said, 'But you're in the business to make money; we're doing it to save lives. We don't care about the money."

Both Seals and Crofts insist the song's message was, simply "don't take life too lightly," to stop and think before going through with an abortion. But the critics tore the record to pieces, and Seals and Crofts with it, deriding it as not only a bad record, but lousy poetry. The single was a commercial disaster; the album shipped gold, but the retail returns were serious.

"It was a double–edged sword," Crofts says of the *Unborn Child* controversy. "It hurt us in one way, and helped us in another. It turns over fans, is what it does. If you're against something, you lose those fans. But if you're for it, you gain some fans. And that's kind of what happened."

"I don't know whether people knew what was in there or not," Seals recalls, "but some of the pro–abortionists called up the radio stations and demanded equal time. Well, that killed the airplay on it. What we had done is we had taken a single issue. Before, we were dealing with the general concept of things. I think everybody in the world, regardless of whether they've previously been a racist, or an atheist or whatever, can accept, without getting too upset, the fact that mankind is one family. We're all here on one dot and we need each other. It's obvious. But when you pull it down and start taking the different really hot issues, if a person is not looking at the overview that you are, then they're not gonna connect the parts together. They just see one thing."

This one thing got Seals and Crofts picketed all across the country. "I think we got more good results out of it than bad," says Crofts, "because a lot of people called us and said, 'We're naming our children after you, because you helped us decide to save their lives with that song.' That was very fulfilling to us."

"I thought either it would be very much accepted, on the strength of the song itself, or that it would be the biggest bomb that we ever had," Seals explains. "But it was incidental by that point, because the music was gone. I was out of gas already. When you get in that position, you really don't know what to do. It happens without a lot of different artists, and I admire those people who have not let that happen to them. We started with a classical–oriented instrumentation, mandolin and guitar, and trying to find ways to use that – and to not use it – with two people was very difficult.

"If you had one person with the freedom of adlib kind of singing, of being able to move through different phrases of music, it's much easier for one person to do it than two. Duos had never been my cup of tea, to start with. Outside of a few records, I don't like 'em. A group, and a single artist, are much easier to manage and to record."

"Unborn Child" hurt Seals and Crofts' reputation – it was as if they had crossed that thin line, that sacrosanct divider that separated their music from their religious beliefs. The single never made it higher than No. 66 in *Billboard*, and the follow–up, "King Of Nothing" (with Crofts on lead vocal), only went to 60. They toured for much of 1974 with the issue hanging over their heads. Often, their concerts were picketed by pro–choice groups.

In April of 1975, damage control began with a new single and album; both titled *I'll Play For You*. As a response to the fires stirred up by the "Unborn Child" single, this one was an innocent, somewhat innocuous pop song, the most neutral thing the duo had ever recorded. "I'll Play For You" squeezed into the Top 20, but the follow–up, "Castles In The Sand," failed to chart at all.

For Christmas that year, *Seals And Crofts Greatest Hits* was issued. It had both of the *I'll Play For You* singles, and "King Of Nothing," but "Unborn Child" was conspicuous in its absence. Buoyed by the plethora of songs from the glory days of *Summer Breeze* and *Diamond Girl*, the album sold well.

Still, Seals says, he could read the writing on the wall. "After *Unborn Child* and *I'll Play For You*, the music just started getting more and more watered down, less identity and this, that and the other," he explains.

"I remember the night it happened. I was in the dressing room, I think it was down in Mobile, Alabama, and I just knew. I said, 'The spirit is gone.' You sense it. I sensed the same finality that I had sensed with the Champs, except it was our music. And it really made me kind of sick."

"But at some point like that, you can't go backwards. And also, if you're a hard rock group, you can get softer, you can go to a softer song, or a softer style, and you can find your way to peace in your soul, or whatever you want to express and you can get away with it. But if you're a soft rock group, you cannot do a hard song and get away with it. Very seldom, at least in those days, was it acceptable."

Still they plugged on, pretending nothing was wrong. Ironically, when they tried a "hard song," it gave them their biggest–selling single ever. "Get Closer," which Seals had written as a Bill Withers–type ballad, was recorded as an uptempo R&B single, with a trio of lead vocalists – Seals, Crofts and R&B singer Carolyn Willis, who'd been a member of the trio Honey Cone ("Want Ads"). "Get Closer" reached No. 6 in April of 1976.

"I always felt like Carolyn Willis' voice was too high for ours," Seals laments, "because she would be singing at the bottom of her range, and us at the top, in order to get three parts." Nevertheless, Seals and Crofts hit the road in support of the gold *Get Closer* album, with a huge band, Willis and background singer in tow.

They both knew it was all wrong. "I tried several times to get him to go out with just the two of us again, after we had been successful," Crofts explains. "The problem with touring, in those days, was the expenses were astronomical. You had to ask promoters for a fortune just so you could make some money. And the farther along it got, the higher the expenses got. I think that's what caused the decline.

"And Jimmy was his own worst critic. He was very critical of himself, and was very hard on himself. Sometime I'd say 'Jimmy, when are you gonna just let go and enjoy this?' He was pretty much of a perfectionist, but Jimmy took it so seriously that sometimes he would badger his own self."

The reason he took up mandolin, Crofts says was to be able to travel without "a bunch of stuff to carry around. I ended up with like three 18–wheeler trucks to carry the stuff that goes with the mandolin.

"It got really insane at one point, and I finally said, you know, this is unbelievable. We've got four pilots, three truck drivers, a road manager, an assistant road manager, a business manager, a creative manager, a band and about 12 roadies. We were taking 30 people on the road. It was like an army."

Warner Brothers tried valiantly to keep the *Get Closer* momentum going with *Sudan Village*, released in the fall. It was a live album, of relatively obscure songs from the Seals and Crofts archives, and the first recording of Seals' "fiddle breakdown," a highlight of their live shows for years.

"We were touring so much that we didn't have time to go in and do a legitimate album," Crofts remembers, adding the album was (badly) recorded over a three–night stint in Las Vegas. "I think it was a pretty lame idea, myself. But there wasn't too much we could do about it, because we were so busy." The album was a stiff, although the single culled from it, "Baby I'll Give It To You" (another trio with Willis) actually charted slightly higher than "Unborn Child."

"We felt like, after the *Sudan Village* album, that we were forcing ourselves to come up with material," Crofts says. "Because, basically, we had said everything we wanted to say already. Our hearts weren't into it, because we'd already made our statement. It puts you under such pressure. The pressure is once you've got a hit, trying to stay in the flow."

By '77, they were flying blind. A friend of the duo's, television writer Charles Fox, talked them into singing a collection of songs he'd written (with lyricist Paul Williams) for the soundtrack of the Robby Benson basketball movie *One On One*. Fox also produced the film, which was not a major success. The single from this project, "My Fair Share," made it to No. 28. They didn't write it, and they didn't like it.

In 1978 came the album *Takin' It Easy*. The uptempo single, "You're The Love," was out-and-out disco, a full 180 from the "wandering troubadour music" of their heyday. Warner Brothers even issued it as a commercial, 12-inch dancefloor single, extended to six minutes in length for maximum boogie-ing down. "You're the Love" was Seals and Crofts' last time in the Top 20, reaching No. 18 in April.

Around the same time, they also cut the theme to the popular television drama *The Paper Chase*. Although it was heard each week by millions of people, "The First Years" never appeared as a full song on a record.

The next year, Seals and Crofts accepted $60,000 each to lay down a vocal for a McDonalds' radio commercial. Crofts: "In those days, it wasn't cool to do a commercial: 'Oh, you're selling out.' Now everybody's begging for commercials. They're killing each other to get a commercial. We kind of did it with a grain of salt. We had offers from Kodak, and Johnson's Baby Powder, and things like that. They were offering us really big bucks."

The end finally came in 1980. Overtly jazz-inflected, *The Longest Road* was to be their last album. "The best part of *The Longest Road* was, for me, working with Chick Corea and Stanley Clarke," Crofts reports. "They didn't have to do the session with us, but they did it out of sheer respect.

"But I think what we were doing there was just grabbing for straws. We had material, but we knew that the material was not up to par. But we had a contract with Warner Brothers; we were supposed to put out two albums a year. And so we threw an album together – that's basically what *The Longest Road* was."

The album, and the single "First Love," got nowhere near the charts. *The Longest Road* was outsold by K–Tel's *The Seals And Crofts Collection*, which was released around the same time. Looking forward wasn't doing anyone any good; it was time to look back.

Warner Brothers dropped them.

"After that, we decided, 'What the hell are we doing here?'" Crofts says. "We're trying to force material, and stay up with the standard we've already established. And why prostitute ourselves? Why don't we just stop?'"

"We just didn't have the material," explains Seals. "And I think Warner Brothers probably looked at their past artists and said, 'How many more have these guys got?'"

Don't hold them to it, but Seals and Crofts have no intention of returning. "Even today, there's not one been able to make a comeback and sustain it," says Seals. "Maybe one album. In those days, a group was good for one, maybe two or three albums. They'd reach a high point, and the rest of it was greatest hits albums; milk it for all you can."

Wiki Commons

6. Mary Hopkin
'She's a Joan Baez type, but we'll soon alter that'

I don't have a lot to add to the original intro, except that at this writing (in 2019) the notoriously press-shy Mary Hopkin has yet to do a more extensive interview, with anybody. No idea how I got to be the lucky one. She spoke to me to promote the expanded-issue CD debut of Apple Records' Those Were the Days: The Best of Mary Hopkin. *This is reproduced exactly as it appeared in* Goldmine *in 1992.*

Mary Hopkin is surprised and flattered to learn that she is something of a mythical figure in America. In the States, general knowledge of Hopkin is pretty much limited to seven singles and three albums she released between 1968 and '72, and even then, you'd be hard-pressed to find too many people who could hum anything other than "Those Were The Days."

Little-heard though they may have been, Mary Hopkin's American releases were on the legendary Apple label, owned, operated – and eventually all but abandoned – by the Beatles. She was discovered, and her career set in motion, by Paul McCartney himself.

And that's enough to put Mary Hopkin in the pop music history books. The fact that most of her Apple records were good, unlike so much of the non-Beatles Apple catalog, only makes her more of a legend.

She was born May 3, 1950 in Pontardawe, South Wales (coincidentally just a few kilometers north of Swansea, hometown of fellow Apple artists Pete Ham and Mike Gibbons of Badfinger) and with her angelic soprano voice sang folk songs with her mates at school. Accompanying herself on guitar, she'd performed on a couple of regional TV shows.

Mary Hopkin's Cinderella story goes like this: Her Welsh agent, Bert Veale, signed her up to appear on British ITV's *Opportunity Knocks* talent show, and against her better judgment (Hopkin said the program was "like the *Gong Show*") she went on, and won. The date was May 6, 1968.

The long-legged and very famous model Twiggy saw Hopkin on that first show (in the weeks to follow, she'd go on to win a record number of times) and told Paul McCartney about it. McCartney happened to be looking for talent for the soon-to-be-launched Apple label, and on Twiggy's recommendation, he tuned in to the next *Opportunity Knocks*, and immediately had his office find Mary Hopkin.

"I got in touch, and her and her mum came down and we had a little lunch in Oxford Street somewhere," McCartney recalled in a 1987 interview. "Mary was really a sort of folk singer, so I said, 'But, for record success, there's this song that's not a mile away from folkie It's got a folkie feel. It could be a big hit, with the right treatment, the right arrangement'."

McCartney told the story of how he found "Those Were The Days" in a London nightclub: "There would sometimes be cabaret clubs. I'd go down late, about 11:30, and catch the early show. It was kind of a good thing to do, you know, because around Berkeley Square there was the Blue Angel. I used to go down there quite regular and check out the cabaret."

One night at the Blue Angel - it was probably in 1966 - he saw an act called Gene and Francesca. "They were an American act, and I'd never heard of them before," he said. "But they did this little song; they said 'Here's a little song of our own that we've worked up.' I always thought 'Ooh, that's a good little song. If it hadn't been written, someone would have to write that'."

He was knocked out by "Those Were The Days," which Gene (Raskin) had adapted from a traditional Lithuanian folk song.

"I got the office to try and find those people," McCartney said. "He was an architect, I remembered. Because it was almost a hobby for them, this little thing they did on holidays. We got a little tape of them singing it, and I worked it all out with Mary."

Produced by McCartney, "Those Were The Days" was released the same day as the Beatles' "Hey Jude" (in August 1968) and went on to sell eight million singles, even knocking "Hey Jude" out of the number one spot in the U.K.

(McCartney, ever hit-conscious, had Hopkin record her vocals in English, French, Italian, German and Spanish, and "Those Were The Days" became an across-the-board international smash.)

Almost immediately, as McCartney's attention began to wane, she grew disenchanted with the singles she recorded as follow-ups. She was a folk singer, not a pop artist, and despite being voted Britain's Top Female Vocalist in 1969, she was miserable making the endless rounds of TV shows and ribbon-cutting ceremonies her Apple handlers sent her on. She lamented about the "sugar-coated" image that Apple had bestowed upon her, and about the things she was expected to do as an "all-round entertainer."

Worst of all were the summer seasons. "A summer season," Hopkin explains, "is a three-month gig at a summer resort, like a beach resort. In this country, we've got Blackpool and Margate, all over Britain wherever the beaches are. Sometimes it takes place on the pier, or in the local theaters. You perform six to eight times a week for three months.

"And unless you like that sort of thing, it's pretty horrendous. You end up singing the most dreadful material."

And then there were the pantomime shows, usually at Christmas, where fairy tales and sundry "light material" were given the musical treatment. Again, for weeks on end.

The low point, for Hopkin, came with her representation of Great Britain in the 1970 Eurovision Song Contest. For this show of shows, she was given the insufferably chirpy "Knock Knock Who's There" to sing. As she said in this interview, such things did great damage to her confidence, but she was young and naïve at the time and trusted the advice of her manager, Stan Skeffington (who was also her brother-in-law).

"Knock Knock Who's There" was the second of three Hopkin singles produced by Mickie Most, who was brought in after McCartney drifted off (his last single for Hopkin, "Que Sera Sera," featured just him and Ringo Starr on the backing track).

Hopkin and Most didn't get along, though, and her next sessions were produced by Tony Visconti, with whom she was able to make an album (*Earth Song Ocean Song*) that she felt truly captured the acoustic flavor she'd craved from the start.

But it was too late. The record got no support from the fast-rotting Apple; Hopkin was booked into another hated summer season and was unable to tour to promote the record. Despondent, she let her Apple contract expire (although in truth there was no one left to stop her).

Today, Hopkin lives in England. She writes songs with her 21-year old son and talks about returning to the music business on her own terms.

As for her Apple period, well, how to be diplomatic? For Mary Hopkin, the memories aren't all bad, but those really weren't the days.

Prior to signing with Apple, you made several records on the Welsh label, Cambrian.

I did a few EPs in the Welsh language, and I think they were particularly enjoyed in the Welsh settlements in America and South America. There was a television program, basically Welsh folk music and contemporary music, and I did a few of those. It was a good experience. And I used to sing for pocket money with the band we'd formed, with three local boys.

We listened to English pop music, mostly. We did actually have a Welsh pop chart, but it was mostly folk music at that time. These days, they've gone on to do covers of a lot of the current American and English pop charts. I think they sound horrendous. In fact, I listen to the stuff I did then, covers of English songs, and they sound awful.

What did you want to be in those days? Did you have designs on a folk singing career?

Joan Baez and Bert Jansch were the first guitar-playing folk singers I ever really listened to; I was introduced to them by a friend of my father's, who was a keen folk enthusiast. I learned to play guitar from Joan Baez records and things, but left to my own devices, I think, I'd have developed into a singer/songwriter. My development was rather halted halfway, when I was thrown in at the deep end of the music business.

The old story is that Howard Hughes was a great fan of your Welsh-language records.

I was rather amused by that. You could picture him as a recluse, sitting with his Kleenex on his lap, listening to his little Welsh girl. Very strange. Very odd.

Your "big break" came on the ITV talent program Opportunity Knocks. **What was that like?**

It was all terribly, terribly embarrassing at the time. It wasn't something I want to be a party to. But I was sort of (talked) into doing it by the agent who was finding us work while I was still at school. Without my knowledge, he put my name down for this show. I was mortified when I heard he had done it. You can't condemn that kind of show, because they can do a lot for people, and certainly it would've taken me a lot longer, if at all, to get into the music business, but the whole thing is terribly embarrassing. I did the audition, because my agent said it would be good experience to attend an audition.

Do you remember what you sang on the show?

The first thing I did was "Turn Turn Turn," the Pete Seeger song. I just went on and did the Joan Baez songs I had learned up to that point. They're a bit show business for my liking, those light entertainment shows. It smacks of cabaret and summer seasons.

I presume this is where Twiggy comes into the picture.

Hmm, yes. She was watching it, one of the many who do watch that sort of program. I'm not one of them. But I am grateful to Twiggy; she's lovely and she certainly gave me a momentous start in the music business. I did the show on the day after my 18th birthday; I was still supposed to be studying for my final exams at school, my university entrance exams. Twiggy saw the show, and I think the next day saw Paul McCartney. He was telling her all about the new Apple label. And she said she'd seen this girl on *Opportunity Knocks*, and he should check me out.

So I received a telegram, two days after the show, which I ignored for a few days. It said, "Ring Peter Brown at Apple Records" and I had never heard of either of them. I was a great Beatles fan, and I'd heard of the Apple Boutique, but nothing else. We didn't know Apple Records was on the way.

I left it on the shelf for three days, and then my mother said it would be polite to ring back. So I did, and I was put on to whom I thought was Peter Brown. And this chap had a distinct Liverpool accent.

I started wondering at that point, making the connection with Apple but he asked me if I'd come to London and sing for him. I said, well, that depends and he realized I was being very cautious, so he asked my mother to come to the phone. So my mother came to the phone, and he said, "Oh, this is Paul McCartney. Would you like to bring your daughter to London to sing for me?"

That was it, really. I was whisked off there the next day and sang for him; we demoed at the little Dick James Demo Studios. I sang a few songs for him; then I was called back about two or three weeks later, and he sang a little song for me, sort of hummed it, and said, "I've had this song lying around for years. It's called 'Those Were The Days'." And he said, "Let's go in and do it."

"Those Were The Days" sold eight million singles. Was there a game plan for your career, for following up its huge success?

It was a bit haphazard, really. I think everyone was taken by surprise by the success of "Those Were The Days." I don't think anyone expected that to happen so quickly, you know. It went straight to the top of the charts, and it was number one in 13 different countries at one time, so I was whisked around the world and spent the next year promoting it.

Did you have the impression that Paul wanted "a girl singer" on Apple, and was trying to groom you, to fit you into the mold?

I'm not sure what he wanted. It was definitely an experiment. I felt as though it was an experiment to see what I was capable of, and that was not very much at that time. I didn't take it that seriously at that time, I thought, "This is all right." I didn't realize I'd spend the next 20 years trying to live it down.

On Post Card, you cut those big, show-stopping songs, like "There's No Business Like Show Business" and "Someone To Watch Over Me." Was Paul pushing those on you?

Not really. Paul and I talked things over. I didn't know what I was capable of anyway, and I thought, "He must know better than I do." I mean, I didn't really question it. There were songs I was obviously much more comfortable with, like the Donovan songs. I was completely at ease with those, and those would've led directly into *Earth Song Ocean Song*, where I did choose the songs.

On that first album, you sang Donovan's ethereal acoustic ballad "Lord Of The Reedy River."

I loved that. The three of us just sat there, it was all done live, and I sang direct from Donovan's lyric book, where he had just printed the words out. It was lovely, and that's the way I would've liked to work. I don't think there were any of their songs on *Post Card*, but as soon as I met Benny Gallagher and Graham Lyle, we clicked. We were obviously on the same wavelength.

Did Paul score all those big orchestral arrangements on Post Card?

Paul was always involved. He would go sit with George Martin and they would work it out. Sometimes it would come from George, and sometimes Paul would sing a little riff and say "this feel" or "that feel." I can't remember who did exactly what now. But Paul was very much involved.

What did sudden success do to you?

It didn't change me very much, I don't think. I was pretty naïve about a lot of things; having grown up in Welsh valleys, you're quite protected and sheltered from the Big Bad World. I was experiencing a lot of new things, but probably because of my solid Welsh upbringing I rejected a lot of the things I didn't want to associate with in the music business.

I remember one quote from Paul in the press. He said, "She's a Joan Baez type, but we'll soon alter that." That didn't go down well with me; even though I thought Joan Baez was wonderful, I didn't want to be too influenced by her. Like all young people, you listen to artists when you're 12 or 13, and you learn their songs, but that doesn't mean you end up being like them. You want to develop your own songs.

The Beatles were having serious problems by 1969. Did you feel that Paul was paying less attention to your career?

Of course. A year went by before he wrote "Goodbye." And that was after I'd said, "Look, how about another single?" But I understood. Obviously his priority was the Beatles, that's natural. He said he wrote "Goodbye" in about 10 minutes. I'm not sure how true that is! It probably is.

The two of you played acoustic guitar together on "Goodbye," right?

Yes, we did. And Paul put a thigh-slap on there – on his own thigh, I might add! It's a good song for its kind, but whether it was suited to me, I don't know. It was easy for me to do those songs. They were fun little pop songs. So it was very easy for me to say, "Oh. Okay. Yes." But as soon as I realized what was happening, I started putting the reins on, and putting my foot down about what material I was going to do.

I trusted Paul's judgment, anyway. I would never condemn him for what he did; because he did what he felt was right for me. And I really enjoyed working with him.

Were you aware of the chaos at Apple, and did it affect you?

I was aware that it was disorganized; I think everyone involved in Apple would agree on that. I think they were just finding their feet; it was early days for them, and a lot of them were new to it anyway. [Beatles publicist] Derek Taylor mentioned in an interview over here that my management setup was pretty dreadful. I had no one to represent me at the time. Eventually, my brother-in-law took over as manager, but there was no one at Apple.

Every time I did a television show, I always had an escort, a sort of acting manager. There were a couple of people, Terry Doran and Alistair Taylor. My sister didn't manage me, which you sometimes read in the press – she was sort of pushed into the position of chaperone-come-spokesman, because I had no one else to represent me.

Did you feel that they were overly concerned with your image?

I don't remember any formal discussions about it. Coming straight from school, I suppose I looked very innocent and little girl-ish. What I didn't think was necessary was extra sugar-coating on the top of that. I felt they were exaggerating the image. If I'd be sitting in a bar with a drink, a glass of wine or something, and a photographer turned up, it would be whisked out of my hand and replaced with a Coke or a lemonade or something, by whoever was with me from Apple at the time.

I thought that was rather silly, because it must've been embarrassing to Apple to have someone like me on the label, anyway. I thought, why exaggerate this image when it's sickly enough as it is.

Tell me about "Que Sera Sera," the last single Paul produced for you.

At the time, it was just one of Paul's fun ideas. It was one sunny afternoon, we were sitting in Paul's garden, and he said, "Do you like this song?" I said, "Well, I used to sing it when I was three!" And he said, "My dad likes it, let's go and do it." And so Ringo came along; it was all done in an afternoon. I was sort of swept along with Paul's enthusiasm, really.

By the time I was halfway through the backing vocals, I said, "This is awful." I really thought it was dreadful and I didn't want it released.

Mickie Most came in and produced the next single, "Temma Harbour."

Had it been done by another artist who'd established themselves in a different vein, had I been an established singer/songwriter, for example, you can then do very twee little songs and get away with it. Like Sting did that 'Happiness" song. Someone like that, because he's established, he can sing a twee song and everybody gets the joke.

But when Mary Hopkin did something like that, the general public wouldn't understand. Now I write very tongue-in-cheek, bitchy little songs. That's what happened with the sugary image that was presented. It made it all very ghastly; songs like "Temma Harbour," anything sugary, are really very nauseating to me.

Why Mickie Most?

The reason I worked with Mickie was that obviously Paul and I agreed that it wasn't going to work out, because he hadn't the time, and I had to get more material out. We came up with Mickie Most, and I thought, "Oh, that might be good," because he'd produced Donovan, who was very sensitive and does beautiful music.

Unfortunately, Mickie took a different approach with me. And that's when the rot set in.

The crunch was when Mickie visited me at my final summer season. We'd been going over some songs to record, and he said, "Choose the keys, and I'll go away and record them. When you've got a chance, you come down and do the vocals." I said no way; I have to be there. I want to discuss the arrangements. I don't want to be a session singer, just come in at the end and stick a vocal on top, thank you very much.

There is a perception that after the Beatles broke up, no one at the label paid any attention to the other Apple artists.

I didn't mind that, because I left Apple, by choice, after *Earth Song Ocean Song*. I was so demoralized by that time, because I'd finally done the album I wanted to, and Apple was encouraging about that, but I was then tied up in doing these horrendous summer shows, which preventing me from promoting that album. So it sort of fizzled out without a trace, because I wasn't there to promote it. I remember reading a lovely write-up in *Rolling Stone*. But by that time it was too late. I'd been pushed more and more into the show business side.

It's very easily done, because when you're surrounded by people who've been in the business for years, handled around to different agents, you say yes, the first time, because you don't know what it's all about. It's hard to explain, but it's easy to be manipulated when you're 18, 19, and people say, "Ah, but you only have to do this one, and then you'll be free to do the kind of material you want." They have their ways of persuading you.

Was it the best of times or the worst of times?

I was so young at the time, I didn't take it seriously. I didn't realize immediately that it might harm me psychologically. I'm not sure how it's harmed me as far as the public is concerned.

You represented England in the 1970 Eurovision Song Contest, and you've said it was a real low point for you.

I did lose my confidence. I really don't want to sound too upset about it all, but at the same time it was unpleasant. I'd say.

The music quality is appalling. The only decent thing that came out of it was ABBA, that kind of music. It was another embarrassing experience, an experience to crown them all really. I wish it had never happened. I was promised that that quality of songs for the competition would be improved, that they would be decent songs.

And what happened?

Well, they were dreadful. I was conned, basically. Not by the BBC, but just by people around me, who said it was very important that I do this. The song was "Knock Knock Who's There." I was devastated when I heard that, because by that time I was committed to doing it.

That's the problem, you see, you weren't told exactly what was going on. So by the time you'd committed yourself, professionally, you couldn't back out. It would be unprofessional.

Aside from a few scattered singles and group recordings, you haven't appeared much on record shelves since the Apple days. What are you doing now?

I'm writing songs now, working either on my own or with other writers, in various styles. The songs that are important to me are the ones I'm writing with my son, Morgan, who's living in New York. He's 21, and he's writing some amazing music. He sends me backing tracks and I write the melody and lyrics. And so far the response has been really good. We're really enjoying it. We're very much in tune. He writes what I hear, what I can't put down, because as a musician he's excellent. I'm fine with vocals, and basic guitar and piano, but I wouldn't be able to put down a whole backing track as well as he does.

Are you considering re-entering the music business?

Although I'm not consciously looking for a record deal – I've had some unpleasant experiences in the past – I'm not interested unless I have full control over what I do. But my idea would be to have them released and do videos, and that's it.

So, how do you feel about the Those Were The Days album being released on CD?

I'm not unhappy it's coming out. Fortunately, I can sort of remove myself emotionally from it. I'm delighted that people who enjoyed the tracks then will get to hear them again. It's always lovely. That's why I don't want to condemn them, really because if it gives people pleasure, it's good. As a singer, it sort of demoralized me, but we shouldn't harp on that, should we? I've moved on.

Do people still recognize you, stop you on the street and say, "Mary Hopkin! 'Those Were The Days'!?"

I'm afraid so, yes. I've never liked that side of it. I've always really liked the music side when I'm in control of the music. Basically, I'm not a performer. I've never been comfortable onstage, really. I am a singer and now, hopefully, a songwriter. I love that. I feel as if I'm finally expressing myself in the way I want to.

So the Apple days were like being in kindergarten, really, just falling over a lot and the whole world witnessing all my spelling mistakes.

(Those Were The Days: The Best Of Mary Hopkin was compiled by Apple in 1972, and in its new greatly expanded form, by Hopkin herself. After our interview was completed, she was asked to comment on each of the 'new' version's 17 tracks):

"Those Were The Days": Good quality. I'm proud of that. It was a delight to do, especially since Pavarotti and his pals sang it.

"Goodbye": Jolly little song. I think slightly in the wrong direction, but it was fun at the time. I think it was good of Paul to write it for me.

"'Temma Harbour": No. No. I did say no to this at the time. It was one of those long drawn-out arguments, really. I lost. Another artist, with some credibility, could've done that really well.

"Knock Knock Who's There": That wasn't Mickie's fault, even though he produced it. That was from the other side of things, nothing to do with Apple. It was just a lot of other people wanting me to do the Eurovision Song Contest. It was the accepted thing, if you were a popular singer then, that you would represent the country that year, you know.

"Think About Your Children": I lost a lot of confidence because of the material I was doing. And I suppose I've only myself to blame anyway, but all I can say is that I was very young at the time, and however much I disagreed, there were about 15 people who would oppose me. It was very hard to stand up to all these experienced businessmen.

"Que Sera Sera": As far as I remember, it's just Paul and Ringo. I don't think he added anything else. It was all finished in that one afternoon.

"Lontano Dagli Occhi": That was another song contest, in Italy. Again, it seemed like a good idea at the time. I had never been to Italy, and I thought, "Good, I'll go to Italy."

"Sparrow": "Sparrow" was lovely, because that's when my friendship with (songwriters) Benny Gallagher and Graham Lyle started. And we've been friends ever since, which is about the most wonderful thing that's come out of my time with Apple. It was a little somber, on reflection, but at the time I was happy with it.

"Heritage": I think that's one of the ones where I just sat in the studio with Benny and Graham on acoustic guitars. I loved everything they were involved with.

"Fields Of St. Etienne": That's one of my all-time favorites. Beautiful song. Apparently, the first time it was released on an album, it was a different arrangement. It might've been the chap who did "Those Were The Days," Richard something. Paul produced the other version, which was a bit over the top. And having been told that they were re-releasing it, I begged them to find the version I did with Benny and Graham. Which I think this is.

"Jefferson": The country "Ya-hoo" song. Pleasant, fun, yes, not their best song. But it was fun working with them; we were great friends by then.

"Let My Name Be Sorrow": I think my friend Ralph McTell found this – a French writer, I think. I loved it; it's all a bit melodramatic, looking back, the way I sang it and the way it was arranged. They were a bit over the top. Vocally, my voice hadn't matured enough to cope with any of these really. Many of the heavier ones.

I can't blame Paul for thinking I should sing light, jolly little songs, really. But there could've been a happy compromise – I could've sung some more of the contemporary folk things.

"Kew Gardens": Oh, that's a delightful little song. That's a twee song, but it's very sweet. It's not one of my all-time favorites, but since Ralph wrote it, it's a very sensitive little song.

"When I Am Old One Day": I haven't even heard it since then. We recorded it, but I think we had enough tracks for the album, and that was one of the ones that got left out in the end.

"Silver Birch And Weeping Willow": Quite honestly, I didn't want to include my absolute favorites on this album, because they didn't fit in with it as a collection of songs. So I chose the lighter songs, really. "Silver Birch" is another gentle, sweet song of Ralph's.

"Water, Paper and Clay": I enjoyed it very much.

"Streets Of London": I wasn't ever happy with my vocal on that. It's a beautiful song, but only Ralph can sing it really. We have this argument, Ralph and I: He thinks I didn't do it justice. It's in this collection because I do love the *Earth Song Ocean Song* album. It had such a beautiful atmosphere there. It has all the best musicians – Ralph, Danny (Thompson) and Dave (Cousins, of the Strawbs) and Tony produced it very well and wrote lovely string arrangements. It was all very sensitive, and that's the way I wanted to work.

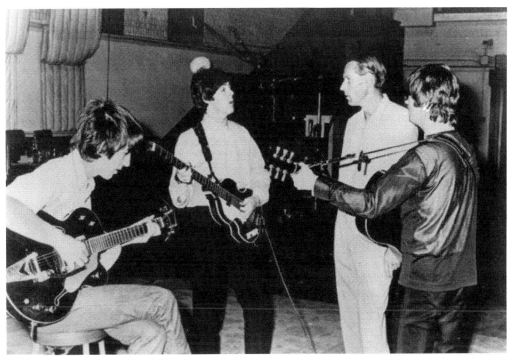

Wiki Commons

7. Sir George Martin:
'These are my boys, the greatest in the world'

Hands down, my favorite interview. George Martin was, in every sense of the word, the Fifth Beatle. Without him, none of those incredible string and horn arrangements, no classical influence, no baroque harmonies, no eager acceptance of new and untried ideas. He was the antithesis of a pop producer in the 1960s in that he encouraged experimentation, and he enjoyed dark humor, and he selflessly nurtured the Fab Four's growth spurts. I thought long and hard about questions for this one – I knew that this would most likely be my only shot at talking with someone so key in the Beatles universe, so I came up with a list of things I had always wondered about, from a serious fan's perspective. The year was 1993, and since it first appeared in Goldmine *this interview has been plagiarized, quoted and misquoted in magazines, books and online fan sites. Usually without attribution, I might add!*

John Lennon used to say that when he heard a Beatles song, it automatically brought him back to the recording session, what he was playing, how he was feeling that day. Is it the same way for you?

Not really. Looking back at all the songs, it's a long time ago, and I purposely over the years hadn't looked back at the songs. My life has been so busy, I've tended to go on and look at tomorrow rather than today, or even yesterday. And I find that you can get too obsessive about the past. I did find, however, that when I did that television program on *The Making Of Sgt. Pepper* a couple of years ago, that of course forced me to look back and see what was going on. And it was the first time, to be honest; in all those years I'd really looked back and started thinking deeply about the past.

When I think of a song – if you play me "Paperback Writer" or "Norwegian Wood" – sometimes I will think about things … in the case of "Norwegian Wood," it immediately brings it back to a hotel in St. Moritz, where John and I had a skiing holiday together. And he wrote the song during the time there, so that's obviously very evocative. But if you take a song that doesn't have that particular kind of nostalgia, it's a kind of blur. "Fool On The Hill," I can remember how we did that … but there were so many, and there are so much of them, that it's all one sort of melting, shimmering haze.

You played piano on a lot of songs during the early years; it's particularly evident on the **Hard Day's Night**–*era tracks. Was that literally because no one else could do it?*

To begin with, of course, none of them knew what a keyboard was like. They were guitar players. When I first met them, I was aware that they were guitar men and I was a keyboard man. And if you're running through a new song for the first time, a guitar player will look at another guy's fingers and see the shapes. You can see what the guy's doing on the fret, and you know what chord he's playing. If you then take that guitar player, and he doesn't know anything about keyboards, what you play on the piano will be completely meaningless to him. He won't understand the chords at all. And a keyboard player, if he knows a bit about guitar, won't understand what the chords are by looking at his hands. There's a hidden language there.

So I actually said to myself, "Hey, I'm going to have to learn the guitar, because I'll need to communicate with these guys on their level." And Paul, at the same time, said the same thing to himself: He said, "I think I'll have to learn piano, to see what George is up to." Because what I used to do, whenever Paul or John sang me a song, I'd sit on a high stool and they'd play it in front of me. And I'd learn it, and I'd then go to the keyboard and I'd say, "Is this it?" and I'd play through the chords and hum the tune. And they'd say, "Yeah, that's fine, Okay," and I'd know the song.

That piano sound was very distinctive.

Piano's a very useful instrument. And, of course, Paul was the one who actually took it up and learned it more quickly and more adaptably than anybody else. I mean, he's such a fine, versatile musician; he could play almost any instrument if he set his mind to it. So that by the time he got to "Lady Madonna," he was doing a bloody good solo. He couldn't possibly have done that in 1962.

And John never really mastered the keyboard. His idea of playing the piano was having a group of triads – you know, three notes that formed a chord – and just go up and down the scale with them. He could play rhythm all right on keyboard, but he wasn't very clever at doing single notes or lines.

It's been theorized that your classical music background, and your work on comedy records, were big factors in making the unprecedented new pop sound that you made.

I tried to turn them on to it. We did get counterpoint into their work. I remember during "Eleanor Rigby," which was quite a breakthrough in a way, when we were actually recording it I realized that one of the phrases could work against another phrase, that, they hadn't designed that way.

In other words, "Ah, look at all the lonely people" actually could come at the end of the piece. Which it does. I put it in; got them to sing it … they were knocked out by that. "Hey, yeah, those two things go together! It's great, innit? It works well." It had never occurred to them; never occurred to Paul. But that was a lesson for him. Because I'm sure that when he came to write "She's Leaving Home," that was, definitely, two lines working against each other. It was one broad melody, and another one kind of answering underneath it. He learned how to use that weaving of lines.

They were like sponges, in a way, weren't they?

They learned so quickly. But when I first met them, I had absolutely no idea at all they could write decent material. They wrote songs that were pretty awful – "One After 909," and "P.S. I Love You," and "Love Me Do" was the best of them. It was pretty rough stuff. I didn't really blame the guy who turned them down so much. In fact, everybody turned them down, more or less, on the grounds that their material wasn't very good, I imagine.

Do you remember exactly when they stopped being your students in the studio and started pretty much calling their own shots, coming to you simply for advice?

There was no one moment. It was a gradual drift. By the time we got to a song like "Walrus" or any of John or Paul's later songs, they would have very definite ideas on what they wanted to do, which they hadn't to begin with. It was a gradual drift so that they became the teachers, almost at the end, and I was the pupil.

What I do remember, though, was that having rejected all the stuff that they had, and accepting only "Love Me Do," I had actually rejected "Please Please Me," in those very early days of 1962, saying "This is no good, this song, it's very dreary. If you're going to make anything of it at all, you need to double the speed and really put some pep into it. Make something really worthwhile. Maybe use some harmonica on it." Because when they played it first to me, it was Paul singing a very kind of winsome, Roy Orbison slow ballad. Which was very dreary.

Well, they learned from that, because when I gave them "How Do You Do It," and we made a record of that, they still wanted to have their material. They said, "We've been working on 'Please Please Me,' we'd like you to listen to it." And the result was good. And that gave them an incentive, then, to do better things from that moment onward.

Had you tried that in 1968, say around "Hey Jude" time, would they have said, "Don't tell us what to do, George?"

I don't think so. I don't think they ever rejected anything I said. All of us in the studio, including Ringo, had equal voices. And the five of us would look at things and try to make things better. They were much more fruitful by this time, so that if I did have something that I didn't like ... in the case of "Hey Jude" I said, "Do you think we're being a bit unwise, going on for seven minutes?" And Paul said, "No, it's there. Can you get it on a record?" I said, "I can get it on, but it's not exactly a single. DJs will fade it." I was being practical, and I was wrong, because he was right, because it was right that it should be seven minutes. And it always has been, ever since.

Curiously enough, Paul and I have always been good friends, and we've often had dinner with our wives and so on. And about eight years later, '78 or '79 I'd say, we were having dinner one night and Paul, at the end of it said, "By the way, I'd like you to produce my next record."

I fell apart and I said, "I'm not sure that's a good idea."

He said, "Come on! Don't be so silly! Why not?"

I said, "Because things have changed now. You're a good producer in your own right, and I don't want to spoil a beautiful friendship, thank you very much."

He laughed and said, "Why don't you think it'll work?"
I said, "Because I don't think you will accept the direction that I have to give you as a producer."

He said, "Of course I will. We know each other too well for that. How could it not work?"

I said, "Well, there's a selection of songs, for a start."

"Do you want me to audition for you?!?!!" he said, jokingly.

I said, "Not quite, Paul." But, I said, "I've got to be able to choose your songs and tell you what's good and what's bad."

And he swallowed. That had never occurred to him. By this time, all of them had got to the stage where everyone revered them so much that they hadn't quite thought anyone would dare to suggest that anything they did wasn't terribly good.

He said, "You're quite right. I've got 14 songs."

I said, "Give them to me, and I'll listen to them over the weekend. I'll tell you about them on Monday."

He rung me on Monday and said, "What about it, then?"

I said, "Well, I've listened to every one of them."

He said, "Good."

I said, "Four are great."

He said, "Four???!!"

I said, "Six need a lot of work on them, and the other four you can throw away."

There was a kind of distant silence. But Paul is a sensible and honorable fellow, and he said, "All right, you and I had better talk about it, and we'd better sort them out." And we did, and we made a very happy album.

I think that people, when they become superstars, they have to have someone to tell them … they're surrounded so many times by people who tell them they're the greatest thing in the world; they need to have an honest opinion. It's the emperor and his new clothes, isn't it?

Near the end of the Beatle years, did you consider yourself friends? Or was the relationship like that of an employee to an employer? This was White Album, Abbey Road time.

The *White Album* was a funny one, because at the time they came back from abroad and they all had a huge collection of songs they wanted to record. And they wanted them done all at the same time. By this time, they were four individuals with their individual songs, wanting to record them with the assistance of the other people, rather than being a group. I couldn't cope with it all at once. We were actually recording in a couple of the studios at the same time, identically. John would be in one studio, and Paul would be in another. And I was running from one place to another. I had a very able assistant by this time, a guy called Chris Thomas, who's now a first–class producer. We shared the work, so I would come in and see what he was doing, and supervise and so on.

But it was such a frantic time; I never really worried about any sort of splits there. The real cracks appeared during *Let It Be*. That was the worst time.

With regard to the White Album, you've said that you tried to get them to cut it down to a single–disc, 14–track album. What would you have cut out?

That's a good question, because it's now such an accepted album. Everyone thinks it's terrific. A lot of people say it's their favorite album. Don't forget, I was looking at it from the point of view of the songs when I heard them, rather than the songs when they were finished. I said to myself, "Let's pick the best and most commercial songs, and let's work on those. Let's forget the other ones for the moment."

I'm not saying we wouldn't have recorded those other songs, but I would like to have made a really great album out of the best of the stuff there, and concentrated and worked very hard on them. But they wanted everything done at once. I thought they were dissipating their energies rather than focusing them. That was my concern. There are one or two items of dross on the *White Album*.

Such as?

I haven't got the list in front of me. You'll have to read them off. Was "Bungalow Bill" on that? "Honey Pie?"

Yes, and "Wild Honey Pie," "Revolution 9," "Birthday."

"Birthday." Well, there you go. You're picking them for me! There are songs that are not at the front rank, put it that way. From other groups they probably would be front rank, but these are my boys, they're the greatest in the world, and that's the way I saw it.

The songs that remain unreleased today: "Leave My Kitten Alone," "If You've Got Troubles," "That Means A Lot." Was there a sense while you were cutting them that they were hopeless? Or were they just culled at the end of the sessions?

There were many instances when they would come in and not get very good results. I don't remember the specific circumstances; quite often, they would be done at the tail end of sessions, or sometimes they would be done because they came into the studio and they didn't have anything else.

Would you like to see that stuff released?

Now that all the water's gone under the bridge and everybody's much older and wiser, we are actually now looking at putting out a kind of definitive, all–encompassing Beatle Anthology.

They've certainly been doing it on film; the boys themselves have been collecting a hell of a lot of footage and interesting visual programming. They've got about six hours assembled so far. And toward the end of next year, or maybe 1995, there will be the beginnings of a television series of hours. It'll be tracing the history of the boys from when they were kids right through to the dissolution in '70.

Now there will be an accompanying series of albums, which will go alongside that. But they won't be the soundtrack, because the soundtrack will be spasmodic and so on. They will be complementary rather than identical. And for that, I'm going to delve, and I'm going to look at every source – bootlegs that are in good condition. I'm going to look at radio broadcasts, live performances, demo records, all sorts of things apart from anything else we did in the studio, and I shall collate, polish, look at, criticize, chuck away, but maybe issue anything that I think is worthwhile, that actually traces their history.

The bootleg CDs that are out now, some of the stuff is pretty phenomenal.

So I understand! And where the material came from in the first place is most interesting. I'd love to know. I've heard some of it, and some of the quality is remarkably good.

You don't think anyone knows how they got out?

I think all these things will probably be incorporated in what I'm talking about. It doesn't make sense for them to go out on bootlegs, does it?

In his 1970 Rolling Stone *interview, John made several disparaging remarks about Beatles recordings, what he called the "Dead Beatles sound." Did that hurt your feelings at the time?*

Very much! John went through a really crazy period. I was very incensed about that interview. I think everybody was. I think he slagged off everybody, including the Queen of England. I don't think anyone escaped his attention.

When I saw him back in L.A. some years later, and we spent an evening together, I said, "You know, you were pretty rough in that interview, John." He said, "Oh, Christ, I was stoned out of my fucking mind." He said, "You didn't take any notice of that, did you?" I said, "Well I did, and it hurt."

He went through a very, very bad period of heavy drugs, and *Rolling Stone* got him during one of those periods. He was completely out of it. John had a very sweet side to him. He was a very tender person at heart. He could also be very brutal and very cruel. But he went through a very crazy time. The tragedy of John was that he'd been through all that and he'd got out the other side. And he really was becoming the person that I knew in the early days again.

I spent an evening with him at the Dakota not long before he died, and we had a long evening rapping about old times, which was marvelous. That's now my happiest memory of him, because he really was back to his own self.

You were recording Tug Of War *with Paul the day John died. Just for the record, where were you when you heard about it?*

I lived about 80 miles west of London, and he (Paul) lived 70 miles south. We were both in our respective homes. It was six o'clock in the morning, and somebody rang me from America and told me the news, which was not a good way to start the day. I immediately picked up the phone and I rang Paul, and I asked if he'd heard it. He had heard it.

And after a few moments together, I said, "Paul, you obviously don't want to come in today, do you?" He said, "God, I couldn't possibly not come in. I must come in. I can't stay here with what's happened. Do you mind?" I said, "No, I'm fine. I'll meet you."

So we went into AIR studios in London. We were supposed to record that day. Of course, we didn't put down a single note, because we got there and we fell on each other's shoulders, and we poured ourselves tea and whiskey, and sat round and drank and talked. And we grieved for John all day, and it helped. At the end of the day we went back to our homes.

Now, one of the ironies and one of the bitter bits about life is that Paul, when he came out of the studio, of course was surrounded by reporters and journalists. He still was in a deep state of shock. They photographed him, and they flashed him, and they said him the usual sort of zany and stupid reporter questions. The question was, "How do you feel about

John dying then, Paul?" I don't know what you're supposed to say to that. And he looked and he shrugged and he said, "Yeah, it's a drag, isn't it?" And went off into the night.

And he was slated for that. He was mercilessly attacked saying, "How callous can you be?" And I felt every inch for him. He was unwise, but he was off his guard. It was tough.

You recently scored Paul's song "C'Mon People." You must have a pretty good working relationship with him.

I don't produce because I'm too old, and he's a good producer anyway. I don't want to produce. In fact, he's asked me if I would. But life's too short. But he had this song and he said, "Would you mind doing a bit of scoring for me?" So I listened to it and I said, "Okay, why not?" And it was fun. It's nice occasionally working together. I wouldn't want to make a habit out of it.

You've done a lot of remastering and CD transfer for EMI on these Beatles projects. When you get to the Phil Spector songs, "The Long And Winding Road" and that, are you ever tempted to twiddle the knobs and just wipe out those strings and choirs?

(Laughing) You bet I am! It's a silly thing, really, because that was a wounding thing. And I don't honestly think those tracks are as good as we should have made them. But hell, they were there, and they're history now. If you're a sensible bloke, you just say, "That's it." And obviously, when you're transferring to CD, it's got to be as it was when it was issued, and that's the end of it.

Maybe you'll get to change some when you do this anthology next year.

Well, you can't really change the artistic content … that would be wrong. My brief was to try and reproduce on CD what we heard on analog. That was my prime motive, to try and make it sound, on CD, with the same warmth and quality we have on analog. Which is not an easy thing, by the way. So when it comes to the question of changing things, no, if I changed it, I would've re–scored it, and all that kind of thing.

On the American LPs, they added all that echo and awful stuff. Did you used to hear that, and throw your hands in the air?

Of course I did, but I was powerless to do anything about it. Capitol ran the roost. And they used to take the credit for it too.

Do you know why they did those things?

Ego? I don't know! I mean, there's a guy who actually put his name on the records, saying he produced them. So you tell me. Eventually, when we do this anthology thing, then we'll go back over all those albums and make sure they're in the right order, and in the original versions as well as other stuff. It'll be quite a big job, but it'll be fascinating to do. The last thing I'll ever do with the Beatles.

You think so?

I guess so. The final thing. The final solution.

So you're content with being known as The Beatles Guy now?

Well, you can't escape these epithets. You get pigeonholed. Some people think I've never done anything else.

MCA Records

8. Tom Petty (1993):
Just the hits

Reprinted by permission from The Gainesville Sun. *The original recording was long lost, but this one had significant historical merit – Petty does a song-by-song review of his upcoming* Greatest Hits *album, which would go on to sell 15 million copies and usurp* Full Moon Fever *as his all-time best seller. At the time, all it meant to him was the last commitment to his contract with MCA Records, with which he had grown weary.*

He was already recording Wildflowers *for Warner Brothers, the Traveling Wilburys' label, and looking far down the road. Things were changing; the band as I knew and loved it would soon lose a key member, among other things. I lost interest after that. I would only speak with him on one more occasion, at the Heartbreakers' 2002 Rock and Roll Hall of Fame induction in New York City.*

It was just about 20 years ago that Tom Petty said goodbye to the old hometown. Along with the four other guys in the band Mudcrutch, he threw his gear in a van and left Gainesville forever. His goal was to become rich and famous.

Oddly enough, that's exactly what happened.

What a long strange trip it's been for the skinny, scruffy blonde kid from the northeast section of town. He's 43 now, an internationally recognized rock star who counts Bob Dylan and two ex-Beatles among his best friends.

Still, he remains closest to the Heartbreakers, most of whom he's known and played with since his nightclubbing days in Florida.

On Thursday, he'll play the O'Connell Center, in a concert that'll be broadcast live around the world on FM radio. The show - one of just three Petty will play this year; the other is Tuesday at St. Pete's Bayfront Arena - is officially part of the University of Florida's Homecoming celebration.

It wasn't supposed to happen quite this way, Petty explains via telephone from his Los Angeles home.

"Johnny Depp talked us into playing one night," he says. "He opened this club on Sunset Strip called the Viper Room. He came to us and said, 'We're gonna have opening night, and I'm gonna give the money to sick kids, and please come play. You can play whatever you want.'"

The band, which hadn't toured for two years, was at that moment in the studio laying down the new songs for the greatest hits album. "With a little arm-twisting I convinced them all to come play," Petty explains. "We played about an hour of just new stuff. We didn't play any old stuff.

"And we got a little buzz behind playing, and we sat around saying it was fun to play, we hope we do it again."

End of episode. Petty then turned his attention back to the solo album he'd been working on before Depp's phone call.

Out next week is his first-ever greatest hits album, including his best-loved tracks with the Heartbreakers, songs from his hugely successful solo album, *Full Moon Fever*, and two new Heartbreakers numbers recorded just for the occasion. A boxed-set anthology is in the works. Petty says his plan was to dig into the solo project, and not come up for air - for any reason - until it was finished, hopefully in the spring of '94.

Still, "I love to play live - I'm not nuts about touring year in and year out. On the last tour, we did a pretty good stretch, and when we got done in Europe we decided we would take a sabbatical from touring for awhile, just so we don't start to feel like 'entertainers.'

"I love playing. That's still what it's all about to me."

The last tour was behind *Into the Great Wide Open*, the ninth Tom Petty & the Heartbreakers album since 1976.

The set was produced by ex-ELO frontman Jeff Lynne, whose distinctive style had invigorated *Full Moon Fever*. But on *Great Wide Open*, the critics carped, there was simply too much Jeff and not enough Tom.

"I loved that album," Petty counters. "You can't help what people think. But it sold quite well! And it seems to have gone down all right with a lot of people. And often times, when that criticism would come up, what they thought was Jeff was me, and vice versa."

During their time together, Petty and Lynne got together with Dylan, George Harrison (and, just before he died, Roy Orbison) to record as the Traveling Wilburys. Petty says a third Wilburys album is being discussed.

Of Lynne, he offers, "I would certainly like to work with him again. Because, really, I have to say that of all the people I've encountered and worked with, he certainly is the best musician and the best arranger - record-maker - that I've ever met."

He has no time for anyone who thinks he and Lynne got too chummy in the studio. "When you're out a long time, people have their favorite sort of periods of what you do, they say 'He should be more like he was then,' but I can't get wrapped up in that," he says.

"I just kind of go where the wind takes me. It's what I've always done, and I'm sure that's what I'll continue to do."

Rick Rubin, founder of Def Jam Records and producer of Mick Jagger's recent album and an upcoming set by Johnny Cash, is producing Petty's solo album. It will be his first for a new label, Warner Brothers.

"When it came time to do the *Greatest Hits*, it was actually Rick's suggestion that we should get the Heartbreakers together and cut the songs live in the studio, like we used to years ago," says Petty. "We had to have two new songs.

"So we took a little time away from the other project, and I wrote a handful of songs for the Heartbreakers. We called 'em in ... I think the list was 30 songs in two days' time. So we had a lot to sift through."

In two days' time, they'd recorded nearly 15 songs. Included on the hits album are "Mary Jane's Last Dance," a bluesy Petty original that features him playing both harmonica and second lead guitar, and a cover of Thunderclap Newman's classic "Something in the Air."

The latter song, a call for change in a world gone crazy, seems as relevant today as it did when it was written, in 1969.

Just days after the 1992 Los Angeles riots, Petty wrote "Peace in L.A.," a heartfelt plea for understanding. He recorded the song with the Heartbreakers, and had it released as a single - with proceeds earmarked for L.A. rebuilding efforts - within a week.

"I do what I can," Petty says. "It's very hard to tell somebody what that was like, to be here when that was happening. It was very disturbing. And it was just my natural urge to do that, and I've always been real glad we did.

"And we still get really nice letters. It obviously made some money for some really good causes."

Although he likes to talk about environmental issues from the stage ("I've never really learned to shut up"), Petty won't go the distance and call himself an activist. He was one of the first rock 'n' roll artists to insist that cups at his shows' concession stands be made of recyclable paper.

"A lot of people used their position to just hip everybody that there is a problem, and here's some simple ways that you can help a little bit," he explains. "But these days, it's almost redundant to go up and say anything about recycling, because everybody does it."
The idea of acting as a spokesman for an issue - any issue - is anathema to him, quite frankly. He's well aware that other rock stars speak out all the time, but that sort of thing is just not for him.

"They're probably much more comfortable in the role of celebrity," he believes, "which I can honestly say I've never sought. And I have no intention of ever seeking it. I don't want to be a personality or a celebrity. I just make music, and that's the end of my job, really. I don't go to things like premieres. I don't want to be on TV."

But Petty's fans hang on his every word. Wouldn't he be able to make a difference?

"Maybe they listen to me because they believe me," he replies. "It's hard for me to ever believe some of these celebrities - I often wonder if it's an actor's business to tell me anything, or a musician.

"I don't know that I'm always right, or that I've got the right idea, but I think somebody's got to speak up every now and then. We still have a lot of things to work out in America -- the gay issue is one, and human rights in general. I think racism still runs rampant in some areas of the country.

"These are things that I would be most interested in helping out. I think most importantly we just have to treat everybody like humans and hope for the best."

And the hits just keep on comin'

"It was kind of fun when I heard it all strung together," Petty says *of Tom Petty & the Heartbreakers Greatest Hits*, which MCA Records will release on Nov. 9.

The song selection was left to Petty himself. "I was sort of flooded with a lot of memories," he says. "I thought they were pretty good little records, really. I don't ever put them on at home. I hear them on the radio, but the first time I'd sat down and really played 'em all in a row, it was kind of nice."

After this one, his new records will be released on Warner Brothers. "It was a nice way to end my long affiliation with MCA," he reports. "I think I'm leaving on a good note - everybody's still friendly and everything. How long was it, 18 years? That's a long time to be there."

Song for song, here's Petty's comments on the album.

"American Girl': I remember we recorded it on the Fourth of July, and I remember a lot of talk about the Byrds when it came out, but Michael (Campbell, Heartbreakers guitarist) and I never really even thought about the Byrds until other people brought it up to us. I remember when we got the take, we were pretty excited about it."

"Breakdown": "I wrote that because, whatever song we did that day, we got done pretty early. And no one really wanted to go. Someone said 'Why don't you write us another one?' and being young and naive I just said 'Yeah, OK.' I sat down at the piano and wrote this 'Breakdown.'

"It was originally put down in this jammy kind of version that was about six or seven minutes long, and the guitar lick Mike played only right at the end of the song. And this guy called Dwight Twilley, he was around a lot in those days, he said, 'Boy, that's a really great lick at the end there, I can't believe you aren't using that more. It's a great hook.' I'd already sent the band home, and I phoned them at 2 a.m. - so they say - and they came back to the studio. We cut the track in a couple of takes, in a much shorter arrangement. We were into very short songs at the time - no excess - because there was so much of that going on in that time period." Petty says he has no idea at all why he sang "Breakdown" with a cheesy Spanish accent.

"Listen to Her Heart": "My wife Jane had gone, with (producer) Denny Cordell, over to Ike Turner's place. And she had been kinda cornered by Ike Turner and barely got away. She was saying it was this wild experience. I don't really think I was writing to Ike. I think it gave me an idea and I took it from there."

"I Need To Know": "I was trying to make a song like Wilson Pickett's 'Land of 1,000 Dances.' That's one of my favorite records. I actually wrote that at Crescent Beach, Florida, at a friend's house."

"Refugee": "'Refugee' was mostly Mike's music. I think I just hummed the tune and wrote it very quickly, in 10 or 15 minutes. I can't remember exactly how long, but I remember thinking 'Boy, this fell together quick.'

"The song hung around for a good year before we ever got it recorded, but we used to play it on the road. It was one of those that really caught on with people."

"Don't Do Me Like That": "Mudcrutch recorded it in L.A. around '74. It was something my dad used to say, 'Don't do me like that.' We never really took it very seriously."

"Even the Losers": "I think that's really a good song. I heard it the other day on the radio. I remember that I didn't have the title when I went to the session. I had all of this song and then the chorus came and I didn't know what to sing. That just sort of blurted out of me on one of the passes and I went, 'All right! There's the title.'"

"Here Comes My Girl": "Another one of Mike's, from the same demo tape as 'Refugee.' I got the idea for the narration from Debbie Harry, who we'd been playing with at the time. She did some deal where she just talked in the song."

"The Waiting": "Don't remember much about 'The Waiting' except ... I think we recorded it on my birthday, because we were interrupted by somebody in a gorilla suit, one of those really awful telegram things. And he wouldn't go away. It was really annoying. We were just, 'Please, never let any more of these in the studio.' We were trying to cut this track, and the guy was trying to do 'his show', and he wouldn't leave until he'd done his entire act."

"You Got Lucky": "Just a little pop song. We'd just gotten the synthesizer, obviously. It was probably the first germ of trying to break out of the bag we were in, musically. That whole album (*Long After Dark*), I think I was impatient with everybody and wanting to do something else. That was the one chance I got to sort of feature the keyboard more than the guitar. It's a pretty hot little single, you know, pretty hot. Pretty good rhythm track.

"I think I was already in the mind to make *Southern Accents* by that time, and there was consensus around that I was maybe being crazy. So I almost felt like I was conceding to do the stuff on *Long After Dark*. Although I enjoyed it; I really thought at the time we probably should've been doing something else, because it was so much like the stuff we'd done before."

"Don't Come Around Here No More": "It's still one of my top three things I ever did. That one's way up there on my list; just as a record it's a lot of fun to listen to."
What are the other items on the top three? "Couldn't say."

"I Won't Back Down": "I like this one quite a bit, too."

"Runnin' Down a Dream": "A terrific driving song, I think. One of the only songs I ever wrote about a car. Del (Shannon) had a good laugh about it. I gave it to him in an airport; he said he put it on, on the plane, and started laughing."

"Free Fallin'": "'Free Fallin'' was really about Los Angeles and the San Fernando Valley. At the time, I was living in Beverly Hills and Mike lived in the valley, and I had to drive over Mulholland Drive, which is this kind of road that looks off to L.A. on one side and Hollywood on the other. It was formed driving down Ventura Boulevard.

"It's a very active road. It's a kind of a trip just driving up and down it. I'm very pleased that I was so embraced by the people of the San Fernando Valley. Anytime I go somewhere, they thank me for the song."

"Learning To Fly": "I love that one. I just think it's one of my better songs. I wrote it with Jeff Lynne, and I loved the record. We had a ball doing it."

"Into the Great Wide Open": "The problem with a lot of them, especially 'Don't Come Around Here No More,' people always think of the video. 'Wide Open' was one of my favorite videos, because it came out so close to what I envisioned. It was exactly like the movie in my head."

"Mary Jane's Last Dance": "I'm still thinking of the right words to explain the song, but I don't know if I've come up with them yet."

"Something in the Air": "It was one of those that we'd only played twice. And when we dug through everything, we all just oohed and aahed over it. We were so pleased with it, and we thought 'You know, this is probably the only chance we'll have to put this out on a record.' Because covers never seem to make the final album cut; the originals just get priority. So we decided to stick it on. I thought it was a nice little message for the end of the album."

Petty understands that not everyone will be happy with his choices. "There was a lot of things that some people wanted that there just wasn't room to put on," he says. "It's really a double album. They'll probably bring out another volume at some point."

Warner Bros. Records (1978)

9. Emmylou Harris
Sweetheart of the Rodeo

A lot of people, myself included, owe Emmylou Harris a debt of gratitude for introducing them to country music. Because she and her musician pals were 180 degrees from what country had become during the 1960s and '70s – big hair and rhinestones, predictable, cookie-cutter songs with inane lyrics and the syrupy Nashville production sound that had come to be derisively known as countrypolitan. She looked like somebody you might actually know. Most of all, Emmy's gossamer voice was like nothing we'd ever heard; she and her band of relatively young guys made cool records out of songs by the Louvin Brothers and Buck Owens and Patsy Cline, right there alongside songwriters with names like Townes Van Zandt and Jesse Winchester and Rodney Crowell. This wasn't the stodgy, showy country music of Robert Altman's Nashville*; this was something, for those of us raised (like Emmy was) on rock 'n' roll and folk music, new and exciting. She opened a door, and we followed her through, not knowing what we would experience next.*

This story was written from a series of interviews conducted in 1996 with Harris, Herb Pedersen, Bernie Leadon, Barry Tashian and Rodney Crowell. A conversation with Linda Ronstadt, written as a sidebar, follows.

Serendipity, what Webster loosely defines as "dumb luck," is an important concept for Emmylou Harris. The most admired and influential female vocalist in modern country music, she refers to her career as a series of fateful incidents, one thing or one person leading to another, and so on. Twenty-one years of peerless recordings, of hard work and diligence and the supreme exercise of God-given talent, and she very humbly passes it all off as little more than charmed good fortune. Serendipity.

Emmylou Harris styled a synthesis of country and pop music that honored and upheld them both, instead of watering one down for the sake of the other. She has explored long-hidden trails on the historical landscape and discovered treasures, then faithfully brought them back to share with everyone. In the mid '70s, when much of country music meant hackneyed pop knockoffs, she sang the songs of the Louvin Brothers, the Carter Family, Buck Owens and Hank Williams, forging distinctive and durable music with those most workman-like tools, harmony and melody.

But Harris and her producer Brian Ahern weren't making archivist recordings – their albums rang fresh, and inventive, and they tossed pop and rock songs into the mix, underscoring the primal emotional links between the styles, which had seemed bitterly polar (especially when filtered through those crossover hits of country radio).

She began as a student of country-rock pioneer Gram Parsons, and after his death took the things he'd taught her about real country music, its magic and its magnetism, and applied to them a gloriously tactile soprano and first–rate crew of backing musicians. From her first "true" album, *Pieces Of The Sky* in 1975, to the recent *Wrecking Ball*, Harris' music has straddled the lines between genres: eclectic, not indulgent, single-minded but hardly one-dimensional.

"It's hard to describe what I was trying to do, because it's an intuitive thing," she said. "I was very inspired by Gram's music. In my own way, I was trying to carry on his music. I didn't know what Gram would have done. I knew that he hated the term 'country-rock.' To him, it implied something that was lesser than the sum of the parts.

"And I knew that he loved the beauty of the traditional music, but he infused it with his own poetry. You take a song like 'Sin City,' it has all the structure of those beautiful Louvin Brothers songs, but the words could've only been written by someone of his generation and his experience."

Although she's never reached the commercial peaks of her pals Linda Ronstadt and Dolly Parton, Harris has managed to make one record after another of astounding quality and resonance. She was a decade ahead of the so-called "traditionalist" movement that swept country in the mid '80s; indeed, she was steadfastly country when country wasn't cool.

Emmylou Harris still wonders just exactly who her fans are. "I think they're people who like all different kinds of music and want to be challenged and want to be surprised," she said. "And are always looking for something different. And I think they want to be moved and changed by music; they don't want it just as background noise in their lives."

Said singer/songwriter Rodney Crowell, one of the links in Harris' serendipitous chain: "There have been a few women who carried that cultural thing that happened in the '60's, where artists like Bob Dylan and John Lennon had that kind of mystique that the poetic artists carry. In a lot of ways, she's been one of the few women to really carry it.

"In the '60s, women country singers did not own their intelligence or their integrity so much. Our society being what it is, women were kind of directed by men. And Emmy was kind of the first country artist to stand up with some sort of integrity and not be directed by men; she certainly collaborated with men, but she wasn't directed by them. Maybe the first feminist, in a way. She doesn't lead with that one thing."

And although she writes infrequently, Crowell said, "Emmylou Harris is a supreme artist. In her way, even as an interpreter, she's a poet. She's very sensitive in communications. She communicates with her songs, poetically. The songs she chooses, the language, the atmosphere. It's her vision."

The artist, true to form, paints herself in more down-to-earth tones. "It's very hard to explain, because I do feel that I'm a channel for music," she said. "I know that sounds a little New Age, perhaps. I know that I'm part of it, but it seems like music comes through us. It's not like, 'This is mine, I'm responsible for it completely,' but it's so much of who I am and the way I express myself and how I see the world is wrapped up in music that I can't imagine who I would be without it."

Just plain folk

The younger of Walter and Eugenia Harris' two children, Emmylou Harris was born April 2, 1947 in Birmingham, Alabama. When Emmy was five, her father, a Marine Corps officer known to his friends as Bucky, was reported Missing In Action in Korea and spent 10 months as a prisoner of war. The family moved from state to state as Bucky's commission dictated, and eventually it landed in Woodbridge, Virginia, where Emmy and her older brother Rutland attended Woodbridge High.

She was a shy, studious girl who worried about fitting in with the cool kids. A self-described "prig," Emmylou nevertheless won several beauty pageants (including the "Miss Woodbridge" contest) and was valedictorian upon graduation in 1965. She thought she'd finally found her niche in drama and she won a scholarship to study the thespian arts at the University of North Carolina in Greensboro.

But music was running in her blood, too. An early stab at piano lessons hadn't produced anything, and she blew alto sax in the Woodbridge High marching band, but Harris eventually got the attention she craved by singing with her little Kay acoustic guitar at parties. Her grandfather down in Birmingham had given Emmy the instrument, her first, when she turned 16. She studied chord books and learned all of her favorite Dylan and Baez songs, and briefly considered leaving school "to become Woody Guthrie."

She had only a passing interest in country music, she recalled. "From sort of a photosynthesis point of view, I got some from my brother, who is a great country fan. I absorbed Buck Owens, Loretta Lynn and Hank Williams and Bill Monroe. But not in the way that I did later on when I started working with Gram. It sort of snuck into my repertoire, into the style that I was accumulating at the time, in my teens."

This serious, responsible girl inside won out and she pressed on, taking courses at UNC and working weekend gigs with a friend, Mike Williams. He played 12-string and she picked a high-strung Gibson J-50 guitar, on material from writers as diverse as Hank Williams and the Beatles, anything that had simple chords and a lyric she liked. Mostly, she recalled she sang because college was boring and she needed the money.

Harris was determined to be an actress, and after 18 months she quit UNC for Boston University, where they had a better drama program. She spent the end of 1966 and the first half of 1967 earning money for school by waitressing in Virginia Beach, near Norfolk, singing and playing when she could get a gig. In time she changed her mind about acting and chucked it all in for New York City. She never went to Boston U.

A five-year subscriber to *Sing Out!* Magazine, Harris thought New York's folk music scene would be thriving when she arrived; instead, she found it virtually nonexistent, as rock 'n' roll and psychedelia were all the rage. Disheartened, she moved into the YWCA.

Still, there was work to be had and she eked out a living ("maybe 100 bucks a week") playing Greenwich Village clubs. In 1968, Harris became a regular at Gerde's Folk City, where she fell into a circle of songwriters that included Jerry Jeff Walker, Paul Siebel and David Bromberg. "Mainly I listened to folk music," she said. "I listened to Bob Dylan to Joan Baez to Judy Collins to Ian and Sylvia. I was really into the singer/songwriters of that era. I listened to folk/blues; I loved Mance Lipscomb and Son House, Robert Johnson, Bukka White, Lightnin' Hopkins, a lot of that. That was my main influence when Gram happened upon me."

In New York, Harris performed on a couple of local TV shows; she took waitressing gigs and even worked in a bookstore to supplement her meager earnings as a performer.

One reason she never became a popular entertainer was her habit of doing songs she liked, rather than choosing them as potential audience-pleasers. "My repertoire would include Paul Siebel, Joan Baez songs, some Simon and Garfunkel and some songs that I had written myself," Harris said. "I had quite an eclectic repertoire. I did some Buck Owens, I did a few Hank Williams songs, but I almost did them tongue-in-cheek, I'm ashamed to say. I didn't get them. I didn't really get them."

She married songwriter Tom Slocum in 1969 and in what seemed like a heaven-sent ticket to the top, inked a deal with the folkie label Jubilee. Recorded in a trio of three-hour sessions, *Gliding Bird* was released in the first part of 1970. Harris was pregnant and her marriage was failing. *Gliding Bird* was made under very strained circumstances and her memories of the experience are not particularly fond.

"The good thing about that record is that it shows that I was very much into songwriting," Harris recalled. "Half the songs on there, they're not the greatest songs in the world, but I'm not embarrassed by them. I wrote like half the album. And I think the song selection, for the most part, was pretty good. I did a Dylan song and a Hank Williams song. So there were some seeds of what was to be." Her soon-to-be-former husband wrote the album's title song.

Although *Gliding Bird* is a gentle, unassuming little folk record (Harris' rather fruity arrangements owed more than a small debt to *Clouds*-era Joni Mitchell), her singing was all over the map, exhibiting none of the remarkable control and phrasing that would come to characterize her later work.

"I was struggling and no one was interested in what I was doing," Harris said. "I got a manager who got me this deal with Jubilee and I made the mistake of not getting a lawyer and not looking into what was going on. I tended to be very passive, as I am still, maybe not so much as I was then, but I just signed the contract and found myself with a company that really wasn't able to do very much for me. Or wasn't inclined to. I went in and did a record in three days and didn't really have a direction, I didn't really have a style. I don't think I really got all those bits and pieces. I don't think that they were forged into anything definable until I worked with Gram."

Her take on Hank Williams' "I Saw The Light" was amateurish, her "I'll Be Your Baby Tonight" no cousin (distant or otherwise) to Bob Dylan's original. She also covered Fred Neil's "Everybody's Talkin'" and at the request of her producer Ray Ellis and over Emmy's own objections, Bacharach/David's "I'll Never Fall In Love Again."

Of course, *Gliding Bird* went nowhere (1,300 copies were reportedly sold) and Jubilee billed the artist for $8,000 to cover production costs.

Pregnant, but clinging to a dream of success, Harris gave up on New York and headed for Nashville, where she worked as an art class model ("fully clothed and holding an umbrella, for some reason") and waited tables in a Polynesian restaurant, before her advancing condition forced her to quit. She landed a few performing gigs, but nothing stuck. And the marriage finally fell apart.

Daughter Hallie was born in the summer of 1970, and when Emmylou found herself buying baby food with food stamps, she realized a change was in order. After eight months in Music City, she and her daughter moved back in with Bucky and Eugenia, who were now on a small farm near Columbia, Maryland, not far from Washington. They welcomed their own little girl back with open arms.

The Fallen Angel

Although her first job was a model-home hostess, it wasn't long before Emmylou began to pick up the pieces of her music career. She made the acquaintance of singer/guitarist

John Starling (founder of the Seldom Scene) and his wife, Fayssoux. Bill and Taffy Danoff (who would soon form the Starland Vocal Band) introduced her to guitarist Gerry Mule and bassist Tom Guidera, with whom she formed a performing trio, arranging an eclectic bag of tunes around her vocals. Guidera moved in with Hallie and her mother; he and Harris would remain romantically involved for several years (his bass work can be found on *Pieces Of The Sky*, her first "real" album, released in 1975).

Washington's Georgetown District was peppered with rock and folk clubs; it was a subculture all its own and in early 1971 Harris found herself with a reasonably steady gig. The trio played six nights a week, up and down the strip, but mostly at a joint called Clyde's, the back room of a singles club, where she could sing her so-called "weird and obscure" songs to an audience that by and large had nothing better to do than listen.

One fall evening Rick Roberts and Kenny Wertz, of the Flying Burrito Brothers, dropped into Clyde's for a beer (the Burritos were playing several nights at the nearby Cellar Door club, which routinely booked big-time acts). Roberts was impressed with Harris's reading of Kitty Wells' "It Wasn't God Who Made Honky Tonk Angels," and the next night he returned with Chris Hillman to show her off.

Hillman, the ex-Byrd who had formed the Burrito Brothers with singer/songwriter Gram Parsons, was at that moment weighing an offer from Stephen Stills to put the band Manassas together. Since Parsons' departure the year before, the Burritos' fortunes had been fading (not that they'd ever been all that successful) and, Hillman thought, something had to happen pretty darn quick.

When he heard Emmylou Harris, Hillman thought his problems were solved. He invited her to sit in with the Burritos the next night, which she did, and considered asking her to join the band, thinking that a Linda Ronstadt-type singer might make the Burritos a commodity after all.

Ultimately, Hillman let it go and went with Stills, and the Flying Burrito Brothers were retired from active duty. There were a few more concert dates to be honored, however, and Parsons, just back from Europe, where he'd been living the high life with Keith Richards and Anita Pallenberg, agreed to go on the road and sing his old Burrito songs one last time.

Parsons was about to begin recording his first solo album and he'd been talking about finding the perfect girl singer, someone with whom he could sing close harmony, the way his beloved Louvin Brothers sang. Like the Everly Brothers sang. Like George Jones sang with Tammy Wynette.

When the Burritos played a date at the University of Maryland at Baltimore, Hillman told Parsons about this amazing girl they'd met in D.C. He suggested his old buddy go over and check her out.

Gram Parsons was never the alchemist he thought himself. A hippie kid from a rich Florida family, he was a rocker who worshipped at the altar of George Jones and his music blended country's passion with rock 'n' roll's intensity. It was not a popular concoction during his lifetime.

He'd tried to make the marriage work during his brief tenure with the Byrds, shaping the seminal *Sweetheart Of The Rodeo* album into something so rural and plain, the group's fans literally didn't know what to do with it (most of Parsons' original lead vocals were replaced by those of audience-friendly Roger McGuinn, anyway). He snatched Hillman from the nest and put together the Burrito Brothers aiming to dig the twang in deeper, but that band never cleared the commercial hurdle, and after two albums he was drugging it up in Europe and Morocco with the Stones, gaining weight and bragging boozily about the solo album he was going to make.

He wanted to call *it These Blues Have Made A Nigger Out Of Me*. His friends were sure he'd lost his mind.

Parsons had a sweet, clear voice with a crack down the middle and a blue, lonesome ceiling. With his charged rock 'n' roll backing bands, Parsons played country like the electric hard stuff. And he looked the part with his long hair and rhinestone suits from Nudie's.
His music wasn't the poppy country-rock of the Eagles, whom he detested (although Eagle Bernie Leadon, a good friend, was a one-time Burrito Brother), but a raw, honestly-felt hybrid forged from something more than a grievous desire to sell his soul to sound good on the radio and sell a million records (although that would have been nice).

Gram Parsons made it work, but it cost him dearly. And before he took his final joyride on the lost highway, he passed the baton to Emmylou Harris.

She was still gigging at Clyde's when he walked in, heard her sing "It Wasn't God Who Made Honky Tonk Angels" and knew, he just knew, that she was the singer he'd been looking for. They performed two songs together at Clyde's that very first night, for five or 10 paying customers.

Parsons and Harris sang together constantly for the last two years of his life. The fey little folkie of *Gliding Bird* learned how to sing country music and to appreciate it. "He turned me on to the Louvin Brothers, which I just immediately loved," Harris said. The key, she continued, "was singing with him and singing harmony with him and learning the phrasing; because singing with Gram required you to be extremely restrained and economical. And I realize now in retrospect that that is a real signature of country music; the emotion is in the restraint; and I believe restraint intensifies emotion, especially in music."

She and Parsons, along with other musician friends, used to stay up into the wee hours, or later, trying to impress each other with one country song after another. Harris was hooked. "I just went completely over the top," she said. "George Jones, Merle Haggard, Tammy Wynette, of course all of the Louvin Brothers' stuff. I just listened to country music all the time."

Parsons' first solo album, *GP*, appeared in 1972 (he'd flown Emmy to Los Angeles to sing at the sessions). In early 1973, his manager Eddie Tickner organized the artist's first (and as it turned out, his only) cross–country tour under his own name. The Fallen Angels (Parsons' suggestion, the Turkeys, had been quickly vetoed) hit the road for a month, playing in second-string nightclubs and "the better hippie honky-tonks of the nation." Emmylou Harris was featured prominently; singing at her own mic, center stage next to Parsons.
"My perception at the time was, Emmy would be standing there next to him staring at his

face," recalled Bernie Leadon. "Staring at his mouth and having the ability to get it by some kind of telegraphic twitch or something; where he was going. And if you listen to those records, I wouldn't be surprised if her enunciation was a microsecond after his."

Leadon said the Fallen Angels opened a few shows for the Eagles in 1973. He remembered the sparks that flew when Gram and Emmy sang together. "Everybody was enthralled with Emmy's voice, because it was so ethereal," he said.

"The harmony, I felt at the time, was principally due to her abilities. Having already worked with Gram, I knew that he tended to never rehearse. To put it mildly, what this meant was he really thought it was okay to just rearrange songs on the moment. So length of intros, number of verses before the chorus, number of choruses before the outro, those were all completely negotiable."

The Fallen Angels went out of their way to ensure Emmy's safety and comfort (such as it was) on their cross-country Greyhound ride. "They may have been protective of her because she was from back east and she had a kid already," Leadon said. "I think everybody cared about her a lot because the all saw that she had this innocence and genuineness. And they may have been protective in a literal sense too, as in, 'hey we don't want any of this rock 'n' roll crap to soil you.'"

Parsons "was always gracious, unbelievably gracious" to Harris, added Leadon. "He really had a southern gentleman quality to him. And he was always extremely affable, you know, he was very pleasant toward women. He was all that."

"When she was working with Gram, she was a little less disciplined than she is now," observed musician Herb Pedersen, who sang on several Parsons sessions. "Because Gram wasn't a real disciplined singer at all. He was an emotional singer. It's like Mick and Keith. You listen to them and it works - it may not be the most in-tune stuff in the world, but there's a lot of heart in it."

Grievous Angel was Parsons' last testament. The album was released in January, three months after he'd overdosed in a motel near the Joshua Tree National Monument in the Mohave Desert. He'd finished recording the album only weeks before his death.

Parsons had planned to put Harris' name prominently on the front cover; his choice for the jacket photo showed the two of them astride a Harley-Davidson motorcycle, shit-eating grins on their faces. Parsons' widow, who had been jealous of Harris all along, reportedly pitched a fit and had the cover changed to an innocuous picture of Parsons alone. The legend "With Emmylou Harris" appeared in large type on the back, however.

"Gram's death was like falling off a mountain," Harris told Cameron Crowe in 1975. "It was a very hard year between his death and the making of my album. A year of throwing myself into a lot of work that my heart wasn't really into."

Emmy moved back to D.C., where Tom Guidera had also become a country music convert. With pedal steel player Danny Pendleton and two other musicians, they put together the Angel Band and started gigging around the clubs, playing some of the songs she'd performed with Gram.

Eddie Tickner made Harris his number one priority and he convinced Mary Martin, an A&R representative from Warner/Reprise Records (the label that had released Parsons' solo work) to investigate an Angel Band show in a Washington nightclub.

Emmylou Harris became a Reprise Records recording artist in 1974; with her daughter Hallie in tow, the Angel Band relocated to Los Angeles to begin work on her first true solo album.

Heartbreak and desire

To produce, Martin paired Harris up with Nova Scotia native Brian Ahern, the mastermind behind Anne Murray's spate of hits in the early '70s. She brought the quiet Canadian to hear the Angel Band, and he recorded the performance on a hand-held cassette machine to study at home.

Ahern was renting a house on Lania Lane, a winding, one-way street in the Coldwater Canyon section of Los Angeles. He turned it into a recording studio; the Neive console was installed in a 19–ton semi truck parked alongside the house. The Enactron Truck, where Emmylou Harris would make her first 10 albums with Brian Ahern, was connected with the home studio via closed circuit TV. The studio band was set up in the living room, in front of the fireplace; solos were cut in an isolation booth inside the truck. The front lawn and driveway were strewn with cables.

The studio band included drummer Ron Tutt, pianist Glen D. Hardin, bassist Emory Gordy Jr. and lead guitarist James Burton, all members of Elvis Presley's backup band, and all of whom had played on *Grievous Angel*; other familiar faces included Fayssoux Starling on backing vocals and Bernie Leadon on various stringed instruments. "Brian lived in a back bedroom, and the rest of the house was all just living space part of the time and recording space part of the time," Leadon said. "That's how they made the album. It was a constant; they might record at any hour of the day kind of thing.

"The truck was parked at a house up in the hills, near Beverly Hills," he added, "although it certainly wasn't the Jed Clampett part of Beverly Hills." Leadon laughed at his recollection. "I guess there was a Jed Clampett aspect to it, all right."

Pieces Of The Sky, their first collaboration, got its name from a line in Danny Flowers' song

"Before Believing", a track recorded with Tom Guidera on bass and a young fiddler from Kentucky named Ricky Skaggs.

Harris wrote the lyrics to "Boulder To Birmingham," a bittersweet adieu to Gram Parsons ("The hardest part is knowing I'll survive") sung in a heartbroken, heartbreaking voice, almost a whisper. Bill Danoff composed the melody (despite a popular story of the day, her line, "I was in the wilderness and the canyon was on fire," was not about Parsons, whose body was stolen by friends and set ablaze in the Mohave, but a reference to the extensive Coldwater fires of mid 1974).

Ahern and Harris purposely stitched together a mixed bag for *Pieces Of The Sky*, including country/rock standards (Dolly Parton's "Coat Of Many Colors," Merle Haggard's "Bottle Let Me Down") a Beatles song ("For No One") that Harris had done since her early sets at Clyde's, and Felice and Boudleaux Bryant's "Sleepless Nights." There was a bouncy song from Parsons' heroes, Charlie and Ira Louvin, "If I Could Only Win Your Love."

At last, she "got" country music. "It's something that you have to listen to; you have to feel it," she said. "It's an acquired taste, especially for those of us who have come to it through the back door, who didn't grow up with it. And I think that's wonderful. If you grow up with it, then maybe you think it has to sound exactly like *this*. What's good about coming to music after you've listened to other kinds of music is you absorb it, you get it, but it fuses with other things."

The playing of *Pieces Of The Sky* was clean and economical, the arrangements tastefully layered, with fiddles and mandolins at every turn. Emmy's angelic soprano had taken on the razor's edge of ache and sorrow, what bluegrass musicians called the high lonesome sound.

Despite the steel guitars and other embellishments of tradition, *Pieces Of The Sky* was more pop than country; but it wasn't rock 'n' roll either. It had little to do with the Eagles' squeaky-clean "country-rock" which was all the rage at the time, or Linda Ronstadt's sheeny pop country, and even less in common with commercial country music circa 1975. *Pieces Of The Sky* had elements of folk, rock 'n' roll and very traditional country music; at the center was Harris' fragile, gossamer voice, breaking from the heartache of "Boulder To Birmingham" and cracking honky-tonk wise (in a mannered sort of way) on Shel Silverstein's "Queen Of The Silver Dollar."

"Aside from having that miraculous voice," wrote Bud Scoppa in his *Rolling Stone* review, "She has great personal charm made up in proportionate parts of intelligence, honesty and self-effacement … Harris' exceptional musical and personal appeal should be sufficient to put her in touch with a good many non–country listeners."

Ahern's production strategy centered around the voice; there were no strings, no Jordanaires-type singers crooning behind her. The album was smartly produced with the focus on the correct instrument.

Most importantly, every song was a good one, and no one in country music was doing that.

Herb Pedersen was a singer and banjo player who'd been in the Dillards, the late '60's band that had been a kind of hayseed version of the Burrito Brothers. When Ahern and Harris were putting together *Pieces Of The Sky*, Pedersen was recommended as a harmony singer by Linda Ronstadt, with whom he'd been recording. Harris had met with him during *Grievous Angel*.

Pedersen recalled that Ahern, a former rock guitarist, was very much in control. "He was very particular about arrangements," he said. "He was a very schooled musician from Canada before he came down here. He did a lot of the rhythm guitar parts that are on there and he didn't take credit for them. He was careful about the arrangements and the key choices and the tunes. He didn't want it to be just another country chick singer."

Harris, Pederson added, "was very definite about what she wanted to do, too. When I would be in there doing harmony parts, she would be there, listening, to see if it would work for her. She was as much a part of that whole thing as he was, I think."

Harris recalled holding her breath waiting for her album's spring 1975 release. "I was pretty nervous about it," she said. "I didn't think anybody was gonna 'get' the record. I did feel that certain people, whose opinion mattered to me, were going to like a lot of it. People like John Starling, I knew that he really loved 'If I Could Only Win Your Love' and I loved that, too. It was just so new to me, making a real record. And it was pretty eclectic."

She wasn't worried, she said, "that the album might be too country for the pop charts, or too urban for the country charts" (that, of course, had been a Gram Parsons trademark). "I don't know if I even thought that big," she recalled, "because I remember I was on a promotional tour, the record had just come out and I was sitting in a Sportsman's Lodge doing interviews when somebody from the record company called me and said, 'You know you're number 120 on the pop chart.' I said, 'What???!!!' I mean, never in a million years … 120, that was okay, just to be on a pop chart. To be on any chart, I couldn't believe it."

"If I Could Only Win Your Love" went to No. 4 country and made her a star. Throughout her career, Harris' singles would hit purely country, her albums sell to a mixed crowd. She was a beacon for fans of progressive country, people who read *Rolling Stone, Musician* and *Crawdaddy* and appreciated the level of musicianship and production standards on her albums.

It all started with *Pieces Of The Sky*. "And that was like day and night," Harris said. "It was like all of a sudden I went from just this person that had a private life that nobody really knew who you were, to being this other person. It was like my life totally changed. The whole concept of everything I was doing just kind of changed."
Nashville, she recalled, wasn't sure how to deal with her; but she never, ever felt snubbed.

"The first time I came to town after *Pieces Of The Sky* was doing well, the community embraced me," Harris said. "I think it was because of 'If I Could Only Win Your Love.' It was like, 'God, here's this old Louvin Brothers song and it's got a mandolin solo. Remember mandolin?' At that time it was like, 'don't put a mandolin on it. People might actually think it's country music.'"

"Musically, I think I've always managed to be kind of an outsider anywhere I would be. I've always managed to do whatever I wanted. I can live anywhere and do that."

She wasn't a star just yet, but something was in the air. "Before that album was released, she did a little show at UCLA Royce Hall," Leadon said. "She opened for the Earl Scruggs Revue, which was really cool.

"Emmy's band was just me and Herb Pedersen and her. So we did it all acoustic, and three-part harmonies. Herb Pedersen just has this unbelievable voice. It's inspiring to open your mouth and sing with two voices like that."

Leadon remembered that "Boulder To Birmingham" was everybody's favorite song at the time. "The context here is she had no validation from sales. She had none. She had been out singing harmony with Gram, but that wasn't her thing. And that wasn't a particularly well-attended tour. She was a single mom from back East and she'd already been to Nashville and already been rejected. She had already moved back to D.C. to be a mom and here she'd gotten hooked up with this country-rock crazy man, on this Rolling Thunder-type tour that they did.

And then she met Brian, this real sort of stable type, even keeled Canadian guy and she met Eddie Tickner, who also is very even-keeled, through Gram."

Today, Harris looks back with fondness at the woman who made *Pieces Of The Sky* so many years ago. "I think it was a really honest record," she said. "And I think it was the beginning of me learning how to be a recording artist. I was so fortunate to be able to work with the musicians I worked with, and with Brain Ahern, who has enormous respect for the instincts of an artist.

"Because I was afraid to say anything, at first. In fact, I remember in particular we were cutting 'Sleepless Nights.' And about seven or eight takes into cutting it; somebody in the band suggested a chord change. And I'm sure it wouldn't mean anything to anybody, but for about the next 10 takes I bit my lip and I sang and I just didn't like it. And finally, I very sheepishly piped up. I raised my hand and said, 'you know, I don't…I…I…I'd rather go back to the way it was.' Everybody just said, 'why didn't you say anything earlier?' Everybody was so cool about it. And we ended up taking one of those takes that had the chord change in it that I didn't like and we meticulously went back in and just for four bars, we overdubbed the old chord.

"And that taught me a lesson, that it was not only okay, it was encouraged for me to give my ideas. And with Brian at the helm, I always knew that my ideas would be considered, and if they were good, he would use them. And if they weren't going to work for another reason, he would tell me. But I always thought that he respected and encouraged my ideas. And I really started the learning process of making records with *Pieces Of The Sky*, so it was a really important record for me.

"And also because it was successful, it gave me the carte blanche to do whatever I wanted for the rest of my career. And I'm still enjoying that because I also happened to be with a record company that supported and nurtured that kind of artist. They wanted you, especially if you had just a minimum of commercial success, they said, 'Well, she must know what she's doing; leave her alone.' I've had that for over 20 years."

Some Like It Hot

The success of *Pieces Of The Sky* gave them all a buzz; sessions for Harris' second Reprise album began almost immediately and she started a touring schedule that would go on, virtually without stop, for seven years.

Harris was convinced to fire Guidera and Pendleton in favor of a top-flight touring group; someone at Warner Brothers had persuaded her to "go out and get a really hot band." To her surprise, both James Burton and Glen D. Hardin accepted, with the proviso that they'd work around Elvis' increasingly infrequent live appearances. Emory Gordy signed on full time as bass player, Hank DeVito took the pedal steel chair, and the elected drummer was John Ware, formerly with Michael Nesmith's First National Band. Harris had to pay their hefty pro salaries out of her own pocket, but decided it was well worth it. She dubbed them the Hot Band.

"Serendipity, I suppose, is the only way to describe it," Harris reflected. "And Gram has to take a lot of the credit for that. Because half that band - Emery, Glen D. and James -

that was the band that he put together to record his album."

Fate still had to play one more card in this latest hand with Emmylou Harris. "Brian brought me up to Toronto to listen to tapes of songs," she said. "We listened all day long, eight hours, to stuff that had completely left me cold. We started laughing about it after a while; we got kind of silly."

Ahern who also owned a publishing company, had stacks of cassettes lying around his office in Toronto. "He said, 'here's a tape of somebody that I just signed; I signed him on the strength of a recommendation of a friend, and I haven't even heard him yet. You want to hear him?"

"So he puts on this tape," Harris continued, "and I hear Rodney Crowell. And I said, 'Okay. Now we're getting somewhere. This guy is great. This guy has obviously listened to George Jones.' It was 'Song For The Life' and 'Bluebird Wine,' those two songs."

A 22–year old vagabond from Houston, Crowell had no prospects at the time and welcomed the call from Ahern. "I went to Toronto and Brian and I flew down to Washington D.C. and I think Emmy was playing at a club with her Angel Band," Crowell recalled. "After the gig, we stayed up all night somewhere in D.C. and played songs till daylight.

"It was pretty much cemented there. I was into all this old music, like the Louvin Brothers, and she was too. It was a little bit of the archivist thing. It was musicology all night. Country musicology. I think Gram Parsons might've been her entrée into it, and I think we clicked so heavily because I came from Texas and I grew up on that stuff."

Crowell's punchy, darkly ironic songwriting reminded Brian Ahern of Parsons; therefore, he thought, the kid might be just right for Emmylou.

"I had a show to do, and they flew Rodney in," said Harris. "And he actually sat in with me and we did some songs. That day, he said, 'I've just written this,' and he played me 'Till I Gain Control Again.' And it's been like that ever since. Rodney will say, 'Oh, I just wrote this' and he'll play me 'Leaving Louisiana In The Broad Daylight.'"

Harris recorded Crowell's "Bluebird Wine" for *Pieces Of The Sky*. When Crowell saw her with the Angel Band at the Armadillo World Headquarters in Austin, she and Eddie Tickner had a surprise waiting for him backstage: a plane ticket to Los Angeles.

"I didn't know what was going on. I just went," Crowell remembered. "And when I got there, I learned that management was going to dissolve the Angel Band and form another band, which I was the first member of, this Hot Band thing."

Crowell was enlisted for rhythm guitar, harmony vocals and, truth be told, because he was a good guy that Harris and Ahern liked having around. And with Rodney close at hand, they always got first crack at his songs.

"I was lucky to have Rodney Crowell all to myself for a couple of years," Harris said. "He was writing all the time. And we sat and sang all the time. We were always singing."

For Crowell, "It wasn't my level as a musician, or even a singer, that earned me that place. I think my songwriting certainly earned me a place there, but I think it was more that I was an extension of Emmylou's creativity at that time. So I collaborated with her on songs, and just on, 'this is what it is. This is what's cool about this music.' So it was a good place to be. I was quite innocent."

Harris cut "Till I Gain Control Again" for her next album, *Elite Hotel*, released in the first month of 1976. And Crowell helped her polish off "Amarillo," a song she had started writing but was unable to finish. "Everything was just instinct then," Crowell said. "You know, there's a lot to be said for innocence. Innocence is a good thing, you can get a lot done."

Several of the songs on *Elite Hotel* had been originally recorded for *Pieces Of The Sky*, including the Beatles' "Here, There and Everywhere." Still, the album (originally to be called *Wheels*) had a tougher, edgier feel than its predecessor. For starters, there were more fast songs, shit-kicking raveups like "Feelin' Single, Seein' Double," Hank Williams's "Jambalaya" and "Amarillo."

Parsons figured in the equation via covers of "Sin City," "Ooh Las Vegas" and "Wheels." She covered vintage country territory, in the form of the heartbreak classics "Together Again" and "Sweet Dreams." It was true to her vision, an eclectic mix. As on her debut, the arrangements and production were flawless.

Vocally, however, Harris was a waif no longer. She was dropping the wounded-bird thing that she'd worn so convincingly on the first album, and on such songs as "Amarillo" and "Ooh Las Vegas" she even managed to sound worldly-wise.

The recording sessions for *Elite Hotel*, noted Herb Pedersen, who sang on more than half the album, were done with an agenda. "It was essentially the same type of focus and essentially the same direction," he said, "but we knew at that point that there was something very good happening. I was a real studio ape at that point, doing a lot of sessions, and I would go up there and it was as professional as anything I'd ever involved myself with."

The Enactron Truck was the place to be. "They were making great records," Pederson said. "And it was very hip, as far as the country scene was concerned, as far as Nashville. We were making great country records in L.A; we weren't thumbing our noses at Nashville. It was, 'Yeah, we can do this too, because we have great musicians out here as well.' Nashville isn't the only place that you need to do country music. You can do it anywhere if you've got the players."

"Sweet Dreams" was included in a version recorded live at Los Angeles's Roxy Theatre. Ahern, ever the perfectionist, dubbed a Bernie Leadon guitar part, cut in the truck, onto the track.

The newly–christened Hot Band took to the open road, with Crowell and Harris singing harmony in best Charlie and Ira/Gram and Emmylou fashion. They opened two Elton John concerts in Dodger Stadium. "Musically," said Crowell, "it was great. We would go from Conway Twitty to Elton John to James Taylor. It's a lot more separated now. We were getting into some good places. It was fun, playing really strange gigs."

Each concert's showstopper was a killer version of the Miracles' "Shop Around," which never found its way onto an Emmylou Harris album. Crowell, the young pup of the group, recalled these as his rough and rowdy days. "We played the gig and went lookin' for trouble," he said.

James Burton's flashy guitar work was also a highlight of each night's show (some people doubtless attended the concerts to hear him, not Harris). After about nine months in the Hot Band, though, Burton's conflicting dates with Elvis became a problem. In the end, Crowell recalled with a chuckle, "James went with Elvis, and Glen D. went with us. Glen D. liked us better."

The Hot Band was actually booked to play in Memphis, August 16, 1977, the day Elvis never came out of the bathroom. "We flew in; we were playing that night," remembered Crowell. "Glen D was with us and we were besieged by the media when he came in."

Burton's replacement on lead guitar was frizzy-haired Englishman Albert Lee, whose fiery and immaculately picked fretwork was to give Harris' music yet another dynamic. A friend of Emory Gordy's, Lee first appeared on the third Harris album, 1977's *Luxury Liner*. *Elite Hotel* won the 1976 Grammy for Best Country Vocal Performance, Female.

As her reputation spread, Emmy began to get calls to sing harmony on other artists' sessions. In 1975, she'd recorded "Star Of Bethlehem" with Neil Young, who returned the favor by adding his own voice to Harris' Christmas single, "Light Of The Stable" released that year. ("That's my favorite thing about 'Light Of The Stable,'" said Harris. "He sounds like a choirboy, doesn't he? He has wings when he sings that.")

She harmonized on *Old No. 1* and *Texas Cookin'*, the first recorded works by Texas singer/songwriter Guy Clark, whose wife Susanna, a songwriter and painter, became one of Harris's closest friends. She sang on "Evangeline" with the Band (and appeared in a "fantasy sequence" built around the tune in *The Last Waltz*).

Her most high-profile session work to date came just before *Elite Hotel*. To her astonishment, Bob Dylan came calling for another voice to add to his *Desire* project, released in the spring of 1976. His producer Don DeVito was a friend of Mary Martin's.

Harris wound up singing on several tracks including "Mozambique," "One More Cup Of Coffee" and a last-minute inclusion, the 11-minute gangland dirge "Joey." Several other tracks were released years later, on Dylan compilations.

She still shakes her head when she talks about her whirlwind *Desire* sessions. "There was no time to be nervous with Dylan," she said. "You sit next to him, you're reading the words off the page that he's looking at, you're trying to watch his mouth and watch the words at the same time, and it was one take, or two takes. So there was no time to be nervous; you just had to keep up with him."

Easy From Now On

Harris and Ahern recorded 19 tracks for *Luxury Liner* that summer; in the end, they included 10. These ranged from Parsons' scrappy little title track (he'd written and recorded it

93

with his mid '60s International Submarine Band) to the Carter Family classic "Hello Stranger," as traditional–sounding an Appalachian folk song as anything she'd committed to wax, with Nicolette Larson and Harris trading lines a la Sara and Maybelle Carter.

Harris was listening to a lot of rock 'n' roll oldies on the road; she and the Hot Band nailed down a fun rendition of Chuck Berry's "C'est La Vie (You Never Can Tell)" for the album. Crowell and Lee sang backup on Townes Van Zandt's haunting "Poncho and Lefty." The Louvin Brothers were represented by an angelic reading of "When I Stop Dreaming," with harmony vocals by Emmy's new friend Dolly Parton.

Harris cut Parton's song "Coat Of Many Colors" for *Pieces Of The Sky*, and Parton returned the favor with a version of "Boulder To Birmingham" on her album *All I Can Do*. During a listening party for that album, Harris was devastated by Parton's song "To Daddy," a heart–wrenching tale of a family torn apart from the inside out. Parton's version stayed in the can, but Harris recorded it immediately, and it would become a hit from her *Quarter Moon In A Ten Cent Town* album in '78.

Released in January 1977, the same month she and Brian Ahern married up in Halifax, Nova Scotia, *Luxury Liner* was something of a high-water mark for Harris. With its disparate song selection, it mirrored the earlier albums enough to keep her growing legion of fans thrilled.

For the first time, however, there were few session guys. Forged into a smoking, cohesive unit by the constant road work, the Hot Band was playing behind Harris as closely as her harmonies had mirrored Gram Parsons when they took off - an Albert Lee guitar solo here, a Glen D. Hardin honky-tonk piano flourish there - you couldn't see the cars for the smoke along the track. The Hot Band more than lived up to its name.

Still, some critics carped that Harris and Ahern were starting to turn out cookie-cutter albums. "I agree that there was something of a formula, but in the best possible sense of the word," Harris said. "Because it was rather open-ended. What Brian and I started with those musicians and our working relationship, reached a real zenith on *Luxury Liner*, at least up until *Wrecking Ball*, were my core songs. In every show I did 'Hello Stranger' and 'Luxury Liner.' I still do 'Pancho And Lefty' and 'Making Believe.' I'm about to work up 'Tulsa Queen.' Those songs became real benchmarks of material and playing, and the kind of sound that I'm associated with."

Crowell quit the Hot Band in 1978 to make his first solo album, *Ain't Living Long Like This,* produced by Ahern and recorded in the Enactron Truck (Lee followed suit a year later and made *Hiding*, with Ahern at the helm. Harris guested on both records).

Crowell had hooked up with Johnny Cash's daughter Rosanne, who was at that time living in Europe. Although he appeared on Harris' next two records, his mind was elsewhere. "I left Emmy's band in September 1978 to get a band together and go out and support my record," Crowell recalled. "But when my record came out, I was in Germany with Rosanne for six weeks. And then I came back and went, 'What? I missed something here.'"

Quarter Moon In A Ten Cent Town took its title from "Easy From Now On," the opening song, which was given to Harris by its writers Susanna Clark and Carlene Carter. Clark also provided the album's evocative cover painting (the same year, her oil work graced the jacket of Willie Nelson's *Stardust*).

"To Daddy" went to No. 3, and "Two More Bottles Of Wine" (the Delbert McClinton song, recorded for *Luxury Liner* but left off) became Harris' third country No. 1. Still, the artist today has few kind words for *Quarter Moon*.

"I have some bad memories of that record, because we mixed it and mixed it and mixed it, it was mainly my fault," Harris explained. "I kept thinking I wanted to hear a certain sound, and I was responsible for, I think, over-mixing that record. When we went back and listened to the rough mixes that we had, there was something happening with that record that didn't ever get out, that people never heard.

"On the upside, it had a kind of a distant sound to it. A distant feel that works for the record. But I just remember long, unnecessary hours in the studio. Brian, in his wisdom, let me learn a lesson. There's a certain point where you have to say, 'This song is done; let's move on.' I had to learn it the hard way, by maybe over-mixing. Maybe every artist goes through that."

She did like the cover, though. "That painting is my favorite part of the record." Harris said.

For the first time, Harris recorded no Gram Parsons songs. Instead, *Quarter Moon* included two by the Canadian scribe Jesse Winchester ("My Songbird" and "Defying Gravity"). She continued to mine the rich vein of Rodney Crowell's songwriting, with his epics "Leaving Louisiana In The Broad Daylight" and "I Ain't Living Long Like This." Willie Nelson added a duet vocal to Walter Martin Cowart's "One Paper Kid," and the Utah Phillips chestnut "Green Rolling Hills" featured harmonies from Fayssoux Starling and from young Ricky Skaggs, who was soon to replace Rodney Crowell in the Hot Band as Emmy's singing partner.

Crowell left, but never really went away. He and Harris had formed a bond - he says they were "instant family" - and had all through the '80s, when his own career was flying high, he continued to play with her when their scheduled allowed.

And he always gave her songs. "I did this version of 'Till I Gain Control Again' with Willie Nelson that was never released, and it was real good," Crowell said. "But other than that, I think Emmylou's version of 'Til I Gain Control Again' is still the definitive version. Crystal Gayle had the big hit with it, but I don't think her version was as soulful as Emmy's.

"Emmy's version of 'Leaving Louisiana In The Broad Daylight' is pretty interesting. But you know what? Value judgments don't serve. Like I don't necessarily think my own versions of my songs are any better than anybody else's might be. It's all subjective. That's not to say I haven't made a lot of money on versions of my songs that gagged me. But never Emmylou's."

Crowell said he'd learned early on that he couldn't fool her. "I wrote a song specifically for Emmy, and I took it to her," he remembered. "And I said, 'Hey Emmy, I wrote this song for you, okay?' And she goes, 'That's good. But I heard this tape of this song "You're Supposed

To Be Feeling Good," and I want to record that.' And I went, 'Oh, okay.'"

"The few times that I've done that, to write something for somebody; it don't work. You just gotta write it 'cause it's there. That's making up songs, as opposed to capturing them. The better songs come from somewhere else; that's an intellectual process, as opposed to an emotional thing."

Crowell's "Even Cowgirls Get The Blues" became a standout track on *Blue Kentucky Girl*, Harris's fifth Reprise album, in the summer of 1979. Although there were one or two old pop songs ("Save The Last Dance For Me," the first single, was a Top Five country hit) *Blue Kentucky Girl* had a more acoustic, pure country atmosphere.

Alongside Willie Nelson's playful "Sister's Coming Home" (the album's token electric raver) and Leon Payne's "They'll Never Take His Love From Me" (a song long associated with Hank Williams), Harris cut Jean Ritchie's aching "Sorrow In The Wind" and the Louvins' "Everytime You Leave." Parsons' most haunting melody, "Hickory Wind," was included too, and Harris' singing had never been so bittersweet.

Blue Kentucky Girl won Harris her second Grammy, for Best Country Vocal Performance, Female. Harris explained why it was an ironic designation. "We got to the time to do *Blue Kentucky Girl*, and I think that was a reaction on my part to things that were coming out in the press that were saying, 'The only reason you're successful as a country artist is because you really don't make country records.' And I took umbrage at that! Because I wanted to do country records the way I wanted to do them. But this idea of, 'Well, if you didn't have a Beatles song on this record, it would've never had the enormous audience that it had…' and all this stuff, and I thought okay, I'll take up that gauntlet.

"So we decided to do *Blue Kentucky Girl*, which was still different from what you'd consider a traditional country record, but very much, in the song selection, very traditional. We still managed to put the Gram Parsons song in there, and the Willie Nelson song, showing that traditional country songs could hold their own in a contemporary setting."

She hit No. 1 on the country singles chart for the fourth time with Dallas Frazier's "Beneath Still Waters," and the album's title track made it to the sixth position.

"Oddly enough, that record initially was a failure," Harris said. "The record company didn't know how to promote it. Until it won the Grammy, it had been written off. No one got it; they said, 'This is just like all your other records.'

"So then we said, all right, we'll go back even further and we'll do a bluegrass record. Which is where *Roses In The Snow* came in."

Ricky fingers

Released the next spring, *Roses In The Snow* turned the clock back even before the time of Hank Williams and George Jones. Its 10 songs were all acoustic - some were bluegrass, and some were traditional Appalachian sacred melodies, adapted by Ahern. There were no drums. The emphasis was on musicianship and vocal harmony. The former came in the form of Hot Band members past and present, with guest spots from the likes of acoustic guitar master

Tony Rice and dobro player Jerry Douglas; the latter from Dolly Parton, Linda Ronstadt, Johnny Cash, the White Sisters (Sharon Hicks and Cheryl Warren) and the by-now-indispensable Ricky Skaggs.

The songs were from the catalogs of the Carter Family, the Stanley Brothers and the Louvins (Harris included Paul Simon's "The Boxer," too, a staple of her folk sets back in D.C.). At the dawn of the *Urban Cowboy* era, when country and pop were about to reach their crossover zenith, Emmylou Harris not only dug down to country's roots, she also foreshadowed the new-traditionalist movement that would follow in the mid '80s. *Roses In The Snow* was almost too timely.

And it nearly didn't happen at all. "Halfway through the making of it, I got panicky," Harris explained. "I was going through eclectic withdrawal! I felt like, I don't know if I can make this record without striking something on there that is left-field. And Brian sat me down and said, 'Look, it's really important that we stick to our guns on this and make a record that is pure in its style.'

"I wanted to put 'How High The Moon' on it. We'd cut 'Millworker' at the same time, and he said, 'If they didn't get *Blue Kentucky Girl* … it's really important that we keep the song selection pure.' The only left-field thing that he allowed me on the record was Willie Nelson's solo on 'Green Pastures.' Which is still one of my favorite guitar solos, of anything. And it's on *Roses In The Snow.*"

On *Roses*, Skaggs' presence is felt at every step. His high mountain tenor blends perfectly with Emmy's soprano, and he performs on mandolin, guitar, fiddle and banjo. It was through Skaggs' bluegrass connections that Tony Rice would up playing on the album, too (the two subsequently made a duet record for the bluegrass label Sugar Hill).

"He certainly solidified my love for bluegrass," Harris said of Skaggs. "I had been doing bluegrass and acoustic songs all the way through. There were things on all the records up until Ricky came into the band that I had been doing. We even did a little bluegrass segment in the show before Ricky came: Emory, Albert, Rodney and I would do a little acoustic portion of the show, with things like 'Angels Rejoiced In Heaven Tonight' and 'Satan's Jewel Crown,' things that we hadn't even recorded. We used them to warm up, because Emory has a great love of bluegrass.

"When Ricky came into the band, he came from serious bluegrass roots, from the time he was 5 years old he'd been playing mandolin and singing, and then moved on to the fiddle. So then it sort of shifted into a higher gear. I think it was Ricky's being in the band that moved us in the direction of doing *Roses In The Snow*. Certainly his input was very important. "But I also think that myself and Brian's involvement with Ricky gave him something, a way of making records, of putting all that bluegrass knowledge, and shifting him into another gear. So it was very mutually beneficial."

Roses In The Snow became Harris' sixth consecutive gold album, and it earned her the Country Music Association's Best Female Vocalist award. Her mind, however was somewhere else: Although she continued well into her pregnancy (check her out in Willie Nelson's movie *Honeysuckle Rose*), Harris had to take some time off when her second daughter, Meghann, was born in September 1979.

"I recorded three albums during my pregnancy. We recorded *Roses In The Snow*, *Blue Kentucky Girl* and *Light Of The Stable* all at the same time," Harris said. "And part of *Evangeline*, actually. I was too pregnant to go on the road, so I went into the studio."

Light Of The Stable appeared in time for the 1980 holiday season. It included her Christmas single from 1975, a new Rodney Crowell song and eight Yuletide standards and mountain hymns cut in the same lovingly unplugged style as *Roses*.

The album, said Harris, is "The best–kept secret in the music business! It comes out every year, and nobody even knows I have a Christmas album out.

"I like that record; I don't think very many people do acoustic Christmas albums. But those songs really lend themselves to acoustic arrangements and instrumentation."

Glen D. Hardin left the touring band around this time; he was briefly replaced by Tony Brown, another former Elvis sideman (and the future president of MCA Nashville). Gordy, DeVito and Brown departed the Hot Band in 1980 to play with Rodney Crowell's Cherry Bombs, formed to work the road in support of Crowell's second album, *But What Will The Neighbors Think?*

The two-record soundtrack to the film *Roadie* was issued that summer, and while the film died a quick (and merciful) death, the music enjoyed relative success. In particular, "That Lovin' You Feelin' Again," a duet by Roy Orbison and Emmylou Harris, went to No. 6. "I was a little nervous about working with Roy Orbison," Harris recalled. "Because there are just a few people that are larger than life, and he was one.

"But you know, what's great about singing and music is once you're actually doing it, you're not thinking about the fact that you're singing with Roy Orbison, you're just singing. And you're carried away by the song, and by what you're doing. I suppose Fred Astaire and Ginger Rogers felt that way.

"I seem to have an innate ability to follow people. Duet singing is something I don't think about. I just jump in. You just do it, and you're carried away by it, and it's kind of a transcendent experience." She and Orbison shared the 1980 Grammy for Best Country Performance, Duo or Group.

In February 1981, *Evangeline* was released (the title track, the Band song by Robbie Robertson, featured Parton and Ronstadt on harmony vocals). Including mostly leftovers from the previous records, *Evangeline* was a hodgepodge of ideas that didn't really gel, a critical disappointment, and it sluggishly became Harris' final gold album.

Three years earlier, Harris, Parton and Ronstadt had attempted to make an entire album together (their provisional moniker was "The Queenston Trio"). Scheduling and other difficulties had killed the project (they finally got it together in 1987). *Evangeline* included a version of the Chordettes' sprightly "Mister Sandman," produced by Ahern for the abandoned trio album. Released as a single (with Harris' re-recorded vocals replacing those of Parton and Ronstadt, for legal reasons), "Mister Sandman" reached No. 10.

For Harris, things started feeling like a treadmill. The Hot Band had been diluted from the hard-hitting ensemble she'd started out with, and her records were suddenly not selling the way they had been. She started to fear artistic stagnation.

At that moment, Ricky Skaggs left for a solo career. "I think it was time for Ricky to go on and do something else," Harris said. "I think our styles diverged because Ricky is more into things being very specific: 'This is the way a song should go, it should be sung like this,' and you don't vary from it; whereas for me, I'm more comfortable with leaving things a little more open-ended.

"Whereas for a while it was very creative and very good for both of us, I think it was time for us to go on to different paths, and take what we'd learned from each other."
Barry Tashian, a New Englander who'd met Harris while she was singing with Parsons, had sung on three *Evangeline* tracks. A guitarist and songwriter, Tashian had fronted a Boston rock band, the Remains, when he was 21; that group's claim to fame was as an opening act on the Beatles' final tour, in 1966.

Almost out of nowhere, Emmylou called him in the spring of 1980. "She said, 'Ricky's gone off on his own and I need somebody to sing and play rhythm guitar,'" recalled Tashian. "The only thing I'm going to ask you to do is play a little banjo, and sing higher than you're used to singing.' That's what she said.

"It was hard at first, because I'm naturally a baritone. But I learned to stretch my range so eventually it became a little easier." He played his first Hot Band show on the Fourth of July. By then, only drummer John Ware remained from the original lineup (he would resign in 1982). Lead guitarist Frank Reckard had taken Albert Lee's spot.

There were other, more significant changes on the horizon. Emmylou's marriage to Brian Ahern, who'd stepped into the Svengali shoes when Parsons died, was unraveling. Although they made three more albums together, and added a half-dozen more hit singles to the canon, the spark was pretty much gone.

It's evident on 1981's *Cimarron*, which yielded three hits (Townes Van Zandt's "If I Needed You," sung as a duet with Don Williams, Paul Kennerley's "Born To Run" and the Karen Brooks/Hank DeVito tune "Tennessee Rose," featuring the White Sisters) but had an overall flat, uninspired sound. "At that point," said Harris, "Brian and I were coming to the end of our … I know it wasn't our last record, but I think that we had maybe maxed out. We were starting to max out on our ability to be able to work together. I like a lot of the songs on *Cimarron*."
Harris had another No. 1 with a vocal version of Floyd Cramer's "Last Date," which became the title song of the live Hot Band album, released in late 1982. Ahern turned the fabled Enactron Truck into a truly mobile console and recorded the group (the credits do not specify where) performing a good chunk of their live show at that time, which included Parsons's "Grievous Angel," Hank Snow's "I'm Movin' On" and Neil Young's "Long May You Run." Harris herself played the Bob Morris lead guitar part on the Buck Owens chestnut "Buckaroo."

Ahern and Harris' own last date was 1983's *White Shoes*, which ranged farther afield than ever before with covers of the Donna Summer hit "On The Radio," "Pledging My Love" (a 1955 Johnny Ace smash) and even "Diamonds Are A Girl's Best Friend." Both "Pledging My Love" and "In My Dreams" (written by Paul Kennerley) reached No. 9 on the country singles chart, although the album was Harris' third consecutive release to miss gold status. "In My Dreams" won her a fourth Grammy. Critics called *White Shoes* her rock album.

Remarked Harris: "There were certainly some rock things on there, but the high point on that record, for me, was the Sandy Denny song called 'Old Fashioned Waltz.' Which I think is worth the price of the record."

Before *White Shoes* had even hit the marketplace, Harris dropped the ax. With Hallie and Meghann in tow (they were 13 and 4 respectively) she left the Enactron driveway for the last time and didn't stop until she got to Nashville. And this time, she arrived a winner.

By any other name

Englishman Paul Kennerley had relocated to Nashville to pitch his songs, after the moderate critical and commercial success of his two country music concept albums, *White Mansions* and *The Legend of Jesse James*. Harris had sung a major role on the latter, produced by Glyn Johns and released in 1980 (the other lead players in Kennerley's "country opera" were Johnny Cash, Levon Helm, Charlie Daniels and Albert Lee, and although they attempted to give the historically-based libretto some weight, it came off as little more than a poor-man's Nashville imitation of *Jesus Christ Superstar*). But Kennerley came into Emmylou Harris' life just as the road was turning and she was wondering where to go next.

On one of the Hot Band tours, Harris' road manager had deterred a fan who thought she had recognized Harris in a bar. No, that's not her, he'd said protectively; that girl's name is Sally Rose. And these guys are her band, the Rosebuds.

It was a road pseudonym they often used - Sally was Emmy's sister, and she'd check into the hotels under that name, and for a while the Hot Band would be introduced for their opening set as Sally Rose and the Rosebuds. After a while, Harris began to create a story for Sally Rose, using, like many fiction writers, easy parallels from her own life. A theme began to form in her mind. Musically, she began collaborating with Paul Kennerley, asking him to help her fill in the blanks.

"I had these songs that were stewing around," Harris recalled. "And there was something that I wanted to say. I knew that I had to just put everything aside and just put the energy into writing that album.

"I had reached an impasse, a logjam if you will, creatively as an artist. For the most part, I am an interpreter of other people's songs, and I'm very happy to do that. But when you do have something to say poetically, and in this case, it was more than one song … I had an idea for a story that was more than mildly autobiographical, but it went into a realm of something else. I became a project, something that I had conceived of and wanted to follow to its fruition."

It was steel guitarist Hank DeVito who convinced a procrastinating Harris to thread all the songs together and make *The Ballad Of Sally Rose* a true concept album. "I kept putting it off, and I knew that I was just going to be treading water creatively, trying to come up with another record as good as the last record," she remembered, "and that that was just not gonna happen until I did this."

The Ballad Of Sally Rose hit the street in February 1985. The story of an impressionable young girl whose parents met near Mount Rushmore ("Through the valley of the shadow of Roosevelt's nose"), the album follows Sally through her musical apprenticeship with The Singer, who takes her into his confidence, his band and his bed. Before long, they're married, and Sally's fame as a performer begins to overtake his. He's a wild man with a deep love for honky-tonk music, but little regard for the feelings of those around him. When he begins to hit the skids and hit them hard, Sally takes off for brighter lights.

The Singer dies in a car wreck, never to know that a hopelessly lovesick Sally was on her way back. She dedicates herself to keeping his unique music alive any way she can.
The press pounced on the story's similarity to that of Emmylou Harris and Gram Parsons (Harris at the time would coyly admit that autobiography was a large part of the inspiration). Although three singles were released, none made the Top 10, and *The Ballad Of Sally Rose* became her first out-and-out flop.

Too bad all around, because several of the songs she and Kennerley crafted, especially the majestic "Woman Walk The Line" and the sinewy "Rhythm Guitar" would have been worthy additions to her book of sonic triumphs with Brian Ahern. She had learned how it was done.

"Having written with Paul Kennerley myself, I can only imagine how much fun she had doing all those songs," said Barry Tashian, one of numerous past and present Hot Band members to play on the *Sally Rose* sessions. "Paul is such an inventive and talented craftsman, I can well imagine she learned a lot through that process. I remember visiting them out at this little barn where Paul used to live, on Mel Tillis' property. They just sat and pounded out all those songs."

Sally Rose meant much more to Harris than a transfusion of new blood. It was a change, a journey into the unknown. "It was kind of frightening," she said. "But also, I was at the point where there were so many things I needed to change about my life and the thing that was pulling me toward the change, and the project that was sort of my crowbar was *Sally Rose*. I came to Nashville with the idea of working on that record."

Tashian remembers the Hot Band taking a longer-than-normal respite while Emmy and Paul were hammering out the songs and the story. "There was as break in the flow," he explained, "and I think it started around August of the year she moved to Nashville. I think I was one of the first ones to move to Nashville, which could've been the reason I would up on that album when maybe some of the others didn't.

"The transition, once it was accomplished, once the album was done, then the band kind of re-materialized. She brought the people together again. (In concert) we played the album from top to bottom, and things resumed pretty much after that." The last holdout from the original Hot Band, drummer John Ware, had departed the year before, and now Emmy had all new guys.

The *Sally Rose* live show (one set of the entire album, the second set consisting of

Harris' best–known songs) was a resounding critical success. And at the end of the tour Paul Kennerley became her third husband.

"There were a lot of changes happening," said Harris. "It was a huge creative step for me. Quite scary, in a way." She thinks of it as one of her best albums, and recommends it to her fans. "If they're interested in what I do and in the left turns that I've taken, I really took a left turn with that one," she said.

"After *Sally Rose* I did *Angel Band* and that was really good. And that was something that was not even a record; we just got together to really get the juices going again, and just sing without the idea of making a record. But it turned out so good that we ended up putting it out."

One of the most unorthodox (and fascinating) albums in the Harris canon, *Angel Band* consists of acoustic renditions of traditional country gospel songs along the lines of "If I Be Lifted Up," "We Shall Rise" and "Where Could I Go But To The Lord." (The well-known spiritual "Angel Band" had given Harris the name of her first post--Parsons group, way back when.)

Produced by her longtime bassist Emory Gordy, *Angel Band* was little more than a simple harmony record, less complex even than *Roses In The Snow*, with Vince Gill adding the Ricky Skaggs tenor to Emmy's soprano. It was a low-key affair, released with little fanfare.

Angel Band wasn't released until 1987, by which time Harris had already put out *Thirteen*, co–produced with Kennerley. "*Thirteen* is a record that probably suffered from me being really tired and exhausted from the afterbirth of *Sally Rose*," she said. "Because I put so much effort into making that record, and then I toured myself into the ground, went way into debt … for all intents and purposes, I suppose, it was kind of a disaster. Except for me, artistically. Then I went in and I made *Thirteen*."

Harris' favorite song on *Thirteen* is Bruce Springsteen's "My Father's House." It continued the fascination with Springsteen's music that began with her version of "The Price You Pay" on *Cimarron* (later she included "Racing In The Street" on *Last Date*, and would go on to cover "Mansion On The Hill" and "Tougher Than The Rest" on subsequent albums).

"Oddly enough," she explained, "it was the *Nebraska* album that Bruce Springsteen did that made me say, 'All right. If I don't put everything aside and finish the *Sally Rose* project, then I shouldn't have my artistic license renewed.' It was such an amazing record. The songs on *Nebraska* were so moving and so beautiful. It was such a brave record for him to make. He was this pop icon, this rock icon, and he made basically 'Luke The Drifter 1980.' He just did something that was so brave.

"But *Nebraska* is still my favorite Springsteen album. 'My Father's House' is just an extraordinary song. *Thirteen* is worth it for me, just for 'My Father's House.' But ultimately, maybe I should've waited before I had nine more like it."

She rebounded from the album's lack of success in a big way during 1987. *Trio*, the album she, Parton and Ronstadt had begun a decade earlier, was finally realized (George Massenburg produced) and became Harris's first (and to date only) platinum album. It climbed all the way to No. 6 on Billboard's pop albums chart.

"We started the *Trio* record in late '77 and 'Mister Sandman' was one of the original things we cut for it. I was dragged kicking and screaming into that. I didn't like the song, and I ended up with the hardest part. We called it the road-map part. What little melody there was, there was less of it on my harmony part.

"But over the years, I've come to at least learn to admire and respect that song, because of how difficult it is. It was like learning to speak Russian or something." The Ahern-produced "Mister Sandman," of course, had been issued in 1981 on *Evangeline*.

Harris, Parton and Ronstadt each sang on one another's solo records in the intervening years. So why did *Trio* take so long to materialize? "We kind of lost our direction," said Harris. "It kind of fell apart. I think we were a bit shy about getting back together again, because we didn't want to have another aborted attempt."

Herb Pedersen was called in as "Vocal Arranger" for *Trio* (John Starling was credited as "Musical Director"). "All three of them were pals, and they didn't want to be the one to say, 'You should sing this,' or, 'You should sing tenor, and I'll sing the bass,'" Pedersen explained. "So I kind of came in and would listen to what the arrangement was, and then suggest, 'Well, maybe Dolly should sing this part because it's more in her range, and it won't be such a strain for Linda, and Emmy can sing the baritone.' It depended on the tune and the key." When he arrived, Pedersen said, the tracking work was all done; his job was purely to fine-tune the harmonies.

"It took us a while to realize that instead of trying to make this great record to end all records, all we wanted to do was make a little acoustic record," said Harris. "We weren't trying to make this huge pop record. What we did best was sitting around singling very simple, melodic songs, with basically acoustic accompaniment. To really give Brian his due, who was initially supposed to produce the record, that was what he said to us. And we said, 'No, no, we have to do this, and we have to do that!' and we sort of self–destructed. The one we ended up making, if you listen, is really all acoustic. Except for maybe 'Telling Me Lies.'"

"Telling Me Lies" was second of four singles from *Trio*; the others were "These Memories Of You," "Wildflowers" and the old Phil Spector tune "To Know Him Is To Love Him." All of them made the country Top Ten ("To Know Him Is To Love Him" went to No. 1). *Trio* took the Grammy for Country Performance by a Duo or Group. Also nominated that year were the *Angel Band* album and "You Are," a single Harris made with Glen Campbell. Harris' version of "Back In Baby's Arms," from the John Hughes film *Planes, Trains And Automobiles,* was released as a single in December, 1987, and she hit the top spot for the last time to date in the summer of 1987 with "We Believe In Happy Endings," a duet with Earl Thomas Conley.

"We Believe In Happy Endings" was issued on *Duets*, released by Warner/Reprise in 1990. This invaluable album collected some of Harris' finest one-offs, including "Wild Montana Skies" with John Denver (a top 20 hit in 1983), "That Lovin' You Feelin' Again" with Roy Orbison, "Evangeline" with the Band and "A Thing About You," a Tom Petty song she'd recorded with the group Southern Pacific.

Among the other gems on *Duets*: "If I Needed You" with Don Williams, "Star Of Bethlehem" with Neil Young, and "Love Hurts," the *Grievous Angel* version, with Gram Parsons.

She released an album in 1988, *Bluebird*, that placed two singles in the Top 20 ("Heartbreak Hill," written by Harris and Kennerley, and "Heaven Only Knows," a solo Kennerley composition). Co–produced by Harris and guitarist Richard Bennett, *Bluebird* was a nice, safe, wake-me-when-it's-over record. She was treading water.

Its follow–up, 1990's *Brand New Dance*, had a little more muscle (and some lovely songs) but really wasn't a quantum improvement (the production chores were handled by Bennett and Alan Reynolds, the same team who produced some of Nashville's more broadly commercial acts). "I got the chance to work with Mary Black and Dolores Keane on *Brand New Dance*," Harris said. "And that was a good experience, because they're two of my favorite singers. We did Bruce Springsteen's 'Tougher Than The Rest.' That might be my favorite thing on that record."

A new beginning

Harris's storybook marriage to Paul Kennerley ended in January 1992. By then she had accepted a position as president of the Country Music Foundation, Nashville's historic archive and country music library. It was essentially a public relations gig; she made TV commercials for the CMF, hawking its reissue album series.

In 1992 Harris was inducted into the Grand Ole Opry. She'd been in Nashville a lot the previous year, working with the CMF, staying home to tend to 11–year old Meghann, and working through the separation from Kennerley. A serious bronchial infection convinced her that something else needed to go, too.

"It made me realize how hard it was to sing over the top of the electric instruments," she recalled. "And I'd been doing it for 13 or 14 years. It made me come face to face with the fact that I was tired, and I was tired of doing the same thing, and there were no new worlds to conquer. The band played great every single night. It was nothing to do with their performance. It was mine."

And so in late 1990, the legendary Hot Band ceased to exist. "She just called me up one day," remembered Barry Tashian, "and said, 'I've done this long enough, and I'm going to dissolve the band. I don't know what's going on with my voice.' A couple months earlier though, I remember she'd had kind of a moody period, where she mentioned she wasn't having much fun. So perhaps it had run its course.

"I remember the house sound man saying, 'I've got to run Emmylou's microphone all the way up.' In other words, she wasn't projecting very much. So she was having some problems there."

Said Harris, "Sometimes I think these events happen to us that can initially be looked on as something that's really bad, but they awaken us to something: You have to make a change. Scott Peck, in his book *The Road Less Traveled*, calls it re–writing your road map. Because you actually are a different person, and you're in a different place, but you're acting as if it was 10 years ago. And we all go through this, in personal things, our professional life, whatever.

"It's very terrifying to make a change from something that is successful and that you can depend on. And you're almost on automatic pilot. But that's death. You have to sometimes just step into the unknown. And it's easy now to talk about it, but at the point of making that change, it was pretty frightening."

She assembled an all–new band, the Nash Ramblers, with Newgrass Revival founder Sam Bush on mandolin, fiddle and harmony. The other members of the five–piece outfit were acoustic bassist extraordinaire Roy Huskey Jr., singer and guitarist Jon Randall Stewart, drummer Larry Atamanuik and pedal steel whiz Al Perkins, who'd been a member of Stephen Stills' Manassas many years before, the group that caused Chris Hillman to disband the Flying Burrito Brothers. What goes around comes around.

"I either needed to take some time off, or I needed to put together a completely different musical unit," Harris explained. "And it was John Starling who encouraged me to put together an acoustic band."

Emmylou Harris and the Nash Ramblers were recorded live in Nashville's historic Auditorium, longtime home of the Grand Ole Opry, April 30-May 2, 1991, before a specially-invited audience. They played more than 20 songs each night, and 17 wound up on *Emmylou Harris And The Nash Ramblers At The Ryman*, produced by Reynolds and Bennett using the New York-based Record Plant's remote truck.

True to form, she picked an eclectic bunch of tunes for the album and the accompanying TNN television special. There was Eddy Arnold's "Cattle Call," Steve Earle's "Guitar Town," and Nanci Griffith's "It's A Hard Life Wherever You Go," and the old Dion hit "Abraham, Martin and John," plus tunes by Bruce Springsteen, Creedence Clearwater Revival and Peter Rowan.

The Nash Ramblers also performed Bill Monroe's "Get Up John," and Monroe himself appeared on the Ryman stage each night to buck dance with Emmylou. "I didn't know how my audiences, who had been coming very loyally to see me and the Hot Band for all those years, were going to respond," she said. "I don't know if I was going to lose any power, because I was used to being in front of a really high-powered bunch of musicians.

"And what I found to my delight, was that these guys were just as high-powered. They just did it with different instrumentation."

At The Ryman won a Grammy in the by–now familiar "Duo or Group" category, and although it didn't go gold, it certainly sold enough copies to qualify as a success; still, Harris and the new upper-levels at Warner Brothers could not see eye to eye, and in 1993 she left the company for Asylum Records, which had recently re–energized its Nashville division. *Cowgirl's Prayer*, her 18th (not counting *Gliding Bird* or the two best–ofs issued during her long tenure with Warner) appeared in September. Again, Reynolds and Bennett produced, and members of the Nash Ramblers played on several cuts.

Harris seemed to be searching for direction again. Mining familiar ground, she cut an old country standard (Eddy Arnold's "You Don't Know Me"), a tune from an up-and-coming songwriter (Lucinda Williams's Cajun-flavored "Crescent City"), a Jesse Winchester song, a Leonard Cohen song and a collaboration with country folkie Kieran Kane. She even muttered through David Olney's bizarre spoken-word parable "Jerusalem Tomorrow," the story of a snake-oil salesman who takes a job with Jesus Christ. With a clarinet solo in the bridge, no less.

Perhaps the most galvanizing song on *Cowgirl's Prayer* was one Harris wrote all by herself. She cadged the chord progression for "Prayer In Open D" from "Norfolk," a tune she'd penned back in her D.C. clubbing days. The story of a search for peace ("I can find no bridge for me to cross, no way to bring back what is lost"), it seemed possibly connected by some emotional thread to her recent divorce. Her voice, deeper now, conveyed both heartbreak and hopefulness along with a certain resignation that had never been there before.

"Prayer In Open D" (played, naturally, in open D guitar tuning) became one of the high points of Harris's Nash Ramblers concerts. It was performed by Harris on guitar, accompanied by Sam Bush playing violin. "Most of my songs, I feel like I need people behind me," she said. "Something like 'Boulder To Birmingham,' I would kind of miss the harmonies. It's not so easy to play by myself. My abilities as a guitar player come glaring through." Although she'd been playing guitar on her own records all the way back, she was always part of an ensemble, where she felt comfortable. "Whereas in an open tuning, I really get up past the third fret, and I can impress people."

In early 1995, Harris embarked on a European tour with a re-united Hot Band (the roster included Rodney Crowell, Albert Lee, Glen D. Hardin and others from later incarnations of the group).

Harris was now seen as a sort of spiritual godmother to contemporary country music (all the new singers, many 20 years younger, sang her praises) and although she remained as hauntingly beautiful as ever, with her almond eyes and model's high cheekbones, her hair, which had been streaked with white since the '70s, was now completely that color. She moved gracefully into middle age.

Realizing that country radio wasn't going to squeeze her in, whatever she recorded, Harris decided to take a giant step in a completely different direction. Instead of playing to an indifferent market, she would please herself. When Asylum Records president Kyle Lehning queried her as to which producer she'd like to work with, if she could choose anybody, she said Daniel Lanois.

Lanois had made his mark creating atmospheric, moody backgrounds for U2 and Peter Gabriel; he'd been at the helm of Bob Dylan's acclaimed *Oh Mercy*, and his solo album *Acadie* was one of Harris's recent favorites.

As always, the first task was choosing songs for the project. Harris brought in Lucinda Williams's deceptively simple "Sweet Old World," Dylan's "Every Grain Of Sand" and Steve Earle's "Goodbye" (she had recently guested on Earle's comeback album, *Train a–Comin'*). Two Lanois compositions, "Where Will I Be" and "Blackhawk," were added to the stash.

Lanois convinced Harris to record Jimi Hendrix's "Waterfall (May This Be Love)," and she in turn overrode his doubts about "Goin' Back To Harlan," written by Anna McGarrigle, one of her favorite songwriters. She championed yet another newcomer (California songwriter Gillian Welch, who penned "Orphan Girl"). And she wrote yet another number with Rodney Crowell, "Waltz Across Texas."

But the album, *Wrecking Ball*, was like nothing Emmylou Harris had ever done before. Every song pulsed with dark and primitive percussion, its background a wash of guitar and keyboard figures. True to Lanois's trademark style, each song was stripped to its essence and re-introduced into a smoky atmosphere. At the forefront, always, was Emmylou's voice, recorded hot and breathlessly close to the microphone, intimate and grave.

She admitted to a certain fearlessness in the studio. "If it was somebody that I trusted that wanted to do it, I would certainly give it a shot," she said, "and if I felt that I could bring something to it … I have a pretty good barometer in me that tells me when I'm comfortable with something. And even something like 'Where Will I Be,' which even Daniel thought was really different for me, I knew it was different but I loved the song so much … as long as people give me a little bit of latitude to maybe change things a little bit, phrasing, and sometimes I inadvertently change melodies and I don't realize I have, as long as they're okay with that, then if I bring something to it that works, then I'm happy to do it."

Neil Young, who'd written the otherworldly title song (Harris discovered it on his *Freedom* album), sang harmony on it; likewise, Williams and Earle played guitar on their own compositions. U2's Larry Mullen Jr. was featured on drums and hand drums, and Lanois himself played a multitude of guitars and basses, and sang lead and harmony vocals.

Just before it came out, Harris told interviewers that *Wrecking Ball* was her "weird record." "At that time I coined that phrase, I was in discussions with Kyle Lehning at Asylum," she recalled, "talking about what record I was going to do next after *Cowgirl's Prayer*. And I said, 'Well, I've got this idea for a country record that I might collaborate with Rodney Crowell on. And then I've got this sort of weird record, because I had these songs that were not country songs, and were kind of eclectic. So when Kyle and I would talk, it was my way of identifying one project from the other. It came from a very innocent source. I wasn't getting *X Files* on anybody, if you know what I mean."

Harris said she was never worried that *Wrecking Ball* might be carrying things a little too far. "I've always been very eclectic, so the song selection was not a very big jump for me. Maybe doing a Jimi Hendrix song was, but that was Daniel. That was really a duet between the two of us. I don't know if Daniel ever did, but I never had any second thoughts, ever."

As for the thought that her faithful fans might be turned off by the new sounds: "I didn't worry about it. I thought that that might happen, but I felt so strongly about what I was doing I felt if I alienated anybody, they probably weren't my fan to begin with. Not in the long run."

Released in September 1995, *Wrecking Ball* didn't land any singles on the country charts and it missed gold–record status, but the album topped *Billboard*'s new "Americana" chart for several weeks. And in March, it won a Grammy Award (Harris' seventh) as Best Folk Album.

A week before the album's release, Harris had joined Earle and singer/songwriters Guy Clark and Townes Van Zandt for a show at Nashville's intimate Bluebird Café. The three Texas legends kept the crowd spellbound with their exquisitely crafted songs. Harris, who sang harmony with each of them, more than held her own with a solo reading of "Prayer In Open D." In the first month of 1995, she brought Earle onto the Grand Ole Opry stage for the first time.

A class act all the way, Emmylou Harris remains, more than 20 years on, delightfully classless.

"It's probably better for me that my success is not calculated by, 'Oh, I had another huge hit," she said. "Or by my sales. It's calculated by an inner thing that I look for, and also getting that sense that my audience is responding, because I don't go by record sales, or whatever. The critical acclaim is one thing, although you shouldn't listen to them, I suppose. But more important, I think, it's looking back and saying, 'I like the songs on this record; I like what I did here.'

"*The Ballad Of Sally Rose* was not a commercial success. And it had mixed critical success. But I stand by that record. I know it has flaws, but I stand by the material. And the fact that I did it. *Angel Band* is a very little known record, yet I have people always coming up to me and saying how that record, you know, affected their lives. It's things like that where you feel it was good that you did something.

"But ultimately, you want to just be excited about music. And I know that there were times when it was a struggle for me to be excited about making music, and I probably should've taken some time off. But I either didn't have the courage to do that (I told myself it was for financial reasons, that I had to make an album and I had to do a tour) but ultimately, I think that that's a copout.

"I think it's scary to remove yourself from something that is very much wrapped up with your identity and who you are. And it's very difficult to be quiet and still. That's something that I've never done."

Warner Bros. Records

10. Linda Ronstadt (1996)
'It was an act of Dolly'

As a sidebar to the Emmylou Harris story, I got to speak with Linda Ronstadt. I knew she loved Emmy and would probably say some wonderful stuff. She did, but I also got an earful about her working relationship with Dolly Parton, the much-loved Trio *album and what was to have been its sequel. This is a short interview; it was never intended to be more than a footnote to the main feature. But it's one of my all-time favorites.*

What did you think when you first heard Emmylou Harris sing?

When I met her, I thought, "I would give anything to be able to sing with Emmylou Harris. I wish we could become the Everly Sisters." Well, she had a singing partner, Gram, and I thought it was a wonderful combination. I remember telling my boyfriend at the time, who was Albert Brooks, that Emmy could sing higher and lower, and louder and softer, and she could phrase a lot better, than I could. She really had country-rock nailed. Country-rock had been my little niche, but I'd been getting pushed very hard to move it more into rock 'n' roll. And I said, 'She just does this so well, I think I'll stop fighting this.' Because she just does it better than anybody.

I made a choice. I decided that loving her music was more important than feeling that I was the queen of country–rock. And then I made a decision that she was my singing sister, and that when I got the chance to sing with her, I would do it. So we sang a duet on "I Can't Help It (If I'm Still In Love With You)." We won a Grammy for that record.

In your opinion, what did Emmylou Harris bring to country music?

She gave girl country singers elegance, taste, class and dignity. I don't mean to demean the girl singers that had been in country music before, but they never appealed to me. I must confess that I wasn't a person who hungered after a Kitty Wells record. With all due respect for Kitty Wells. I was raised as Emmy was; we had a little bit more refined upbringing. To me, those women didn't seem like real country singers. The seemed like girls who'd gone to the city, hung around the bars and became very jaded. They seemed hard; their makeup was on too thick. I didn't like it as a role model, and their singing was too twangy, too hard and too nasal. Because of the hardness of their lives and their attitudes.

Emmy brought more country fresh air, a real rural style. More like the Carter Family and Jean Ritchie. And with it, elegance and dignity that came from the more refined upbringing, which doesn't have anything to do with being hoity-toity, or rich, or anything like that. It just has to do with having been raised like a lady. In the meantime, she could go into the honky-tonks with the best of 'em.

Her approach was totally new. She was really responsible for bringing a lot of that stuff back. And she was uncompromising and tireless. And another thing I've always loved about Emmy is that she has campaigned for other singers and songwriters, very unselfishly. She's been sending me tapes for years.

She's got the profound respect of the entire musical community. There isn't anybody that's more revered, in a lot of ways. If you call up Keith Richards and say, 'Emmy needs you to come over and change the cat box, tomorrow morning,' he'll get on a plane and come over and do it. He thinks she hung the moon.

You first attempted a trio record with Emmylou Harris and Dolly Parton in 1977, with Emmy's then-husband Brian Ahern producing, but it was never released. What happened?

I think we had pretty much a whole record. There were some real problems there. I think that Brian is an excellent producer, (but) I don't think he was really on track with that one. He wasn't a good communicator. And I'm used to working with somebody where you can talk about stuff. The control booth was out in the truck, and we were in his house ... and there were a lot of mind–altering things going on in those days. I'm not saying we were exactly taking them, but they were around. It was a different mentality.

It was actually a difficult thing for Emmy to be married to the producer, because there were times when she didn't agree with him, and she felt she had to side with him. And things would go farther than they needed to. I think that was very hurtful for Brian, and for Emmy, and for all of us that it was an aborted production. But it was mine and Dolly's decision on the phone to stop it. We didn't feel the record was worthy of what we wanted to have.

"Mister Sandman," on Emmylou's Evangeline *album, was salvaged from those sessions. Were there any others that got released?*

"Mister Sandman" was one of the problems. We didn't sing in tune. It wasn't a good version of it. I thought the version she did that was all hers was dramatically, infinitely better.

"My Blue Tears" came out on my record. I asked for that track. That's what I thought should define the direction of what the trio should be. "Even Cowgirls Get The Blues" was one of them too, and "Evangeline." I remember Dolly at the time saying the album was too cluttery, and I agreed with her.

You three finally made your album together in 1987. I guess you felt it was special enough to wait for.

It was a thrilling sound. The only problem was that Emmy and I are both passionate about material. And that would be like two ganging up against one. Unfortunately, Dolly's tastes often didn't jibe with ours; she has different ideas of what's pretty, and fancy and impressive. For us, it was uncomfortable often to sort of get around her taste without hurting her feelings, or making her feel like we thought we were better than she was, or hipper than she was. And I thought we did a masterful job with it. There were never any fights.

Did the trio ever go on tour?

We had a tour planned, and it was cancelled. I don't think her manager thought that was the best move for Dolly to make. It's not up to us to say what they should value. He convinced her that it was more important for her to do a variety television show.

Feels Like Home*, your 1995 album, was originally to be the sequel to* **Trio***, wasn't it? Emmy sings on that one.*

Emmy wanted to do a project that wasn't a trio project. She wanted to involve some of the writers and singers that we loved, like the McGarrigle Sisters. I had suggested Alison Krauss.

We invited Dolly as a courtesy, to see if she wanted to sing on some tracks. And she was busy, but about six months later she sent word that she wanted to do it. I said, great, maybe this should be a trio record. And Emmy, who's always more practical than me, was remembering how difficult it had been to get our schedules together, and how difficult it had been to schedule time to promote the record, which we'd felt was really crucial. And we thought that if Dolly was on the record, and then pulled out and couldn't promote it, the two of us couldn't go out and promote it, if it was a trio record.

So Emmy strongly wanted to keep it a record of ours. Plus, she remembered the taste discrepancy. I felt that what the trio had done was so stunning, I would love to repeat it, so I fought for that.

I asked Dolly if she would sing on a couple of tracks, and Dolly said, no, she wanted to be full-on trio or nothing. And then Emmy said, "I really would rather not do that. Don't let her talk you back into a trio record." And Dolly talked me back into a trio record, because she's very charming and I loved that sound and thought it would be a wonderful thing if the three of us could go and promote it.

Bob Krasnow, the head of (my record label) Elektra, wasn't a fan of Dolly's. He didn't want us to do another trio record, either. But I said, 'We'll ram this record down country radio's throat. We'll make it sell.'

I asked for Dolly's personal word of honor, and she gave it. I showed up, Emmy showed up, and the night before we started, Dolly sent us a fax, saying there was something wrong with her infomercial and she had to go back for 10 days.

I had booked all these triple-scale players from Tennessee, and it was going to be very expensive to put them up. Emmy stayed at my house, so that we could save money.

When she did arrive, Emmy and I took her in another room, sat her down and said, "Look, we don't feel like you have the same commitment to this project that we do. We're asking you now to tell us whether you're going to really give us three weeks of time at the end of the record, for promotion and a short tour. We have to have the release date written in stone."

And she gave her word. Her exact words at the time were, "I get so many irons in the fire, sometimes I burn my own ass." And we thought, how lovely. But we had her word of honor. Krasnow was still very reluctant and said, "She has a reputation for being unreliable." I said, she gave me her word, that's good enough for me.

We got to the point where we had only Dolly's vocals to record. We had a week left to do them. She cancelled again. It cost us another $20,000. It was 20 grand every time we got one of those faxes. Emmy was gone off on the road, and she was grieving terribly because her father had just died. I'd been in there night and day working on it with George Massenburg, and I was exhausted from being up with my new baby. Dolly did her vocals and we had two mixes left to do. Then she put out her live record right on top of our release schedule at the beginning of August. She said it was going to sell so good and would help the trio record sell.

Well, we somehow did not agree with her. And we couldn't get her on the phone. Another week went by. Meantime, we'd run out of money, and out of time. We started dumping her tracks as fast as we could. We had to somehow come up with a finished record. I started replacing her parts, Valerie Carter started replacing her parts. We couldn't get her on the phone.

Finally, we had a three-way phone conversation. Emmy and I were in the same room. Dolly said, "How can you do this to me? My schedule is so overwhelming." I said, "Dolly, you've made a choice." She said it was like an act of God, like when you break your leg or something. I said it was an act of Dolly. Emmy said, "Dolly, we can't ever get this time back. You took this time away from us."

Krasnow was very upset. It made me look like a fool, because I had given him my word. I'd vouched for her, personally. I was hung out to dry, basically. It broke my heart. George Massenburg was so deeply hurt and discouraged, after how hard he'd worked. He did some of his best work on that record. He moved mountains.

Guess that means you won't be making any more records with Dolly, eh?

I can't work with her. She didn't represent herself as being reliable. Emmy doesn't want to work with her, because she doesn't feel that she values what we did as much as we did. It was her choice. It was not our choice. That's how that record didn't come out. And Dolly then went in the *Ladies Home Journal* and called us very unkind names. She was very unkind and uncharitable to both me and Emmy, and I think she owes us both an apology.

Chumley Records

11. Dave Mason
We just disagree

Dave Mason's Alone Together *is a seminal singer/songwriter album, one of the great ones, and it was a big hit back in '70; it was pretty much all downhill from there, however, and he never again reached those lofty heights, artistically or commercially (notwithstanding his late-period hit single, which gives this chapter its title). These interviews were conducted in 1996, when Mason — truly the Leonard Zelig of rock 'n' roll — had joined*

Fleetwood Mac (you remember that, don't you?) I can confess that he hated this story when it appeared in Goldmine – *he told me so, getting rather angry in the telling.* Alone Together *is still one of the great ones. So there's that.*

In rock 'n' roll, the road may go on forever, but the shoulders are littered with carcasses. To be a survivor, a rock musician has to be able to take the bumps, bruises and creased fenders, to clear hurdles and cross bridges, all the while keeping the gas tank from running dry. There are temptations, frustrations and eliminations, and if you can't run that gauntlet, baby, you might as well put it in the garage and pull down the big door.

Dave Mason has taken hits from every direction, and over the course of his nearly 30–year career has stared down the twin high beams of triumph and tragedy so many times he doesn't even blink any more.

Dave Mason is a songwriter, singer and guitar player; some might quibble with the sequencing of those titles, but no one can argue that his sharp and singular sense of style has served him well as a composer, vocalist and instrumentalist. As a founding member of Traffic, and through more than two decades as a solo artist, Mason has produced some of the most exciting and consequential rock music committed to tape.

Getting there was never easy. In his career, Mason made one bad business move after another, picking the wrong managers, signing the wrong contracts. He had the usual problems with drugs and alcohol, and with relationships with lovers and band members, but at the end of the day, as always, it was the music that mattered.

"His own career is sort of like Fleetwood Mac," observed Mick Fleetwood, one of Mason's oldest and closest friends. "He's been here, there and everywhere, but he's always found a way of prevailing.

"There's a lot of things between Mason and myself. We've had some severe ups and downs, and had crazy times. He's a survivor. And I like to think, in the good sense of the word, that I am. Dave's kept his integrity as a person, and as a player."

History, like the music business, hasn't treated Dave Mason very well. Although many of his best songs ("Feelin' Alright?," "Only You Know And I Know") are considered classics, he's written scores of others equally as provocative, only to see them fail in the marketplace and disappear from record store shelves. His high–profile solo deal with Columbia Records ended in 1980.

The 51–year old Mason is philosophical about the hard knocks he's weathered. "I think I got what I deserved, what can I say?" he mused. "I'm not interested in the victim mentality we have in this country. I haven't got time for the Kurt Cobain kind of thing; I can't hold people like that up as something to be awed at. The guy didn't have the guts to live. He didn't have what it takes to make it through life.

"As for me, if I'd have known better, I'd have done better. It's all been lessons, and everybody's got their lessons to learn. I'm trying my best, and I'm certainly trying to learn from my mistakes. But I'd like to thank all the people that fucked me, because it's been quite an education."

Traffic jams

David Thomas Mason was born May 10, 1946 in Worcester, in the farm belt of the English Midlands, not far from Birmingham. His parents, Edward and Nora, operated a candy store for 46 years. Nora worked in the shop, but Edward, who was 52 at the time of David's birth, was a racing nut who, Mason recalled, spent virtually all his time at the horse track.

David, the younger of the Masons' two children, was a lonely and solitary boy. He was overweight, and prone to crippling migraine headaches, and spent a good deal of time in his room, reading and making up stories of his own.

He remembers his childhood as a "Tom Sawyer existence, running around fields and building rafts and treehouses. But never really talking too much. I was very introverted."

The lonely lad found his way out of the shadows through the guitar, which he practiced night and day in the confines of his room. "I sure as hell didn't want to go and work for somebody from nine to five," he recalled in a 1979 interview. "Plus, I was fat in school and I figured playing the guitar would be a great way to get next to the girls. There's a multitude of reasons when you're 15 years old."

He and his first band, The Jaguars, made an instrumental single out of the classical music standard "Opus To Spring" in 1963. A local record shop pressed the disc, with the necessary financial backing from Edward and Nora.

Drummer and vocalist Jim Capaldi, from a nearby township, was David's mate. Capaldi had a band called the Sapphires. He and Mason joined forces in 1964 as the Hellions. "After I got into it, I knew it was going to happen," Mason said. "I knew I was going to make something happen out of it. Or I knew I wasn't going to stop until something did."

The Hellions were good enough to play in London clubs and eventually took the preordained English bar–band trip to Hamburg, where they rocked the Star–Club. Despite the release of two or three singles, nothing special happened to the band, and it split up in 1965. Mason sat in with Capaldi's next band, Deep Feeling, which also included flute and sax player Chris Wood, while plotting his next move (he was already thinking of going to America). In early 1966, he road–managed the soulful Spencer Davis Group from Birmingham, whose lead singer and organ player, Steve Winwood, was a teenaged legend. Winwood was a fellow everybody knew was going places.

Early the next year, Winwood left the Davis Group to form a new band with his jamming pals Mason, Capaldi and Wood. As Traffic, the quartet spent six months living in a communal home in Berkshire Downs, "getting it together in the country" to make their music without the strains and hassles of the city.

"This house had no water, no electricity; all stone floors," Mason recalled. "There was nothing in this place. And gradually, we rebuilt, put electricity in there. We created a whole lifestyle for ourselves, a way of living, out of which came the music."

Traffic's first single, the odd psych/soul "Paper Sun," was released in May 1967. Written by Winwood and Capaldi in a hotel during a Spencer Davis Group tour (Deep Feeling had been on the same bill), "Paper Sun" featured Winwood's breathless vocalizing and Mason's sitar, and reached No. 5 on the British pop charts. Mason's trippy "Hole In My Shoe" followed, ultimately reaching No. 2. "It was the first song I'd ever written," Mason said, "just a cute little nursery rhyme kind of song. It was perfect for the time."

The others thought Mason wasn't getting into the communal groove; he tended to write alone and bring in his own songs, finished and ready to record. In a band of eccentrics, Mason was the most eccentric of all.

Winwood and Capaldi particularly disliked the poppy "Hole In My Shoe," and Traffic never performed it live. ("It was some trite little song that didn't mean anything," Winwood said years later.) Mason left Traffic before the first album had even been released. "That first time, it was too much success too quick," Mason recalled. "And I couldn't handle it. I was too young, 18, 19, and I was just from a rural town."

The band's debut on Island Records, *Mr. Fantasy*, was issued in December, but by that time Mason was well into an extended visit to the United States at the behest of his new friend Gram Parsons. Parsons, whom Mason had met during a British Byrds tour, took him to the famed Palomino Club in Los Angeles, where Mason was enthralled by the Delaney and Bonnie and Friends band.

Traffic, as a trio, toured the States with Janis Joplin and the Grateful Dead.

In March, Mason went to Hedra, in the Greek Islands (where he came up with his two-chord classic "Feelin' Alright?") and then headed back to the States. And there, wouldn't you know it, was Traffic. "I ran into them in New York," said Mason. "They were at the Record Plant doing the second album and they only had five songs."

He reluctantly agreed to re-join, delivering "Feelin' Alright?," the country–rocking "You Can All Join In," and a collaboration with Capaldi, "Vagabond Virgin." The second album, *Traffic*, was issued in October and was an immediate hit; it's still considered a classic. Mason played one weekend gig with Traffic at the Fillmore East just as the record was being released, but he and Winwood simply couldn't resolve their differences. Mason thinks Winwood was jealous that Mason was writing all the hits. "It just happened that the way I wrote was commercial," he said.

"In the end," Mason concluded, "it was basically a fact of Steve and Jim calling me to a meeting one day and saying 'We don't want you in the band. We don't like your music, we don't like what you do, so we really don't want you in the band anymore.' And that's why it ended, basically."

In November, Winwood dissolved Traffic altogether to record as Blind Faith with Eric Clapton, Ginger Baker, and Rick Grech, and together Mason, Capaldi and Wood assembled a band in London with keyboardist Mick Weaver. The quartet, Wooden Frog, also known simply as Mason, Wood, Capaldi and Frog, never recorded and soon was history ("I got hung up very quickly with that band, because it wasn't handled right," Mason said later, adding that he'd tried without success to get the others to emigrate to the United States and make Wooden Frog an American group. "The general feeling wasn't that good, anyway," he recalled.)

The 1967–68 period in London was magical, Mason said, with pop artists of every stripe hanging out in the clubs and visiting one another in the studio. Mason attending several recording sessions for *Sgt. Pepper's Lonely Hearts Club Band*, and he has a distinct memory of singing on a Beatles session for "Across The Universe" in early 1968.

Traffic's producer, Jimmy Miller, had him along for the Rolling Stones' session for "Street Fighting Man," and Mason can be heard in the recording, blasting a horn and beating a drum in the fadeout. He and Miller co–produced the debut album by the band Family, *Music In A Doll's House*.

One of Mason's clubbing buddies at this point was Jimi Hendrix, and the two of them happened to be at the same London party when Bob Dylan's *John Wesley Harding* album was first unveiled. Mason recalled how Hendrix was taken, as were they all, with Dylan's spooky and hypnotic new song "All Along The Watchtower."

"And during that time that I had left Traffic, Noel Redding was going to leave; Jimi was going to replace the bass," Mason said. "I was going to join them on bass. And their management sort of put a stop to it."

Indeed, Mason played acoustic guitar and bass on Hendrix's searing "All Along The Watchtower," released the next year on *Electric Ladyland*. Mason recalled that Rolling Stone Brian Jones was in the studio as an observer. Mason also sang in the chorus on "Crosstown Traffic," and played bass and sitar on a couple of titles he isn't sure ever got released. He's not listed in the credits, but there's a picture of Mason and Hendrix jamming inside the original *Electric Ladyland* LP sleeve (the notes on the reissued CD, however, say that Mason's bass line was later re–played by Hendrix himself).

In 1974, on his fourth solo album, Mason would record his own version of "All Along The Watchtower," using the Hendrix arrangement. To this day, it's one of his in-concert staples. "There's nothing to the song," he said. "There's no arrangement. It's just the same three chords, and they never change." He paused and laughed again. "It's sort of like 'Feelin' Alright?.'"

He saw his chance in early 1969. At the urging of Gram Parsons, he bade farewell to England and caught a flight to Los Angeles, where he hoped, he might find something better. "After that whole thing with Traffic and their attitude and stuff, there was no other band to be with," Mason said. "There really wasn't much point putting another band together, 'cause it was such a good creative band. I thought. And I figured that I'd just go to America, since it's where rock 'n' roll started."

The Land of Opportunity

"Gram and Cass Elliot were the two people that I knew in L.A. and I didn't really know anybody else," Mason recalled. He fell in with the Delaney and Bonnie crowd, at that time the hot commodity on the L.A. club scene. "They were just a kick–ass band," Mason said. "Originally it was Bobby Whitlock playing keys, and Jimmy Carstein on drums, Carl Radle on bass and Bobby Keys on sax. That was the original band. I went down there and sort of sat in with them."

Alan Pariser, one of the city's legendary scenesters and one of the architects of the Monterey Pop Festival, was Delaney and Bonnie's manager. Soon, Pariser was managing Dave Mason's solo career, and the first thing he did was sign Mason up as lead guitarist in the touring band.

Ironically, Delaney and Bonnie and Friends scored the opening slot on the one and only tour by Blind Faith, Steve Winwood's new group. Halfway through the tour, Eric Clapton began spending more time with Delaney and Bonnie Bramlett than with his own band members. When the tour finally stammered to a halt, there was no more Blind Faith, and Dave Mason left the Friends to record his first solo album for Blue Thumb Records.

In September 1969, he sat in with Stephen Stills at the Big Sur Folk Festival (they played Mason's new song, written in open-F tuning at Elliot's house, "Only You Know And I Know"). Eric Clapton stayed on and replaced him as Delaney and Bonnie's lead guitarist, and then recruited Delaney to produce his eponymously–titled solo debut.

Blue Thumb was the maverick independent label operated by former Kama Sutra Records president Bob Krasnow (he would go on to successfully run Elektra for many years in the '70s, '80s and early '90s) and A&M expatriates Don Graham and Tommy LiPuma. The label's first signing in 1968 had been the eccentric and counter–commercial Captain Beefheart; later acquisitions include Tyrannosaurus Rex, Mark–Almond, Ike and Tina Turner and Dan Hicks and His Hot Licks.

Alan Pariser was a partner in Group 3, a management and design firm, with Barry Feinstein and Tom Wilkes. Feinstein and Wilkes operated Camouflage Productions, too, which became Blue Thumb's house art department.

In 1969, Mason was being courted by all the major labels. Because of his association with Pariser, he went with Blue Thumb, which bought out the remainder of his contract from Island Records head Chris Blackwell, who was only too glad to see him go (Blackwell retained publishing on "Feelin' Alright?" and Mason's other Traffic tunes, however).

Tommy LiPuma was elected to produce Mason's Blue Thumb debut. "When we got together, and he played me most of the stuff from the album, the material was just ridiculous," LiPuma recalled, meaning that in a good way. "He had just bought a 12–string, and he was really in love with it. The songs were just so strong, forget it. You had to be deaf not to hear it."

Mason delivered a half dozen spiritually deep pop songs, some of the most moving things he would ever write, all coming from the perspective of someone keenly aware of the cultural climate in which he lived: "World In Changes," "Can't Stop Worrying, Can't Stop Loving," "Sad And Deep As You," "Shouldn't Have Took More Than You Gave" and the jubilant "Only You Know And I Know."

The album, *Alone Together*, was recorded in the spring of 1970 in Los Angeles. LiPuma spared little expense in recruiting the best session players of the time, including Leon Russell,

Jim Keltner, Jim Gordon and most of the Delaney and Bonnie band. "He was such a great player and songwriter, people were so in awe that when we started these things they just fell right into it," said LiPuma. "Everybody couldn't help but hear what was going on in there. And a lot of the stuff just really fell right in like within an hour in the studio. Within an hour, for each tune, there was a groove happening and we were recording."

Alone Together was superlative pop, 1970 style, because of Mason's unusual open tunings, his unexpected shifts in melody, because of his simple but somehow cosmic lyrics, and because he (and, to give credit where it's due, LiPuma) had a talent for layering electric and acoustic guitar sounds. Mason's lead playing developed its trademark simple, repetitive figures at this stage, something he's still known for.

He's a man of few notes, but the ones he pulls have a multitude of colors.

Colors were on the brains of Feinstein and Wilkes, who at Mason's urging had developed a unique packaging for the *Alone Together* album. Mason wanted the jacket to fold out over several layers into a sunrise, with the actual disc serving as the sun; Camouflage turned this into the "Kangaroo Pack," which could be hung on the wall like a poster (it came with a little pre–drilled hole on top, just over the cut–out picture of Mason, in a top hat, peering over the San Bernardino Mountains).

The design team really outdid itself, though, in preparing the vinyl on which *Alone Together* was pressed. It was Feinstein's idea to elaborate on Mason's sunrise idea, to make each copy of the album different by swirling together the colors in the big vat of bubbling plastic where the records were pressed.

LiPuma remembers going, with Krasnow and Feinstein, to the pressing plant and selecting color pellets from jars on somebody's desk. As the presses were rolling for *Alone Together*, the three of them stood over the vat and dropped pellets in one by one. Mason loved the effect. "There was no way to actually control the colors, so every one of them is different," he said proudly.

LiPuma: "They had to break down a press or two presses in order to do this; because when they were finished doing a run, they had to clean the machine up so it wouldn't show up in the next run of records they were doing for someone else that were black."

Advance order in the United States for *Alone Together* totaled 100,000. The album eventually went gold and became Blue Thumb's biggest hit ever. "That fuckin' package costs us like two to three times what you'd normally spend on a record," said LiPuma, who thinks it might be the best production job he ever did. "Not just the vinyl, the Kangaroo Pack."

Mason, for his part, thought his singing on the album was dreadful, and the week it was unleashed on the public he was back in England, hanging out with familiar company. "I had to keep a career going, somehow," he said. "I did the solo album, but I wasn't looking to be a solo artist."

On June 14, 1970, Mason played the first of two or three dates (he can't remember exactly) with Eric Clapton in his new band, Derek and the Dominos (the Dominos were Carl Radle and Bobby Whitlock, mates from the Delaney and Bonnie band, and Jim Gordon, who'd joined the Bramlett troupe after Mason's departure and had performed on *Alone Together*.

Derek and the Dominoes cut several tracks with Mason on second guitar, "but we were all pretty individually into our own sort of private hells," Mason recalled. "That's when Eric was pretty fucked up. And there was just never any rehearsing. I just got bored. I just said fuck this, I'm going back to the States. I came here to do something, let's do something, if we're gonna do this."

Before he left in disgust, Mason accompanied Clapton to a session or two for George Harrison's *All Things Must Pass* album, and Mason added his guitar to his first ex-Beatle project (there would be another). In time, Clapton would scrap the Dominos tracks with Mason and remake them with Duane Allman on second lead guitar.

Back in L.A., Mason fell into his old routine of hanging out at Cass Elliot's house, smoking dope and sitting on the lawn in a ring of acoustic guitar players. "Her house was a sort of meeting place for all kinds of people," he said. "It was nuts up there."

It was in August 1970 that Mason and Elliot decided to cut an album together. According to Mason, the whole thing happened organically and spontaneously. "I really liked her," he remembered. "She was a great lady, very funny, and we just sort of got along together. I just did it because I really liked her and her career wasn't happening, musically. An odd collaboration but …"

The duo act debuted at the Hollywood Bowl in September and played a short tour that included an *American Bandstand* appearance and a date at the Fillmore East (where Mason had dead-ended with Traffic two years earlier).

Dave Mason And Cass Elliot was released on Blue Thumb in February 1971, produced by the singers themselves and promoted with a single, the fa-la-la poppy "Something To Make You Happy." As part of the deal with Elliot's label, Dunhill, the single credited to Mason and Cass, was issued by that company. Blue Thumb had just secured a distribution deal with Capitol/EMI that wouldn't last a year.

Despite the presence of several good Mason tunes, the album was not received well, and the duo went its separate ways. In early summer, Mason joined Winwood, Capaldi and Wood for six gigs on English college campuses. The shows were held in the lunchrooms, which is why the resulting album was called *Welcome To The Canteen* (the original quartet was augmented by Jim Gordon, Rick Grech and Rebop).

"I've tried to get Traffic together," Mason told *Rolling Stone* from the road. "I've tried to work in units and it's obvious, for some reason, they don't work. So I must go and develop me as myself, and have it accepted for whatever it's accepted for. I hope it won't be 'Dave Mason, ex-Traffic.' It would be nice to drop that."

At the time, he said, the snail's pace was just too much for a restless sort like him. Just like Derek and The Dominos the previous summer, he couldn't get Winwood and the others to work harder, or do more shows. He got angry and returned to the States again. "It was just one gig a week, which is stupid because you'd get onstage and it would take half an hour just to warm up into it," he complained.

Are you feelin' alright?

The Mason and Cass project had failed to yield a hit single; indeed, the album was roundly booed by critics and fans alike, and shortly after its release started turning up in cutout bins across America, where it was a depressingly common sight until the start of the CD age in the mid '80s.

Upon his return from England and the disappointing episode with Traffic and *Welcome To The Canteen*, Mason went through two managers, Don Sherman and Billy Doyle, and "because I was young, drugged-out and not thinking straight," wound up in court with the latter. Eventually, Mason lost all the rest of his publishing to Doyle, and was ordered by a judge to pay his former manager a settlement of $350,000. Mason could only stare at the judge in disbelief.

In October 1971, Delaney and Bonnie hit the Top 20 with a raucous version of Mason's "Only You And I Know." Several weeks later, financially strapped but buoyed by the song's success, Mason started looking closely at his various contracts, and grew indignant over the 1969 deal with Blue Thumb. He and LiPuma were halfway through the follow-up to *Alone Together*. It was to be a double album, half new studio material, the other half live tracks cut with Mason's freshly-minted band at the Troubadour club in Los Angeles.

This rockin' new set, *Headkeeper*, was in theory going to increase the fan base established by the success of *Alone Together*, while (hopefully) making people forget about the Cass Elliot debacle.

Instead, it almost ruined Mason for good.

Mason recalled: "*Alone Together* became a big hit. Because of the experience I'd had with Chris Blackwell on Island, I figured, 'Well, since you've got a big hit, I want the contract re-negotiated.' I was in the middle of doing *Headkeeper* and I took all the master tapes and hid 'em in a vault. I said, 'I want you to re-negotiate this shit, otherwise I'm not gonna do anything else.'"

Drummer Rick Jaeger, who'd been hired just weeks before the Troubadour recordings were made, remembered getting the news about *Headkeeper*, which was to be the first of his many studio projects with Mason.

"I got a call from Dave in the middle of the night telling me that he had split with the tapes," Jaeger said. "He'd walked in when nobody was around, picked up the masters and walked out, because he didn't want to work with Blue Thumb anymore.

"He said, 'I'll go to court and win, 'cause the judge will understand that I'm an artist.' He was lucky he didn't end up going to jail. That's a federal rap. He lost everything on that." No one in rock 'n' roll had ever gone into a recording studio and absconded with their own master tapes; at least nobody could remember if it had been done. What happened next, well, it's a lesson that all recording artists, and record labels should commit to memory.

Headkeeper, the new Dave Mason album, appeared in record stores, from your friends at Blue Thumb Records, in February 1972. Packaged in a cheap, purple psychedelic jacket with a blurry concert picture of Mason on the front, the single LP was studio on side one, live on side two.

Mason, who was aghast that Blue Thumb would actually issue an unfinished record, today puts the blame squarely on Bob Krasnow's shoulders. "He took the masters from the studio side – he had some copies – and just rough, 7–1/2 IPS tapes of the live side, and went ahead and mastered an album off that. He just put it out." Five more studio songs were in the works, Mason recalled; the remaining live tapes became *Dave Mason Is Alive*, issued by Blue Thumb in 1973, long after Mason had extricated himself from the label.

(Mason remembered fondly that he'd started talking with the American Bank Note Company to print the labels for *Headkeeper*, "which would make it a federal offense to bootleg it.")

Tommy LiPuma still gets angry when he talks about *Headkeeper*. "We did half an album. The album was fuckin' great. It was great. And halfway through the album suddenly they went to the studio and took the tapes. Now, you can ask any record company, or whatever: These tapes don't belong to the artist, they belong to the record company. The record company pays for them."

Mason maintains that his beef was never with LiPuma, but with Krasnow, who he saw as the villain. "I wasn't trying to rape him," Mason said. "I just wanted a fairer royalty rate. I'd already been fucked over by Chris Blackwell and his promises with Island, but I was very young then." Blackwell, he says, had promised the young Mason profit-sharing in the fledgling Island label, way back when.

"I'm just one of a thousand stories of that in this business," Mason reported. "I said, 'Here's the deal: If we're gonna stay together, and I'm gonna keep making records and we're gonna have a successful relationship, you'd better come across with something that makes me want to stay here.' He didn't want to do it."

LiPuma figures Mason was getting bad management advice. "They took the tapes and they sued us, because at the time they were trying to get out of the contract," he recalled. "Because Columbia was waving seven figures in front of them, I'm sure. And that was the deal. In the meantime, we had done a live album, because the band was so hot. And the live album came out great. These guys were just gonna walk. And we decided to put the album out."

LiPuma produced *Headkeeper* from safety masters he'd made of the session tapes; the live material was dubbed from two–track tapes (LiPuma always recorded live shows on both multi–track and two–track; Mason had walked out with the multis but left the two-tracks).

LiPuma was pleased with the results, such as they were. "If you're not happy," he said, "you come to somebody and you say, 'I'm not happy,' or, 'This isn't working out. How can we work something out?' You just don't go and take the tapes. We got all kind of heat for that," LiPuma added. "And the reason they gave us heat was because we blew the deal. In other words, they couldn't go and make a deal with Columbia at that point."

Mason, in the rock music press, called Blue Thumb's *Headkeeper* a "bootleg," and urged his fans not to buy it. They didn't, but it was probably due more to the half–finished project than any urging from the star himself.

The studio songs were by and large strong ones: "To Be Free," which had appeared in a clunky pop arrangement *on Dave Mason And Cass Elliot*, was now an elegantly poetic lyric framed by delicate piano work. "Here We Go Again" featured some dazzling acoustic guitar playing, and Mason laid a ringing slide guitar on "In My Mind."

Still, the live side certainly confounded fans who recognized the titles as retreads from *Alone Together*; here again were "Just A Song," "World In Changes," "Can't Stop Loving," all from the first album, along with Mason's most famous older song, "Feelin' Alright?"

While the case was being litigated, Mason was legally unable to record for anyone; he kept his band on the road virtually nonstop. On his side was Columbia Records president Clive Davis, who was, as LiPuma suspected, angling to align Mason with his label once the Blue Thumb situation was resolved.

Krasnow, meanwhile had signed a distribution deal with Gulf and Western, which had decided to go into the record business. All parties, Mason included, attended a meeting at Gulf and Western headquarters in New York City.

"The meeting was to say 'I want out of this,'" said Mason. "I was there, he was there, Gulf and Western's attorney was there, and I was saying, 'Listen guys, this is not going to work. If I don't feel like I can give you my best stuff, then what's the point of having me here? Negotiate a buyout, and let me go somewhere else.'

"It went on and on and on. I finally said, 'You know what? If you don't let me off this label, I'm going to go in the press and you're going to read the worst publicity you've ever read in your life.' Their attorney jumped up and said, 'Are you threatening us? Are you threatening us?'"

San Francisco attorney Brian Rohan, representing Mason, got him out of the Blue Thumb jam by having him declare bankruptcy and shake off his creditors by going into double default. At the last moment, Clive Davis rode in on a white horse and bought up his contract.

The signing of Dave Mason to Columbia Records in July 1973 was one of Davis' last acts before the board of directors ousted him on various charges of mismanagement. Mason got another manager, a "Barnum and Bailey" type named Jason Cooper, who "took care" of some of Mason's leftover business dealings (Mason said he "got involved with some shady people" when he needed money, and Cooper smoothed everything over for him).

At long last, he was free to record again, on a big label, and at a wage he figured he was worth. Columbia, it was reported, had big plans for Dave Mason, its newest star. "I never got into this to be a star," Mason said. "I've been doing this since I was 15, and I like my work. That's my work, and I created it, and that's my integrity. And I don't want anybody fuckin' around with it. I don't think that's too much to ask."

Here we go again

Clive Davis gave Mason a sizeable advance, money to help tidy up his business problems and to get on the stick with his first Columbia album.

After staying briefly in New York City, where he wrote several new songs, Mason began the sessions in Los Angeles with drummer Jim Keltner and bassists Carl Radle and Greg Reeves (a recent expatriate from the Crosby, Stills and Nash camp). The bulk of the songs on *It's Like You Never Left*, released in October, were recorded by Mason with drummer Rick Jaeger, bassmen Lonnie Turner and Chuck Rainey and pianist Mark Jordan (from the *Headkeeper* band).

The year before, Mason had laid a distinguished lead guitar line on "Immigration Man," a hit single for his pals Graham Nash and David Crosby. Nash returned the favor by singing high harmony on "Baby … Please," the rollicking number that opened *It's Like You Never Left* (Mason had played on Nash's *Songs For Beginners* album. Nash, for his part, had done a bit of harmonizing on *Headkeeper*).

"It's Like You Never Left" (the title song) was Mason's winking acknowledgement of the "missing years" since *Alone Together* had almost made him a household name; it highlighted Mason's talent for mixing acoustic and electric guitar sounds, and for writing complex arrangements for essentially simple songs. His sense of melody was in full evidence on the haunting "Maybe," his arranging chops on glorious display in the horn chart for "Misty Morning Stranger."

Another sprightly acoustic-based tune, "Silent Partner," was a rewrite of "Here We Go Again," from *Headkeeper*, but nevertheless an improvement. And the song, "Headkeeper" itself was even re–recorded, in a bacon-sizzling, pulse-pounding arrangement featuring Mark Jordan's piano, and harmonies from Nash.

One of Mason's all-time finest ballads, "The Lonely One," featured brilliant harmonica soloing from Stevie Wonder (he'd been recording *Innervisions* down the studio hall, and Mason, who'd never met Wonder before, asked him point-blank if he'd mind helping out on "The Lonely One."

George Harrison, in Los Angeles to do promotional work for *Living In The Material World*, laid a stinging slide guitar on "If You've Got Love."

Dave Mason's "comeback" failed to get any higher than No. 50 in the *Billboard* charts, no hit single appeared, and the reviews weighed heavily toward the negative ("a major disappointment," whined *Rolling Stone*). And Mason's relationship with Columbia began to sour almost immediately after Davis' ouster; there was nobody at the label he felt comfortable with.

"I think the problem, really, was that Clive was so good - he was a great record guy in terms of music - he became individually very powerful within the corporate structure," Mason said. "And as soon as one man becomes that, it's like signing your death warrant. And they started to hire people from the legal department to run the company, who weren't record people.

"I'm more from that era when people who started record labels were music freaks. Then the business started to get run by attorneys and accountants. If you want loyalty, buy a dog."

Still, a career was a career, and Mason had signed a contract with Columbia calling for a ridiculous two albums per year. "You make a record deal, and they put up the money for you to do an album," he complained, "And the company makes money from record one sold. They're recouping the cost of making the album from your royalties. So in essence, you're paying to make your own album. But you don't own anything."

The first order of business was to put together a good, solid road band and get to work. Rick Jaeger, the drummer who'd anchored the *Headkeeper* band, had moved to the San Francisco area from Wisconsin in the late '60s (he'd hit the road with the Everly Brothers when he was just out of high school). Jaeger introduced Mason to many of his musician pals from Marin County, including organist Mike Finnigan, Mark–Almond bassist Bob Glaub and most importantly for Mason, singer/guitarist Jim Krueger.

A native of Manitowoc, Wisconsin, Krueger had come west with a bunch of musician chums. When Jaeger joined Mason in Los Angeles, Krueger had stayed in Marin. Krueger and Jaeger also played together in flutist Tim Weisberg's band (Weisberg's flute added a nice touch to "Show Me Some Affection," on the 1974 album *Dave Mason*).

Krueger, despite his nickname, Bruiser, was a shy, introverted guy, a talented songwriter and a pure tenor vocalist who could match Mason's distinctive style and follow him note-for-note. His harmonies were almost as good as Nash's; this was not lost on Mason. Krueger and Mason hit it off immediately, and their relationship was to last an unbelievable (for either of them) 19 years.

Mason: "He was a great guitar player. It just musically worked. But there was no real personal relationship. I mean, there was, but we didn't hang out, we weren't really like friends." According to Finnigan, the Mason/Krueger alliance was "very complicated. Jim was an excellent guitar player, and Dave is a great guitar player. Totally different styles. And Dave used to give Jim some blowing room.

"And as songwriters, they were different too, but kind of the same in some ways. I think there was a mutual respect there, but also tinged with a little bit of resentment on Krueger's part, which was only natural unless you're a mentally healthy giant. Unless you're totally without ego, and I don't know anybody that description fits."

Still, Finnigan said, "Whatever bad feelings he might've had toward Dave from time to time were obviously counterbalanced by a certain respect, and certain financial realities."

To wit: Mason and Krueger needed each other.

The new band recorded the *Dave Mason* album and Columbia had it in the stores in October, allowing Mason to keep his two-albums-per-year commitment. Barely. The album was a stylistic move away from the sheeny pop/rock of *It's Like You Never Left* and the earlier collections; Mason's songs were tinged with bluesier guitar lines and more soulful singing.

A highlight, and one of three singles released from the album, was Sam Cooke's "Bring It On Home To Me" with Mason, Krueger, and Finnigan on three-part harmony. The band cut a searing version of "All Along The Watchtower" using the same arrangement that Mason had done with Jimi Hendrix back in 1968 (it would quickly become a staple of the Mason band's live shows).

And, perhaps because Mason couldn't come up with enough new songs to meet Columbia's imposed deadline, the track "Every Woman," which had been a standout on *It's Like You Never Left*, was rearranged with pedal steel guitar, an extra chorus and Krueger singing Graham Nash's harmony part. Overall, the impression, completely intentional, was that *Dave Mason* was a *band* album, the result of four guys playing, rather than a studio confection.

"I think I had some influence on his singing," said Finnigan, "just because I was around him a lot, and I sang a lot. I noticed a change in his approach vocally. I think he became a little freer, and I think he got a little bluesier. I wasn't really aware of it until some other guys I know pointed it out to me: 'Hey man, he's startin' to sound like you.'"

The band hit the road hard, taking second and third billing to every arena-rock act on the 1974 American landscape. It was Bob Glaub's first extended tour, and to this day, he hasn't forgotten it. "It was the most fun I'd had," he said. "I had a ball during that period. It wasn't just another gig. We always came to play; we probably overplayed - we were playing like we were getting paid by the note or something. But it was really fun. The four of us in the band really got along well."

Finnigan remembered that first tour. "We got a bus, and all it had was a couple of rollaway beds, tied to the sides. And then the rest of it was regular bus seats. Except for one area that was a card table. Our opening act was Gabe Kaplan, the comedian. Rough job, opening for rock 'n' roll shows. I used to think, 'Man, this guy's got more balls than Mike Ditka.'

"We played cards with him a lot. We'd sit there and play poker with Gabe Kaplan, and it seemed like he won all the time. We couldn't beat the fuckin' guy. Years later of course, he won the World Championship of Poker, and I didn't feel so bad."

The show must go on

The years 1974-76 were spent touring, recording, and touring and recording some more. Incredibly, even though he hadn't had even a minor hit single, Mason could fill arenas - he and the band sold out New York's Madison Square Garden, the Spectrum in Philadelphia and the Capital Center in Washington, D.C. "I had a big live following," Mason observed, "unlike a lot of people who might have big hit singles but couldn't fill anything."

In January 1975, Mason was visited backstage in New Orleans by young Scottish guitarist Jimmy McCullough, who was in town with Paul McCartney and Wings, recording the *Venus and Mars* album. McCullough, a big Mason fan, invited the guitarist down to the studio late that night. Mason found McCartney and company recording "Listen To What The Man Said," an uptempo track that required a hooky, pop-flavored lead guitar figure. And that's how Dave Mason got himself on a worldwide No. 1 smash by another ex-Beatle buddy.

Split Coconut was released in September, and although it failed to go gold, as Mason's two previous CBS albums did, it brought him some of his best critical marks thus far.

The title song was a mostly instrumental funk fest (the words "split coconut" constitute the entire lyric) and set the tone for what was essentially a fun, throwaway record (Mason had visited a Jamaican restaurant called Split Coconut in London while on tour, and was inspired by the atmosphere). For his necessary cover tune, Mason arranged Buddy Holly's "Crying, Waiting, Hoping" with a calypso beat, creating a medley with "Peggy Sue Got Married." He played 12-string folk guitar on the ballad "Long Lost Friend."

Bob Glaub and Mason parted company just before *Split Coconut* was recorded. "He was headlining arena tours, and paying us very little for the money he was making," Glaub said. "But we were still having a ball. I didn't feel like I was getting ripped off at the time, 'cause I was too ignorant to know any better."

Mason, Glaub added, was never into hanging out. He almost always traveled separately from the guys in his band. "He's a very aloof guy, basically. Not a real people person, which is unusual for what he does. He didn't really connect with a lot of the people he was working with, he just worked with 'em. And then he'd have other people that he traveled with, just to hang out with. We called them 'rent-a-buddies' at the time."

Mason agrees with at least the sentiment of Glaub's statement. "We spent so much time on the road," he said. "You're with them all the time. And I've just got my own thing that I want to do. When I come off the road, I want to be left alone. I've spent my life out there, practically."

In the studio, recalled Mike Finnigan, who would remain a stalwart of Mason's band for five years, "Anything was allowed to be tried. Dave's input was usually more in terms of, 'I don't think that's such a good idea,' as opposed to, 'Do this!' I think he knew what he wanted until he heard what he didn't want."

What Mason wanted more than anything was a hit record. Although his albums were good, and he had solid fan support, he couldn't get on the charts. And that bugged him. Still, said Jaeger: "He was always pretty up, because the band was so damn good. It was amazing that we were staying on top of it like we were. The money was still coming in and without a hit, it was amazing."

For his 1976 project, Mason went the way of every other CBS Records arena rocker: He cut a two-record live album. There were several reasons for this: One, he had a fantastic live band (Gerald Johnson had replaced Glaub on bass, but Jaeger, Finnigan and Krueger remained). Two, he could turn a whole new audience on to his classic old songs (the logic being if they didn't go for "Split Coconut," maybe they'd flip for "Feelin' Alright?")

Three, the terms of the CBS contract were killing him. To come up with two albums every year, he had to record other people's songs at a rate he didn't care for, and record them quickly. "You can't," he fumed at the time, "paint a fucking Mona Lisa every other day."

Behind the enigmatic smile on the cover of *Certified Live* was a financially desperate man; Mason filed for bankruptcy for the second time in 1976, breaking his Columbia contract in the bargain. Unlike before, it was only a short pause, and despite serious negotiations with Atlantic Records president Ahmet Ertegun (who, according to Mason, loaned Mason $50,000 of his own money), Columbia made the best offer and re-signed him for another couple of albums.

At any rate, reprising the chestnuts via *Certified Live* gave him little breathing room to get his next collection off to a good start. Engineer Ron Nevison, who would soon become one of the leading lights of '70s rock 'n' roll, was hired to produce something "more commercial" for Mason's 1977 album. He needed that elusive hit, damn it, and Mason's management thought Nevison might just be the guy to happen.

Let It Flow was released in April, preceded by the single "So High (Rock Me Baby And Roll Me Away)." Written by "Drift Away" composer Mentor Williams, "So High" was a superbly played and sung pop record, featuring gritty vocalizing by both Mason and Krueger. It wasn't to be though; the single didn't even make the Top 40. And out of the box the *Let It Flow* album looked like another stiff.

Then, in August, Krueger's wistful ballad "We Just Disagree" was released as the second single. The melodic song about no-fault divorce featured Krueger's 12-string guitar prominently; the author also sang the harmony under Mason's anguished, too-proud-to-cry lead vocal.

"He first played it to me and it was like I could've written it," Mason recalled. He related to "We Just Disagree" on several levels, he said, both personal and financial. He knew he could get under its skin. And he thinks Bruiser sang the song with Mason's style in mind. "I thought that song was too good a song to be a hit," said Mason "although some promotion guys at Columbia at the time really busted their ass to make it a hit. And actually," he said, "*Playboy* voted it the worst record of the year."

"He was very careful in terms of selecting tunes," Finnigan said of Mason, "and we used to rehearse a lot. I remember we must've played 'We Just Disagree' 50 times before we recorded it. Before we even got to the studio. There was not too much left to chance by the time we got in front of the microphones."

"We Just Disagree" struck a quiet nerve in the middle of the disco era, and in November it reached No. 11 on the *Billboard* chart.

Here's how Jaeger remembers it: "Thank God that Bruiser's song came along when it did. It renewed it. Immediately after that, Dave just fucked it all up. He was on a self-destruct thing. He stopped listening to me - I got Finnigan, I got Krueger, I knew these people - and somehow he convinced himself that he was a genius, and that he needed people around that he selected. And that's where it started falling apart."

Mason bought a Spanish-style mansion in Malibu from composer Leonard Rosenman. He named it Villa Mariposa and recorded many of the songs for his next album in his backroom studio (it was the first house he'd ever owned; and to this day he still hasn't purchased another one).

In March 1978, the Mason band played to 250,000 people at the massive California Jam concerts.

Finnigan and Krueger took a breather and cut an album with guitarist Les Dudek; Krueger made a solo album in 1978, too, but it met with the same critical and commercial reception as the Dudek project (no one liked it or bought it) and Krueger was soon back in the Mason camp.

Mason took no interest in either album, nor did he contribute musically in any way. "I think Dave Mason treated everybody pretty much the same," recalled Finnigan. "He wasn't as egocentric as a lot of people I've worked with, certainly. I mean, he was a little weird in some ways, and kept to himself on the personal level. But he was easy to be around; he had a good sense of humor and nobody tiptoed around him. And he gave as good as he got."

Also in 1978, Mason wrote and recorded two songs for the disco movie *Skatetown USA*, starring Patrick Swayze (in his first feature film role) and Linda Blair. Mason appeared in the movie, too, singing his song in a dream sequence as nubile young girls skated in circles around him.

Wipeout

In the summer of 1980 came *Old Crest On A New Wave*, Mason's seventh Columbia album. Co-produced by Mason and Joe Wissert, the album attempted to rock a bit harder than the previous *Mariposa de Oro*, without any obvious attempts at "We Just Disagree"-style balladry.

Krueger, for the first time, played guitar but was not featured, with one notable exception, on the harmony vocals he'd provided so well since 1974 in his Mason-parroting style. The background vocals were done by former Vanilla Fudge keyboard player and singer Mark Stein, who'd replaced Finnigan halfway through the *Mariposa de Oro* sessions (Finnigan had gone off to do the project with Les Dudek and Krueger, and then stayed on with Crosby, Stills and Nash).

Interestingly, Krueger's prolific pen came up with the uptempo "Save Me," one of the better melodies on *Old Crest*. Krueger and Mason sing the rollicking chorus in unison, joined in scat-style by yet another Mason mystery guest, Michael Jackson.

"He was in the same studio, Hollywood Sound, cutting *Thriller*," Mason recalled. "And I needed somebody to sing a high part, and I asked him. He said, 'Man, I'd love to. When I was seven years old, I did a TV special with Diana Ross and we did 'Feelin' Alright?' So he came in and sang. Paul McCartney was not the first white guy to sing with Michael Jackson."

Despite its release as a single, "Save Me" could not do just that for Dave Mason, and by the time he and the band took off on the North American leg of the *Old Crest* tour, Mason knew that Columbia was about to pink-slip him.

(According to Jaeger, the drinking and drugging in that period was ferocious. He remembers Mason playing everything "way too fast" and seeming not to care about how the band sounded). The well–oiled machine that had made *Certified Live* was now teetering on the edge of certified obsolescence.

To top it all off, Jaeger said, Mason fired him over the phone just days before the band was to leave for Japan. "He is one cold motherfucker," said Jaeger, who moved back to Wisconsin and remains there today, part of Milwaukee's busy musical scene. "I said, 'Hey man, at least let me get through this Japanese tour, so I can pay a couple of bills.' After nine years, I figured he owed me that."

Columbia did indeed drop Mason after *Old Crest* turned up lame. The recording career that had begun so promisingly with *Alone Together* 10 years before was now, to all appearances, a lost cause.

"It was all over when Clive left," Mason said. "When you see a label like Columbia dropping Chicago, who must've made God knows how many millions of dollars for that label … They just arbitrarily dropped them from the roster."

Down, but not out, Mason used his fading celebrity to latch onto Miller Beer. In 1981, he and Krueger cut a series of radio commercials for the company. Then they took to the road, just the two of them and their acoustic guitars (they couldn't afford to pay a band), making Dave Mason, and he's very proud of this, one of the very first "unplugged" acts. "It was good to do because I'd always been sort of hiding behind a band - not hiding, but having the support of a band," Mason said. At all the shows, he let Bruiser play lead guitar while he himself strummed a 12–string and crooned.

In 1982, Mason moved to Chicago (Krueger was just a brief plane ride away, in Manitowoc, his Wisconsin hometown).

He made two albums in 1987. The first, *Some Assembly Required*, was self–produced on the Canadian label Maze (distributed by A&M in the United States). Krueger, by Mason's side as always, played guitar and banjo and sang backup; both Finnigan and Stein sang but did not play.

Krueger, curiously, was nowhere to be found on *Two Hearts*, which Mason made for MCA in the second half of 1987. Augmented by the single "Dreams I Dream," a duet with Phoebe Snow, *Two Hearts* was produced by Mason and Jimmy Holz.

Although the songs, nearly all Mason originals, had something to say, the album was decidedly lackluster. Instead of Mason's trademark guitar runs, the tracks were rooted in electronic keyboard sounds, obviously in an attempt to make Mason seem more "contemporary" (it was after all, 1987). "I should've done it with a band," he said, "instead of programming it."

Steve Winwood, of all people, laid down his best "While You See A Chance" synthesizer tracks for the song "Something In The Heart" from his Nashville home/studio (he sang backup on the song "Two Hearts," too, although at no time were he and Mason in the studio at the same time, the "collaboration" being Mason's then-manager's idea of a hip gimmick).

The album was a failure, a comeback attempt that was roundly forgotten by one and all a year after its conception. Within 12 months, he had struck out twice. He never got a third pitch.

"There's no interest or desire from anybody to sign me," he explained. "I'm not a valuable commodity to them, because I'm not 18 anymore. Which is really stupid, because they don't understand there's a whole age group of people out there. The thing is, when I started making records, we were making records on four-track tape. Rock 'n' roll had only started when I was about 10 years old. So rock 'n' roll is not a very old music at all."

He's had absolutely no luck with label honchos or A&R departments; today, he said, having a track record as long as his means hardly anything. And contemporizing (see *Two Hearts*) just won't work; he's a songwriter and guitarist out of the late '60s classic school.

"It's all perception," he explained. "To them, I'm just yesterday's news. For the most part, the music business is totally centered in either L.A., New York or Nashville. Nashville not so much, because country is more of the people's music, and they do stay loyal …

"But where you're dealing with quote-unquote-pop, they're just a little secluded, isolated group of people who think there is nothing else going on but what's going on in their little group. And that whole mass of space between New York and L.A. don't matter. They don't know what the hell's going on out here."

It's like you never left

The wheel began to turn for Dave Mason in 1993. After more than a decade of "unplugged" tours with Krueger, of trying to meet the meager payroll of such ventures, of moving from Chicago and back to Chicago, of filing reject slips from uninterested record labels, fate was about to force his hand.

Back in Manitowoc, Bruiser went into business with his brother and bought a liquor store. When his dance card wasn't filled with Mason dates (and it wasn't, increasingly) he played in several local bands, including Normal Adults and the Happy Schnapps Combo, a comic polka group.

On March 29, 1993, Jim Krueger died in a Manitowoc hospital, from complications of pancreatitis, a disease commonly associated with alcoholism. He was 43.

Bruiser's death was totally unexpected. "He was supposed to be leaving, in like a day or two, to go out on tour with Dave," said brother Rich. "They were going to start a nostalgia-type tour with Poco and Richie Havens.

"He had no idea he was ill, because he was leaving the next day. He thought he was getting out of the hospital in a day, and 48 hours later he was dead. Our parents had no idea he was in the hospital."

Krueger and his brother often spoke of Mason's arrogance, spitefulness and bouts of sulking. Mason, he'd been told, would often hurt those closest to him.

Still, Bruiser loved Dave.

"Jim did a lot of babysitting for Dave, trying to keep him straight," Rich Krueger said. "He kind of covered his butt a lot of times." The "intimate evening" tours, Krueger added, always seemed to come up "when Dave needed money."

Rick Jaeger, who lived in nearby Milwaukee, saw Bruiser often. "Jimmy was a recluse," he said. "A very shy person. And he did not have it in him to go out and hustle. He was never meant for Hollywood; he couldn't stand all the bullshit, and the insincerity."

According to Jaeger, "We Just Disagree" was Krueger's "lifeline" and his increasingly tenuous link with success, and with reality. It was on his solo album, and he proudly played it with his Manitowoc groups.

"Toward the end, it was breaking his heart," Jaeger recalled. "He'd call me and say how Dave owed him money." Jaeger said he was surprised to hear from Mason the morning of Bruiser's funeral. After a long talk, full of reminiscences, they made plans to attend the service together, in Mason's car.

But Mason, who was living three hours away in Chicago, didn't show up at the funeral. "The morning I was going to drive up there, the weather was just the worst," Mason explained. "It was unbelievable. I found that it would've taken me five hours in that weather. And the other reason was I didn't want to be around all those people. Because they're all … I mean, you want to talk about drinking!

"I didn't want to be around it when they were all celebrating afterwards, because that was his whole life. To them, there was nothing wrong with it. They didn't understand that alcohol is another health–destroying drug, the same as any other one."

So he stayed in Chicago, wondering what to do next. And he grieved for his long lost friend. "Jim's there every night I get up and play," Mason concluded. "I sing 'We Just Disagree' every time. That's the best way for me to remember him."

With Bruiser gone, there was little of the old way left for Dave Mason. He decided to return to California and "try and reestablish something. And one of the things I did was call Mick Fleetwood, just to say hi. I hadn't spoke to him in years."

Fleetwood was in the midst of auditioning guitarists and singers to replace Billy Burnette, Rick Vito and Stevie Nicks, all of whom had left Fleetwood Mac (Christine McVie left too, but eventually decided to become "the Brian Wilson of the band," according to Fleetwood, and make records without going on the hated road).

"Dave was leaving Chicago, I think," Fleetwood recalled. "There was a big party at his house in Chicago. It was a drag. And that moment is my catalyst, in the modern-day era, for when our friendship really struck up again. He came to stay with me, and lived in one of the cottages at my house in Malibu for about a year." It was, Fleetwood said, a bonding thing.

Fleetwood and Mason tell this story slightly differently, but the ending is the same. In 1993 Dave Mason officially became a member of Fleetwood Mac.

"We had lunch, and he was telling me, 'I'm trying to get the band back together' and all this stuff," Mason said. "He said, 'I'm rehearsing all these young guitar players and they're all notes and no content. I can't stand this anymore.' He said, 'I'm almost tempted to ask you.' I said, 'Well, ask me.' And that's basically how it happened."

Fleetwood: "All I did was sit 'round the pool, listening religiously to players who'd sent tapes in. There were a couple of people who got fairly close to joining Fleetwood Mac, but it didn't happen for whatever reason. I said, 'I'm getting a bit frustrated, Mason,' and I jokingly said something along the lines of, 'I'll have to put you in the band if I don't find anybody.' And he said, 'Mick, in all seriousness, I would love to do that.'"

At this point, Billy Burnette, who'd gone to Nashville to take another stab at a solo career, came back to L.A. and asked Fleetwood if he could re-join the band. Fleetwood says sure, Bill, we haven't really been doing anything anyway. There was literally nothing to lose, and everything to win. Bekka Bramlett, Delaney and Bonnie's 25 year-old daughter, was brought in to sing in Stevie Nicks' place.

Mason, said, Fleetwood, fit right in with Bramlett, Burnette, Fleetwood and John McVie. "He's a darn good guitar player, good sense of melody, and God knows he's a good writer," Fleetwood said. "So I thought, 'Hmmm, this is adding up. And he looks like me, so that can't be bad. You put me, John and Mason in a row, without stretching it too much we might be very possibly related. We've all got ponytails and beards, and we're all going bald, you know. Although, I'm long since bald."

The "new" Fleetwood Mac spent a year touring, to work out the bugs, before venturing into the studio for *Time*. "It's not awkward at all," Mason said. "There's nothing about it that's out of place. I'm very song-oriented and so are they; there's a little bit of blues in both of us. It's not an off mix at all. It works really well."

He enjoys singing with Bekka Bramlett, too. "She was two years old when her parents did 'Only You Know And I Know,' which we do together now in the (live) Fleetwood Mac thing," he explained.

Recording *Time*, Fleetwood said, was relatively painless after the lengthy road test (they did the same thing with Nicks and Lindsey Buckingham before cutting the landmark *Fleetwood* Mac album in 1975). According to Fleetwood, Mason had some "teething problems" at first, adjusting to a democratic system, but he's "made the transition" to everyone's satisfaction.

"We call him The Bull," Fleetwood reported. "He has learned, I think to be in a band. He always used to fantasize when we were hanging together. He'd say, 'I miss being in a band. On the other hand I like calling the shots, and I can control this and that.' But eventually it gets lonely – talk about alone together – and he was ready for a change."

"I don't want to say anything bad about this project, because it's an ongoing thing," Mason explained before offering: "To spend a year and a half in a studio, making a record, to me is absurd." He was excited about making the Fleetwood Mac record, but at the same time frustrated.

Mason is putting his all into it. He probably won't be doing any more solo concerts for a while, because he's committed. "That's fine, that's great," he said. "I need this Fleetwood Mac thing to put my profile up. I wasn't too happy with the laboriousness of the recording process, but the bottom line is that this is a great band. It feels great. It doesn't have to be all on me anymore. I liked being in a band in the first place. I liked the whole Traffic idea, except they didn't."

And apparently, they still don't. In the spring of 1994, Steve Winwood and Jim Capaldi made an album under the name Traffic, *Far From Home*, and criss-crossed the country on a huge and well-publicized tour (the album and tour were, to be diplomatic, less than successful). Chris Wood, the other original member of the English quartet, had died in 1983. Mason didn't have that kind of excuse. He was, quite simply, not invited to participate.

"I always, for years, in an attempt to make it work again, tried and tried but it never went anywhere," Mason recalled. "I'd spoken to Jim the year before, and he'd mentioned something about it. I would've thought that if they were going to attempt a Traffic tour in the U.S. that it would have been smart to have done it with as many original members as possible." Mason knows Winwood's quote by heart: "When *Billboard* asked him about me, he said, 'Well, Dave Mason was never anything more than an invited guest in Traffic.' It wasn't anything close to that."

Today, Mason is classified as an "alien resident." He never became a U.S. citizen, although he says there's not much Englishman left in him, and he has no family in his homeland anymore. "I don't think about it," he insisted. "I'm like my dad, who was a real conservative. He had a little sticker on the back of his car that just said 'Citizen of the World.' That's how I feel. People are people, they're either good people or they're assholes."

Dave Mason has been called both – numerous times, in fact – and he's happy, more or less, with the way things have turned out. "I've been through four earthquakes, three marriages, two bankruptcies, one major hurricane and I've survived the music business," he said. "That's a pretty good record."

Jim McGuire (1974)

12. Guy Clark
Susanna Clark
Step inside my house

I spent a good chunk of 1996 with Susanna Clark, the bright-eyed, hilarious, wonderfully charismatic wife (and muse) of the great Texas songwriter Guy Clark. Susanna and Emmylou Harris were close friends, and after Susanna read my Goldmine *Emmylou profile, she decided - in the way that ideas just landed on her shoulder like little birds and sang in her ear — that the amazing story of how she, Guy and their lifelong pal*

Townes Van Zandt had arrived in Nashville in the early '70s, and how the home they shared turned into the center of gravity and attention for some of the greatest singer/songwriters who ever picked up a guitar, should be told in a book. I was nominated for the gig.

So with no clear-cut idea of what we were doing, we got started. In Nashville, I stayed in the Clarks' guest room. Susanna flew to Florida a couple of times. We spent one memorable weekend in her East Texas hometown, where we wandered into her family's long-ago church on Sunday afternoon, and accepted the preacher's invitation to stay for a pot-luck dinner.

She and I recorded many hours of interviews. She told me a lot of personal things that I'll never let out of the vault. Mostly, we laughed. She was so damn funny. I was on the floor a lot of the time.

The project, sadly, was never finished. Van Zandt died suddenly on Jan. 1, 1997, and so great was her grief, she canceled every plan she had. Many of my interview tapes – including those with Townes himself – had been transcribed and re-used (something we poor journalists did in those days). Susanna never forgave me for that; on those tapes were some of the last conversations they'd had, and she desperately wanted them, to have and to hold.

Many years later, I discovered one 60-minute cassette in a box. On one side was Susanna chatting happily away; Guy was on the other. He was never much of a willing interview subject, but because this was for Susanna's project, he opened up just a little bit.

Susanna died in 2012, followed in 2016 by her husband.

This is all that remains of our book.

Tell me how you met Susanna.

I was dating her sister, Bunny. I met her once, seems like, when Townes and I would go up to Oklahoma City and play music. I met her once there. And Bunny and I continued seeing each other long distance. I was working in Houston at a TV station, Channel 11 – I was the art director. And when I was still living in San Francisco, Bunny had come out there and hung out for a while, and then we got a driveaway car and drove it back across the country.

Anyway, Bunny was coming to see me one time – I'd bought her a ticket – and the next thing I knew, I got a call from Susanna that Bunny had killed herself. Out of the clear blue sky. (long pause)

So I went up there to the funeral, and that's how Susanna and I got together.

That's where it took off from.

Was it a gradual thing for you and Susanna, getting through this event …

I don't know, we just kinda fell into it. I mean, it wasn't gradual, it was immediate. Probably because of the high emotional intensity of the moment, you know? We have kind of an anniversary on the Fourth of July. I went up to Oklahoma City and got her, and brought her back.

You were at the TV station then. What were you doing with your music?

Just playing at night. I had been living in San Francisco, working in a guitar shop and playing music. Been divorced for a couple, three years. And it just got to the point where I had to make some money to support [my son] Travis. And so I gave up that street-hippie life and went back to Houston, got a job at this TV station. I had some experience, I had worked at one before, when I was married.

This was before computer graphics, so we're talking about … the logo on the front of the desks?

Uh-huh, and the sets, and the stationery, billboards … I got a whole resume, what do you call it, a portfolio of stuff I did back then. I'll show it to you.

You must have been writing quite a bit by then.

No, not really. Not much. Not anything I ever kept. I was playing a few of the songs I had written at the time, and mostly traditional folk music. You know, Bob Dylan songs, the same thing everybody else was doing. Yeah, I was continuing to write, actually. Doing that kind of job, it … television is so … it doesn't wait for anybody. Shit goes on the air every minute whether you're ready or not. I ended up working 16 hours a day. I mean, I had two or three people working for me. But still, it was like if I didn't do it, it didn't get done.

And finally I just went crazy. Nuts. So I quit, and I continued to freelance for the station because I was doing this real neat series of newspaper ads that they really liked. Just illustrations. And I continued to do that.

I'd met a couple guys from the music business in L.A., who'd come through Houston looking for talent. I just quit everything, fixed up a Volkswagen bus and drove out there. It was an old one, a '63 or '64. But I was into rebuilding those engines. I could rebuild an engine on the side of the road with what I had in my toolbox.

I spent most of the time driving around trying to find a job to support us. And finally got a job working at the Dobro factory in Long Beach.

Had you worked on guitars before?

Mm-hmm. The first guitar I had, I took it apart. It was just always something I've … doing things with wood and stuff has always fascinated me. When I was a kid in West Texas, the first thing you got was a pocket knife; you learned how to sharpen it, then you learned how to make your own toys. Carve out little guns and little airplanes.

But how do you qualify yourself as someone who can work on guitars? Do you just take one apart in front of them during the job interview?

(laughing) It's mostly just say-so! I was driving all around southern California, and I met John Dopera, who had a shop in Escondido. Just a repair shop. I asked if he needed any help, and he said no, but his brothers had the Dobro factory in Long Beach, and they were always looking for help.

Basically, the Dobro is kind of like building toasters. It's not like building guitars. My job was to take all the different parts from the other guys that worked there (there was only six of us) - the neck and the body and different things – and assemble it into a playable instrument that they could ship to the music store. I could do like six a day. But you could hire somebody who doesn't know anything about guitars to do that.

Did you feel like, "I'm in the music business now"?

No, because every time I'd get a chance to get any time off, I'd drive into L.A., get an appointment with somebody, and play songs for 'em. We lived in a little garage apartment in Long Beach. I could walk to work.

What songs had you written then, that are still with us?

None. The first song I wrote that I kept, I wrote out there. Which was "That Old Time Feeling." Well, I'm sure that was part of getting the deal that I finally got, but I wrote that out there, and I think it's the only one I still do that I wrote out there.

What would the songs you wrote then have been like? Obviously, you didn't think enough of them to keep them around …

Well, I did at the time. I remember a Saturday, I was off work, just sittin' there drinking wine, and "Old Time Feeling" just came. I've got the original paper I wrote it on. And it was just like, "All right, there's one." (laughing) You know? It was just like a quantum leap "OK. Now I see."

Actually, the first song I wrote, in Houston, Lyle Lovett remembers. He still does it. I mean, the very first song I wrote. Somehow, he got a tape of it from Houston. Called "Step Inside My House." Matter of fact, we were doing a songwriters' show in New York, me and Lyle and Joe Ely and … I can't remember who else. Anyway, one of the questions by this moderator was "Play a song you wish you'd written." And Lyle started playing this song. He was two verses and a chorus into it before I realized it was my song. I didn't even remember it.

How come you never recorded it?

I never thought it was that good a song! But when Lyle does it, it sounds pretty good.

Where was Susanna in the middle of all this?

She was right there. She was painting that shirt painting in L.A. And a couple other paintings.

Was she helpful to you? Encouraging?

Oh yeah! She was totally behind it.

So you're making the rounds of the publishing companies …

Yeah, didn't have any tapes. I'd just take my guitar in. I did that for almost a year. This guy I'd been to see, he kinda liked the songs, he called me one day and he said "Listen, the president of the company's coming into town. I want you to come down and play him some songs." A guy named Gerry Teifer. The president of Sunbury-Dunbar, RCA's publishing company. Sweet guy. So I got off work, I went in and I sat down and played him four songs. He looked up and said "That's enough. How much money you want, and where do you want to live?"

It was that simple?

Yeah, to actually get to the guy that was president of the company, to cut through all the bullshit, and the next day I had a check in my hand.

I was like "All right!" because it was finally happening. And his attitude was "We got offices in New York, L.A., Nashville, Paris … you can be anywhere you want." I didn't particularly like L.A. and that whole scene, and the only person I knew here (in Nashville) was Mickey Newbury. So I just said "Nashville."

You knew Mickey from Houston?

Mm-hmm. And Mickey was very successful. He had "Just Dropped in to See What Condition My Condition Was In," and a lot of serious cuts.

This was a publishing deal, not a recording deal, so you were ostensibly going to write songs for other people.

Fifty bucks a week. Matter of fact, Mickey was instrumental in it. The first "real" recording I had was on the last Everly Brothers record they did together. "A Nickel for the Fiddler." I mean, I had one minor thing on some small label by a guy, but that was really the first one.

Was that written for the publishing company?

No, it was written about a day I spent in a park in Berkeley, every year on the 21st of June. Summer Solstice. High holiday. I didn't write it for them, I wrote it for myself. But it was about that day, of seeing all the Jefferson Airplane guys and all these San Francisco bands playing county music.

Townes came down to be the best man at your wedding in '72, and he wound up staying with you …

For eight months.

Why did he stay? What was his gig then? He was in New York?

Yeah, he was living in different places – Colorado in the summer, and New York, no permanent residence that he paid rent on. It was just, wherever. He stayed because he's my best friend, and he became Susanna's best friend, and he's the smartest, brightest guy you ever met in your life. And the funniest. And the best songwriter. And it was more fun than not doing it (laughs).

You were bringing in 50 bucks a week, and you had child support to pay. How could you expect to live on that?

I mean, we just did the best we could. At times we got food stamps. Stealing from mini-markets. And a lot of bean surprise. And the odd gig at the old Exit/In. I remember the first time I made 80 bucks one night, it was just like "Wow! We made it!

Who would come to see you in those days? Was there a buzz going?

I guess there was some kind of buzz going. I remember Kristofferson would come. Other songwriters, you know? And they were probably all getting in for free. It was never sold out or packed, but it was …

Susanna told me about how you'd go to record company parties and steal liquor. Pretty lucrative.

(laughing). Yeah, at Christmas it was Big Time.

Were you waiting for something to happen? Waiting for somebody to buy a song?

Yeah, to record a song, or to get an album deal. Which within a couple of years I got, with RCA, because they had the publishing. A lot of it was due to Chet Atkins. He was helpful. And my relationship with the publishing company. They had a vested interest. They were trying to make it happen.

She was painting the whole time? What was your favorite of her work?

Well, actually I think she finished that shirt after we moved here. It was kind of a work in progress from L.A. to here. She painted constantly, but she took months to do a painting. But she got into writing. While we were living on Chapel Street, she wrote "I'll Be Your San Antoine Rose" and had a hit. Townes and I were still just like …… *fuck*.

What about "L.A. Freeway"? Is every line of that one true?

Well, it's as true as I could make it. While we were living in California, I was playing in a little string band, just real traditional country music. Not even as sophisticated as bluegrass. String band music, real old-time music. And we got a gig one night in San Diego, a place called the Heritage Coffeehouse. Matter of fact, Tom Waits was the doorman. And I had just written "Old Time Feeling."

Anyway, we played that night. And we're driving back, in the back of this guy's beautiful old restored '53 Cadillac. Like 4 o'clock in the morning. We were almost back, and I dozed off. I just kinda raised up and looked around, and I said "Let's get off this L.A. Freeway without getting killed or caught." It just came out of my mouth. And I got Susanna's eyebrow pencil, and a napkin or something and wrote it down. I carried it around in my billfold till we got to Nashville. Just that line.

And the landlord, that was all true. Skinny Dennis was the bass player in the band, and I thought I'd never see him again. He heard the song, and all of a sudden I had a new best friend.

And that other, last line in there, "Love's a gift that's surely handmade," that was a painting Susanna did. It was the letters … a painting of the words.

Susanna

I remember walking into my living room, and sitting on the couch were Guy and Townes. As friends of my sister. I don't know how they got there, but there they were. And I thought to myself, "These are two of the most unhealthy-looking guys I think I've ever seen in my life." They looked tired, and they looked exhausted, and they looked skinny. And my first words to Guy Clark was "Would you like some vitamins?" He said no.

I think they were waiting on my sister to get ready to go someplace. She was in another room, and I didn't know how to talk to or what to say to either one of these guys. I guess it was up to me to make small talk or somethin' as my sister was getting ready to do something.

At the time, I was painting in my living room. And I had a painting all set up. Well, these guys were just kinda slumped on my couch, and I thought "Well, they don't talk much, and I don't know who they are or what they do or anything about 'em." So I thought well, I'll just go ahead and do my work. So I just started painting. I got stuck at one part, and I said "I can't make this foreground come forward in this painting."

Guy got up and said "Aw, you know what to do." He said "You can do this, do that, you mix this color with that color …" and I thought geez, I like him. First of all, he's interested in painting. And second of all, he called me on it, "You know what to do, come on." And I went well, I guess if I thought about it, I did. I hadn't run across a male who cared about the fact that I painted. Much less knew something about it. Much less called any bluff I was throwing out there. So I liked him.
And that's how I met him.

What were you painting?

It was a wheat field. I was into Andrew Wyeth, and I remember I had read an article of Andrew Wyeth that (said) "If you can get where the wheat – or a blade of grass - has blown over a certain amount, and capture the moment just before it goes back, not just standing there, if you can capture that, then you're getting there." I was fascinated with that one sentence of Andrew Wyeth's. So I was going to capture the moment of this blowing wheat.

I really had not much contact with Guy after that. Now Townes claims, and always has claimed, that he's the one responsible for introducing us. I'm not sure if that's true or not, but he claims that. Maybe he met Bunny the night before at a party or something and introduced her … I don't know, but that's what Townes claims and he says it's true.

Bunny and Guy kept up a correspondence of sorts. In a way. There would be letters and cards that came in the mail from her friend Guy in Houston, Texas. Just things like that, I think. They became friends.

What happened then was my sister committed suicide. She shot herself in the head. That's another story.

And that having happened, nobody in the family knew about her friendship with Guy. I did, and so I called Guy to tell him. And I told him. He said "My God, I can't believe this week. The man who was like my grandfather…" The guy in "Desperadoes Waiting For a Train" – his grandmother's boyfriend, who had raised him while his father was at war – had also died that week. His name was Jack Prigg. And Guy was going out to Monahans for the funeral. He said "I'm on my way out to Monahans for the funeral – what do I do?" And I said "Would you come to Oklahoma City? I feel horribly in grief, stricken and depressed and everything like that." And he said "Yeah."

So he came up that weekend, having just buried Jack Prigg. And he stayed at my apartment. And that was the beginning of our relationship. We were both of us quite devastated from the whole situation – he was from his, and Bunny as well. He was shocked at that. And I was from mine.

In that torn-down state of sadness that we were both in, we sorta fell in love.

He went home in a couple of days. And we talked on the phone every single day for two or three months. He came up again, and I wanted to get out of Oklahoma City because I couldn't stand all the reminders of my sister. And I moved back to Houston with him. I moved in with him.

Warner Bros. Records

13. Neil Young (1997)
'The world does not need another awards show'

Young was barnstorming the country with Crazy Horse, yet again, when I managed to get him on the phone in 1997. They were part of the H.O.R.D.E. tour (if anyone cares, it stood - awkwardly - for "Horizons of Rock Developing Everywhere") alongside young bands du jour like Blues Traveler, Squirrel Nut Zippers, Big Head Todd and Screamin' Cheetah Wheelies).

It's short and sweet, but like every conversation with Neil, it's funny and fiery, too.

Earlier this year, you declined to go to the Rock and Roll Hall of Fame for Buffalo Springfield's induction. Was that something you had to think about, or was there never any question that you would go to the ceremony?

No, I went back and forth several times, trying to make up my mind. But there was always something stopping me from getting excited about going; there was always something there. Finally, what it really came down to was the television of it. I just didn't want to go.

I'd already been to four or five of those things where it wasn't televised, and I knew how cool it was. Then I was at one where they televised it, and I could see the difference.

Then, when it went to VH1, you know, the world does not need another awards show. So who cares? I'm saying it's great to be in the Hall of Fame. I'm already in it. It's great to be in the Buffalo Springfield, but I've already been in the Buffalo Springfield.

And here I'm talking to guys in the Springfield who would like to bring some of their families with them, but can't afford it because the seats are so expensive. And then the place is filled up with all these high rollers, and it's all on VH1's bill, or the TV station, or whoever the heck it is. They all make the money; everybody gets the big sponsorship money, and people in the bands can't afford to bring their families to the ceremony. There were a lot of things about it that kind of bothered me.

Now, it was expensive to go to the Waldorf in New York, but there wasn't a big television thing involved in it. No 'We're going to cash in,' or 'We're going to make a donation to the Hall of Fame to shore up the building' or something. I don't know. So I left that off my itinerary of things that I thought were cool to do.

Did Dewey, Bruce and Richie understand when you made your statement, or were they just pissed off?

Well, I know Dewey and Bruce understood. I guess everybody else understood it, I never really spoke to Richie about it. But I did speak to the other guys about it. I just told them where I was at with it. And they're used to me.

What was it Stills said onstage: 'Well, Rich, he quit again.'

Yeah, right. That was great.

Your induction as a solo artist, and performance with Pearl Jam, had been televised just two years earlier. I remember thinking that was great TV. You said you could tell it was different then. How was it different?

What's different is that your speech, whatever you want to say, this is the moment of a lifetime for a musician. Did you see the Grammys when they gave Frank Sinatra his Lifetime Achievement Award? How did you feel about that?

Pretty upset.

Well, television. That's the way television has to be. They have a corporate thing going there, they got their commercials, they got their slot, and with VH1 it was even worse because they didn't even do it live. I mean they didn't even have that excuse.

Later on, they went in and Editor D, from Room C, was designated by Executive A to leave half of some guy's heartfelt speech on the cutting room floor. And cut out almost everything that he said, and put in just what VH1 thought was cool. As far as I'm concerned, that's not hip. Doesn't get it for me.

It reminded me, and a lot of people, of this 'This Note's For You' thing with MTV. That was the last TV controversy I could think of involving you.

Well, you know, there's a place for 'em. They do a good service to the community. (laughs) Wasn't that diplomatic? You won't be seeing any of my videos on VH1, I'll tell you that.

As I remember, MTV didn't play "This Note's For You" until it won their big award.

Yeah, they didn't play it until it won Video of the Year, so they aired it.

How did you feel about that?

For me, it was a lucky break. I didn't have to have anybody see it, so they didn't recognize me when I was walking down the street.

How much of Lionel Trains do you own?

Well, the partners and I have control of the company.

How did you get involved with Lionel? I know it had something to do with your son.

Well, I bought part of Lionel along with my partners, Wellspring, an investment group. I had a history with Lionel before that, where I developed a control system that the company uses for controlling the trains. It was developed with an eye for doing a lot of things with my son, using a controller that was accessible to a physically challenged individual. Who had different ways of accessing switches.

So I came up with this idea, and came up with concepts for supplying auditory feedback, and visual feedback, for every command issued. So that every time you made a command, you heard or saw something happen. You got action back.

And then you can select the commands by remote control, with a wireless controller, that can be accessed by your physically challenged friend. And so whatever you do with the controller, then when they hit their switch, it happens. So there's no plugging things in or changing things. It's fast and easy.

Were you a model train aficionado before this?

Yeah! I sort of developed this because of that. I kept thinking how all my kids loved trains so much, and I did too, so we just enjoyed playing with them.

And I just happen to have this son, Ben, who's physically challenged, and wants to have a lot of fun. So we share this together.

And it just turns out that through the development of it, it's made it possible for a lot of other things to happen for everybody who plays with trains. That really couldn't happen before.

There's a tent at H.O.R.D.E. with a train setup.

Yeah, Lionel has a display of electric trains, and a thing called LionelVision, which is cameras mounted in the trains. The trains fly around with little color cameras and stereo microphones mounted in them, listening and looking everywhere they go.

So will we eventually see your face on the packaging? 'Neil Young says….'

No. (Laughing). No, I don't think so.

You're 51 now. What does life look like to you?

Well, I love playing. I love playing music, and I love being around lots of other people who play music. That's why the H.O.R.D.E. tour is so much fun.

It absolutely feels just as good.

You turned down the Lollapalooza tour. What appealed to you about H.O.R.D.E.?

Really, the diversity of the music. There's just so many different bands out that are all so different, and all of the different kinds of music, from the Mighty Mighty Bosstones to the Squirrel Nut Zippers, and on the tour we've had other groups that have visited and stayed for two or three weeks, like Beck, Primus, Blues Traveler.

There's always new bands that nobody knows too much about, which is always cool, because their energy is so good, and they're so positive. It's just good to be around all of that, for me.

Does that make the audience primed and already vibrating when you get out there?

Well, actually, they get a day of music that's all different, so they're wide open by the time I see them. So it works real well. I just like the energy out here.

Is it a younger crowd, or is it really mixed aged groups?

Oh, it's definitely a younger crowd. I have to say that at least 50 percent of the people I play for have never seen me. So that's great, that's a big plus. Because it's just more of a challenge it's just different. And at this stage, something different is something great.

Does it have to be Crazy Horse for this audience; could you, for example, have used the acoustic band or the Bluenotes for H.O.R.D.E.? Is that what makes the most sense for you?

Yeah, I would say that's true, that Crazy Horse is the band for this. And that's had a lot to do with us choosing this, and doing it this way. Whereas the Bluenotes would have been great, but not as the position I'm in, as the headliner. They would have been a great band to play during the day or in the afternoon, if it wasn't 'Neil Young.' The band itself, without having to drag my name along with it, would've been fantastic at this show. Because the same kind of diversity represented in that band is represented all over this show.

You're doing a lot of re-arranging lately. It was nice to hear "Barstool Blues" again, on the live album Year of the Horse. Can you take any song out of your bag and say 'Crazy Horse could do this'? An acoustic song, or something from Trans, for example.

Well, "Barstool Blues" was a Crazy Horse song in the first place. And Crazy Horse was on a lot of *Trans*, on the songs I sang with the vocoder, so it would be possible.

See, they're there all the time. People seem to think that through all these changes and everything that they're gone, but the core of Crazy Horse is always around, on most of the albums. And of course the other albums that I've done that don't have this core music thing happening, that I have with Crazy Horse, a lot of those songs don't fit with Crazy Horse.

The opposite to that is true of the album I did with Pearl Jam, where most of the songs on that album fit great with Crazy Horse. I just go through my songs to figure out what would be the right ones to do that night.

Down the road, does that mean Crazy Horse might play songs from Harvest Moon? Is that conceivable?

Hey, anything's possible.

Six of your catalog albums remain unavailable on compact disc. Recently, you told an interviewer you would burn the tapes before you let them come out on CD. Why?

Until we get the technology. I'm pushing for better technology. And CDs don't cut it, to me. HDCD is a real great improvement on digital sound, no matter what the format of the sound is. That's a process you can make CDs through, and it makes them sound more detailed. If you have an HDCD playback system, it sounds incredibly more detailed.

Is that one of those technologies that we'll 'see by the year 2000'?

It's out there now. There's about 40 different companies, small audiophile companies that make stereo equipment that carries the HDCD chip.

There are something like 15 of your albums out on CD on Reprise. How come they're out, and these six aren't?

Those were made during the beginning of CDs. When it hadn't really dawned on everybody how inferior the CD was. But during the mastering of all of those, and listening to what we ended up with compared to what we started with, everyone became aware of the problems. And that was maybe more than 15 years ago. And there's been no improvement, in 15 years, from a bad standard.

Meanwhile, we got 64-bit video games, and 32-bit this, and 16-bit sound. Running at a slow speed. So we really need to get a standard together for recorded sound that doesn't destroy it.

But Reprise is still making those discs.

Oh yeah, that's right, you can't stop that. But I'm not gonna do any new ones until there's a standard.

Let me play devil's advocate. Since you're committed to this, can't you just put a stop to those that are still in print? Can't you tell the label 'They sound like shit; let's take 'em out'?

You can do that with the new ones. When you put out a master, you put it out, OK, it's out. Until then, you have it.

You know, those six albums aren't available on vinyl or cassettes, either. They've all been deleted.

I'm trying to use that leverage to get some tonal quality on the recordings.

Well, what can I do? I'll make a call. As a fan, it bugs me that I can't put, say, American Stars 'n' Bars on the CD player.

It's tough for me, too, but I'm not gonna put out "Hurricane" sounding like a piece of shit. That's the way it is. There's the ability to have it better, and I can make a statement. I'm not gonna let it keep happening.

What about your long-rumored multi-disc Archives project?

It's the same thing there. We're close enough to the new standard. There's all kinds of people throwing ideas for the new standard around. The latest new standard that came out for sound is worse than the CD. That's the DVD. That is totally a piece of crap. A thousand times more distortion, and I'm not exaggerating. That is a clinical number.

It's a terrible thing, and they say that you can play CDs on it. You can play 'em, but they have to be interpolated and translated and everything before your ear hears 'em; by then, they're so distorted, they're just not there any more.

So what they've done is, they're killing an art form through greed, and not being able to focus on using a decent standard. They're more interested, it seems, in putting out more product, and more real time information on a disc, than they are in putting out more quality on a disc. And one plays against the other.

So a lot of things have to be worked out before the new standard is set, but the wheels are turning right now, it's happening.

Didn't you record Time Fades Away digitally in '73?

No, it was recorded through a Quad-8 CompuMix board, one of the first computer boards. It was mixed directly to masters; instead of copying masters, it made masters over and over again. But actually it was kind of a misfire.

Tell me about the Year of the Horse movie. Was Dead Man your first collaboration with Jim Jarmusch, and did it lead to this?

Dead Man was definitely first. That was just getting to know Jim. And we did a video together, *for Dead Man*, and then we did a video for *Broken Arrow*, And then we decided to do this … actually, we didn't really decide to make a film, we just decided 'Let's film some stuff and see what we get. If it looks like it's gonna be good, and fun, we'll keep going.'

You cut your hand a while ago. What was the deal with that?

It was just a regular accident. If I hadn't been so famous, it wouldn't have made any difference. I was slicing a sandwich.

And you had to cancel some dates in Europe?

Yeah. If it had been Joe Schmoe, it wouldn't have made any darn difference, but now I gotta live with people going 'Hey, you cut your hand a few months ago." Pretty soon it's gonna be like 'Hey, back in '97, you cut your finger." When I'm 88.

Warner Bros. Records (1978)

14. Rodney Crowell
The Houston kid

What turned out to be the final installment of my Nashville saga is about a singer/songwriter I had revered for years. Rodney figured prominently in the epic I'd done on Emmylou Harris, and we'd already sat down to talk a little for my (never to materialize) Susanna Clark book, so we were on reasonable terms. He is a well-spoken and clever fellow, and has - in spades - that dry humor common to so many Texas musicians. And he's

151

friendly and chatty, so this story seemed like a natural. Guy, Susanna, Emmylou, Albert Lee, Tony Brown and others went on the record here. And speaking with Rosanne Cash, his former wife and musical partner just made a good story – and I think this is one of my best from the period – even better. From Goldmine, 1997.

He's written songs that reach in deep and massage the heart, songs that bring on tears, songs that bring on laughter, songs that bristle with electrically charged emotion, like he went to some dark, hidden place of energy just to find the switch and throw it. His songs are happy, catchy, friendly, playful, fearful, fretful, thoughtful, mindful, visionary and blind, and the records he's put on the air, and on jukeboxes, have made the country music standard of living a little richer, made the lives of everyone who's tapped into his talent a little more interesting.

As a writer of the highest standard, Rodney Crowell is a national treasure. The singer/songwriter has long been an important presence in country music, from Hank Williams and Lefty Frizzell, to Merle Haggard, Willie Nelson and Charlie Rich - and Rodney Crowell can stand up there proudly in line. They all started with naked truth on a scratch pad and went on, with varying degrees of success, from there. His contributions to the development of country music as a contemporary force can't be measured. Gram Parsons is often described as the father of country/rock, as the guy who put the square peg in the round hole and came up with something that fit more or less comfortably. But Parsons died young, still trying to get it just right, and it took another generation - a generation that included Rodney Crowell - to realize and perfect his dream.

Rodney's musical education consisted of as much rock, folk and rhythm 'n' blues as whole-cloth country. At his father's knee, Crowell learned all the old country standards, how they were put together, what they meant and why they were great. He was a teenager when the Beatles and the Stones arrived on American shores, and even down in the Deep South, where Rodney and his family lived, their influence and their energy got in the bloodstream of every guitar-strumming teenager.

From Bob Dylan, he learned to put thoughts and music together. From Guy Clark, he learned to reach for poetry, not just words. Harmony, humility, perseverance and professionalism, he learned those from Emmylou Harris.

He joined Harris' celebrated Hot Band in 1975, at the age of 24, and stayed less than three years. "I wanted him very much to go out and sprout from that tree of artists and writers who came from that country place but who were infused with their own poetry of their own time, their own generation," says Harris. "That were going to push the frontiers of country music, and infuse it with something very much current, and their own.

"He had the vision to do it, he had the songwriting talent, and he had the voice. I always thought Rodney was a great singer, a very underrated singer."

Crowell met Clark at a time when Nashville was telling its scribes to keep it short, sweet and stupid. Rodney had already mastered that particular hat trick - and when he connected with Clark, he learned about putting words on a page like the strokes of a paintbrush. The secret, he discovered, is to stay away from pretentiousness by remaining connected to your own heart and your own sense of irony. Care about what you write. Stay true and, by God, the picture will paint itself.

Over the 25 years of their friendship, Crowell and Clark have co–authored a dozen songs. A songwriting partner, explains Clark, "has to be somebody you can trust, because when you're writing there's a lot of experimentation, and off-the-wall stuff you have to verbalize. Which won't always be used in the song, but it seems to be part of the process. That's something you don't have to worry about when you're writing by yourself.

"There's some very good friends of mine, we've tried to write together and, nothin.' And sometimes I've written with strangers and it's just come off wonderful. I'm not quite sure what the chemistry is, but for some reason Rodney and I have always been able to do it."

MCA Records Nashville President Tony Brown, a longtime friend, believes Rodney was always destined for big things. "The first thing I noticed about Rodney was his eyes," Brown says. "It was almost like you could see into his brain, they were just clear and amazing.

It felt like I was meeting somebody really special. A very charismatic guy."

Brown, who co-produced all five of Rodney's No. 1 hit singles, hit further paydirt with other artists including Reba McEntire, Wynonna and George Strait. "People ask you what makes stars," he says. "Some people have that, and most people don't. And Rodney has it. He's probably Gram Parsons reincarnated."

Perhaps the quality that sets Rodney Crowell apart is his willingness to wear his heart on his sleeve for the sake of his art. Very few writers use their vulnerability as a tool, as Crowell has done many, many times over the course of his songwriting career. The songs, he says, come to him - rarely does he go looking for them. So he writes from a deep and genuine place, even when it hurts.

"I never considered any other kind of work," he says. "I did a lot of different kind of stuff before. I was a dishwasher and a busboy at a Friday's restaurant in Nashville, and I quit in the middle of the day. I told my boss, 'Look, I'm sorry to do this, but if I can't make a living making music, then I'll just starve.' I was committed to that, and this is what I've done ever since. So I guess that kind of commitment is what you gotta have."

His career has gone up and down more times than the Space Shuttle, but he's learned to put it in perspective. Sensitive and self-aware, Rodney Crowell wasn't too surprised to find that his greatest commercial success coincided with his most intense period of personal unhappiness. When all was said and done, however, he got a couple of good songs out of it. Oh, yes … he knows how to have fun, too. "Rodney is able to put exuberance in a song without being perky," enthuses Harris. "Without over–simplifying the positive.

"There's still a quality to Rodney that no matter how old he gets, he'll always be the Houston Kid. There's always going to be a kid in there."

Meeting the muse

He was born Aug. 7, 1950, the only child of James Walter and Cauzette Crowell. Rodney's father, whom everyone knew as J.W., was from Arkansas and grew up in southwestern Kentucky farm country, in a town called Murray. He'd met Cauzette Willoughby (from Buchanan, Tenn., just "a mule ride away" across the border) at a Roy Acuff concert at the Buchanan High School gym. Many years later, Rodney introduced his mother to Acuff, backstage at the Grand Ole Opry, and was proud to say "Mr. Acuff, if it wasn't for you, I wouldn't be here."

Both J.W. and Cauzette had left school in the 8th grade, to help out on their respective family farms, and after they got married they high-tailed it out of there. Times were hard and jobs were few for young people in those post–Depression years, and if you had a lick of sense, you went where the work was. First stop was Detroit, where J.W. took a position on an auto assembly line. It didn't work out, and soon the Crowells were on the move again.

"They wound up in Houston, because Houston was a port and there was lots of menial labor," Rodney explains. "He went to work there as a laborer."

The Port of Houston was one of the busiest on the Gulf of Mexico, with nearly all of Texas' oil products eventually shipping out via the city's tremendous man-made channel. The Crowells' tiny house was near the channel, on the "wrong side of town," packed with refineries, warehouses and beer joints. J.W. did whatever work was at hand. "On my birth certificate, his occupation is listed as 'truck driver,'" says Rodney. "What he was really doing was delivering ice."

The senior Crowell, his son remembers, played the guitar and sang, and was pretty darn good. "He was, basically, an encyclopedia of songs from a certain period. His area of expertise was the Roy Acuff era, from Jimmy Rodgers, probably from 1930 to 1965. He just knew all of that country music."

J.W. performed at home, in what spare time he could find. "I think it's what he really wanted to do," Rodney says, "however, he grew up the son of a sharecropper, and the Depression hit those people so hard that I think my dad was locked onto this thing that he had to have a job.

"And that's what he did, but I think what he really wished he would've done is gone to Nashville and 'made it.'"

J.W. gave his boy the gift of music without even realizing it. "Later on, when I found my own love for it, the foundation that had been laid, just through osmosis, all of those songs … one thing about my dad, he didn't write 'em, but he knew 'em. I think I became a songwriter because I absorbed so many songs when I was little that eventually I had to just re-assemble them and turn them into something else. I had a body full of songs just from osmosis. He had those rabbit in the graveyard, trace her footprints in the snow, all of those dead baby songs, a real wealth of authenticity in his repertoire."

Rodney Crowell remembers a musical household; "Hearts of Stone," by the Fontaine Sisters, was a favorite record. "I remember hearing that record when I was like real little, I must've been 3 or 4. Or younger.

Mostly, there was country music. "I remember Hank Williams 78s. There was some sort of crude record player there, and we had these Hank Williams 78s, no dust cover or anything on 'em. I just remember music."

By the late '50s Rodney's dad had a band, J.W. Crowell and the Rhythm Boys, to play weekend dates at the local drinking establishments. "These were dives, with no barmaids, with that alcohol lunatic fringe," Crowell recalls. "It's sort of an under-culture of its own down there, a seaport town. There are a lot of those ice houses and beer joints that Merchant Marines hung around, in the part of Houston where the ship channel ended, where I grew up. It was honky-tonk country music, from the Hank Williams era through to middle Merle Haggard."

Years later, Rodney's friend Guy Clark wrote a song about the Crowell family, "Black Diamond Strings," proclaiming that J.W. played "two nights a week in a hillbilly band."

Not the case. The Rhythm Boys gigged maybe five nights a month. And never, ever on school nights, because in 1961, the group took on a new drummer, 11–year–old Rodney.

"My dad came home one day with a pawn shop kit, set 'em down and showed me how to do it," he remembers. "I practiced for a little while and then went and started playing with him. I would say within a week's time I was playing drums, a goofy 11-year-old kid."

Although he never saw a serious fight, never experienced a real "barroom brawl," Rodney didn't like going to the beer joints. "I felt a little put-upon. I wasn't entirely happy about it. I was kind of 'made' to do it. And like in Guy's song, Cauzette didn't like what J.W. was doing, taking the kid to a honky tonk. So she went to keep an eye on me. She thought the devil lived there." Rodney often fell asleep in the back seat of the family car, on the drive home.

J.W. drew from his vast repertoire of country classics to keep the tempo going, Rodney says. "Watch me," his dad would whisper, "I know how to keep the dance floor full." Requests would be written on one-dollar bills dropped into a cigar box in front of the stage. "At the end of the night when they split up the dough, there wasn't any coming my way," Rodney chuckles. J.W. had deduced that by adding his little boy to the band, that was one less musician he'd be required to pay.

So when he was 14, Rodney quit the Rhythm Boys. The Beatles and the rest of the British Invasion had reached Houston radio. "It was like plugging your finger into a light socket," he says: "Ah … the guy out front gets the girls." He was attracted, he says, to the energy.

J.W., predictably, said the Beatles were "bullshit," but his harrumphing couldn't keep a guitar out of Rodney's hands. His first band was called the Arbitrators, and the played Beatles, Beach Boys, Animals, Yardbirds, whatever big-beat stuff happened to move them. And they were moving plenty. Rodney Crowell's teenage years were a combination of Arbitrators rock 'n' roll, baseball and bull-riding (which he wasn't much good at, although that didn't stop him from taking rein in hand).

After a light bulb snapped on over his head, he realized he could put his dad's influence to good use and started a second group, a rodeo dance combo, using a couple of the Arbitrators as sidemen. "That band was Merle and Buck," he says. "I knew those songs. I'd get up there and slam those songs." He played some rock 'n' roll, and some country music -

foreshadowing the "supposed fence-straddling," he points out, of his later years. "This is not schizophrenia; it's real. I was doing that when I was a teenager, to make money."

Rodney was one of Crosby High's 46 graduating seniors in 1968. And although he had composed a tune at age 15, a "childish song in D minor," his first big lunge at the pen came at graduation time.

One night the senior class was to vote on the class flower, the class this and the class that. It occurred to Rodney that they'd probably go for a class song. "That morning I got up and I threw a song together. I went and played it at this meeting, and they all voted that that was going to be our class song. And God, it was blood awful. It was very Beatles-derivative and it was … it was bad. It was really bad. And I got up there with a cap and damn gown, with a guitar on, and sang that stupid song."

Now, let's fast–forward … "I went to my 25th class reunion, and there was a woman who taught a little English and home economics, and was kind of the only cultural icon that we had around there. Her name was Miss Hansen. Her daughter was my age, so I saw here there.

"A lot of these classmates were saying 'Sing the song, Rodney Crowell!' and I said no, I'm not going to. And Miss Hansen was standing there, and she said 'Wise choice, young man.' I said 'It really was bad, wasn't it?' She said, 'Awful.' And I said 'Thank you for supporting me.'"

It was at Stephen F. Austin College in Nagadoches that Rodney met Donivan Cowart, his first in a series of soul mates. Donivan was a history major; Rodney was ostensibly studying political science and English. In reality, they spent their time "getting high, skipping class and writing songs." Rodney got a job playing guitar in a Holiday Inn group; eventually he took over the six-nights-a-week gig, adding Donivan and a drummer. They called themselves the Greenville Three, only because Donivan had written a song called "Greenville, Tennessee." It made enough sense to go by.

"We got fired regularly because we played our own material," Crowell says. "And the clientele that started to come see us was young hippies, and the young hippies had their inebriants before they got there. So they would just sit and listen to the music, and not buy drinks. They'd fire us and then hire us again.

"We would ditch the 'Jeremiah was a Bullfrog' crap and start playing our own songs. And the crowd would dig it. And we'd get fired, and literally re-hired the next day."

Eventually Crowell and Cowart drifted east to Houston, in Donivan's '65 Impala to look for work, college having become a dead issue. And there they met Jim Duff, whose claim to fame was having engineered a 13th Floor Elevators record. This was as close to the music business as the young musicians had got, so when Jim Duff offered to manage them, they readily agreed. Signed on the dotted line. "We loaded up the car and drove to Crowley, LA to J.D. Miller's studio, where he did all of those race records, those party records," Crowell recalls. "And they did a whole lot of Cajun records over there. We did a record with Jim Duff.

"Well, as it turned out, Jim Duff was a real bad alcoholic - the poor man was an ill alcoholic - we made this record and came back to Houston, and he said 'OK, I'm going to go to Nashville with it.' Donivan and I were working as a duo at Popeyes, a supper club in Houston, and making some pretty decent money - we were doing covers but could sneak in our original tunes.

"We got the call from Jim Duff: 'Hey, I'm signing you to a 10-year recording contract with Columbia Records, and you're going on the road with Kenny Rogers and the First Edition. Get up here.' "Well, we quit Popeyes, jumped in the car and headed to Nashville, man. Slid in sideways, doors flew open, 'Where's Jim Duff?'"

"We couldn't find the guy anywhere. We were like 'What the fuck?' I had spent my last dime buying this really fine Martin guitar - hey, I gotta have a good guitar if I'm going to do this, right? - we slid in sideways to Nashville with 15 bucks. No Jim Duff."

Both in their early 20s, Crowell and Cowart didn't know anybody, didn't have any prospects, and they sure as hell couldn't find their mentor and his Columbia Records contract. They assumed Kenny Rogers was waiting somewhere for them, looking at his watch and impatiently tapping his foot.

Having no money, "We lived in the car out at Percy Priest Lake, Donivan in the front and me in the back, and came into town," Rodney remembers. They took baths in the lake. In time, they started picking up a little change by passing the hat at Bishop's Pub, a legendary watering hole on the west end. Owner Tim Bishop liked their enthusiasm and gave them free hamburgers in the kitchen.

Soon a mutual friend - well known to be a speed freak - drove all night from Houston, just to tell them the truth about Jim Duff and their big-time opportunity.

"It was a lie. What he'd really done was, he came up and didn't get nothin' going, so he sold the publishing for $100, for a bus ticket back to Houston.

"We found out that the tapes and the songwriting contracts were on top of a drawer at Surefire Music, which was the Wilburn Brothers' publishing company.

"We went in at lunchtime, and Donivan charmed the receptionist. And I slipped into that office, swiped the tape and the publishing agreement on the songs, and we scooted out of there with our tapes and our songs."

The write stuff

Bishop's Pub was a mecca for the new breed of songwriter then immigrating to Nashville and living the dirt-poor but artistically rich lifestyle. The pub was dark, and the beer was cold, and Tim Bishop would let any of them get onstage and play for the hat. A supportive group of like-minded individuals - many of them from Texas - began to orbit Bishop's Pub. Central to the coterie were Guy Clark and his wife Susanna, herself a gifted songwriter and painter, and the Clarks' compadre Townes Van Zandt, who'd already made a couple of albums on the tiny Poppy label. The three of them shared a small house on 34th Street, just around the corner from Bishop's Pub, so they could just walk over whenever they felt like it. Mickey Newbury, Billy Joe Shaver and Richard Dobson were regulars, too.

"It started to get cold, and me, Skinny Dennis Sanchez and Richard Dobson got a house on Ashland Avenue together," Crowell says. "And all of the songwriters started crashing out there.

"That's when I started working at Friday's. As a dishwasher, I'd get off at 2 in the morning, and from drinking all those half-empty drinks that came through I'd be smashed when I came home. I would be just perfectly oiled up for what was already going on at the house. We'd play music till dawn, sleep all day, and then I'd work at night."

There was never a dull moment at Rodney's place. "For a while, there was an acrobat and his assistant living in the front bedroom," he remembers. "I think Richard Dobson went off on one of his literary trips, and sublet his front bedroom to these circus performers. I can't remember their names, but they were just out, just perfect for the whole bizarre atmosphere that was going on around there at the time."

Guy Clark had already written "L.A. Freeway," which included a line about Skinny Dennis Sanchez - the Californian bass player who wound up sharing the house with Rodney - but his first album was still two years away.

Susanna Clark remembers the first time she and Guy ran into Rodney and Donivan, at the Ashland house. "Everybody was in the kitchen, doing what they did, and these two were in the walk-in front hall, looking kinda weird. I just sat down and said 'Hi!' I was young and in the way, too. Still innocent and friendly.

"I just thought Rodney was this twinkling, beautiful angel. And I said 'I'll play you a song, if you'll play me one.' I played him something, I don't remember what, and he played 'There's Glue on My Stool.' He only played that one for me - he wouldn't dare play it for anybody else.

"We started talking, and he was bright and cheerful, and stars started poppin' all around his head. And I said 'I like you!' And he said 'I like you, too!'" In the Clarks, Rodney was to make the best of friends. "Susanna and I started talking," he says, "and we hooked right up. I think Guy was passed out on my bed, face down with his boots hangin' off the end. That's how I met Guy."

Guy Clark's disciplined, no-words-wasted songwriting had an immediate effect on Rodney, who eagerly joined in the all-night sing and booze-alongs. "I would venture out a few of these twerpy songs, and there was Guy Clark songs, Mickey Newbury songs, and Townes Van Zandt songs. I was exposed. My shortcomings were exposed in a big way.

"There was no suffering fools there. I wasn't tolerated at all - I was ignored. I think the talent was present, and my knowledge of music was present - I think Guy kind of locked in on that, he saw that I had real roots, and that kept me around - but the songs that I was writing were just an embarrassment. I was smart enough to realize it."

"I thought he was very good when I first met him," says Clark, who calls Rodney one of his "real, true" friends. "I can't remember exactly where I met him - I remember he and Donivan came over to our house in East Nashville - but I always thought he was great. I always knew he was capable of it."

According to Rodney, the late-night songwriters' gatherings were friendly, but competitive. "It was intimidating. Townes was extremely competitive. Townes was more overtly competitive than Guy - those two were very competitive with each other. But I think I was just young enough, and guileless enough, I took my beatings in the proper spirit of learning."

He was, after all, only 22 years old, the runt of the litter. Eventually, however, things began to change.

"I remember quite clearly when I played this song called 'Bluebird Wine.' Which is not a great song, but it's a good start. It was one of those nights, and I got Guy's approval with that. And of course, Townes wasn't giving any approval on it."

"And then the next time around, in some setting, Guy would go 'Hey, Rodney, play Bluebird Wine.' So then I was in. I had a song that Guy would say 'Play that.' I think that fanned the flame a little bit."

In Clark's view, Rodney blossomed quickly as a songwriter. And their friendship, a symbiotic affair, grew deeper as time went on. Rodney told interviewers later that he could very well have gone into business writing cheap, glittery, radio—friendly country songs at that point, but for connecting with Guy Clark and coming to understand that you could write about what was inside of you, reaching deeper with each pass until you found it. He learned about songcraft. From the beginning, Rodney described Guy as his mentor. "I never thought of it as a student—teacher thing, never wanted it to be," Clark says. "I learned a lot from Rodney. He has a really good sense of music, and a great catalogue of knowledge from having played as a kid. He's got a real energy."

Voila, an American dream

In the spring of '73, Rodney was eking out a living playing clubs, after giving his notice at Friday's. Somebody, he doesn't recall who, asked him if he could yodel; he said yes, of course he could! He would've done anything by that point to make some cash.
He went to Opryland, which was just getting ready to start its first summer, and auditioned for their big summer revue, based on the life of Jimmie Rodgers. His yodeling carried the day, and he was awarded the part of the "Blue Yodeler" in the summer spectacular. A steady paycheck seemed assured.

"But I happened to be playing Happy Hour at the Jolly Ox, and I was expressly forbidden to play my own songs," Rodney recalls. "One night I clenched through my teeth 'I'm gonna play one of my own songs.' So I played this song called 'You Can't Keep Me Here in Tennessee,' and at the end of that set Jerry Reed's manager came and said 'We'd like to record that song tomorrow, and if you're not signed, we'd like to sign you as a songwriter.' I said 'OK, yeah. Good timing.' I think that was a crossroads." He has often reflected on how his life would've turned out differently if he had become the "Blue Yodeler."

True to his manager's word, Reed cut Rodney's song the very next afternoon. "I speculate they were sitting around at Happy Hour at the Jolly Ox going 'God, we need a song for tomorrow…'"

Vector Music paid him $100 per week to turn out the tunes. Although he wrote several that would later prove pivotal, including "Song For the Life" and "'Til I Gain Control Again," none got recorded at the time. Still, Vector was a learning experience, and he met Chet Atkins, Jim Croce and even Buford Pusser, and super-session drummer Larrie Londin (later a close professional and personal friend) during this period.

Skip Beckwith, who played bass with the Canadian country/pop diva Anne Murray, came through Nashville in '74 and wound up crashing at Rodney's house for a week. The two became fast friends, and when Beckwith flew home to Toronto, he was carrying a cassette demo of a couple of Crowell songs. His intention was to play them for Brian Ahern, Murray's producer.

But Ahern was knee-deep in a new project. He had agreed to produce the first solo album for Emmylou Harris, the former harmony singer for country/rock pioneer Gram Parsons, who had died from bad living the previous fall.

It was a fateful meeting, and one Harris remembers well. "Brian popped the tape into the machine, and 'Bluebird Wine' came on," she says. "There was something in Rodney's voice that I really liked. There was something about the energy and the song that I really liked. So we listened then to 'Song For the Life' and I said 'Now, here's somebody that has obviously listened to George Jones.'"

Crowell was tracked down in Houston - he still has no idea how they found him there - and within hours of Ahern's call he was on a plane to Toronto. He came face-to-face with Emmylou Harris for the first time at the rural Virginia home of guitarist John Starling, of the Seldom Scene.

"We sat up all night and played songs," says Crowell, "'Do you know this one?' We both were into all those brothers - the Everly Brothers, the Louvin Brothers, the Wilburn Brothers, John and Paul, all of those duet singing teams."

Immediately, they both knew they had to sing together. It was too good.

Harris: "We would sit there and bang away on the guitars, and he would jump in with the harmony. In the way that Gram used to play me songs, and I would jump in on the harmony. Or then Rodney would sing the song and I would start harmonizing with him."

During that first session at John Starling's house, Rodney sang "'Til I Gain Control Again," and Harris was stunned. "At this point, I felt like I had probably found the mother lode. Because for somebody at his young age to be able to write a song like 'Til I Gain Control Again.' … I always felt that Rodney was an old soul, that he was able to write songs that you can appreciate when you're young, but they really age well because as you get older, and life gets harder, and you get more and more worn around the edges, the songs take on even more levels of soulfulness and poetry. He really has always had a phenomenal talent for the lyric and the melody."

Susanna Clark remembers the first time she heard Emmylou Harris sing. "Rodney called us over to his little apartment, and he said 'Sit there, Susanna. I'm gonna play you something. You have to be still.' All of a sudden there was this piercing, beautiful, angelic voice, singing 'Til I Gain Control Again.' And he said 'See? They like me up in Canada.' I knew how he wrote it, and why he wrote it, but I'd never heard it like that before, ever, ever."

Eventually, Crowell was Choice No. 1 for the Hot Band, which Harris and Ahern were assembling to back her on her first album. He readily agreed to move to Los Angeles, where the sessions were to take place.

"Being a harmony singer was such an integral part of what my real musical education was about," Harris points out. "So much of what we did was built around singing those harmonies. And having somebody to bounce songs off of, and bounce harmonies off of, having somebody to harmonize with … That whole duet thing was a real important part of my identity, the way I approached music, the way I thought of myself.

"I found myself center stage because of fate and circumstances, but I always felt that I was sharing the stage with Rodney. And the whole rest of the band. I always thought of myself as a member of that band."

The Hot Band was aptly named, as it included several members of Elvis Presley's touring group, guitarist James Burton, bassist Emory Gordy Jr., pedal steel player Hank DeVito, drummer Ron Tutt and pianist Glen D. Hardin. And Rodney Crowell.
All but Tutt agreed to tour with Harris - Burton and Hardin on the condition that they be allowed to work around Elvis' schedule. Gordy, DeVito and Crowell, in particular, formed a bond that lasts to this day.

"It's interesting that everybody focuses on the Hot Band, and the hot players, and rightly so," Harris says. "Everybody in the band was so important. But Rodney brought something to the band - I think he became the spirit and the personality. He had such a wonderful, open, playful quality about him, and yet he was so talented as a songwriter. Everything just fell into place, and somehow it was real pivotal around Rodney."

Harris recorded "Bluebird Wine" for that first album, *Pieces of the Sky*, and "'Til I Gain Control Again" for *Elite Hotel* in '76. For the next decade, Rodney Crowell's songs figured in nearly all of her records - Harris was the first to record "Ain't Living Long Like This," "Leaving Louisiana in the Broad Daylight," "Even Cowgirls Get the Blues" and numerous others.

"I was like a kid in a candy store," she enthuses. "I had this great young writer that nobody else knew about, and I had first dibs on anything he wrote. In fact, sometimes I was the first person to hear the song."

Rodney's first recording sessions were as backing vocalist on Guy Clark's RCA Records debut, *Old No. 1*. Clark had recorded the entire set, then decided he didn't like it and cut the whole thing again. By the time of the re-make sessions, Crowell was living in Los Angeles with the Hot Band. He flew back and forth to Nashville to help with *Old No. 1*.

"He brought a lot of good, positive energy," says Clark. "And he made the record better."

Crowell also figured prominently in the recording of Clark's historically underrated second album, *Texas Cookin,'* in '76.

Onstage, the Hot Band was re-papering the walls between country and popular music. Burton, DeVito, Gordy, Hardin and Crowell were more than mere backup players. The virtuosity onstage was astounding, and audiences from coast to coast to coast responded.

Crowell: "It was fun. It was heady. At that time, we were a country rock band opening for Elton John at Dodger Stadium. We were out with James Taylor. We played a lot of the rock venues. At that time, it wasn't so segregated. And it was real cool.

"I was young and impressionable, and I learned a lot. I think that's the period where I became a record producer, because working with Glen and James Burton and Emory and all of those guys, it was a group of arrangers.

"I could only claim that I was a songwriter and a little bit of a vocalist at that time. But being around those guys, I actually learned how to arrange. And combining my sense for songs and what I learned about arranging, being in that band, has really served me pretty well for a while."

History has re-assigned the Rodney Crowell of that period the role of surrogate Gram Parsons; Harris, it's suggested, needed a strong male vocal presence on the stage to make her comfortable, and Rodney filled the bill.

"That was a completely different deal," Crowell says "Gram Parsons needed Emmy. He sang melody and she sang the third harmony part. It doesn't work without the third. And with me and Emmy, Emmy sang the melody, and I sang usually the fifth beneath her. It's a different kind of harmony configuration.

"Whenever I took the melody, and Emmy sang harmony with me, I think we had that particular sound. I think I was basically the same kind of singer as Gram Parsons, in that timbre."

Crowell thinks of Parsons as a "James Dean character who died a flamboyant death," and that's about it, thank you. He never met the guy. "I wasn't a surrogate Gram Parsons," he says. "We were just working, making music."

A brief marriage, in 1975, to his Nashville girlfriend Martha didn't last long, but it resulted in the birth of Hannah Crowell, who was brought up by her father. "She left and I got the kid," Rodney says proudly. "I raised her up solid."

By any other name

The next year, he met Johnny Cash's 21-year-old daughter Rosanne, an aspiring singer/songwriter herself. It happened at a party at Waylon Jennings' house, where Rodney and Emmylou were the center of attention. "They trotted us out and we sang duets for them," Crowell recalls. "While Rosanne and Willie Nelson sat under a pool table."

He didn't really notice her, he says, although she later told interviewers she took an instant liking to him. "There was too much going on to really dial it in," Rodney says. "Me and Emmy were kind of performing for everybody, so I don't think I was terribly receptive. We were performing for Willie and Waylon, really. And I don't think John and June (Carter, Rosanne's stepmother) were there."

Brian Ahern sat in the producer's chair for Rodney's first solo album, *Ain't Living Long Like This*, for Warner Brothers in the spring of '78. The album featured many of the virtuoso players that made up the Hot Band. To pursue his own dream, Crowell left the touring band, to be replaced by young Ricky Skaggs, who found himself referred to by the press as a "surrogate Rodney Crowell."

"Honestly, I dropped out thinking that I would just do what Emmy was doing," remembers Crowell. "Get myself a great band and go out and play all those great places she was.

"That was not at all what happened. I put out that first record and it didn't do anything for me, personally, but the songs were good and they all got covered."

Within three years, "Leaving Louisiana in the Broad Daylight," "Ain't Living Long Like This" and "Voila, An American Dream" would become huge hits for other artists. Harris herself cut "Leaving Louisiana" and "Ain't Living Long" on her fourth album, 1978's *Quarter Moon in a Ten Cent Town*. It went gold.

But Rodney Crowell's album gathered dust on record store shelves across America.

Perhaps it just swung too wide - along with the sharply etched originals, Crowell included covers of Dallas Frazier's "Elvira," Porter Wagoner's "I Thought I Heard You Calling My Name" and Hank Snow's "A Fool Such As I," all of which he'd learned at his father's knee.

"'Elvira,' and 'Candy Man,' which I did years later, were songs that I learned off my Aunt Mary's stereo down in Houston," says Crowell. "She had a collection of R'n'B singles, back there in the late '50s and early '60s, that was uncanny for the kind of woman she was. These R'n'B records from New Orleans. She had Frogman Henry and those things." Aunt Mary's son, Larry Willoughby, followed Rodney into the music business.

Everyone involved was stunned at the failure of *Ain't Living Long Like This*, which never sold more than 50,000 copies. "It was a great record," believes Emmylou Harris. "And just about every song was lifted by somebody else and made a hit.

"But for some reason, that door that had opened for me when I kind of surprised everybody, including myself, and there was an audience for this new kind of country - the door kind of closed somehow. And I don't think the record company knew exactly how to promote that record of Rodney's. I don't know what happened, because certainly it was a good record."

To add insult to injury, the Oak Ridge Boys took their revival of "Elvira," using Rodney Crowell's arrangement, to No. 1 in 1981, earning "Single of the Year" honors from the Country Music Association.

Success somehow eluded Rodney Crowell. "I think I just sort of assumed it would come," he laughs. "Maybe I was presumptuous about that."

In retrospect, Crowell believes he doomed *Ain't Living Long Like This* because he didn't promote it; rather than hitting the road, he flew to Munich, Germany, where Rosanne Cash was making an album for the Ariola label. As a favor, he had produced her demo recordings. When a friend in Munich played the tape for someone she knew at Ariola, Rosanne was offered a record deal. Crowell always believed they were trying to cash in on the fact that she was Johnny Cash's daughter.

The first sessions went badly, and soon Rosanne called Rodney and begged him to come to Germany and help her finish the record. He did, and during their stay in Munich romance blossomed.

Rosanne's self-titled Ariola album was issued worldwide, and died a worldwide death. That, they figured, was that. They both hated it, anyway.

Back in California, Crowell had formed a bond with Albert Lee, the English guitarist who'd taken over for James Burton in the Hot Band, when Burton opted to keep his calendar open only for Elvis. "There were mixed feelings when I joined the Hot Band, because I was replacing James Burton," Lee says. "James wanted to do both gigs, really, and they forced him into a decision. So I was fortunate enough to get the gig with Emmylou, which was perfect for me. It was the kind of music I'd always wanted to play.

"But I had to replace one of my all-time favorite guitar players, and play a lot of his licks. Which was fine up to a point. But there were certain people in the band - I won't name names - who were putting pressure on me. But Rodney was certainly on my side, and a big fan. And we became fast friends right from the word go."

Rodney and Albert weren't together in the Hot Band for very long. But they enjoyed singing together; they dubbed their weekend act "Rodney & Albert."

"In Emmy's down time, we started playing down in Redondo Beach, at the Sweetwater," Crowell recalls. "It was me and Albert, (drummer) John Ware, Emory Gordy and Hank DeVito. Rosanne sang harmony and played guitar with us. That was what eventually became the Cherry Bombs."

Some nights, Rosanne was so nervous she turned her guitar amplifier off and only pretended to play.

Tony Brown, another former Elvis sideman, had replaced Glen D. Hardin as the Hot Band's pianist. When Emmylou cut down on touring because of her pregnancy, Brown took a desk job with RCA Records in Los Angeles, joining the Hot Band for their infrequent gigs, most of them in California. He hooked up with "Rodney & Albert," too, and by simple virtue of his presence became a charter Cherry Bomb.

Between 1979 and '81, the Cherry Bombs barnstormed the California club circuit, played some big shows, and re-organized with a slightly altered lineup each time. "We would play for anything from a dollar a night to whatever our fee was, just to be in that group, with Larrie Londin on drums," says Brown.

"The Cherry Bombs didn't become the Cherry Bombs until we brought Larrie Londin out from Nashville to the Record Plant in Sausalito," Crowell adds. "That's when I got on the idea to call the band the Cherry Bombs: 'We'll tour the whole world!'" Vince Gill, who was just then starting to sing with Pure Prairie League (his explosively successful solo career was still a decade away), often played lead guitar with the Cherry Bombs.

"I first met Vince at the Troubadour in '76," recalls Crowell. "I went down to see Byron Berline, and Vince was on the stage. I walked in and got me a place in the balcony up there, and Vince started singing 'Til I Gain Control Again.' And I went 'Wow, that was good.' He sang it REAL good. Vince must've been 20 or 21 at the time.

"When they came off, I went and introduced myself. He was, I think, just starting to date Janis from Sweethearts of the Rodeo, and I knew them from the Long Beach Bluegrass Festival days. When I was a judge, and I voted for 'em. They were the Sweethearts back in '75."

In early '79 Rick Blackburn, then the head of Columbia Records, was at Johnny Cash's house in Nashville. Proud papa pulled out the Ariola album, *Rosanne Cash*, and put it on the turntable. Blackburn didn't care for the record's trendy pop sounds, but he liked Rosanne's voice, and he was particularly drawn to one song, "Baby, Better Start Turnin' 'Em Down," written by Rosanne's new boyfriend, Rodney Crowell.

Rosanne was signed to Columbia Records, and it took some persuading, but Blackburn eventually allowed Crowell to produce her debut, *Right or Wrong*.

He tackled his first major production in the Enactron Truck studio, the very facility where the newly-married Ahern and Harris made their masterpieces (it was indeed a truck, parked in the driveway of the house they leased on Lania Lane in Beverly Hills).

Right or Wrong was a punchy, heads–up concoction merging country/pop ballads and uptempo ravers. Rosanne covered her father ("Big River"), used one of her own songs ("This Has Happened Before") and hit a blue streak of great Rodney Crowell tunes ("Baby, Better Start Turnin' 'Em Down," "Anybody's Darlin,'" "Seeing's Believing" and "No Memories Hangin' Round").

A duet with Bobby Bare, "No Memories Hangin' Round" was Rosanne's first hit single, reaching No. 17 in September '79, two months after she and Rodney tied the knot in Los Angeles. Rodney's daughter Hannah moved in with them, and daughter Caitlin was born later in the year.

The Cherry Bombs backed Rosanne on her record, too. "He had an idea what he wanted, but obviously he put a lot of trust into the players," recalls Albert Lee. "He knew what he could get from the players. He relied on us."

Lee's chicken-pickin' electric guitar, as well as his piano work and vocal harmonies, were used on every Crowell record, as an artist or producer, during this period. "All the times

I worked with him in the studio, he never really grilled me at all," says Lee. "It's always been very easy. He knows what I do, and he always seems happy with what I deliver."

Rodney's focus once again became his solo career. In '79, he was besotted with Elvis Costello. "It was songwriting far beyond all those punk guys," he says. "By that time, I'd been to England a few times and hung out with Dave Edmunds and the Rockpile boys, and got introduced to pub rock sensibilities. I went back to California thinking we were too soft."

On a trip to London, "Hank and I went down to Dingwall's, and they had 'Pump it Up' blasting, and it was like 'Man, this is the hippest stuff I've heard.' And of course, we started going 'Well, now we've got to upgrade our shit, here.'"

So Rodney Crowell and his Cherry Bombs moved into a rented house in Sausalito, armed with a handful of freshly-minted compositions, and "started bashing away." The result was *But What Will the Neighbors Think*, a punchy, poppy record that bears little resemblance to the lighthearted and decidedly country *Ain't Living Long Like This*.

Rodney's vocals had something new, a compressed, filtered quality. "That's me trying to get tough with it," he says. "I think that's me being influenced by Elvis Costello and those guys."

The album was produced - virtually live in the studio - by Craig Leon, who'd made records with the Ramones. Rodney liked what he'd done on one of Moon Martin's albums and sought him out.

"This artist travels outside the borders of country music, a move that jingoistic outlawism would consider an implicit betrayal," read the rave *Rolling Stone* review of *But What Will the Neighbors Think*. "Yet rock 'n' roll and even English folk balladry are of a piece with Crowell's concerns."

The music was heads-up different-sounding, but Rodney Crowell the songwriter was right there where he should've been, dead center. "On a Real Good Night" ached with beautiful desperation, "Here Come the '80s" looked forward with skewed optimism and humor. The covers were great, too, especially Guy Clark's "Heartbroke" and Hank DeVito's "Queen of Hearts."

But Juice Newton soon had a huge pop hit with "Queen of Hearts," and Ricky Skaggs made "Heartbroke" his third consecutive No. 1 record.

Rodney managed to get to No. 78 on the pop chart with "Ashes By Now," the first of two singles from *But What Will the Neighbors Think*. Even that had been left over from the first album; in fact, the original recording was the B-side of "Elvira" back in '78. Brian Ahern later replaced Rodney's lead vocals with Emmylou Harris' and released "her version" of "Ashes By Now" as part of her *Evangeline* album.

In the meantime, two more singles from Rosanne's *Right or Wrong* were Top 20 records.

Crowell: "I was certainly frustrated, and disappointed and hurt, but you know what? Every time I did something that the public or the writers perceived as such a devastating thing, to make me such a negative, nasty person, it just wasn't true. Because I would just get over it and get on to the next thing I was working on. I was producing something else or I was touring with the Cherry Bombs. I was always optimistic.

"I was certainly disappointed, and I was going through the trials and tribulations that you do in marriage, when you're young and getting too screwed up, but I think there's this general stamp to put on me in that time.

"And it's not fair, because I was always optimistic and always writing more songs, and onto the next thing."

He wore his producer's hat for two new projects, Guy Clark's *The South Coast of Texas*, and Rosanne's *Seven Year Ache*. Early in the year, Clark had made an album, *Burnin' Daylight*, with Craig Leon, but it wasn't a hit with anyone who heard it (especially the nit-picky Clark) so it went back in the can, and Crowell was enlisted to re-make it. And that was *The South Coast of Texas*, issued by Warner Brothers in the summer of '81.

"I played him what we'd done, and explained how much I didn't like it, and he said he thought he could do it," Clark recalls. Craig Leon's wafer-thin vocal sound didn't suit Clark's bare-bones songs.

Ultimately, Rodney would produce two albums for his friend - and today, Clark doesn't care for either one of them, either. "There's just too much stuff," he says. "I never did like that kind of thing, just trying to do what too many different people wanted. (And) he was trying to learn to be a producer on me; it wasn't totally a labor of love. He had an agenda."

Clark, who now records with a primarily acoustic sound, says he and Crowell agree today that the big–production thing - drums, electric guitar and pedal steel - was a well-intentioned mistake.

A breakthrough was on the horizon, though. Under Rodney's careful production, *Seven Year Ache* was a slick, masterful updating of the rockin' country sound Harris and Ahern had developed for Harris' early records. But Rosanne's style was more urban, her choice of songs and her delivery less rooted in the traditional. The music was more sophisticated.

The album had saxophones instead of pedal steel guitar, but the players were, as always, the best — members of the Hot Band and the Cherry Bombs. With *Seven Year Ache*, Rosanne Cash became the poster girl for contemporary country in the 1980s.

Three No. 1 singles emerged, including the feisty title song (inspired by Rodney after one of the couple's many arguments), a cover of Asleep at the Wheel's "My Baby Thinks He's a Train," and another Rosanne original, "Blue Moon With Heartache." Rodney and Hank DeVito contributed the lovely "I Can't Resist," later covered by Sweethearts of the Rodeo.

Rodney issued his third album that year, too. Containing some of his best songs yet, including "Shame on the Moon," "Victim or a Fool" and "Stars on the Water," *Rodney Crowell* appeared with little fanfare from Warner Brothers, virtually no publicity, and zero radio play. Its two singles scraped into the lower reaches of the Top 30.

The Cherry Bombs continued to plug away. "I think about then Albert might have started playing with Eric Clapton," says Crowell. "Actually, there were three guitar players in that band that kind of rotated: Richard Bennett, Vince and Albert. Probably the one who did the most work was Richard Bennett, because Albert got real busy and Vince was in and out. There were nights that they were all three onstage."

Recalls Tony Brown: "I felt like I was barely hanging by a thread to be able to play with those guys. I had that whole Hot Band bunch way up on a pedestal, and I was just hanging by my fingernails."

Always the bridesmaid

Waylon Jennings took "Ain't Living Long Like This" to the top of the country charts, and the Oak Ridge Boys did the same with "Leaving Louisiana in the Broad Daylight." Then Crystal Gayle's version of "'Til I Gain Control Again" went to No. 1.

Rosanne's success was the capper. The party line, in the press, was that Rodney Crowell had the magic touch - at least when it came to other recording artists. As a performer himself, he couldn't get arrested.

Having the touch wasn't entirely what he craved. "There were always times when I remember evaluating: To be a producer is to actually get into the art of helping someone else realize what they're trying to do," he says. "I always thought that was a pretty noble undertaking, and I still do. It's a part of me that's always been there - I like collaborating with other people, kind of a midwifery. And I always kind of viewed it like film directing, producing records. I always really enjoyed it artistically. Still do."

He was to reach the brass ring, but not for a while yet. "I got perspective on this," he says now. "Having big hit records myself later on didn't satisfy, so there you are."

As Rosanne's star ascended, his stayed on the ground. It made good copy, and the public could buy it -hell, it made sense on the surface - but Crowell insists that household envy just wasn't the case.

"It was my success, too, because I in the early part, I was a real driving force in those records," he explains. "She later on matured and started taking on a little more … she eventually became her own producer.

"But in the beginning, I enjoyed the satisfaction of seeing them succeed."

Recently, Laurence Leamer's book on country music, *Three Chords and the Truth*, reiterated the old story about Rodney's "bitterness" in those early years, watching Rosanne score hit after hit. The book steamed him like a clam.

"I wasn't jealous of that," he says. "I was frustrated with myself. It was 'How come I can get this to work so easily, but when I put the spotlight on myself, why do I trip up?' I couldn't figure that out, and it took me five more years to solve that."

After he produced albums for Bobby Bare (*As Is*) and for actress Sissy Spacek (*Hangin' Up My Heart*), Rodney, Rosanne, Hannah and Caitlin loaded up the truck and moved to … Tennessee, on the Fourth of July, 1981. "We started having children, and L.A. just didn't seem like the place to be to do that," he explains. "A little too sprawling. A little too much time in the car. Not very big yards." The couple's second daughter, Chelsea, was born in Nashville.

Renewing his friendship with Guy and Susanna Clark, Rodney then set about making himself known in Nashville. He produced an album for his cousin, Larry Willoughby, and one for Albert Lee (both were eponymously titled). He did *Somewhere in the Stars* for Rosanne, and *Better Days* for Guy.

Then Bob Seger's smoky cover version of "Shame on the Moon" became a huge pop hit, at the end of '82. Not long afterwards, the Dirt Band hit No. 1, country, with Rodney's "Long Hard Road (Sharecropper's Dream)."

He and Rosanne were addicted to cocaine by then. It wasn't fun around their crib. "So much of my frustration was self-induced, and the self-induced frustration was also fueled by drugs," Crowell reports. "It became pretty much of a black hole situation for me. In the late '60s, in the beginning, I started writing because of it. It was a fuel for that.

"But by then, it really became a real negative thing. I was allergic to cocaine, yet I kept on doing it. I made the decision that I don't care if I never write again, I gotta quit doing this." The world turned on New Year's Eve, 1984. "When she went off to treatment, that's when I stopped using cocaine myself," he says. "And I haven't used it since."

How did he kick such a destructive habit? "I stayed home with the kids," he chuckles. "She took the high road, and I took the low. I remember waking up in the middle of the night with sweat and thinking 'Ah, I'm withdrawing here.' And I actually started writing better. Got more focused. I could actually finish a block of thought."

Cash emerged from the detox center clean and sober. Crowell maintains that even though their drug daze fogged some of their records (listen to the lackluster *Somewhere in the Stars*, for example), they still created a good percentage of solid material in that period.

"I think I managed to do some good work as a producer," he offers. "Where I think it held me back was personally. It was my own stumbling block, my own inner conflict that kept me from being able to create for myself what I wanted.

"Truth is, I know that what was going on for me at that time was not about her, it was about what was going on with me. I was self-inducing some real serious blocks. That's why I don't go with the old tried-and-true story that her records took off and I was jealous. That just wasn't true."

He threw himself back into his work in 1984, proclaiming, hand on the Bible, that he wasn't going to "be a producer" any more. He wanted that solo career, and with a new clarity of vision, he went after it.

The album he and co-producer David Malloy came up with, *Street Language*, was delivered to Warner Brothers at the end of the year. Label president Jim Ed Norman promptly handed it back.

"There was a little cheese factor in what we did," Crowell reflects, chuckling. "It was pop in a way that wasn't whole. Sorta inorganic.

"I don't think David and I really hit on it, you know. We took it to L.A., and their reaction was 'We can't really do much with this.' Jim Ed was very gentlemanly then - I've kept him in the highest regard - and he said 'We can't put this record out, but we'll give you a budget to make another record. Make us a record that we can work in Nashville.'"

Instead, Rodney negotiated a release from his Warners contract, and a deal was struck with Columbia Records, Rosanne's label. "That record went on the shelf, which I've always been grateful for," he says. One track from the rejected *Street Language* album, "I Don't Have to Crawl," was released in 1989 on the Warners compilation *The Rodney Crowell Collection*.

The first order of business was re-making *Street Language*. Booker T. Jones, who'd played organ on the *Rodney Crowell* album, agreed to co-produce. Crowell had met him during the sessions for Willie Nelson's *Stardust* back in '77 (Jones produced that seminal marriage of pop and country, the album that made Willie a crossover star).

The re-made *Street Language* leaned heavily on rock 'n' roll and big, electric arrangements. Columbia wasn't sure how to market the thing.

"I was still kind of headstrong that I didn't want to make a country record, per se," Crowell says. "I wanted to make my own record, right? So when we finished it, we took it to New York, and it was kind of a "co-" between Nashville and New York. And that never works, on any huge level."

Neither the New York or Nashville brain trusts could get *Street Language* off the ground, despite a huge promotional campaign that included countless interviews on "hip" college radio stations, and a tour (in the summer and fall of 1986) with the Hooters and the BoDeans.

As eclectic in its own way as *But What Will the Neighbors Think, Street Language* betrays very little country influence - most of the songs, from the rollicking, horn-driven "Ballad of Fast Eddie" to the Beatle-esque "Stay (Don't Be Cruel)" owe their souls to rock 'n' roll. "Oh King Richard," re-recorded from the first version of the album, was a "modern folk tale" about race driver Richard Petty.

Crowell: "One of my favorite things I ever did was 'Oh King Richard.' To me, that was folk/rock at that time, and I loved that. And I really liked 'Ballad of Fast Eddie.' I look back on 'Let Freedom Ring,' and I think (co-writer) Keith Sykes and I had seduced ourselves. We were in New York and it was Springsteen fever. When I hear that record, I want to cringe.

"'When the Blue Hour Comes,' that wasn't Booker's fault, that was my fault. That thing was totally overdone. Because I did a demo of it recently, with this girl singing, and I discovered it to be a real sweet song. But to me, the way it was all dressed up on that record, we killed a perfectly good song."

"When the Blue Hour Comes" was a three-way composition with Will Jennings and Roy Orbison. "Will Jennings was mine and Orbison's friend, and he kept saying 'You guys are so much alike. I gotta get you together.' He saw us as Texas boys, so he instigated that.

"Roy was black and white, Roy was. Working with him one day, it was like 'God, this guy! I can't wait to get out of here. He don't like me, Will. What made you think that we would get on?'

"And then the next day, he was like the funniest guy in the world. I was so relieved. Every joke he told, I'd laugh till I cried."

"Ballad of Fast Eddie" was inspired by Peter Sheridan, a hulking, Harley-riding "character" who found his way onto Willie Nelson's tour bus - "a cowboy bus in the New York zoo" - in the late '70s ("Fast Eddie" was the crew's code name for Willie). On his east coast swings, Rodney and Rosanne spent a lot of time with Willie, who recorded the Crowell composition "Angel Eyes (Angel Eyes)" for his *Honeysuckle Rose* soundtrack album in '79.

Sheridan was killed on his motorcycle in 1982, and Rodney's song became a tribute to his intimidating, hipster-cliché-spouting presence in their lives.

Around the time of *Street Language*, Rodney was enlisted to "produce" an album recorded in Europe by Orbison, Johnny Cash, Jerry Lee Lewis and Carl Perkins. *Class of '55* was nothing to write home about. It had probably looked good on paper.

"Somebody recorded it in Germany, and they brought the tapes to me and said 'Make a record out of this,'" Crowell recalls. "And then Jerry Lee Lewis comes in with his entourage, puts a pistol on the console and says 'I'm gonna be on Side One.'

"But he came in late in the show, so the biggest job was cutting Jerry Lee Lewis onto Side One of the old 33 1/3. And then we spent a week working on matching the audience sounds, so that it sounded like he came out for the fourth song of the set."

All three singles from *Street Language* tanked, and Rodney's career didn't advance a millimeter. Meanwhile, Rosanne hit No. 1 four additional times, and was being treated like royalty, as Nashville's hip young queen.

Oh, they'd say, and her husband is a great writer and producer. Maybe you've heard of him?

Sometimes it's diamonds

The Columbia Records office was across the parking lot from MCA Records, where Tony Brown was staff-producing one great, and successful, album after another. One afternoon in late 1987, Rodney Crowell tapped on his old buddy's window.

Brown: "He asked me 'Hey, why don't you produce one on me? Let's cut some hits.' And when he came and started playing me things, he was so fired up. He was in a good space at that point. I was so excited, I was levitating. Which I guess, probably, inspired him."

Practically overnight, Crowell had experienced an epiphany. "Harlan Howard and I had written a song called 'Somewhere Tonight,' that that group Highway 101 recorded," he says. "It was the kinda Bakersfield-sounding thing, and I really liked it. I'm talking to myself: 'I have a natural feel for that stuff. I really like that stuff.'

"And about that time, Steve Earle came along and made *Guitar Town*, and I liked the kind of directness. I wrote 'I Couldn't Leave You If I Tried' and 'After All This Time,' and Guy and I had that old song 'She's Crazy For Leaving,' and at that time the songs, and where I was, and what was grabbin' my attention and holding up a mirror, that's the music I wanted to make.

"I don't think I made that music to grab the brass ring, but it did. I think my motivation for doing it was artistic, as opposed to material."

Tony Brown had produced *Guitar Town*, and he was a musical compadre, so why the hell not? Together, they recorded, mixed and mastered *Diamonds & Dirt* in four weeks.

"We went in the studio, and I guess it was the only record he ever made that fast and didn't second-guess it," Brown remembers. "He did the vocals quick. He just flew through it. "Because Rodney will sit and second-guess. He's the kind of guy that when the record has been out a year, he wants to re-cut Side Two one more time."

There was no master plan, nobody saw it coming, but *Diamonds & Dirt* proved to be the record that broke Rodney Crowell. Broke him wide open. "Tony Brown and I got on the same page," he recalls, "and I said 'I want to make a real cool country-sounding record.' And it worked."

He had steadfastly refused to make a straight-ahead country record for so long, when he finally did it, it was as if the country music audience had been waiting for him all along. The hunger had built up and reached a fever pitch. He was an overnight sensation, in gestation for 10 years.

With its shuffling honky-tonk sound, *Diamonds & Dirt* was a natural for the period, when artists like Dwight Yoakam and Randy Travis were putting more traditional sounds back on the radio. And Rodney knew that kind of music inside, out and all kinds of ways backwards. For some fans, however, the album was a disappointment. After the passionate eclecticism of Crowell's earlier records, it sounded like an overtly commercial appeal to the radio.

"But it didn't sound contrived," says Brown. "I think it just sounded like real accessible Rodney Crowell. Everybody had sort of made him a left-of-center act for sure. When I played it for people who knew Rodney, their first response wasn't 'What a commercial record,' their first response was 'God, Rodney sounds great.'"

Brown has nothing but compliments for Crowell's abilities. "I really hadn't come into my own," says the man who would later become Nashville's most successful producer. "For Rodney to ask me ... he was one of my mentors. A lot of my production things I copied from him and (Jimmy) Bowen. I took Bowen's ability to organize himself, and to say there's no one you shouldn't hire. Fly 'em in.

"And I took Rodney's way of looking at the creative process. I studied that. So they were my mentors."

Between January and October 1988, Rodney Crowell had five consecutive chart-topping singles. First out of the chute was "It's Such a Small World," a duet with Rosanne Cash.

They'd avoided recording a duet for years, mostly because that was what everyone in country music, conservative or contemporary, did eventually. "I remember saying 'Nah, we're not going to try to capitalize on that,'" says Crowell. "Whatever made the change happen, I don't know. But as I look back on it, it was natural casting. I coulda got Emmy to do it, maybe. But we were both on the same label."

"It's Such a Small World," ironically, was the most pop-sounding track on *Diamonds & Dirt*; still, the duet with his famous spouse served as a proper introduction to country radio, which didn't know Rodney's voice at all.

Afterwards, in rapid succession, came "I Couldn't Leave You If I Tried," "She's Crazy For Leavin'" (the original, produced by Rodney, was on Clark's *The South Coast of Texas*), "After All This Time" (eventual winner of the Best Country Song Grammy) and a cover of Harlan Howard's "Above and Beyond" (a honky-tonkin' hit for Buck Owens in 1960).

Suddenly, it was Rodney Crowell this, and Rodney Crowell that. He was in print, he was on TV, he was on the radio every time you punched a button.

Success should have been sweet. Predictably, perhaps, it wasn't.

"I was too busy trying to keep up, to do what was coming as a result of it," Crowell says. "It really brought in a tough time for me, actually. That was when that marriage started to go down the drain."

Says Susanna Clark: "When he got hot, he was physically unavailable, but it seemed like psychologically he needed you more."

The fall of '89 brought *Keys to the Highway*, which should have been a blockbuster followup. "Well, I got a little more miserable," Crowell reflects. "After I did *Diamonds & Dirt*, I really wanted to break out. I kind of like what I tried to do with *Keys to the Highway*, but that to me was just a little too much a following ... I think that record was more trying to stay in the marketplace than *Diamonds & Dirt* was. I think *Diamonds & Dirt* was just making a record because I felt like it. And then after I made it, I kind of had to do a follow-up. And I'm not too good at follow-ups. And I wasn't too happy about where I was."

Again, Tony Brown co-produced. "With *Keys to the Highway*, he and Rosanne had just started going through some problems," he remembers. "And face it, if you go through any artist's career, in any genre, and you see a little cycle of where there's a dip, nine times out of 10 there's something in their lives that's personal that's interfering.

"His father passed away. A lot of things happened. I remember when we were in the studio and had just finished recording 'Things I Wish I'd Said,' he just broke down in front of the entire band. It was a really emotional moment."

"Things I Wish I'd Said," written as a tribute to J.W., barely charted at all. "Many a Long & Lonesome Highway," another one with poignant lyrics about his father's passing, went to No. 3.

Even the album cover was downbeat; unlike the happy-go-lucky Rodney Crowell who strolled toward the camera on *Diamonds & Dirt*, the guy on the front of *Keys to the Highway* looked grim. There wasn't a single picture of his million-dollar smile anywhere on the package.

The uptempo "If Looks Could Kill" reached No. 6.

Things carried on, for all intents and purposes, like nothing had changed. Daughter Carrie was born in 1989; Rosanne, who preferred not to tour, stayed home in Nashville while Rodney worked the road with his Dixie Pearls Band, virtually for two years straight, massaging his newfound celebrity. "That just didn't sit well at home," says Rodney. "It wasn't a good time.

"I had all those No. 1 records in a row, and two of them from *Keys to the Highway* were Top Five, and boy, it just didn't do anything for me. I was actually more miserable. That was the most miserable time in my life.

"Rosanne's perspective on this would be her own, and I wouldn't project ... I always felt that I was more supportive of her than she was of me. If you ask her, in fairness, she might say 'No, I was more supportive of him.' But I stayed."

Rosanne moved out of the Nashville house in 1990. She went to Connecticut, and then to New York City, where she's lived since her divorce from Rodney became official in mid-1991.

When Roseanne wrote: "I wonder where you are/Do I exist for you?/If that pain that never quits/Ever gets you too?" her husband finished the song: "I see my past just like a mask I wore/I hardly know how to be myself anymore."

"The thing about Rosanne and I, we just kinda wrote about our experience," says Crowell. "I was writing about my experience - it wasn't all about her, or answering to her, it certainly had a lot to do with her because she'd been a big part of my life.

"I'll say this: Her impact on my life was very positive. I see it as very positive and not negative. She's the mother of my children, and I don't have anything bad to say about her." His marital postscript was 1992's *Life is Messy*.

A sometimes brilliant, sometimes painfully honest collection of songs, it brought to mind John Lennon's classic *Plastic Ono Band* album: Maybe it was a little too personal in places, but there's a lot to be said for the naked emotion in the grooves.

Like Rosanne's *Interiors, Life is Messy* quickly became known as Rodney's "divorce" album. And even though it sent the single "Lovin' All Night" into the Top Ten, it was not a critical or commercial success. This was just four years after the career-making juggernaut that was *Diamonds & Dirt.*

"Here's what I think about *Life is Messy*, having the benefit of hindsight," he says. "If I could take parts of *Street Language,* and parts of *Life is Messy*, I could make one really good record. For me. To me, I have some of the same feelings about them both: There's some really high moments for me, as a recording artist, and some parts that just fall really flat for me.

"I hedged the bet a little bit by putting in 'Lovin' All Night,' 'It Don't Get Better Than This' and 'The Answer is Yes.' I could have made a whole album of darkness. Looking back on it now, I should've made a completely dark record. Who would care? It would sell a lot of records and I could look back and say 'Boy, I made 10 songs that were just committed to that pathos.'"

Despite Crowell's commitment to promoting *Life is Messy* with more TV appearances than usual, and with another concert tour (which found him mixing his ultra-personal new songs with such cheery and familiar fare as "I Couldn't Leave You If I Tried" and "She's Crazy For Leaving"), the album marked the end of his brief but productive relationship with Columbia Records.

He gave it his all, but quickly found he needed his all back.

"Everything was taking a downturn, it looked like then," he remembers. "I look at it now and I go, 'ah, you just hit a rough patch. Toughen up, dude.'"

Rosanne's departure had left a hole in his life, and a hole in the way he got things done. Upheaval was the order of the day.

"I made *Life is Messy,* and Donny Ienner at Sony, up in New York, said 'Come up here and be our Don Henley.' Those were his exact words. And I went 'Awwww … I don't want to be somebody's somebody,' and I just quit: Fuck it, I'm going home."

Coming back

He spent about two years (between 1992 and '94) looking after daughters Caitlin and Chelsea. "I went home and became a single parent, and I spent two years single parenting. Eventually came back out with *Let the Picture Paint Itself,* but there was a period there where my kids needed me more than music did. I was a little overwhelmed at that time, because I had some responsibilities that were outside of chasing fame and fortune."

He'd always considered himself a good father, despite his frequent absenteeism. During the *Diamonds & Dirt* days, the glory days, he sometimes chartered a tour bus just for him and the girls, while the Dixie Pearls band traveled separately.

But now, with the career in a ditch, he went home to Nashville, actually telling a group of journalists -only half in jest - that he was retiring from the music business. "I had to improve my skills in other areas," he says. "I had to get tougher. It was easy for me to be a good-time dad, but I had a teenage daughter I had to start getting tough with."

In '92 Rodney received a call from film director Peter Bogdonovich, who was putting *together The Thing Called Love*, a fictional movie set in the very real Bluebird Cafe, Nashville's plain-jane listening room, where singing/songwriting stars are made overnight.

"He called me to retain me as a consultant," Crowell says. "That didn't take much of my life. I kept telling him to make the River Phoenix character a cross between Dylan in *Don't Look Back*, and Waylon. I took River over to my house and showed him *Don't Look Back*. He'd never seen it, and it blew him away."

Instead, the Phoenix character, James Wright, comes across as a surly and only marginally talented performer - more a testament to Phoenix's own palpable arrogance and increased drug intake (*The Thing Called Love* was the last movie to be released during his lifetime) than to Rodney's songs-for-hire. Altogether, three Crowell originals were included in the film, performed by Phoenix: "Standing on a Rock," "Until Now" and "Lost Highway." The latter was Rodney's favorite, and the only one he didn't record and release himself, with his own vocal track.

Crowell's versions of "Until Now" and "Standing on a Rock" were included on Giant Records' *The Thing Called Love* soundtrack album; he re-recorded "Standing on a Rock" for his Columbia *Greatest Hits* package, because he felt the movie version "just didn't get it."

River Phoenix, then 21 years old, had been writing music of his own for half a decade; he had his own band, Aleka's Attic, in the Florida town where he spent his non-movie time. As a writer and singer, he was heavily influenced by bands such as XTC, R.E.M. and Elvis Costello & the Attractions.

The actor had offered to create songs especially for *The Thing Called Love*.

"They couldn't use the songs River was writing," Crowell recalls. "But I really liked 'em. They were out there. I couldn't sing you a note of 'em, but it was like, 'Wow. That's coming from another planet.'

"I guess if he would've organized it, put it together, he would have had himself a real out-there alternative thing."

Phoenix checked into the Gram Parsons Heavenly Hall of Fame in October 1993. By *then The Thing Called Love* had crashed and burned in movie theaters, and Rodney Crowell was looking at the other side of his serious, stay-at-home single dad period.

He cut several new songs for *Greatest Hits*, including his 15-year-old "Even Cowgirls Get the Blues," and a new one, "Talking to a Stranger," that recalled the Everly Brothers (Emmylou Harris, Vince Gill and Mary Chapin Carpenter helped out with harmony vocals on the new material). He took a month in '92 to produce the debut album for Lari White, who'd been a Dixie Pearls backup singer.

When 1994 dawned, Tony Brown was president of MCA Nashville, and his production had given Reba McEntire, George Strait, Wynonna, Vince Gill and just about every other MCA artist that golden touch. He was the hottest thing going, and he was quite naturally permitted to sign whoever he damned well pleased.

So Tony Brown added Rodney Crowell to the MCA Records roster. "I think he's such an important artist in this town," Brown says. "I really think he's been responsible for a lot of things that happen in this town, the way people write songs, the way they cut records … and I felt like if we did *Diamonds & Dirt* once, we could do it again at MCA."

Let the Picture Paint Itself (1994) repeated the *Diamonds & Dirt* formula: A lot of uptempo, bouncy, hook-laden honky-tonk songs balanced by a couple of pensive ballads ("Stuff That Works," a killer lyric co-written with Guy Clark, was the song that got him started after his "retirement") slicked over with Brown's sharp, shoe-black production, radio-ready and good on the jukebox, too.

But Garth Brooks and his generic Wal-Mart country music was well into its trail ride to the national consciousness. "Young Country" had become the pop music of the '90s, and literate, smart, musicianly guys like Rodney Crowell had no place in that rodeo ring. *Let the Picture Paint Itself* was stillborn. With all the Marks, Tys and Tracys out there, the public - which had turned over several times since the *Diamonds & Dirt* days - said 'Rodney Who?'

"Hindsight on MCA: It looked really good on paper," Crowell says, "with my old friend Tony there, and my cousin Larry in the A&R Department, but it was going backwards in a lot of ways.

"Some of it was a step forwards, and some was a step backwards. Truthfully, MCA gave me a lot of money - basically, the deal was to go back and do *Diamonds & Dirt*. A contemporary version of that. I tried to be a good guy, and honor the deal, but it just wasn't right. I don't blame that on Tony, or even on myself."

With the title song, "Let the Picture Paint Itself," released as a single, "I was trying to make a hit record for country radio, and that's the only time I ever did that."

When the album tanked, says Tony Brown, "I wasn't disappointed, I was pissed off. Once again, they had painted him like a left-of-center. I was pissed off at our label, and at myself for not having the ability to make it happen.

"I think in Rodney's mind, and in a lot of people's minds, they think because I sit in this chair that I have a magic wand. And I don't."

By that point, Brown says, "I started to feel intimidated by Rodney the producer. It's easy to feel like a second-class person around certain producers to this day, when I'm around a Don Was, or a Hugh Padgham, or Rodney. I'll probably never get over it, but it's probably the thing that drives me to make better records."

The second MCA album, 1995's *Jewel of the South*, jumped stylistically all over the map (although Crowell believes "Please Remember Me," the set's big ballad, was a "bona fide hit single" that MCA simply couldn't make happen).

With *Jewel*, Tony Brown's heart wasn't in it any more. "I told him hey, just do what you want," Brown says. "He had artistic freedom. And then he basically just went underground again."

The life I have found

Whether he "went underground" by design or because his diminishing returns made it necessary, Crowell won't say. But after the failure of *Jewel of the South* (which is, ironically, a stronger record than *Let the Picture Paint Itself*) he asked for, and was given, a release from his MCA contract, which had called for three albums.

He'd finally climbed the hill, only to find he was over it. "Success is determined by a lot of different things, in my mind," Brown says. "You can have a record that's a piece of shit, but it makes a lot of money and you're successful, or you have a record that has critical acclaim but doesn't sell that much.

"If it's got serious critical acclaim, you can make a living. People will come out and see you. There are a lot of artists in our business who don't really sell a lot of records who make a real good living playing live."

And that, in a way, is where Rodney Crowell went in 1996. After producing for his good friend Beth Nielsen Chapman (*Sand and Water*), he called together three of his closest musician friends - bassist Michael Rhodes, drummer Vince Santoro and guitarist Steuart Smith - and recorded an album under the name *The Cicadas* (that's a locust-like insect, one variety of which gestates in the ground for something like 13 years before coming out to croak from the treetops).

Warner Brothers Records released *The Cicadas* in the early weeks of 1997. Although Crowell wrote or co-wrote all the songs, and co-produced the album with guitarist Smith, it's actually drummer Santoro who takes most of the lead vocals.

The album is very eclectic, mixing Beatle-esque pop sounds with Everly Brothers harmonies and the infrequent country-sounding guitar lick or vocalization. It swings and it bounces, but there ain't no twang.

The Rodney Crowell of *Diamonds & Dirt* is, literally, nowhere to be found on *The Cicadas*. "It was the way to re-invent," Crowell explains, "and the way to use that glaring self-consciousness that comes with 'solo singer/songwriter.' I wanted to re-invent what I was doing in a way where I could eliminate all that 'You should' business.

"Joining a band, making a record as a band and collaborating on that level really removed that stuff. I enjoyed it in the best kind of way. It wasn't like I was making a Rodney Crowell record, and I had to go get a haircut, or go get my shirts cleaned. I didn't have to do all that shit."

Besides, he laughs, "It's like Michael Rhodes said, it's cooler being in a gang than being by yourself."

For a single, Warner Brothers released to radio "We Want Everything," which Rodney wrote - all in one sitting - as a reaction to the suicide of an old friend, New Orleans folksinger Harlan White. He and Santoro sing the song's verses in unison, an octave apart, in the style of Squeeze's Chris Difford and Glenn Tilbrook.

The Cicadas also covered the classic "Tobacco Road," Rodney's "Nobody's Gonna Tear My Playhouse Down" (which had originally been cut as the B-side to one of the *Life is Messy* singles), the Crowell/Clark collaboration "Our Little Town," and a song Rodney co-wrote with former Tom Petty & the Heartbreakers drummer Stan Lynch, "Through With the Past."

Indeed, Crowell seemed to be saying he was through with it, once and for all. "The re-invention is not so much for image as it is for creativity," he explains. "I haven't done much to re-invent an image, I'm just trying to re-invent the work techniques and the message, so that I don't go into the studio trying to make 'Young Country' records. That's not where I am. I'm more mature than that."

He says he's committed to the Cicadas for as long as it takes - but, one thing's for sure, nothing will be heard from Rodney Crowell, solo artist, for a good while. "It doesn't concern me at all," he says. "I don't have any desire for that."

As for *The Cicadas*, "Warner Brothers is very supportive in that they realize it would be easier to market the record as 'Rodney Crowell,' but then it'd just be the same old shit, you know? I want to move on." He's producing albums for his cousin, singer Brady Seals, and for vocalist Claudia Church, his girlfriend of five years, whom he met on the set of the "Lovin' All Night" video.

The blonde and blue-eyed Church, a former model, is also a writer and a painter, "a real Renaissance woman," Crowell gushes. "I love Claudia. Claudia's great. We're gonna get married. She's the coolest woman that's ever come into my life."

He says producing records for other artists, and singing on still more (including the Hackberry Ramblers and Chip Taylor), is all the "career chasing" he needs right now. "I'm helping other people to realize that goal for themselves. It just ain't mine anymore."

He contributed a fine rendition of Elvis' "All Shook Up" to the charity album *Blue Suede Sneakers* in 1994, and the recent *Jim Croce: Nashville Tribute* included a Crowell interpretation of the Croce classic "Operator." For the *Stone Country* compilation, he turned in a sizzling "Jumpin' Jack Flash."

He figures he's finally got a handle on things. "Where I sit today, I'm a happy man, with the way everything has happened, good and bad. Most of the mistakes, failures or flops or whatever, they were all learning experiences. Equally as valuable as the success stories.

"So with all of that taken into account, I'm blessed. Like I can make a cup of tea and go 'God, I'm going into the studio,' or 'I'm going to write,' and I love it. I love my work. That's the only thing that I have to judge it by. I actually love my work more than ever."

Addendum: Things I wish I'd said

"Songwriting," offers Rodney Crowell, "is the art. Permit me to wax, but I think of myself as an artist. My life is an artist's life. Making records is just hanging your paintings up at the show. The best work that I've done as an artist has been in the area of songwriting - and probably songs that I've never recorded, songs that are still in the bag."

Sometimes, the song won't let you sleep. Sometimes it comes after you. "To the point of tapping you on the shoulder and saying 'Go somewhere and tune everybody out and get this."

Other times it's just a matter of throwing open your arms and giving in to the muse: Turn off your mind, relax and float downstream.

"I think those songs exist in their whole state, somewhere other than where we are right now, consciously," Rodney says. "I'm talking about the area of the unconscious, the Thoreau area. The collective unconscious.

"I believe that the really good songs exist out there already written, in their purest form, word for word, melody and words perfectly matched up. And I think my job is to bring it through to this side. And how well I succeed at that really varies. Sometimes I bring the first half of the song in, and then have to construct the second half. And sometimes the whole things comes in, whammo. And I say gee, I sure am glad I do this.

"And then sometimes it's like hammering nails from the start. And sometimes that shit I made up is not a bad song."

Here are Rodney's comments on a few of his most famous pieces, art or otherwise:

'Til I Gain Control Again: Don't remember writing it. I know I wrote it, back in Nashville in the early days. A real mythical experience with that song, and I still perform it.

Song For the Life: First song I ever wrote that I kept. My first keeper. I wrote it when I was very young, and it was writing into the future about maturing. When it was finally a hit record, a couple of summers ago, I had lived to the age that I was writing about. That was something I enjoyed.

Ain't Living Long Like This: I like that song. That's a good piece of writing. Every word of it's true, although my father didn't die in a stock car! I'm glad I wrote it; I think that's a classic country rock song.

Voila, An American Dream: That was shortly after 'Song For the Life.' Maybe the second or third keeper. It's just a poor kid, livin' on $100 a week in Nashville, who wishes he could go somewhere. The only way to travel is through imagination.

Leaving Louisiana in the Broad Daylight: Wrote that one night during a break in a session; we were recording Mary Kay Place. That's where 'Mary' came from. She was an Oklahoma girl who liked to string phrases together. Mary and I hooked right up. We would get together and just be glib, just talk and run stuff together. We started it during a break, and I woke up the next morning and finished it.

On a Real Good Night: Early song. 'Sleeper wherever I fall' is a good line; the song to me today is a little self-conscious. But at the time I liked it a lot.

Anybody's Darling (Anything But Mine): Some songs are unfinished, to me. 'You're Supposed to Be Feeling Good' is sorta unfinished, and 'Anybody's Darling' is unfinished to me. As is 'Shame on the Moon.' They're real kind of impressionistic, subconscious first. Some of those songs don't come all the way home for me.

Even Cowgirls Get the Blues: Well, I was reading the Tom Robbins book. I was on the road with Emmy, and she was so much like the character in the book, in a lot of ways. I actually wrote that for her. Oddly enough, it was about Emmy and Susanna Clark. I had the two of 'em to write it toward.

Stars on the Water: I don't think it's a great song, but it was inspired writing at the time. Because I was buying all these books on impressionist painting, and reading everything I could. Gaining knowledge about all of their work, and using, in the process of writing, how they blurred reality a little bit. In order for it to give you an impression, as opposed to a focus. That, to me, was what stars on the water were: If Monet lived in Mobile, what he would see on those nights when the lights were reflecting on the water.

Shame on the Moon: Big song, big hit. Well known and shit, I still wish I could figure out the last verse. I just didn't get it. Mac Davis insulted me once. He said 'Man, you shoulda had me around when you were writing that last verse.'

Ballad of Fast Eddie: Peter Sheridan got killed on his motorcycle. He came to me in a dream, he was sitting there on the other side of this river. He was telling me 'I have something I want you to do,' and I wrote it the next day, on the plane to Hawaii. Emory Gordy and I put the music together. You'd ask him 'Peter, where are you from?' And he'd say 'A little place called Lonely, man.'

It's Such a Small World: I went to see this play called *Nine*, with Raul Julia. It's a play about Fellini, the Italian film director. And I was totally gassed by the dialogue. I was sitting in the second row. I said 'I want to try my hand at writing a song that's dialogue.' And that's what happened, it was sort of an exercise for me, based on being inspired by that play.

I Couldn't Leave You If I Tried: OK song. As country songs go, pretty good. It's just a nice shuffle, I'm not too attached to it. It's not really about anything I've ever lived.

If Looks Could Kill: Oh, that was real. That was coming from real shit. I like that song better than 'I Couldn't Leave You If I Tried.'

She's Crazy For Leavin': Guy had that song when we were going to make one of his records. That was mostly Guy's writing - I didn't do much on that song, and I got rewarded for it real well. Probably, Guy got screwed on it.

After All This Time: I started writing it late '70s, when I was hanging around Willie a lot. It was just so Willie influenced: (Singing) 'There were trains ... and we outrun 'em.' And then I lost it, or just forgot about it. Moved to Nashville and had an office. I was opening boxes just to see what was in there, and I found this notebook. I opened it, I remembered the melody, and I sat there right on top of those boxes and wrote the rest of the song. And that was why I called it 'After All This Time.'

Many a Long & Lonesome Highway: Will Jennings and I wrote that. Most of the songs that Will and I wrote together are his melodies and my lyrics. So that was Will's melody - he had that chorus, too. I just wrote the rest of it.

Things I Wish I'd Said: I sat with my father for four days in the hospital while he died. And he really died in my arms. It was really a great experience. When we got him buried, and I got my Mom settled, I went home and I wrote that in 20 minutes. That's a good piece of writing, I think.

Alone But Not Alone: I started that song in Westport, Connecticut. That's where Rosanne lived when she split. I booked passage to Albequerque. I went to Albequerque and rented a convertible and drove around. I went up to where Georgia O'Keeffe lived and painted. I spent about 10 days out there in New Mexico, just by myself. From there, I went to L.A. and hooked up with Larry Klein, and he helped me finish it off.

I Hardly Know How to Be Myself: I came home and the first two verses were sitting on my desk. I don't know if it was a plot, or whatever. But I sat down, I looked at it and I just wrote the rest of the song. I thought 'God, this is great. I hope nothin's going on.' Rosanne came in and I said 'What about this? I don't know if you had a melody, but I've written it.' She said 'I don't even remember that.' It's like both perspectives work - two opposites looking at an issue. Either side you look at it from, each individual's point of view works. It's pretty much the same point of view.

Life is Messy: I was sitting at the piano with one of those little recorders, and I just sang for 45 minutes. A bunch of crap, and I just kept playing it over and over and screaming out 'life is messy.' It was sorta like one of those John Lennon primal scream things. And everything that was on the song, I'd screamed into that little tape recorder. 'Life is Messy' doesn't hold up for me. I think 'life is messy' is a great line, and I know what I was driving at, but …

Let the Picture Paint Itself: We may have dressed it up a little too 'cute country,' but I can strip that song down and just play it on a guitar, and what it says is important. For me.

Still Learning How to Fly: It's the other death song. Maybe some of my best songs are for people who died. 'Things I Wish I'd Said,' 'Ballad of Fast Eddie,' 'We Want Everything.' 'Learning How to Fly' was Ernest Chapman, a friend of mine who had cancer. So I got real involved with his death process, because he was trying to put up a good fight as a legacy for his son. While at the same time, he knew he was leaving. So the song is about the dignity of that fight.

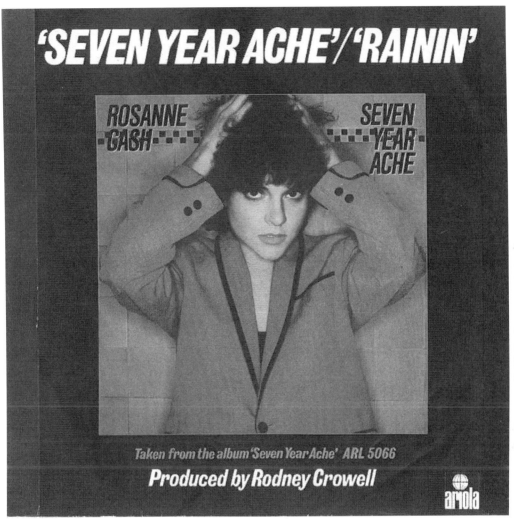

Ariola Records

15. Rosanne Cash
Love Hurts

Original 1997 introduction as published in Goldmine:

The daughter of Johnny Cash and Vivian Liberto, Rosanne grew up in Southern California, and when she met Rodney Crowell they were both in their '20s and hot to get going on something good. With her wonderfully pliant voice and his ear for a good song, they started making records that married every style that felt right. In 1979, they married each other because it felt right. Gut feeling counted for a lot in those days.

Starting with Seven Year Ache, *her third Crowell-produced album, Rosanne found her audience, and between 1981 and '89 she scored 11 No. 1 singles on Billboard's country chart, all but one of them produced by her husband (that was 1985's "I Don't Know Why You Don't Want Me," which they wrote together). After their 1992 divorce, Rosanne moved to New York City, where she lives today with her second husband, writer/producer John Leventhal, and daughters Caitlin and Carrie - both, like her great recordings, collaborations with Rodney Crowell.*

We all know there's a wonderful synergistic thing that can happen with one artist and one producer, where everything clicks. Was it that way with you and Rodney?

From the first record. I think in retrospect we got in less conflict than would have been assumed. We were really young, we didn't know that much about making records, and we kind of learned together. And we had our personal relationship; it would've been really easy for it to just detonate.

But it didn't. I think the work we did together was a kind of stored energy in our relationship, and it was always good, even when everything else was shit. I always knew work was a safe place for us to be, even if we were struggling or having conflicts. It never got polluted.

Is it true that (CBS Records president) Rick Blackburn had to be talked into letting Rodney produce Right or Wrong, *your first album for the label?*

Oh yeah. Not only that, on the second album, we had to talk them into releasing 'Seven Year Ache' as a single. We were swimming upstream in a lot of ways. We didn't have a lot of conscious knowledge. We were still just letting whatever came out, come out. Except for the song 'Seven Year Ache,' I remember we worked a very, very long time on that. We recorded the entire thing and ended up stripping it back down to the bass - not the drums, the bass. And we re-recorded the whole song from the bass up.

'Seven Year Ache' was your first No. 1. How did you write that song?

There is a famous story where we got in this fight, and he left me outside of a restaurant on Ventura Boulevard. But the real inspiration came for me because Rickie Lee Jones' first album came out, and I was so moved by it, and so inspired, I thought 'There's never been a country song about street life, about life on the streets.' So I started writing it, a very long poem, four pages, and then I turned it into a song.

How did you choose the cover material for those first albums?

We were both songwriters, and both passionate about great songwriters. And that's what we drew from. We were pretty snobbish about material, so we'd go to our own wells, like Keith Sykes songs.

I assume you got first dibs on Rodney's songs.

Yeah, it was great. I didn't realize how great it was at the time. It was a blessing.

Wasn't it awkward to be married to the producer?

We fought in the studio, definitely, but it was always a really positive arena. Rodney really loved my voice, and he took great pains to get it recorded correctly. It just made me feel so good about myself that he cared that much about my voice, and it gave me a tremendous amount of confidence. He loved me as an artist, and of course I revered him as a writer. It's just something really, really positive we gave to each other.

I would sulk sometimes, or we would go into separate rooms. I remember throwing the headphones down.

Those early singles scaled the country charts, but they were very much pop records. Did you consider yourself a country artist, or were you just making the best records you could make?

I was just making the best records I could make. Because Nashville signed me, it didn't make me a country artist, as far as I was concerned. Because, you know, I got my definition of country music really, really young. And I didn't fit it. Out of respect, I wouldn't have called myself a country artist! I loved Loretta Lynn and Patsy Cline, but I knew that's not what I was doing.

People think that we really pushed the boundaries, and we opened doors for people, and we started this thing. In a way we did, but it wasn't conscious that that's what we were doing. We were just bringing our hybrid influences to record-making.

It was purely collaborative. So much of that was due to Rodney. There were things I would've never chosen to do on my own that Rodney, with his very eclectic passions, wanted to work out through me. I would have never done 'Tennessee Flat Top Box,' or 'My Baby Thinks He's a Train.' Or 'I Wonder.' But I was happy to do it. Truthfully, a lot of my energy was caught up in mothering, and Rodney felt stronger about things than I did at certain times.

There's a book out now, **Three Chords and the Truth***, that talks about Rodney's bitterness and jealousy when your records were successful, and his weren't.*

But he was producing Number One records! He was pretty damn successful.

He was really frustrated, and he said 'I want a chance to do what you've done as an artist.' And it kind of scared me, because I thought 'Well, that means he's going to go out on the road … and that's my big alarm bell.'

Why?

Well, put two and two together. My dad was on the road for my entire life. It was pretty scary.

But **Three Chords and the Truth** *paints Rodney as a bitter man, an unpleasant guy at that time.*

No. He had his frustrations, and resentments came up at certain times, but no, he wasn't bitter. I would never use bitter to describe Rodney under any terms.

Rodney hit in 1988, and suddenly he was The Thing. Was that pretty much the beginning of the end?

Yep. It was. I can't say how much of it was like your fears coming true, that if we spent that much time apart that it was gonna break us up. That had something to do with it, I'm sure, but the main reason I think Rodney and I completed our work together, both personally and professionally, is that it was done. It was done. We couldn't do anything more with each other.

We had reached a point of diminishing returns; we had done such great work together, on both levels, that we both had the grace to know when to quit. That's how I look at it.

Were the Interiors songs about your relationship?

The nature of writing, I think, is when you lose any sense of time and place, and all parts of your present. Part of it was about me and Rodney, but I was so shocked when everybody started saying 'Oh, it's a divorce record.' I couldn't believe it, because I wasn't there in my life yet. It was really appalling to me.

The story about 'I Hardly Know How to Be Myself' is that you'd left the first verse on a desk, and Rodney came home, worried about what you'd written, and then finished it off. Did you leave it there for him to see?

Not consciously. We both worked up in the same room, and I was really in a lot of pain about him being gone so much. So I started writing this thing. And I thought it was beautiful that he finished it. I love that song.

Isn't the great irony that Rodney wanted success as an artist, but when he finally got it, the cost was enormous?

I wouldn't frame it like that, because it makes me seem like a martyr, in a way. And besides, it's not that simple. It's far more complex. Like I said before, we had completed with each other.

There's nothing left undone with Rodney. I talk to Rodney every other day, and there's nothing left undone. Mostly we talk about the kids. I value what he gave to me so, so much. I would never be the artist that I am if it hadn't been for Rodney.

Photo by Bill DeYoung

16. Merle Haggard
Pride in what I am

Man, was he a great storyteller. We spent hours on the phone in 1999, and I was overcome with how relaxed, and charming, and funny he was. He'd never met me before and had no reason to be so forthcoming (we did meet shortly after the story came out in Goldmine *magazine, and that's when I took this photograph).*
The story is mostly Haggard talking – with a lot less narrative interruption from me – because who was going to tell the story better than him? I also spoke with Willie Nelson, Asleep at the Wheel's Ray Benson, and Hag's right-hand man and woman Fuzzy and Bonnie. I love this one.

They say that all the events in your life contribute to who you are. Joy, sorrow, love and loss are part of the fabric of every living person. To turn those emotions inside out, paint them in different colors and hand them back to society, is the gift of the artist. The artist knows the four corners of the soul, and whether or not he's afraid to visit them is irrelevant because visit them he must – the artist is compelled to share the journey, to tell people what it's like inside his own dark recesses.

In some ways, the country music artist has the toughest job. To create a country song, like a TV jingle for mass consumption, is easy – the hard part is coming up with a line, an image or a musical reality that won't slip away, because it speaks to something deep inside the listener. And when the songwriter has himself walked the walk, and talked the talk, it seems like so much more than a nice melody and a clever turn of phrase.

Merle Haggard has managed to turn his thoughts, beliefs and experiences into songs – hit songs – for more than 30 years. Restless, stubborn and plagued by self-doubts, his journey has not always been an easy one, and many times he's been sidelined by his own frailties both emotional and physical. His track record is not perfect.

It is, however, astonishing. Haggard released 38 No. 1 singles between 1966 and 1987, nearly all of them self-penned, and they echo the dreams and journal the anguish of the working man, the branded man, the wounded lover, the patriot and the poet. He is all of them.

For Merle Haggard, it's never been about stardom, although he's certainly had his share. It was never about conforming to someone else's vision of what a singer/songwriter should be, especially in country music, where the roots run underground all over America.

"I guess I didn't do my homework," Haggard shrugs. "Had I known more about quote-unquote country music, maybe I'd've went to Nashville. But country music wasn't centered in Nashville in my mind. Never was.

"I grew up in Oildale, California, and the only thing that connected me with Nashville, Tennessee was WSM and the Grand Ole Opry that came on once every week, on Saturday nights. We got an hour of it – I didn't know that the show went on all evening. But we'd listen to Roy Acuff and Red Foley and those people back then, my Dad and I at 7:30. But every night of the week, and every day of the week, several times during the day, we had Bob Wills & the Texas Playboys.

"I grew up as a small kid loving Bob Wills and Bing Crosby and Frank Sinatra, and there was this hillbilly show that came from Nashville on Saturday night. I liked that too. But I didn't hear any singers on there that I wanted to sing like. Bing Crosby had probably the best voice at the time of anybody I'd heard."

Merle Ronald Haggard was born April 6, 1937, the third child and second son of Okie immigrants who went west to seek a better life, away from the Dustbowl poverty that choked the life out of so many back home. James and Flossie Haggard settled in Oildale, a nondescript suburb of Bakersfield in Southern California, and Merle's father found work with the Santa Fe Railroad. The family lived, not dirt-poor but on the lower end of the middle-class spectrum, in an abandoned refrigerator boxcar that Merle's father converted into a cozy house at 1303 Yosemete Drive. Mother planted flowers in the front yard.

"My family was a musical family," Haggard says. "They didn't concentrate on one particular type of music. They liked mainly gospel music; they were a religious family and all that, but they were into the popular music of the day and they bought records of that type. I heard 'Rhapsody in Blue' and all the classical stuff."

Among the mainstream country crooners of the '50s were Eddy Arnold, Jim Reeves and Tennessee Ernie Ford. Young Merle was partial to the nasal honky-tonker Lefty Frizzell. "The thing that made me like Lefty more than Tennessee Ernie, was Tennessee Ernie sounded refined," Haggard recalls. "He sounded like a very good singer. My mother would've said 'Tennessee Ernie has a much better voice than Lefty Frizzell.' I was pretty sure that most people probably agreed with her. 'Cause a lot of people would say well, Lefty sounds like he's singing from his nose. And I'd say I don't give a shit if it's comin' out his ass, it sounds good to me.

"When I was a kid, and there was Eddy Arnold and Bing Crosby, Tennessee Ernie Ford and all those great singers, my mother listened to all that. Well, she bought an album of Hank Williams. An album in those days was like four 78s. With eight songs. It included 'They'll Never Take Your Love From Me,' "I Can't Help It,' 'Lovesick Blues,' 'Never Again Will You Knock At My Door' and a couple of other ones – 'A House Without Love is Not a Home.' And I actually learned to play the guitar, I think, open chords, with Hank Williams and Bob Wills music. I had 78 records of Bob Wills, 78 records of Hank Williams, and I learned all those songs."

Merle's father died when the boy was 9; with no discipline to speak of, his adolescent years were full of increasingly serious run-ins with the law. He ran away from home and rode the rails, hanging out with hoboes, getting drunk and stealing cars. He spent months at a time in juvenile facilities, and by the time he staggered out of public school for good he had a serious criminal record. No one, except maybe his mother, thought Merle Haggard would ever amount to anything.

Always, though, there was music. "Many was the time I've wondered if I could've written songs better had I listened to my English teacher and learned all those things," Haggard says. "They try to teach you a description of what you're saying. They've got a name for the line I'm using right now. And I never have found any use for it yet. I couldn't understand the use for it then. It's like the stack on top of the stack of the stack, it just kept on making no sense to me."

He put together his first song at age 12. "I was actually writing earlier than that," he says. "I was unable to put it into a song until I learned a few chords on the guitar. Eleven or 12 was the years I learned to play a few chords on there, and until then I couldn't really structure it and call it a song.

"Even in my third or fourth grade classes in school, in my report cards – I look at 'em now and I know what it was – they said 'He's looking out the window. He does real good in school when he pays attention, but he's always looking out the window.' Well, I was trying to write songs. I was bored with what they were doing, and I would turn around and pay attention just close enough to get a passing grade.

"I never got good grades, I always got just passing grades. Because I was busy. I wanted to write songs as long as I can remember anything."

But a serious lack of self-confidence meant Haggard the hoodlum was dominant, and musically Merle was more or less content to play guitar and sing Hank Williams, Lefty Frizzell and George Jones songs with his drinking buddies up on Bakersfield's Beer Can Hill.

In December of 1957, Haggard was 20 years old, married with two small children, and living the life of a petty criminal – his family, he says, had all but given up on him.

On Christmas Eve, he and a buddy broke into a beanery on Highway 99, prying off the back door with a crowbar. Unfortunately, the would-be thieves were so drunk they hadn't noticed that the place was still open – it was not yet 11 p.m. – and the local sheriff easily rounded them up.

For this, Haggard would do nearly three years of a five-year sentence in San Quentin, one of the toughest penal institutions in the country.

Finally, the fear of God himself was in him. After San Quentin, there could be nowhere else to go but up. "I'm not sure at what period I felt safe from the life I'd been caught up in," he recalls. "I got out of prison in 1960. The percentage points of a man staying out, at the time, were very low. Something like less than two percent of all the prisoners who go to the joint ever recovered as a citizen, become a full-fledged American citizen. Well, I've always been one who wanted to prove the odds wrong. I've always been that way.

"Well, when I went out of the joint they said 'We'll see you in a few days.' Guys that I knew in there were the only friends I had. There's a weird part about being in prison that a lot of people don't talk about, and you can always find out if a man's telling you the truth by just asking him a few things about his first few days out. First of all, you've built a life inside there, and all the friends you have are there. Your meals are taken care of, and you have a place to sleep.

"All of a sudden, you walk out of this place, and you're 21 years old, you got paper shoes on and a bad pair of pants that don't fit, and a coat, and $15. And that echoes in your ears as you walk away from that prison: 'We'll see you in a few days.'

"They're pre-programming you. People didn't talk about things like that in the 1960s." He didn't know what he was going to do; dig ditches alongside his brother, he supposed. But no way was he going back to B&E work. "I walked out of there, and first of all I was pretty disappointed – my wife wasn't there. She was supposed to meet me, and she wasn't there. It broke what was left of my goddamned heart. I stood around there and kept waiting for her to show up. And one of the damn guards said 'Hey, what's going on! You want back in?'

"Well, the ride never did come, and there was a voice came to me, sort of around behind my back. I turned around and there was a lady sittin' there saying 'Would you like a ride over to San Francisco?'"

Haggard thought the lady in the car, whom he figured was about 35 or 40, looked like the actress Joanne Woodward. "She told me 'My family would be very upset if they knew where I was at – I'm a lady who has everything, I have a family, my husband's wealthy, and this is sort of the way I pay back.'

"She said 'I come over here every Tuesday and I wait for the guys who don't have a ride.' I said 'Well … That's kinda dangerous, innit?' And she said 'I've never had anybody show any signs of wanting to harm me or anything.' I said 'Somewhere, you'll get a big bonus in your life.'"

In the spring of 1999, Haggard received a fax from this woman, who explained that she was, at that time in 1960, the wife of San Quentin's warden. "Had he known I was picking up convicts and carrying them to San Francisco," she explained in her note, "he'd have had a conniption fit."

Brother Lowell picked Merle up at the bus station in Bakersfield. Soon Merle and his hotheaded wife, Leona, were trying to make it work, and Merle was digging ditches and wiring houses for Lowell's contracting company. In the evenings, he sat on the living room sofa and played his guitar. He could do a pretty good imitation of two of his heroes, Jimmie Rodgers and ol' Lefty.

Bakersfield in the early '60s, partly because of its large population of expatriate Okies who'd come to work in the oilfields, had developed into a center for west coast country music. The hardscrabble honky tonk music favored in the dancerooms and lounges was raw and urgent, and millions of miles away from the mannered "Nashville Sound" that was coming out of Tennessee.

Bakersfield had its own stars to go along with its own sound. Buck Owens was the biggest, with his pleading whine of a voice and the crackerjack dance rhythms of his Buckaroos.

Everyone in Kern County, and all over the San Joaquin Valley and into Los Angeles, watched Cousin Herb Henson's *Trading Post Show* on TV five days a week, just before the evening news came on. The Trading Post Gang included many of the area's top musicians, including guitarists Tommy Collins and Roy Nichols, singers Ferlin Husky and Dallas Frazier, steel guitarist Charles "Fuzzy" Owen and Owen's cousin, vocalist Lewis Talley. Buck Owens' former wife, Bonnie, was a regular, too.

"I was a viewer," remembers Merle Haggard. "I was this kid that came out of the joint. I was 22, I guess, and I'd been home maybe three weeks." One afternoon, he was home alone, enjoying the *Trading Post* show. "And a guy walked up and knocked on my door, a skinny guy, and he said 'Is your name Merle Haggard?' Hell, I thought it was the goddam law or something. I said yeah, I'm Merle Haggard. He said I hear you're a guitar player and a singer, and a frontman.

"I said where the hell'd you hear that?

"He said my name's Jack Collier. We got a band, and our frontman and guitar man quit. We got a little gig down here at a place called the High Pockets …

"And I never did ask him where he heard about me. I don't know who in the hell he heard that from.

"He said let me hear you sing something. Well, here's two guys standing in front of the front room of a little old house, never seen each other before … my wife was gone, again … and he asks me to sing something.

"I had a wire recorder; we didn't have tapes yet. I said I just made a little ol' recording here …I'll play you what I just did, right before you got here. I played him that, and he listened to it all the way through and he looked at me and he said that ain't you, that's Lefty Frizzell." Collier admired Haggard's Merle Travis-style picking and single-string lead work, and soon the young ex-con was making $10 a night working four nights each week with the High Pockets house band. Added to his ditch-digging wage, he felt he was doing alright. What he was, was reformed. He was scared to death of going back to prison.

"It wasn't long before I was working the top joints in town, and working with the best guys," Haggard recalls. He got on the radio, and eventually on the *Trading Post* TV program. "I was working eight shifts a week, and five days a week we did this 45-minute television show. So within 10 months of the time I was released from prison, I was doing all that."

As a parolee, though, he still couldn't drive, and technically he wasn't supposed to be in bars at all. He had to get special permission from his parole officer to perform.

Lewis Talley was the richest man Haggard had ever met. Talley owned a restaurant in Bakersfield, and ran a Saturday night dance in Fresno, and most importantly he had his own record label, Tally Records (today, no one seems to remember why the "e" was dropped). When Haggard was 17, he'd brought his homemade demos to Tally's studio; although he was politely rejected, Haggard was impressed with Louie and his cousin Fuzzy, who'd encouraged him by telling him to quit trying to imitate Lefty Frizzell.

Now that he was a semi-professional, he renewed their acquaintance.

Fuzzy had recorded a couple of vocal duets with his girlfriend, Bonnie Owens, on Tally, and eventually came to run the label itself for his cousin. Owen produced the first Merle Haggard single, "Skid Row," in 1961, with one of his own compositions on the B-side. The single (Tally 152) didn't do much outside of Kern County, and Owen told Haggard he would record him again once the right song came along, or if he was to write one.

Haggard: "One of my first big breaks was fixin' to happen to me. I'd been in Bakersfield about a year. It was a Saturday night. My friend Dean Holloway came by the Lucky Spot, which I was fixin' to get on the stage and work five hours, it was about 8:30 and you worked from 9 to 2.

"He said I'm fixing to go over to Vegas and see Roy Nichols, Wynn Stewart, Ralph Mooney and all them guys, and Red Simpson, who was a piano player and singer, a friend of mine, was standing on the sidewalk and said 'Why don't you go on, I'll work the gig for you here?' And we went inside and checked it out, and they said OK, go ahead.

"So we went over there – it's only a five-hour drive from Bakersfield to Vegas – and we got there probably about midnight. I walked in the front door of the Nashville Nevada club and Roy Nichols spied me the second I walked in. He just went to wavin' and almost throwin' his guitar at me, a double-necked Mosrite. He had a big ol' bird painted on the back of it. Where Ernest Tubb had "Thanks," he had a big ol' fuckin' bird.

"I went up there and he said 'Hey, take this son of a bitch, play it for a minute and let me go to the bathroom.' Hell, I couldn't say anything, I had to take it.

"It was like a guy being thrown into the New York Yankees, and they say hey, pitch one. I looked around, and here's Yogi Berra, and all the greats. These guys were recording artists. I just looked from one to the other, and Ralph said 'Can you sing?' I said yeah, I believe I can sing something, let's do 'Cigarette and Coffee Blues.' I never asked him if he knew it, and before I had it out of my mouth, man, he had it kicked off. And I was into it.

"We did three songs. The third song was 'Devil Woman,' a Marty Robbins song that you won't hear too many guys singing because it's got a high note in there that will embarrass you if you can't hit.

"I was doing that song, and in the middle of the dance floor I looked and here was Wynn Stewart, standing looking at me with his arms crossed, and his head kind of cocked over to one side. And a funny look on his face.

"Well, I said we're going to take a short intermission and I got out of that deal. The curtain closes on a half-moon bandstand, and from the side of the curtain Wynn Stewart comes on. The first thing he says to me was 'I've been all over America looking for somebody to replace my bass player. I walk in my own joint, and the guy's standing on the stage, singing. Where in the hell are you from and what's your name?

"I told him, and I told him I'd been working over in Bakersfield – of course, he knew all the guys over there that I knew – and he asked me what I was making over there. I said well, about 125 a week, somethin' like that. And he said I'll double that if you'll come play bass.

"I said shit, I don't know how to play bass; I'm just a guitar player and singer, man, I can't do that. Not with this band. And he said yeah, you can, this band'll teach you how to play that fuckin' bass. And it went on from there."

After about six months as Stewart's bass player, during which time he had moved Leona and the kids to Nevada, Haggard found the song he was looking for. Stewart had written a weepy ballad called "Sing a Sad Song," with a caught-in-the-throat octave jump, and everyone in the band knew it was a hit in the making. Stewart, who'd had a half dozen Top 40 hits, was planning on making it his next single.

But Merle Haggard had other ideas. "We were standing in that same spot where he hired me, and I said to him these words: Hey Wynn, tell me something. If you had it within your power to make me a star, would you do it? And his mouth just dropped open, and he said well, sure I would.

"I said well, you can. Let me have 'Sing Me a Sad Song.' And he said, you got me. It's yours.

"So I went directly to the phone. I called Fuzzy over at the Lucky Spot and I said Fozzo, we got the song."

Released as Tally 155 near the end of 1963, "Sing a Sad Song" reached Number 19 on the national *Billboard* chart. Over the next 13 months, Haggard would cut three more singles for Tally, all of them charting (one, "Just Between the Two of Us," was a duet with Bonnie Owens) and in the spring of 1965, Capitol Records' Ken Nelson bought out Haggard's Tally contract.

"(My Friends Are Gonna Be) Strangers" became the title song of Haggard's first album, on Capitol. The album included most of the Tally masters, which Nelson had acquired as part of the deal with Lewis Talley and Fuzzy Owen.

"Ernest Tubb mentions me on a live album, *On the Road With Ernest Tubb*, in 1965," Haggard says. "He said I want to mention a fellow that has a song out called 'My Friends Are Gonna Be Strangers.' He said I made a prediction when I heard Hank Williams that he was gonna be a star. And I made a prediction that Little Jimmy Dickens was gonna be a star. And I'll make a prediction that Merle Haggard's going to be a big country music star."

A branded man

"You're only as good as your repertoire," Haggard says. "If you're a storyteller, you gotta know a lot of stories. And if you're a singer, you gotta know a lot of songs."

His first Capitol albums included one or two mainstream country songs, and the Tally stuff, and some from Haggard's Bakersfield buddies like Fuzzy Owen, Dallas Frazier and Tommy Collins. "Swinging Doors," his second single for the label, was a Haggard original.

"I told Fuzzy I think I've written a good song for Buck Owens," recalls Haggard. "I took it down and at the time I had just signed with Buck Owens' publishing company, with hopes that he would record my music 'cause he was the Number One act in America at the time. Well, he didn't do that. I went and sang him 'Swinging Doors' and he said he liked it and everything, but he didn't do any handsprings, or backflips or anything. I didn't really pay much attention to him saying that, so I went and recorded it myself.

"Buck tells it a lot different. He says I came in and played it for him to get his opinion, and I ran down to the studio and recorded it the next day. Not so – I waited for a period of time to see if he was gonna cut it. And he didn't cut it, so I went and recorded it. Fuzzy said 'That's probably your first big record.'" It reached No. 5 in April 1966.

"Swinging Doors" was followed by "The Bottle Let Me Down," and then, in the last month of 1966, Haggard hit the top spot for the first time. The song, "The Fugitive," was written by Liz Anderson, who had provided Haggard with "(My Friends Are Gonna Be) Strangers." Anderson also wrote "Just Between the Two of Us," a duet with Bonnie, who had become the second Mrs. Merle Haggard in June.

Inspired by the TV program *The Fugitive*, Anderson's song was about a man running from the law, running from his past. Later re-titled "I'm a Lonesome Fugitive," it became Haggard's first signature song, and the blueprint for some of his best and most personal work. (Once he was on Capitol, Haggard's touring band was summarily dubbed the Strangers. Bonnie sang harmony; Haggard's old crony Roy Nichols was on lead guitar.)

"The very first time I heard him, I thought he was so insecure," says Bonnie Owens today. "He didn't sing insecure, but he was insecure in his personality, actions and everything. He wasn't very patient with anything."

On top of that, he was an ex-con, a fact he felt was probably tattooed somewhere on his forehead. Haggard thought people were staring at him.

"The first couple of years of recording and doing shows and everything like that were kind of hard for him," Owens remembers. "I'd notice a certain mood, and he'd say I can't seem to shake the feeling that there's gonna be somebody in the third row sayin' Hey! 745200!, or whatever his number was. He said I don't know if I'll be able to handle it if it happened.

"That was when we were playing nightclubs. And when we did finally get into playing auditoriums, that's when he began to panic a little bit. And he decided just to come out with it, and write about it."

Somewhere between 1966 and '67, Merle Haggard's prison record became public knowledge. Far from killing his career, it became the cornerstone of his lifelong mystique. "Fuzzy told him the very best thing you can do is get it out there," Owens says, "so nobody can say you're trying to hide anything."

Liberated from his secret, Haggard followed "The Fugitive" with a self-penned song navigating the same waters of paranoia, "Branded Man." It reached No. 1 in July, 1967, the first in a string of 40 consecutive Top Ten singles.

Although he continued to record other people's compositions, in the mid '60s Merle Haggard began to blossom as a songwriter, and whatever he tapped within himself – sometimes it was blue, sometimes bleak and sometimes just sweetly melancholy – it somehow connected with blue-collar America, in a way that no other country singer had before. He was real, and listeners could hear it in every line of his songs, which never seemed contrived or calculated for radio or jukebox play.

"It seemed like every time I liked a song, I noticed that the same guy's name was written real small down underneath the big name," Haggard points out. "And I put it together, and I said you know, I think he sings this song better because he wrote it. It didn't take a genius to figure out that a man could play a part in a film a lot better if he was playing his own part. Than he would quit trying to learn and project and interpret the story from somebody else's mind.

"I realized that, real young on, and I thought boy, there's two or three things I need to do. And one of them's write a song."

Although "The Merle Haggard Show" was on the road almost constantly, Merle and Bonnie made their actual home in Bakersfield. Haggard continued to drive the streets he'd roamed as a boy, to patronize the same local businesses, to fish his beloved Kern River. His mother stayed in the area, too.

As a songwriter, he began to focus inward. He wrote "Mama Tried," about his youthful restlessness and his shame at spending his 21st birthday in prison; he wrote "Hungry Eyes," about the Okie labor camps his aunt and uncle had lived in when they'd first moved to California; he wrote "I Take a Lot of Pride in What I Am," about an uneducated man standing tall. "Some of those songs are the wails of a man in pain," he says, "because of the lack of the childhood that I would have liked to have had."

Haggard began to demonstrate a sensitivity that only his closest friends knew existed. Some of his best songs from the '67-'69 era, like "I Can't Hold Myself in Line" and "I'm Looking For My Mind," are the work of a man who's comfortable exposing his soul to the outside world. "Sing Me Back Home" was a heartbreaking prison ballad, and Haggard would use it as the title of his first autobiography in 1981.

He continued to wear his heart on his sleeve. A 1968 single, "The Legend of Bonnie And Clyde," was the result of nothing more than Haggard's infatuation with Faye Dunaway in the *Bonnie and Clyde* movie.

For his *The Legend of Bonnie and Clyde* album cover, he even re-created the famous photograph of Bonnie and Clyde posed against a 1930s roadster, grinning with their machine guns. More than one journalist had already pointed out Haggard's resemblance to Warren Beatty – both were dark and handsome, with wavy hair and smoldering eyes.

Haggard's appeal was equal between male and female fans. To the men, he was rugged and no-nonsense, the kind of guy who said what was on his mind and did what was right. And he didn't have the shiny suits and perfect, poufy hair of most big-time country singers.

Women saw Haggard as thoroughly masculine, but not afraid to let his softer side show. There was clearly something thoughtful going on behind his eyes.

For a while, everything Haggard did was a smash.

"You can't imagine," he says. "From about 1963, the wheels started to turn a little faster. And things just began to happen. I could barely keep up with it. In fact, I'll leave something out if I tell about it. There were so many great things that began to happen. And if you don't believe in the old man upstairs, you got to be some kind of a fuckin' idiot.

"These things were thrown at me – the right moments, the right people, the gift of writing. I didn't write any hit songs until I got ready for 'em. I wonder if that's accidental? You know, 'Workin' Man Blues' came along just when I needed it. The whole thing is like somebody mapped out a script, and if it wasn't documented I don't think anybody'd believe me."

"Workin' Man Blues" (July '69) was the first of Haggard's "Everyman" songs, and would lead him into darker, more controversial territory. It's the story of a regular, beer-swilling joe who would like to "throw my bills out the window" and "catch a train to another town" but, hell, he's got to stay and work to keep his family fed.

Every country music fan in America could relate to one of the taglines in "Workin' Man Blues"; even better, Roy Nichols' snarling lead guitar made the record bristle and snap out of a jukebox speaker. Haggard had found the nerve, and it fell to him to touch it whenever he had a mind to.

"He was so much fun when he was writing, because he was so intense with it," Owens explains. "All I had to do was write it down for him. He'd come over and look at it. When he finally asks what do you think, then you can say what you think. But you don't want to say anything, because eventually he comes around and gets it anyway.

"I didn't want to offer any lines of any kind, because I didn't want to throw him off when he might be seeing it in a different way."

Because they were always working, Haggard did most of his writing on the tour bus. "I wish I'd-a put a mileage meter on my ass about that time," he laughs, "because it'd be interesting to know how many there would be."

"In those years, it seemed like we had a mental telepathy," offers Owens. "I just wrote down almost everything he'd ever say. Sometimes it turned up in his songs.

"I'd be in the back of the bus, writing or listening to tapes or something, and he would be up in the front. And I'd say I'll bet he wants to work on 'Shelly's Winter Love.' We'd meet in the middle of the bus, and he'd say 'Do you have the words to what we were workin' on the other day, 'Shelly's Winter Love'? That happened lots and lots of times."

Owens is modest about the part she played in Haggard's golden songwriting age. "I'm not gonna pat myself on the back, but I know a lot of songs he would have forgotten if I hadn't written 'em down," she says. "Because it doesn't stay with him to the finish. He has to get away from 'em, and think about 'em, and come back to 'em."

In 1969, in the middle of his red-hot streak, Haggard turned in an album that Capitol, where they were used to giving Haggard his way, had reservations about issuing. *Same Train, A Different Time* was a two-record package of songs written and popularized by "America's Singing Brakeman," Jimmie Rodgers, sung in the original, circa 1930s style.

Rodgers, like Lefty Frizzell and Bob Wills, was a boyhood hero of Haggard's; one of the favorite albums at the old homestead in Oildale had been Lefty's own Rodgers salute, *The Songs of Jimmie Rodgers* (1951).

Haggard: "When he did his tribute to Jimmie Rodgers, my mother heard it. I said mother, listen to Lefty's new record. And she said no, no, that's a Jimmie Rodgers song. I said who's Jimmie Rodgers? I'm sitting there 14, 15 years old and never heard Jimmie Rodgers. "My life changed, of course, when I heard that."

Haggard says no one at Capitol ever came right out and said *Same Train* was going to be a hard sell. "I don't think they'd have let me do that if I hadn't been highly successful. You know, the Beatles was in rein at that time … there were artists all over the world being shook off the label like peaches off a tree. We could name artists for 30 minutes that dropped in the period when the Beatles came in.

"Well, here I came, in contrast to everybody else, right up through the middle of Beatlemania, on Capitol, on the same label, with these damn songs that just wouldn't lay there. The people wanted 'em."

Much of the credit for giving Haggard full creative run of the studio must go to producer Ken Nelson, who signed him back in '65 and produced nearly everything he cut for the label. "Ken Nelson was another milestone in my career," Haggard believes. "He could've been another way. Had he been another way, then he could've been the block in the road that kept me from being myself. He could've been one of those 'producers' from Nashville and you'd've never heard Merle Haggard.

"But I can't say enough good about Ken Nelson in relation to my career and to my friendship with him. He had the knowledge and the sense to let me be myself. All he'd do was just make sure we was in tune. He'd let me pick the musicians, he was so kind to me.

"In those days, singin' was so easy for me. We'd go out there in this great place, this wonderful studio where Nat 'King' Cole and Frank Sinatra and Dean Martin all recorded. Man, you think I didn't know that? Studio A at Capitol Records is still the greatest studio in the entire world. At the time, they had a physical echo chamber no one could match.

"I'd find myself in this moment in time, and it was like my brain would stop and take a picture of it. Looky here: I'm standing here with Glen Campbell singing harmony, and James Burton's playing guitar, Roy Nichols and Ralph Mooney on guitar, this great band all around me and the best equipment in the world."

With Nelson in the producer's chair, Fuzzy Owen was the man at mixdown time. He was – and still is today – one of the few people with Haggard's absolute trust. "He would stay on the mic in there and say hey, you sounded like Hank Williams, you sounded like Lefty Frizzell, you sounded like Marty Robbins, how 'bout doing me one track Merle Haggard?" recalls Haggard.

"And I'd say I don't know quite what you meant. He'd say try it again and just sing the song. Think about the words; don't think about who you could sing like. So he said the right things to me, and so did Ken. Ken would say 'A joy to behold! Come in and listen!'"

On the other side of the musical fence, psychedelic rock 'n' roll had given way to a stripped-down, rootsier sound. The same members of the younger generation who grooved to the rural acoustic music of *John Wesley Harding* and *Music From Big Pink* had discovered Merle Haggard, who was about as far away from slick, sappy Nashville as he could get. On purpose. Just as America's young people were digging the *Pride in What I Am* and *Same Train* albums, Haggard took a hard turn to the right. Nobody saw it coming. Not even Merle himself.

He was on the tour bus, as always, rolling through the heartland from one gig to another, when a sign for Muskogee, Oklahoma caught his eye. In no time, with a lyrical assist from Strangers drummer Eddie Burris, Haggard had the song that would make his career, polarize his fans and cause a stink that's still wafting in the wind today.

The fightin' side

Once "Okie From Muskogee" hit the national consciousness in August, 1969, Merle Haggard's life would never be the same. On the surface, it's a right-wing, hippie-baiting celebration of American small-town life in the days before drugs, long hair and Roman sandals had screwed everything up ("leather boots are still in style for manly footwear," it said, addressing the latter issue).

When Merle Haggard sang "I'm proud to be an Okie from Muskogee," it seemed to conservative middle America like the Poet of the Common Man was pitching his tent right there, in Squaresville. To the young people who'd begun to discover Haggard through his adventurous recent albums, it sounded like he was telling them where to go.

In truth, it was all of neither, and a little bit of both.

"It came from the shoulder," Haggard reveals. "A lot of times, you contrive and you write. And that's an art that you develop. But 'Okee From Muskogee' came too quick; it was like a picture appearing on a paper. And the artist standing there and saying hey, where did that come from? It came in a matter of less than 10 minutes – seven or eight minutes, I wrote the thing down. And then read it back, and got up and sang it to a melody that's still there. There was no work, no honing of any sort.

"I sang it to Fuzzy – he was drivin' the bus at the time – and I said what do you think this sumbitch needs? He said it needs to be out. And this is the guy that always says 'Well, I don't know … that's pretty good but it's not a hit song.' When he said 'it needs to be out' I like to have fell out of the bus. This is old hard-nosed Fuzzy talking.

"See, I was coming from the point of view, once again, of my father. I was coming from their point of view, all of my family, the ones who had the religious orientation. The Arkansas/Oklahoma attitude that I'd grown up with, not necessarily agreeing with. But I thought boy, I don't necessarily agree with every word in this song, but this son of a bitch is a motherfucker! And it was.

"Over the years, I've had people tell me five or six different messages out of the song I didn't even know was there. One night Willie Nelson said to me, 'Are you tired of singing Okie From Muskogee?' I said, why? And he said 'Well, if you are, I'll take the son of a bitch for the next 30 years.'"

"Okie From Muskogee" hit the top of the chart in October 1969, stayed there for four weeks and became the best-known song, and best-selling single, of Haggard's career. In the spring, the Country Music Association named it Single of the Year.

Far from being irked at the media calling him The Paul Harvey of Country Music, Haggard took the attention as a compliment, and immediately started writing more conservative, line-drawing songs in the vein of "Okie From Muskogee."

"If you're a songwriter or if you're a pole vaulter, and you do something right, by accident, only a fool would vary far away from that which is working," he says. "In other words, we'd had 'Working Man Blues,' 'Hungry Eyes,' 'Mama Tried' and a few pretty nice songs that were autobiographical, but all of a sudden we had this 'Okee From Muskogee' which was controversial. Well, then all my years of songwriting went to work, don't you see. Because hey, first of all, I'm a songwriter. I said 'Hey … I have a following now. A political following. OK.

"The song was written in a way that didn't describe me. It made me mysterious. And the curiosity built up, and it's been there ever since. Of course, the next song was 'The Fightin' Side of Me.' There's one that was written off the cuff, but the moment I wrote it I knew it was the next followup. I wrote it comin' from L.A. to Bakersfield in a car. Lewis Talley was with me – and he said man, that's it, that's the next song."

("If you're runnin' down this country, man, you're walkin' on the fightin' side of me…")

The album *The Fightin' Side of Me* was released in early 1970. Done up in a red, white and blue cover, the album was recorded live in Philadelphia – "The Cradle of American Liberty!" Intentionally or otherwise, Haggard had re-created himself in the image of the blue-collar patriot, which the record company was only too happy to capitalize on.

One manifestation of Haggard's newfound, mainstream recognition was his invitation to appear on TV programs such as *The Ed Sullivan Show*. Haggard remembers Sullivan staging a salute to Rodgers and Hammerstein's *Oklahoma*:

"They had me casted for Curly, and Curly was just not me. And we didn't know about it until the sixth day of rehearsal, but I told them in the beginning it's by choice that I don't do choreography. It's not because I can't do it, I said it's because I choose not to. I don't want to do it, and don't expect it. If you don't expect it, I'll try to play this part for you. But it'll be different than it's ever been before. And they said OK.

"But every day they kept adding a dance step. I was in some sort of a promenade position with Minnie Pearl on one arm, and Jeannie C. Riley on the other arm, and we're dancing like idiots through this garden. And one of the gay fellas reached out and pinched me on the ass.

"Well, I'm not here to bash gays or anything, but when I went around Fuzzy was in the wings, and I said 'Fuzzy, this is the last trip around. Meet you at the bus!'

"So I went to the bus and I said hey, I'm not gonna do that. I think it's a big mistake. He said well, it's gonna be pretty serious here, they've got you contracted. And I said well, just let 'em do whatever they have to do.

"I said I got truck driver fans and old buddies that I sing songs for, that wouldn't have any idea why I did this. And I'm not going to explain it."

During this period – perhaps he was feeling invincible – Haggard put together a sprightly country tune about interracial love. Fuzzy Owen and Ken Nelson convinced Haggard that "Irma Jackson" was probably too much of a hot potato to pass to the public – maybe it would be pushing Haggard's luck, after "Okie" had caused such a stir. Although it was intended as a single, "Irma Jackson" was relegated to an album track.

"I've always admired black women," Haggard says. "They always were just as sexy to me as white women, for some reason or another. And I tried to imagine some young kid who had a father with a plantation, falling in love with some little black girl that he grew up loving all of his life. And trying to justify the reality of adulthood, and finding out that in America they were created less than the whites were. And I tried to put into a few lines how love could transcend the two races and bring us all together somehow, I guess."

Next, Haggard recruited several members of Bob Wills' original Texas Playboys to play alongside his own Strangers, on *A Tribute to the Best Damn Fiddle Player in the World, Or My Salute to Bob Wills*. Here Haggard re-created 12 of his favorite Western Swing tunes, like "Stay a Little Longer," "Roly Poly" and "Right or Wrong," faithfully to the original Wills style he'd loved since his childhood days in the San Joaquin Valley.

Haggard, whose father had played fiddle in a dance band back in Oklahoma, had been teaching himself to play, much to the general annoyance of Bonnie and everyone else on the tour bus. Nevertheless, he stepped up his rehearsals and tried to be ready in time for the recording dates.

Haggard had started sawing away on the instrument back in '65. "It was a disease," he says. "When I decided I wanted to do that, I knew it was a seven-year decision.

"I looked around, I'd been playin' five years and I was doing what I wanted to do. I was 33, and I said if I can be doing what I want to do by the time I'm 40, then I'll be in the driver's seat. Because I knew the power of that fiddle. Roy said you may not get anybody's attention throughout the entire show, but you pick up that damn fiddle, they might not like it but you're gonna get their attention."

Up in West Virginia, a bunch of hippie musicians calling themselves Asleep at the Wheel heard Haggard's Wills tribute, and it changed their lives.

"Everybody knew that there was this guy named Bob Wills that their parents liked, and maybe they even knew one of the songs," says Ray Benson, leader and frontman, then and now, of Asleep at the Wheel. "Really a superficial knowledge. But that record turned us on – George Strait tells the exact same story – because we were huge Merle Haggard fans.

"It was the pivotal moment for Asleep at the Wheel. That's the album we heard in 1970, and we went from doing just two Bob Wills tunes to doing every song on that album." Today, Asleep at the Wheel carries the torch for Wills' music, and it all began with Merle Haggard's album. In the '90s, Haggard would be a guest vocalist on both of the Wheel's own Texas Playboys tribute albums.

Paying tribute, whether directly or through involuntary impersonation, is a big part of the way country music works. "Every single country singer today," says Benson, "from George Strait on back, is from Merle Haggard. Who is from Lefty Frizzell. So that's the great link. Nowadays, you hear 10 guys in 10 hats, and they're all trying to sound like Haggard."

Immediately after *Best Damn Fiddle Player*, Haggard began to return to more conventional country music – for him, anyway. The hits kept on coming – early '70s chart-toppers included the autobiographical "Grandma Harp," the jukebox favorite "It's Not Love

(But It's Not Bad)" and the pop ballad "Carolyn" – but Haggard continue to confound his listeners as much as he delighted them.

He released a single, "Street Singer," that had virtually no singing – just the sound of Haggard cracking himself up while he picked lead guitar on a hillbilly raveup with the Strangers (nevertheless, it made the Top 10). "Jesus, Take a Hold" was followed soon after by *Land of Many Churches*, a double album of gospel and religious songs, recorded live in four different Appalachian houses of worship.

Although he had shied away from overtly political issues since the "Okie" furor of '69, Haggard again touched on a sensitive subject. "I Wonder If They Ever Think of Me," written from the viewpoint of an American soldier in a Vietnamese prison, was a No. 1 hit in the last month of '72.

"If We Make it Through December," perhaps the loveliest song he ever wrote, was inspired by an offhand comment from Roy Nichols, who always seemed to get divorced in the 12th month.

In "Daddy Frank (The Guitar Man)" (No. 1, 1971) Haggard sang in first-person about a family band fronted by a deaf mother and a blind stepfather. Haggard began conceiving the tale after hearing Bonnie talk about her own hearing-impaired mother.

Mostly, Haggard explains, "Daddy Frank" was "an attempt to write a song about the Maddox Brothers and Rose." The singing family of transplanted Okies, 10 in number, had been a popular dance act all over California in the '40s and '50s. Rose Maddox was a good friend of Merle and Bonnie's.

Haggard, of course, put his own spin on their story. "The only one in the Maddox family that was never mentioned, and never got any notoriety, was Dad. Dad rode a bicycle to work in the shipyards, during the war, and the Maddox Brothers and Rose were the hottest act on the west coast. They traveled in two Cadillacs, five in each one, and he rode a bicycle to work!" As usual, Haggard was drawn to the underdog.

"I thought what if he were blind, and a real good player. Then he'd be there with them, and he'd be the hero, rather than the guy that's ridin' the bicycle … and you can see where it went from there."

The live show continued to pack 'em in. Although he rarely spoke onstage – a product, he says, of his natural shyness – he was animated during the actual songs. A longtime audience favorite involved Haggard impersonations of Marty Robbins, Hank Snow, Johnny Cash and Buck Owens.

He had to be careful when performing his autobiographical songs, not to forget where he was and start thinking about the time and place described in the lyrics. "If you keep your mind focused on that thought, you'll fuck up," he laughs. "So what you have to do, when you're singing a song that's emotionally disturbing, you have to think about your income tax. Or you have to think about something else, because being emotional is not really something in your favor, it's a handicap."

Although his career was hotter than an Oklahoma firecracker, Haggard spent much of the '70s in personal turmoil. He and Bonnie separated and divorced in 1974, during which Merle developed a serious crush on Dolly Parton – he wrote "Always Wanting You," a No. 1 hit in early '75, for Dolly. A happily married woman, she declined to get involved with him. Eventually, Haggard took aspiring singer Leona Williams as his third wife, a relationship that would give him no small amount of heartache.

His prison experience continued to gnaw at him. In '72, California governor Ronald Reagan granted Merle Ronald Haggard a full and unconditional pardon – more of a public relations move than anything else – and Haggard and the Strangers performed at a White House function for Richard and Pat Nixon, who appeared to enjoy the concert (no one was really sure).

But the imagery in Haggard's songs continued to be haunted, scared, running. He was a millionaire recording star, a friend of the president's, but in his mind he remained a branded man, something less than everyone else.

Even today, Haggard can't completely forget what it was like inside the San Quentin walls. "It's very, very claustrophobic," he says. "It's like being smothered with a pillow. And I have recurring dreams, it's been 40 years and I have recurring dreams, sometimes as many as four or five times a month still yet. And I'm always there, and I'm always disappointed that I'm back in there, and that I've somehow fucked up again. There I am and I can't get out.

"I think maybe it's the involvement in this demanding, successful career that I have. I think psychologically I'm imprisoned. I have no choice, really. It would be impossible for me to retire from this business. And so it is, in fact, a prison in some way."

Misery and gin

When Haggard's tempestuous marriage to Leona Williams began in 1978, it was only the latest in a series of changes he insisted on. Feeling his creative juice stagnating, he left Capitol after 11 years and signed with Jimmy Bowen and MCA.

Saxophonist Don Markham became a Stranger in 1974, and Haggard persuaded the elderly ex-Texas Playboys Tiny Moore (mandolin and fiddle) and Eldon Shamblin (guitar) to join the band, too. They played with Hag for 12 years.

He made his peace with Bonnie, who came back to the touring band (along with Markham, she's still there today – Moore and Shamblin have both passed away).

Markham's saxophone became integral to the Strangers sound around the time of *I Love Dixie Blues*, an album Haggard cut in New Orleans in 1973. "If I didn't get to do that, I couldn't stand it," Haggard says. "I couldn't stand to just walk out there, play 'The Bottle Let Me Down' and leave. The performer, in order to get a good performance, has got to be enjoying himself, I think.

"The sax takes us away from this particular sort of music that we're categorized in, for a moment, and it seems to be accepted. I've never had one person say they didn't like it. Not one."

Haggard was on MCA for four years, and he landed some big hits there, including "I Think I'll Just Stay Here and Drink," "Red Bandana," "Rainbow Stew," "Misery and Gin" and "My Own Kind of Hat."

But most who were listening could tell the label switch hadn't revived him; although there were some nice moments, the MCA period wasn't much of an improvement. Haggard began the 1980s living, with several members of his band, on a houseboat he'd brought up to his property on Lake Shasta, in northern California. Leona left, and besides Haggard preferred to be alone with his buddies, and with copious amounts of liquor and cocaine. These were the binging years.

A switch to Epic produced some of his best material in a decade. His first single for the new label, "Big City," was a gentle shuffle, the kind he hated during the old days playing the Bakersfield bars. Nevertheless, it made the top of the charts in 1982, as did "Are the Good Times Really Over (I Wish a Buck Was Still Silver)," a gentle reprise of his pro-America material of the late '60s.

Haggard's voice had aged and mellowed, growing deeper and more resonant, and as he became an elder statesman in those days when *Urban Cowboy* was forcing all but the very best of the old guys off the radio, he commanded newfound respect.

A one-off pairing with George Jones produced *A Taste of Yesterday's Wine* in 1982; the next year, he was in the studio with Willie Nelson, whom Haggard had run into, off and on, on the touring circuit in the early days.

"I heard his records a long time before I met him," Nelson says. "I was touring when his first stuff came out, 'All My Friends Are Gonna Be Strangers,' back in that time. I think we played Vegas one time about the same time, but I really didn't get to know him until years later when we came together on a tour. We'd play poker and sing and play together."

In 1982, both Nelson and Haggard were veterans who knew what it was like to fight and do penance for something you believe in – in their cases, it was writing, recording and even living outside of Nashville.

"We come from different parts of the country, but we're both a long way from the store," Nelson observes. "Nashville was where we were all told we'd have to go sell our products. We had that in common."

Together with producer Chips Moman, they were halfway through a duet album in the summer of '82 when they agreed they still didn't have their key song. "We had run out of songs," says Nelson. "Merle had gone to bed, and we still hadn't done the song we thought should be the title song, the single, all that stuff.

"Lana, my daughter, went home and got a copy of Emmylou Harris' 'Pancho and Lefty' and brought it out to the studio. We sat there and listened to it. I went over and woke up Merle. He was over in the condo next to the studio – I sent somebody over, I wouldn't do it – and I got him back into the studio and we recorded 'Pancho and Lefty.' Merle was still about half asleep."

The following spring, "Pancho and Lefty," Van Zandt's mysteriously moving song about a pair of outlaws and the federalis who track them, became a monster hit.

Part of the allure of their version of the song was the setup – it's not really a duet. Nelson sings the first three verses, with Haggard taking his first and only solo on the fourth.

"I think it happened because I was giving him time to learn the song," laughs Nelson. "I did the whole song for a long time, and when he thought he was ready to come in I said 'We'll do the last verse.' It sounded real good that way; it made him like more of the character than a duet singer. It made him more Lefty."

"We discussed the fact that he was gonna be on the record more than I was," Haggard recalls. "It passes the point where you think a duet is going to occur. And that's what I liked about it. You think it's going to be Willie all the way – then the storyline takes a bend, and here's this new guy. After you quit looking for it, it hits you upside of the head."

The '80s had their ups and downs for Haggard. He and Nelson followed the *Pancho and Lefty* album with another, *Seashores of Old Mexico*, he and Leona divorced, an unsound business deal (he built a resort on Lake Shasta and lost his shirt) shook him.

He got off cocaine, married his maid Debbie Parret (the marriage, one both parties admit was more out of convenience than for love, didn't last long, and she still works for him today). At its apex, the Strangers included 12 musicians.

Always, there was the music. "Kern River," one of Haggard's most achingly beautiful autobiographical songs, was one of his last hits for Epic, in 1985.

Haggard: "One morning I woke up in a truck stop in Bakersfield, my hometown. We'd been asleep there for two days. Now, people who make a living in another way might not understand sleeping for two days. But we'd probably been up for five.

"And I woke up there, after two days of being in a bus sleeping. It was like four in the morning, just starting to see a little gleam of light over in the east. It was on a road that I used to take on the way to Kern River to fish. After playing a nightclub in Bakersfield all night, I'd stay in a little coffee shop and wait for daylight, and then I'd run up the canyon up there, get my exercise, go down there and fish till about 10 o'clock, then come home, go to bed, sleep till five in the afternoon and start all over again."

In 1985, looking through his bus window, Haggard starting thinking about the Kern. It begins on Mount Whitney, a high peak, and sends more than one million gallons per minute straight down for about two miles before evening out. "It's not deep nor wide, but it's a mean piece of water, my friend," the song says.

"I read about my little river in the *Chicago Tribune*, about how it was the fastest falling river in the United States ... I didn't know that," Haggard says. "And I wondered if I'd ever get to fish Kern River again. I thought about the sign posted at the edge of the canyon, that told the number that had been drowned. *Fishing* became *swimming* pretty quick ...."

("I may drown in still water, but I'll never swim Kern River again.")

Haggard got into a shouting match with Epic's president, Rick Blackburn, over this song. Blackburn thought it was counter-commercial in the days of Randy Travis and Clint Black. Haggard held firm and the record was released. Within three years, he was off the label. That wasn't the only factor. Nearly all the old guard – Haggard, Jones, Nelson, Johnny Cash – lost their place on American country radio in the late '80s. Never mind tradition, it was a video-centric business now, and guys with faces like Mount Rushmore just didn't make videos that sold records that got played on the radio.

A move to Curb Records produced a couple of good albums, but Haggard and label chief Mike Curb parted ways acrimoniously in 1996, without any hits to speak of.

He hasn't been on the radio, steadily, for a decade. The younger guys have taken over.

"Let me say this," he says. "I'm goddam glad they don't play me among that shit. And I'm sorry whose feelings get hurt. Dwight Yoakam and Garth Brooks and people like that, who everybody knows make good records, after you leave that, man, I don't want to be associated with that stuff that I'm hearing. I'm not built like those guys are, and I can't make videos like they do, because they won't be as sexy! But I'll tell you what, I'll match 'em on the stage anywhere in America. I don't care if they play me on the radio or not.

"If it never happened again, if they turned the lights out this minute, it's been the greatest trip in the world."

For the record

Not long after he started turning out one hit after another, Merle Haggard was approached by the Grand Ole Opry, the self-appointed holiday-table centerpiece of country music. At the time, the Opry was still based in Nashville's venerable old Ryman Auditorium, where all the greats had performed. The same people who'd fired Hank Williams and Johnny Cash both, told them they'd never amount to anything in country music, came to Haggard with an invitation.

"They had chosen Doyle Wilburn, one of the Wilburn Brothers, as their delegate," Haggard recalls. "And Doyle Wilburn called Fuzzy Owen, who was my personal manager and still is, and said 'It's time you come and join the Grand Ole Opry.' And Fuzzy laughed right in his face. He say hey, Merle Haggard don't need the Grand Ole Opry, the Grand Ole Opry needs Merle Haggard."

Haggard chuckles at the recollection. "I don't mean to put 'em down. If they were to ask me, I'd probably join. But at the time, it made me feel really good when I heard Fuzzy say that to them. He said to me, before that phone call, you got a chance to become someone that that whole town will know, if you stay out of there. You go down there, he said, and we'll get lost in the shuffle. Just like the rest of 'em."

Haggard did live in Nashville, for nearly two years at the start of his MCA period in the 70s, but he felt his skin starting to crawl, being that close to the music business, and he couldn't get back to California fast enough.

Along with Willie Nelson, he was inducted into the Country Music Hall of Fame in 1994.

Today, Haggard and his fifth wife, Theresa, live with their 9-year-old daughter and 6-year-old son on the Lake Shasta property, 500 miles north of his hometown. They have a cabin, a recording studio and the houseboat he used to party on. Haggard figures he'll build a house one of these days, but whatever the reason, he hasn't got around to it

"I've been all over the whole United States," he says. "I lived in Bakersfield for 35 years. The north part of this state is totally a different world from the southern part. There's no war of wills up here. The only problems we have up here is people cuttin' down the damn redwood trees."

Forest conservation has become an issue with Haggard, who's still fighting for what he believes in. He and Theresa are devout Christians, and this year he recorded a gospel album, *Cabin in the Hills*, and made it available through his website.

The '90s haven't been especially kind to him, but as the decade draws to a close, Haggard feels invigorated, full of the old piss and vinegar. After two operations on his heart, he's back to the only things he ever did full-time: fishing and playing concerts.

"I had a couple of deals happen two years in a row," he says of his bypass surgeries. "Not sure that I needed it. I think I may have been a victim of the fact that I fit the criteria of people they do surgery on. That happens about 60 percent of the time in America. If you happen to be a guy that can pay the bill, they'll find something wrong with you.

"One of 'em I think was necessary, and one of 'em I'm not sure about. How do you prove things like that?

"Hell, I might drop dead in 20 minutes, but I believe I'm OK."

He's in love, and content, and although he's cranky as ever, he claims he's no longer suffering from what he used to call white line fever. "When I was a child, I dreamed about traveling. Now I'm grown, and after I've lived 40 years on the road, I dream about never having to leave anywhere again."

Haggard's tenure as a Curb Records artist ended after the *1996* album in 1996. Because of his soured business deals in the '80s, Haggard was forced to file Chapter 11 bankruptcy, and to dig himself out he was persuaded – against his better judgment – to sell the publishing to nearly all of his songs.

He says he's never learned to do things halfway, and in the past it always got him into trouble. "If we go camping, before long we'll have a city built out there in the middle of the woods," he laughs. "We came to Shasta to go fishing and wound up owning two houseboats and building a resort. Made a total dilemma out of our playground."

A gambling addiction that reached its peak in the years just after "Muskogee" has played itself out; just as fortunately, cocaine and alcohol are things of the past, too.

In the '80s, Haggard earned a reputation for being nearly as unreliable as his pal George Jones. Sometimes he'd play a ragged set and stomp off the stage after 30 minutes, angry, leaving the Strangers holding the bag and the audience cursing his name.

Sometimes it was booze or drugs; more likely, it was his terrible mood swings. Especially during his years with Leona Williams, he was likely to explode if anyone happened to say the wrong thing at the wrong time. "I was very hyperactive," he says. "I never had to have any sort of stimulants or anything like that, because of my natural-born energy. And I like to about have drove everybody crazy, I'm sure. I stayed up one time and played fiddle for 48 hours.

"And I hired three or four bands, they were all on dope trying to stay with me. I can verify that."

At 62, he could quit. He thinks about it all the time. "With all honesty, I've become used to a certain quality of life," he confesses. "And I would be like a spouse if I was to suddenly be cut off from this sort of income. You know, money is necessary. You only have freedom in America if you have money to afford it. Otherwise, you wind up in jail. You wind up one of the statistics in the hospital or in the jail if you don't have money to remain free. And that's the truth.

"I have rich tastes, and I've developed even richer tastes. I have to make a lot of money, and also, I could lean back in a chair pretty easily and become an old man pretty quick – out of shape and unable to do anything – and you can't really come back at 62. You've got to maintain some sort of a level of performance or the muscles will give up on you and it'll be all over. So my life really depends on me going to work, I think."

He mulls over the possibilities – he could go into television, he says, or open a restaurant. Maybe start over with a brand-new band, calling it something other than Merle Haggard & the Strangers.

The idea of getting off the bus for good appeals to him enormously. "I've got to look up and see that I don't have any dates,' he says. "And no responsibilities. And then see what kind of a choice I make at that point. That's what I'm trying to get myself ready for, I guess.

"And I want to see if there's anything else Merle Haggard can possibly organize besides this out-of-control monster that's got a hold of me."

Wiki Commons

17. Stephen Stills
As I come of age

As time went on, and advertising fluctuated, Goldmine *began to reduce the number of pages it would allot for feature interviews. I conducted nearly five hours of interviews with Stephen Stills for this story, concurrent with that cutback, and so a story that should have come in at 12,000 words — I'd done one on Kenny Rogers at that length — was limited to a fraction of that.*

Stills, of course, is one of the great rock 'n' roll artists, and if anyone's career deserved the long look, it was his.

I was, however, dealing with the laws of commerce, as they applied to journalism (not for the last time, either). So I quit writing after I'd reached my allotted limit, 6,000 words. It appeared in 2000.

I'm proud of this one – Stills is gruff, honest and forthcoming – but it could have, and should have, been more than twice as long. And, naturally, the actual tapes have long since disappeared.

There exists a bootleg recording of Crosby, Stills & Nash's performance at the Big Sur Folk Festival in 1969 that perfectly illustrates the inherent differences between the three men.

Stills is tuning his guitar when a heckler begins haranguing the trio for "playing for money, man." Crosby and Nash engage the guy from the stage, trying to gently explain that they're on his side, they're doing the show for free.

Suddenly, the exchange is interrupted by loud cheers from the audience. "Stephen," Nash shouts, "if you push him in the pool, I'll never forgive you!"

Stills is in the crowd, in the heckler's face.

A gifted singer and songwriter and a brilliant guitarist, Stephen Stills has had a career with more ups and downs than the mountains of the moon. While he can be fiercely independent, his most lasting works have always been as a collaborator. His relentless perfectionism, confrontational spirit and mile-wide stubborn streak have caused him to be his own worst enemy at times; his talents have brought forth some of the most shimmering and beautiful music made in the rock 'n' roll arena.

That's the way it is with art.

For what it's worth, Stephen Arthur Stills was born in Dallas on Jan. 3, 1946. His father, William "Otie" Stills, was the kind of man who took on all kinds of work - selling, driving, building, fixing - and uprooted the family when he got bored, or went broke.

So Stephen spent his young years in Louisiana and Illinois, and his high school years in Florida, and graduated from a tony prep school in Costa Rica.

As part of the early '60s New York folk scene, Stills joined the Au Go Go Singers, a sort of poor man's New Christy Minstrels. They cut an album for Roulette in 1964.

Eventually, several of the Village folkies, including Stills and his 12-string buddy Peter Tork, relocated to Los Angeles, hoping to find some action. Stills recalled answering a "cattle call" ad in the fall of 1965, for a new television program called *The Monkees*.

"I didn't want to be in the TV show - even if they're trying to be hip, it's not gonna *be* hip," he said. "So I went to see the guy, and I'm kind of too cool for school, but I want to find out who's writing the songs. And they already had a deal with somebody.

"I said well, I'm not really interested in this, but I know somebody you would like, he's very, very charming and I'll send him up. I called Peter and I said 'Peter, you ought to go check this out. It could put you on the map, and even if it only lasts a couple of seasons you'll have a career.' Little did I know."

Contrary to legend, Stills wasn't "turned down" for *The Monkees* because he had bad teeth. He's always loved that story, though.

The same year, fate had introduced him to Neil Young. "The leftovers from the Go Go's formed a group called the Company," Stills said. "We got a little tour through these coffeehouses in Canada. And the first one was in Fort William, Ontario, which is now called Thunder Bay.

"On our second night, this kid comes in and wants to do a set in between our two shows. He was doing folk music on an electric guitar, a Gretsch."

The "kid" was writing his own songs - something Stills hadn't even tried yet - and his combination of musical intensity and off-the-wall humor convinced Stills and his fellow Company man Richie Furay they'd made an important new acquaintance.

At that time, Stills said, "Neil wanted to be Bob Dylan. I went back to New York City and worked it out with the Night Owl to get Neil a visa, and hire him for a gig.

"And I called Neil's mom, and she said 'He's broken up the band and he's living with some folksinger.' She was really vexed with him. She said 'I can't find him, Stephen, and I know that you've gone to all that trouble.'"

Non-plussed, Stills went back to Los Angeles and started plotting. "I called up Richie and I said 'OK, we're gonna get a band.' He came out, and it was me and him. Next, the gods intervened, and Neil Young is on Sunset Boulevard right in front of me." Young and bassist Bruce Palmer had driven west in Young's black hearse, looking for Stills. They found each other in traffic.

Buffalo Springfield had a turbulent but productive 18-month existence, bringing together folk, rock 'n' roll and country music. Stills and Furay's Everly-like harmonies, balanced by Young's dark tenor, drove the band into wonderfully unexplored places.

Stills came to life as a writer and guitarist in this period; his songs "Rock 'n' Roll Woman," "Bluebird," "Four Days Gone" and "Hung Upside Down" displayed a keen virtuosity, and the Springfield seemed poised for superstardom.

Despite two innovative and richly textured albums, however, the band only managed one hit single: Stills' protest anthem, "For What It's Worth." The world was just not interested.

"Bruce Palmer was the heart and soul of it," Stills recalled. "He was the glue. And he kept getting thrown out of the country. He would have a traffic accident and get busted and thrown out of the country. We had managers, and they were too fuckin' stupid to go get him an H-1 visa. Every time we'd start to get someplace, we'd have to fuckin' replace the bass player."

But Palmer's problems - usually drug-related - weren't the only forces working against Buffalo Springfield.

"Neil was afraid to be trapped in a group. We were about to do the Johnny Carson show, which would've kinda put us on the map, because we were a really good band. And Bruce was even back.

"Carson was taping in New York then. And the night before we were supposed to leave, Neil quit the band."

The mercurial Young returned, then left again and came back, and after the Springfield's spring '68 tour as support act for the Beach Boys, he bailed for good. "The inside story on that tour was Mike Love turning into this Svengali influence on Neil," Stills said. "It was weird. They were always off in a corner, whispering. And Mike Love is just a spooky character."

The band's third album, *Last Time Around*, was released posthumously.

"I wanted to get on with it," Stills said. "I had all these songs showing up, and I was getting a vision of the kind of thing I wanted to put together, at least for that period of time. And Neil had a different vision. And we weren't breaking through. We were one-hit wonders so far."

Stills spent 1968 jamming and making demos. He cut the *Super Session* album with Mike Bloomfield and Al Kooper; he turned down an offer to sing with Blood, Sweat & Tears.

Ex-Byrd David Crosby was one of his running buddies - "he always had the best pot" - and he was soon adding harmonies to Stills' new compositions. They sang together at parties.

Stills explained what happened next. "Mama Cass was the one who plotted and schemed the whole thing," he said. "She came to me outside the Troubadour one night. She said 'Do you think that you and David would like a third voice?' And I said, if it's the right thing. She said 'Just when David calls you and tells you to come over to my house, drop whatever you're doing and do it. That's all I'm going to tell you now.'

"Now, I had known Cass since New York. We used to stand out in front of the Night Owl and just crack wise about the passers-by and the musicians. We would entertain each other for hours. The funniest person in the entire universe.

"She said 'I've got an idea, but David's got to think it's his idea. You know how his ego is.'

"We had all been to see the Hollies about a week before. Neil went too, and we all sat up in the front because we were crazy about 'em, they sang so fuckin' good, and that guy with the high voice! The one that looked like Stewart Granger…"

The guy turned out to be Graham Nash, who was unhappy in the Hollies. The British pop band wasn't evolving fast enough for Nash, who had been hanging out with Cass and the L.A. hipsters.

When he added his voice to those of Stills and Crosby on a song called "In the

Morning When You Rise," everyone in the room had to stop and do a quick inhale.

"We couldn't get through it the second time, we were laughing so hard," Stills remembered. "All the answers were there. It was like, it's all over, we don't have to worry any more.

"John Sebastian was off in what he called the mogul chair, that little chair with floats, laying in the pool. And I said 'Sebastian, you ought to get in here and be in this!' And he said 'No, I'm doing good.'"

Atlantic Records president Ahmet Ertegun green-lighted their album.

Manager David Geffen told them *Crosby, Stills & Nash* would be the one to put them over the top. "There's a whole undercurrent of marketing philosophy that says if you cop that attitude, it happens," Stills said. "Geffen just reiterated it over and over like a mantra: We've got to call it a supergroup. They're not going to know what it is, but keep telling them it's great and they're just gonna roll over. Watch."

Stills' seven-minute "Suite: Judy Blue Eyes" was an instant FM radio classic.

The album went straight to No. 1, and the guys were in business. "We were trying to figure out how to go on the road, because we wanted a band," Stills said. "We had Dallas Taylor on drums, and we needed a good bass player - we went through a couple of bad ones.

"We were looking for a really good keyboard player, and Ahmet said 'Why don't you just get Neil?' And I said 'You've gotta make that call. You call him and see what he says.'"

As Crosby, Stills, Nash & Young, they played Woodstock, and Altamont, and their reputation as the most creative (and literate) of the hippie-era bands was cemented by the release of *Déjà vu* in the spring of 1970; another million-seller, it showcased the differences in their writing and performing styles, as well as the brilliant cohesiveness of their harmony singing.

Stills sang lead on Joni Mitchell's "Woodstock," the first of four smash hit singles. Overnight, they'd become the American Beatles.

When *Déjà vu* hit the stores, Stills was in Florida, easing his stress by working as a stableboy at the racetracks he'd known as a youth. He rose at 4:30 a.m. and started shoveling shit.

A visit to England turned Stills' world upside down. He fell in love with the country, and purchased a 14-room estate in Surrey from his new best buddy, Ringo Starr. The house had stables, so naturally Stills cast about for some trotters.

It was at this point - he was a "country squire," riding horses, playing polo and working on a solo album (*Stephen Stills*) with Hendrix and Clapton in a London studio - that *Rolling Stone* interviewed him at length.

Although Stills was allowed to do a little pre-publication editing on the piece, "I still left in the part where I offhandedly described Graham and David as 'my harmony singers.' The term was really offensive to them. I didn't mean it that way.

"My horses experience led to a kind of an unfortunate turn in my career. I looked elitist in the middle of the hippiedom and anti-war movement."

The comment, he said, "resonated in ways that were totally unexpected. Being young and oblivious, you tend to do that - you say things and they make print. And suddenly your friends get very hurt. Apparently this affected David and Graham.

"Actually, I had some satisfaction from it, because between that and the fact that I'd made my solo album, it kicked them in the ass to make the *Crosby Nash* album, which is a beautiful album."

That album was made in the aftermath of the group's first official breakup, which found Stills and Nash at loose ends over the affections of singer Rita Coolidge. There were musical reasons, too - Young wanted out, and everybody was interested in solo projects - but the main reason was that they were too stoned and their heads were all too, too big.

In London, he buddied up with Jimi Hendrix, another expatriate American. "He kind of taught me how to play lead guitar," Stills said. "Even though his hands were twice the size of mine, he was left-handed and I could sit in front of him, like in a mirror. And we would sit, hanging around in hotel rooms and stuff.

"He was a pretty shy guy. He either kept to himself or went out to a club, took it over and started to play, and then would leave. He really wasn't into hanging around the scene."

At one point, Stills was to join Hendrix's Band of Gypsies; at the time of Hendrix's death, the two were planning to do further studio work. "He was fucking drinking and doing those fuckin' Mandrax, and those things are dangerous as shit," Stills recalled. "I kept telling him, 'Don't you take everything that everybody hands you!' God damn it.

"And sure enough, I'm out at the beach house in Malibu and I see it on TV. I just went 'Fuck!' I threw the television into the ocean."

Stills was not involved in the assembly of the 1971 live CSNY album *Four Way Street*. "I said dudes, if we don't have the class to go in and make the effort to clean up these harmonies - I couldn't listen to it. It was so out of tune and so all over the place. So I just basically bowed out and let it go."

After two hit singles ("Love the One You're With" and "Change Partners"), as far away from Crosby, Nash and Young as he could get, Stills in 1972 began assembling another band, something bigger, more ambitious.

"I basically wanted a partner," he said. "I wanted a running buddy besides Dallas. Somebody that had a sense of songs. Chris Hillman invented the phrase 'the lyric police' and was a tremendous help.

"But I was still on that real powerful, energetic, 'let's go I know what I'm doing' kind of thing. Chris realized it was my band, and it was OK for him." Hillman, another former Byrd, had been one of Buffalo Springfield's staunchest supporters.

Stills dubbed the seven-member aggregate Manassas. "Manassas was, if not the first, the best version of what Nashville rock is now," he said. "We had a steel guitar, and Al Perkins could make spectacular slide guitar soloing on his steel. And Fuzzy Samuels, being from the Third World, added a different thing to the mix. Joe Lala provided me the ability to reach into my real Latin roots."

The *Manassas* album covered plenty of stylistic ground, with Stills' sandpaper voice and distinctive guitarwork always to the fore.

"Everybody said 'Why are you doing a double album?'," said Stills. "I listen to it now - it overreached a little bit. It didn't quite get there, but it was sure damn close. Live, we were just great."

The two-record album sold nearly one million copies, "which with a double album is quadruple platinum."

The band toured and toured, and had spectacular success in Europe, but Stills clashed frequently with manager Geffen over Manassas' relative failure. "Somehow, it sort of died on the vine," he recalled. "I said, I really would like to have what I'm trying to do focused upon, rather than just being a sort of respite from the mothership, that group.

"We did work a lot, but it was never a big deal, you know? If you're really paying attention you make your entrances a big deal. Which David Geffen was always serious about. It kind of just got sloughed off, so I fired him."

Stills refused to wax too negative about Geffen. "We worked hard, and we worked together," he said. "It was just a broken promise that I contributed to by allowing myself to deteriorate into believing the Rolling Stones' biography. Trying to do everything they did and getting entirely too high."

Cocaine and whiskey were running Stills' show by '73, and he was dealing with a massive tax bill, and his marriage to French pop singer Veronique Sanson that year only amplified the stress. After a limp second effort from Manassas - "it's all over the place, and it's obvious Chris is waiting for a ride" - Stills decided to start afresh, signing with Columbia Records.

"I was done with Atlantic," he recalled. "I felt like I was being dissed. I felt like I was being pressured into making my peace with David and Graham, which was going to happen as it would, in time."

Meanwhile, Crosby and Nash toured and recorded as a duo. "There was a lot of hurt and misunderstanding, and drug-induced confusion, on everyone's part at the time," Stills said. "And it just sort of all collapsed."

Crosby, Stills, Nash & Young attempted a studio reunion in the fall of '73, but the old bitterness reappeared and it failed. By the following spring, however, they were rehearsing at

Young's ranch for what turned out to be the first all-stadium rock 'n' roll tour.

"We did this wonderful, monstrous tour, but no album came out of it," Stills said of the summer '74 jaunt, which had many fans bitching that the foursome been brought back together - remember that guy at Big Sur? - for the money.

Stills has an answer. "We grossed $11 million," he said. "But we were getting away with a profit margin of less than 20 percent. They were spending so much money on this grandiose shit, and the parties, and the backstage, and taking care of all of their friends.

"We didn't do enough press; we were not doing the right things because everybody was too hip for that or something. I found that a little disconcerting. There's such a thing as too cool."

He tried to get the band to rehearse a proper set. "The rehearsals were like jam sessions. I was the burr under the saddle, and the irritating force that kept telling them 'could we please get a cogent arrangement together here?'

"And the potheads were all about 'oh, just let it happen.' This is my perspective - please take it in context - we've got this enormous opportunity to get up there on the tall dogs' level. So I'm of a mind that there's a certain amount of discipline that should be exercised."

Today, the stadium tour is remembered for the unruly crowds, drowning out the acoustic sets; and for the fiery electric guitar interchanges between Stills and Young.

"By this time, I'd played with Hendrix, I'd been playing lead guitar in my own band for a while, and I didn't suck," Stills said. "Like I did before.

"There was a lot of manic energy around. The same kind of stuff that used to have the Who beating the shit out of each other, the same kind of stuff that broke up a lot of other bands. We kind of steeled ourselves to it.

"But I was angry a lot. There was one time after a show where I thought I'd really played good, and we walk off the stage. On the stage I'd gotten a lot of stink-eye from David, and Neil said 'You played all over everything.'

"There was this 'CSNY' made in ice backstage. There's a picture somewhere, and I've got an expression on my face that says this guy is ready for a fight.

"They start giving me shit, and the show blew. We were playing too loud and the harmonies weren't together, we weren't using any methodology to get ourselves singing correctly. There was too much of everything around, including old girlfriends, every sycophant you could possibly imagine - each camp had its own set of sycophants. We were just buying into the whole act.

"I walked backstage and I was so frustrated, I took this thing apart with backfists and knuckle punches and karate. I took it apart right in front of them. This thing had to be 10 inches deep and four inches wide. I went through the 'N' with one punch, and it just shattered.

"Because I knew they were going to come after me about something that I'd done wrong on the stage, and I just put an end to it."

Stills' first Columbia release, originally called *As I Come of Age*, was released (as *Stills*) in 1975. Song for song, it's probably his strongest record. He followed the album - his last solo work to make the Top 20 - with a marathon tour.

In '76, Neil Young sat in on a couple of shows, and the gigs were so strong that the old mates decided to make a record. Studio time was booked at Criteria in Miami - where Stills had worked since the first *Manassas* sessions - and the album came together quickly.

"I feel that when I do my thing, and I'm at my confident best, I bring shit out of Neil that he doesn't get to with Crazy Horse, or with anybody," Stills said. "Maybe when he worked with Pearl Jam, or with Booker T & the MG's.

"The two of us have this marvelous way of working, and *Long May You Run* almost got there."

The Stills-Young Band hit the road in June; it was not the earth-shattering event everyone expected. "When you've got a band, and you haven't played in clubs, you've worked in the studio, you get a set," Stills said. "You get a really good, flowing set, and you stick with it for a little while. So that you get comfortable with transitions and stuff.

"And then, you get 10 or 12 shows under your belt and then you start to fuck with it. But you get everybody comfortable first.

"Neil felt restricted by the set that always worked. And every time we fucked with it, it would die. Believe me, I'm not putting this off on everybody else. I certainly participated in it. But he just had to get out of there."

So he did, leaving Stills a terse note in his dressing room.

Stills is circumspect about the incident. "You've got two choices. You can let it fuck with you psychologically, you can go into that place of being betrayed, or dissed, or you can realize that you have a responsibility and a commitment to the promoters that have put the cheese up."

He finished four more concerts on the tour by himself, wondering what was up with his old friend. "I could not do that. I couldn't just bail and leave a note. It's not in my makeup," he reflected.

"I can't say as I blame him. It wasn't that he was wrong; it was getting a little static. But my recollection is that it was right on the verge. We'd just done the first third. I thought OK, let's get some long soundchecks together and go a little further back towards the Buffalo Springfield."

The debacle couldn't have come at a worse time, either - Stills' wife, bored with rattling around their Colorado home (they'd sold the place in England), filed for divorce. And his record sales were slumping (*Long May You Run* wasn't received well by the critics or the public).

And both Crosby and Nash were livid; at one point, the Stills-—Young album was to be expanded into a full-blown quartet reunion, but Stills and Young had wiped their partners' harmonies from the finished recordings.

"I went down to see David and Graham's band in Denver, and just sort of went and made my peace," Stills remembered. "And not longer after that tour, Graham's wife Susan did a Cass Elliott. We meet up somewhere and she says 'Come over to our house, and sit with Graham, and you guys get drunk.' So we did, and we cleared away a lot of garbage."

And so before '76 was up, Crosby, Stills & Nash were back in Miami, with new songs and renewed friendships.

"We were into something good," said Stills. "But there was this feeling over in our end of the building that we were making the album of the year. And I didn't hear it. 'Shadow Captain' was a good song, and there were a couple other good songs.

"We didn't practice enough. Neil loves that 'hanging it out over the edge.' Going in the studio and getting a bunch of people and just sort of jamming the song. He loves that immediacy. And I like that too, but I like to go work stuff."

When Nash's "Just a Song Before I Go" hit the Top Ten, the comeback was complete.

After the protracted *CSN* tour, Stills returned to solo work, issuing *Thoroughfare Gap* in 1978 and taking to the road with a band that included Bonnie Bramlett on backing vocals.

In an Ohio bar after a show, Bramlett ran into Elvis Costello, and another page in Stills history turned.

"I missed it, and I was glad that I did, because I was drunk," Stills said. "She was in the program, so she was stone cold sober and proving it by hanging out at the bar with the guys, drinking iced tea. But she's also a good old southern Illinois shitkicker, and this guy starts cracking wise. He was being real surly, and I just walked off and went upstairs. I knew better.

"And apparently he kept at it. It was basically 'Well, what do you think of…?' various artists. He basically thought American rockers had all lost their edge, and they were all fuckin' rrghh, rrghh, a drunken rant, you know?

"She said 'What about Ray Charles, at least?' And he said 'The guy's nothin' but a blind nigger.' And at that point she reaches back into somewhere in East St. Louis and hits him with a right cross that puts him through about three people. Cold-cocked him. And I was just as proud of her as I could be."

Crosby, Stills & Nash turned the decade with a monkey on their back that would have crippled lesser men. Crosby's drug problems had become so bad that *Daylight Again*, their 1982 release, started out as a Stills-Nash album. The record company insisted Crosby be involved.

"It's horrifying to be around," said Stills of his compadre's crack addiction. "We propped him up for a while. Interventions weren't so popular then, and he ran away a few times, and then got in trouble in Texas.

"It was terrible to watch. We did a tour of Europe that was just horrifying. We couldn't do anything about it, so we stayed away from it."

After Crosby's release from a Texas prison, Neil Young made good on a promise and re-joined CSN in the studio. The album, *American Dream*, underwhelmed just about everybody.

Including Stephen Stills. "David and Graham didn't think I had enough songs. Neil thought some of them were fabulous. We worked on it but we couldn't find the right rhythm section, Crosby had that energy of the newly sober, and we just didn't quite all click. Neil and I were trying our best, but there was a lot of pulling in different directions.

"When we had the final playback of what everybody thought the final album was, I went '(Sigh). It ain't there, boys. If you want to put this out, do so over my objections.' The old cranky asshole Stephen Stills would've said 'over my dead body.' Having gotten the picture that I had to modify my behavior some."

Part of the problem with such reunions, Stills said, is that each of the four men uses a different method of writing and recording - they're set in their ways.

"Graham's incredibly fast, David's pretty fast, and more inventive, and I bring the beef," he said. "We've gotten into the bad habit of doing our parts separately, and then doubling it and tripling it. That seldom works.

"I just don't put it to one side or the other. There's some of the methodology that Neil likes to employ that I don't like. I like to practice for a day or two, then put it away and come fresh after tennis or something. And then I'll nail the sumbitch down in two or three takes.

"It's like horse training. To me, there's a little bit of that in eliciting performances in the alien environment of a recording studio."

A similar set of cross-purposes arrived while the foursome made 1998's *Looking Forward*.

"That was sort of like that last Springfield album," Stills said. "Neil came in with finished pieces, and then we complemented them, and then vice versa. And then we cut some new ones. And it almost happened. We were just a couple of songs short. We had this division of labor, how many of who's songs, blah blah blah.

"And at the end of the day, we dropped the ball on the album. It was like, we're too young to be living legends and too old to compete, and the record company didn't quite know what to do with that."

Stills is currently finishing up his first solo album since 1991's *Stills Alone*. He plans to issue the music on Gold Hill, his own label, via the Internet, and hopes that the next Crosby,

Stills & Nash album will be made available the same way (the band severed its ties with Atlantic in the mid '90s).

"An artist that's been around this long, there's no pigeonhole for us," he explained. "Why should we even try to compete with the Backstreet Boys or 'N Sync, or any of that shit? I can't move like that any more. But I sure could when I was young."

And after the successful *Looking Forward* tour in 2000, he said, Crosby, Stills, Nash & Young started talking about recording again. "I don't want to talk out of school, but we ain't done by a long shot," Stills said. "It is still the mothership, and it's way too much fun."

Several years ago, Stephen Stills became the only person to be inducted into the Rock and Roll Hall of Fame twice in the same evening, as Buffalo Springfield and Crosby, Stills & Nash were honored.

He's not proud of every step he's taken, but he's not ashamed, either. "Hey," he shrugged, "the story is the story."

Koch Records (2002)

18. The Bangles
Girls keep swinging

The quintessential "why did the band break up?" story. Not that I knew it when I made the initial enquiries about talking to the former Bangles. This was a group whose records I loved in the '80s – All Over the Place was one of my college-era faves - and it was common knowledge that when they'd split in '89, it had been acrimonious.

In 1999 came a new Bangles recording, out of nowhere, on an Austin Powers *soundtrack album. Far from being a one-off, it was the start of a full-on reunion. It would take them three years to finish up the project, a brand-new album called* Doll Revolution.

They were just getting back together when we did these interviews, and asking them about why they'd gone their separate ways touched a nerve. Well, four nerves. Turns out they were all of them eager to explain everything, in detail.

The postscript is that the reunion album, while exceptional, failed to light the world on fire, and a dispirited Michael left for good. As of this writing, the others are still out on the road as the Bangles.

(This story appeared in Goldmine *in 2000 under the title* California Dreamin,' *which I hated.)*

Anyone who thinks rock 'n' roll is strictly men's work hasn't given a lot of thought to the Bangles. Nourished in equal amounts by the creative wellspring of '60s pop and the fast-food franchise of '70s punk and "new wave," the Los Angeles quartet made a decade's worth of wonderfully bright music that honored the historic and celebrated the contemporary.

That's rather a pointy fence to straddle, as many a "retro"-style band with no hits can tell you, but the Bangles managed to top the charts, sell millions of records and write a place for themselves in the history books. Their vocal harmonies, recalling the Mamas, Papas, Byrds and Springfield of rock's golden age, were textured over sparse, hooky Beatle-esque arrangements that reverberated with cool guitars and a big-beat drum sound.

Far from being mere revivalists, the Bangles were good songwriters, great singers and, as it turned out, exciting performers. They made two No. 1 singles, two more that hit the Top Ten, plus two platinum albums and a string of classic videos.

The Bangles were - and are - women.

Ten years after their acrimonious breakup, the Bangles have kissed and made up, and are about to go into the studio to make another record.

Don't call it a reunion, though. The Bangles believe they are merely picking up the pieces. "We're expecting to get hit from all directions," said guitarist Vicki Peterson, 41, "and yet we're hoping that the people who actually have been waiting for a new Bangles record will be very pleased with what we come up with."

Said guitarist Susanna Hoffs, 41: "It's about going back to the original concept, which is to be a band. And knowing that all of us have outlets for breathing room, our families or other musical outlets, is what enables us to give ourselves so wholly to the band. I think that's the balance that was missing."

In 1989, when the group disbanded, they were tired, stressed and easily swayed. "We shouldn't have let ourselves be manipulated, but we were young and we didn't understand," said drummer Debbi Peterson, 39, Vicki's sister. "Everybody's learned since then, and now we know, hey, if it doesn't work out, see ya."

Bassist Michael Steele, 46, hopes the world accepts a "new" Bangles album, but like her bandmates, she insists she's not doing it for the fans, she's doing it because she believes in the music they made together - and can still make. "How many times can you regurgitate the past? That's the danger," she said.

The band is playing a 10-date "test the waters" club tour during September. "I want this band to have a new life and to make new records," Michael added. "I'm determined that we're not going to become some Dick Clark oldies band, from the Golden '80s. Ay-yay-yay!"

They all swear they don't care if their reformation, after more than a decade, is received with indifference. "If you can face that in Hollywood, you can face anything, I suppose," Michael said. "If we make a really good record that we like, and nobody cares, we can still say we care, so fuck 'em."

Vicki and Debbi

Born two years apart, Vicki and Debbi Peterson always shared a passion for '60s pop music. According to Vicki, their house in Northridge, in Southern California, was "extremely groovy and modern," and their father, an aerospace engineer at TRW, kept Top 40 radio playing near-constantly on the intercom system wired throughout the place. The Petersons rarely went into town, because Dad was a serious do-it-yourselfer, and the four kids usually spent weekends in the yard, helping him do it himself. The radio was always playing out there, too.

(You could also reverse the intercom and eavesdrop on other rooms, which got the Peterson girls in trouble on more than one occasion.)

Although she was a member of Red Cross Youth, and had dreams of going to veterinary school, Vicki's love affair with the guitar began in the 4th grade, when her parents bought her an Electro guitar (a near-perfect Rickenbacker copy) and an eight-watt amp. The guitar was rarely out of her hands; she slept with it sometimes.

In high school, she was a cheerleader, and sang harmony in the madrigal group. But she had discovered her older sister's record collection, and was writing songs in the style of Simon & Garfunkel, Cat Stevens and Donovan. Turning her back on radio - after all, it was the '70s - Vicki began to seriously absorb that which had come before. She and little sister Debbi adored the Buffalo Springfield and the Byrds, and became card-carrying "Beatles freaks."

"My parents really tolerated my hideous high school bands," Vicki said with a laugh. "It was almost considered like one band that started when I was 15, and ended somewhere in 1989, when the Bangles split up."

Ironically, rocking and rolling was an idea that came late - her early bands played mostly Vicki's original songs. They only started working up covers to get jobs.

Vicki and her best friend Amanda Hills, the group's bassist, graduated from Rolling Hills High in June 1976; the band - at that time called Crista Galli - was having trouble nailing down a drummer.

Debbi, the "annoying kid sister" who hung around the band, liked to play air drums at their garage rehearsals.

Remembered Debbi: "Amanda said 'What about your sister?' to my sister. Vicki had never thought about that. We had some friends who were in a band as well, so I sat down on the guy's drum set and started playing.

"And I guess it must have been all those years of being air drummer, I must have somehow figured it out. Vicki's like 'You're in the band!'"

"Vicki had tremendous respect for Debbi as a musician from that moment onward," recalled Amanda. "Because when Debbi sat down behind the drums, she could do it. She just could do it. It was uncanny. The guy in this band showed her a couple of things to play, and she just played them. It was as though she'd been doing it since birth. I remember standing there, looking at Vicki like 'Oh my God. We have a drummer.'"

Equipment was a problem. The group's drummers had always shown up with their own gear. "I saved up some money from my job bagging groceries at Safeway and bought her a little kit, that she still has," said Vicki. "And about nine months later my boyfriend, who was also in the band - bad idea - said 'You know, she should pay you back for those. You spent $250, and she owes that to you.' So she got a job at McDonald's, God bless her."

"I wanted to play guitar, too," Debbi recalled. "But this was an opportunity that I couldn't pass up."

As Aisha, the group continued, mostly at school functions and parties. They had a big year in '78; Vicki and boyfriend Joel split up and Joel left the group, and Vicki and Amanda enrolled at UCLA and got an apartment together. The group's name became The Muze, and they started getting real club bookings.

When lead guitarist Lynn Elkind joined, early in '79, they switched to The Fans. Vicki, an English major, was bored at college and dropped out to concentrate on The Fans.

"She was absolutely convinced we were going to make it," said Amanda, "which was very funny, because in retrospect there was absolutely no reason why we would. And because she was convinced, we were convinced, too. It was just when, rather than if."

"From a very early age, I knew that this was all going to happen," Vicki says. "It was just sheer, wonderful blind faith, and blissful ignorance. I rarely, if ever, actually allowed myself a moment of doubt. Whatever form it took, I was going to make this my life, my work."

From a review in *The View* newspaper, Nov. 8, 1979: "The Fans are a pretty (very pretty) refreshing group in a musical age of lost horizons and general lack of taste, or anything else that once supported our '60s values."

The Fans gigged all around the Southern California club circuit - the Sweetwater, the Troubadour, Club 88 - and often the musicians, most of whom were under the legal drinking age, weren't allowed to leave the stage or their backstage "quarters."

"Not that we ever did," Amanda said. "We were so clean, it was unbelievable."

Vicki was energized by the punk and new wave movement of the late '70s. Playing in sweaty clubs, she thought, was like being at the Cavern. She craved that direct link to the past.

Debbi, Vicki and Lynn took an apartment together on Detroit Street in Hollywood in early 1980. The group, now called Those Girls, was featured in a brief story called "Meet the Girl Groups" in racy *Oui* magazine. "We don't wear sexy outfits," the band was quoted as saying, next to a photo of Vicki, Debbi and Amanda wearing black leather. "We're not a tits-n-ass band and we're not gay."

Sometime that year, Lynn left the band, although she remained a Peterson housemate. Amanda announced her decision to bail, too - she intended to stay in college. The Petersons were determined to forge ahead.

To hunt up players for a new group, Lynn put ad an in the free local newspaper, *The Recycler*. For grocery money Vicki worked in the maintenance office at Laird Film Studios, where she liked to carry a clipboard and roam around in places she shouldn't (she once, for example, watched Steven Spielberg direct a scene from *E.T.*).

It was Dec. 9, 1980, the day after John Lennon's murder in New York City. Vicki was at home when the phone rang with a response to Lynn's *Recycler* ad.

"I call this stranger on the phone, and I don't get the person whose name was listed in the ad, but I get Vicki Peterson on the line," recalled Susanna Hoffs.

Everyone was thinking about Lennon that day. "I couldn't have found a more compassionate person who really was going through the same emotions as I was," Susanna said. "I was looking to be in a band with someone who really was connected to the same stuff that I was."

"We found ourselves on the phone for over an hour, sympathizing over Lennon's assassination, and many other things," explained Vicki. "I realized the person I was talking to was intelligent, and completely in synch with what I want to do. It was sort of like I'd intercepted something very cool, but in order to be ethically correct I passed on the message to Lynn."

Lynn and Susanna spoke briefly the next day, but it was clear they did not have any chemistry. Guilt-free, Vicki called Susanna back, and within days Those Girls were set up in the Hoffs family garage in West L.A.

"Susanna knew of the Guess Who, Grass Roots, Arthur Lee and Love," Vicki said. "We had lots in common. Harmony singing was a breeze. We left that night thinking 'This is it. We got it.'"

"My memory," said Susanna, "is that we played 'White Rabbit.' I didn't even know how to play it, but it was pretty basic. Vicki showed it to me, and boom, suddenly we're playing a song. There's a drummer, there's two guitars, there's voices. It just all came together so fast. It sounded like such a good fit, so natural. And I think we decided to be 'a band' that night."

Susanna

Susanna Hoffs was born to a rich family in a tony Los Angeles suburb. Her parents, Joshua and Tamar, met at Yale in the '40s, and when Joshua went to UCLA for his residency, they got married and moved to California together. The only Hoffs girl, Susanna arrived between brothers John and Jesse.

Although Susanna loved classical music, and started taking ballet lessons when she was quite young, it was Top 40 radio that became "the soundtrack to my childhood - early Dionne Warwick, 'Downtown,' 'To Sir With Love,' those things had a huge impact on me."

And in 1964, when Susanna was 5, "The Beatles had an enormous impact on my brothers and I. My brother John had a friend whose mother worked at Capitol Records, so we got records very early on. She would bring home an extra copy for us. So we had a large collection of Beatles records.

"I remember getting that *Meet the Beatles* record and we listened to it over and over again, and just were so affected by it."

Tamar Hoffs' brother Carmi, who visited from Chicago, was the siblings' "hippie uncle." He was, in Susanna's estimation, a "pretty good guitarist," and he taught them all simple chords, "Tom Dooley"-type stuff, which Susanna loved, and refined around the bonfires at summer camp.

Carmi Simon eventually went to work for McCabe's Music Shop and became a master dulcimer builder.

While Susanna kept up at ballet, music was something she didn't take too seriously until she discovered the poetry of Joni Mitchell's records. "I really taught myself to sing by just copying Joni, Linda Ronstadt and Bonnie Raitt in the '70s," she said. "And other people too. But there was a point, I remember very clearly, where I really focused in and tried to learn all the little riffs and stuff they were doing. And it went from there."

Throughout high school, she had friends that would play and sing folkie-style music together. She learned about singing harmony in the school choir but never even considered rock 'n' roll.

When Susanna went off to Berkeley to study theater and dance, she became involved with David Roback, a guitar-playing kid from the old neighborhood and one of brother John's buddies.

John Hoffs had left for Yale; on winter break in 1977 or '78, he brought his sister a stack of albums: "It was the Ramones, Blondie, Talking Heads," Susanna recalled. "It was like 'OK, I know those three chords the Ramones are playing.' It was mind-blowing. It really was an unbelievable turning point." Suddenly, it was as if music could be more than a passive interest.

Susanna, John and David began harmonizing together - Susanna's favorite album at the time was Nico's *Chelsea Girl*, and they worked up a Nico-like arrangement of Bob Dylan's "I'll Keep it With Mine" for her to sing, along with the Velvet Underground's "I'll Be Your Mirror." "We would do these excruciatingly slow versions of things," she recalled. "Very dreamy."

It was a band - sort of. "We were very intellectual about it," Susanna said. "It was more sitting around imagining what the band would be. We were gonna be called the Unconscious, or the Psychiatrists. We wanted to have this kind of like name that was referenced the fact that our dad was a psychiatrist."

But the family bond snapped. "What happened was my brother was sort of irritated with David and I for becoming a couple. I was his kid sister, and suddenly I'm stealing his best friend away. So then it was just David and I, and we never did get a bass player or a drummer. We never did a show, and all we did was make some living-room tapes."

It was those tapes that Susanna played for Vicki and Debbi that day in December of 1980 as a sort of audio resume. "That made them kind of go 'OK, cool, we're on the same page here.'"

For the better part of a year, as The Colours and then The Supersonic Bangs and finally just The Bangs, they rehearsed as a trio. Their debut performance - and the very first time Susanna Hoffs ever played guitar before an audience - was at a Laird Studios party in '81 (with a borrowed bass player). Vicki and Susanna's friendship blossomed and they started turning out songs, together and separately, and with Debbi, they would work out intricate harmony parts, giving each other goosebumps when something hit the spot.

Around this time, the group members decided that there would be no more men in the ranks. "I can't say that it just worked out that way, because that would be ridiculous," Vicki explained. "It was obviously intentional.

"But the intent was less to make it a 'groovy gimmick' than it was being done with the awareness that a man changes the dynamics. A man would change the chemistry. It was a girls' club, and it felt more natural for us to keep it a girls' club than to let that psycho-sexual thing happen … it's no different than when a bunch of guys are sitting around in a room, and a woman walks in. It's going to change everything."

Just before Christmas 1981, the Bangs issued their one and only record, a single called "Getting Out of Hand" (written by Vicki) backed with "Call on Me" (credited to Peterson-Hoffs-Roback), on the independent L.A. label Downkiddie. Susanna sang lead on both.

Recorded at Radio Tokyo, a tiny studio in Venice, the single was rough, but the hooks were unavoidable. Vicki and Debbi each played bass on the record, and David Roback took the pictures of the band for the picture sleeve.

The Bangs were determined to be like Vicki and Debbi's father and do it themselves; hence, Vicki managed the group herself and handled all the bookings.

Vicki went to England to visit a friend, leaving specific instructions for Susanna to place "Getting Out of Hand" in the hands of influential disc jockey Rodney Bingenheimer, who played up-and-coming music on his KROQ show Saturday and Sunday nights.

"Even though I grew up in L.A., I almost never ventured east of Westwood," Susanna said with a laugh. "I was always a west-sider. So it was a big thing to go by myself in my car, with the little 45 record of The Bangs and get it to this guy. He got tons of records from everybody, so there wasn't any guarantee that he would ever play it."

When Bingenheimer didn't play the record that first weekend, she worked up the courage to call him and ask, nonchalantly, what'd you think?

Susanna explained: "It's pretty good, he said. You sound like the Mamas and the Mamas. And he got the sort of Paul McCartney bass-influence that was on the record. He played it that weekend, and he played it the following weekend, and then he continued to play it for a year, every show."

(At Radio Tokyo, the Bangs cut a 30–second KROQ commercial for the local fanzine *No Mag*, singing new words to the melody of "Getting Out of Hand." They frequently dropped in to chat with Bingenheimer on the air.)

The local success of "Getting Out of Hand" necessitated steady live appearances, and bassist Annette Zilinskas was hired on. "She didn't really know how to play bass, but she was totally into the same music as we were at the time, and she was very eager to learn," Susanna remembered.

The others bought Annette a Vox Teardrop bass - very '60s, naturally - out of *The Recycler*.

They finally got to play one of their dream gigs, at the famed Whiskey A–Go–Go club, as opening act for The Last. They played on bills with everybody. "We got booked with punk bands because Downkiddie's distributor, Faulty Products, worked with bands like the Circle Jerks, et cetera," said Vicki. "It happened pretty quickly."

The Bangs grew into a popular club act. Their natural buoyancy, combined with their talent for songwriting and their effortless '60s harmonies, made them stand out in a club scene increasingly packed with bands whose sound and look was strongly influenced by mid to late '60s pop. People started calling it the Paisley Underground.

"We went from having to beg our friends to come to some out of the way club on a Monday night, and buy them beer so they'll dance," Susanna said, "and we worked our way up to playing packed clubs. And it became a real scene, and it was really fun."

Michael

After enduring disco and wave after wave of metal bands with big and bigger hair, Michael Steele - born Susan Johnson - found the Paisley Underground much more to her liking.

A native of coastal Newport Beach, where the '60s meant Beach Boys singles blasting from every radio, Michael played guitar and bass, and flute in her high school band. Both poet and rocker, she loved the Beatles and the Beach Boys, and fell hard for Joni Mitchell, but it was the British folkie band Fairport Convention, with singer Sandy Denny, that made Michael think seriously about making music of her own.

She entered show business in the summer of 1975 by answering an ad for girl singers. It had been placed by entrepreneur Kim Fowley, who'd dreamed up the idea of an all-female rock band.

Michael auditioned as the Runaways' lead singer, and strapped on a bass during a rehearsal when no one else seemed interested. With Joan Jett on guitar and Sandy West on drums, they played "Wild Thing" for Fowley. "Joan was great, even then," Michael said.

As for the Runaways, "It was one of those things, a girl band made up by a guy. Which kind of sucks. Because it was coming through his twisted concept of what women were."

Fowley worked his girls hard. "He was hilarious," said Michael. "One day he came to rehearsal and he started throwing garbage at us. He said 'Better get used to this.'"

It wasn't long before Fowley replaced "Micki Steele" on bass. "I got booted out for various reasons," she explained. "I found the whole Hollywood scene was a bit … I think I was just pretty overwhelmed by the whole thing."

It was, she insists without elaboration, a "casting couch … it was kind of like sexual harassment before they called it that."

Fowley recorded the first trio of Runaways on a crude reel-to-reel tape recorder, and the material was issued on CD many years later under the title *Born to Be Bad.* "Kim continues to make money off of me and various other unfortunates who were young enough not to know any better," Michael said.

Burned by the experience, Michael ran back home to Newport Beach. Within a year, she started seeing The Runaways in magazines.

"The injustice of the thing just enraged me, so I finally said 'I'm gonna show 'em. I'm gonna go back out there and just start playing with as many bands as I can, and try to become a good bass player.' Because one of the things this guy said was I was a good singer, but I couldn't play bass for shit."

Michael played with a dozen bands in the late '70s and early '80s, and became a regular at the clubs; two of her favorite groups to check out were the Bangs and the Dream Syndicate, whose musicality and dedication to '60s ideals were very close to her own with hers. David Roback's band, Rain Parade, was another big draw.

In 1982, at the invitation of her friend "Spock," Michael moved into a new apartment, which Spock shared with Vicki and Debbi Peterson. There was a rumor going around that the Bangs might need a new bass player soon.

"I was like well, you know, this might happen, and I'd like to be there if it does," Michael said. "And of course it didn't happen for about a year after I moved in - oop! But that's OK, it was a nice place to live. And I was beginning to know a new bunch of people, and that was a nice thing."

Miles From Nowhere

Miles Copeland, the head of Faulty Products, managed the Police and other acts under the LAPD (Los Angeles Personal Direction) banner. Miles' brother Stewart Copeland was the Police's drummer.

In 1981, Copeland was also running IRS Records, and the label's biggest act, the Go–Go's, was an all-female pop group from Southern California whose members were chummy with the Bangs.

A friend brought Copeland to a Bangs gig at the Café de Grande. "I went in with a couple of people, all of whom said 'Don't do it,'" Copeland remembered. "Which immediately made me think well, this is exactly what I'm gonna do. Because they had the energy, and they had the songs. I immediately thought it was great.

"Sure, there was a comparison with the Go-Go's, because there weren't that many all-girl groups. But my view was look, this is a pretty good group with good songs. The fact that they happen to be all girls from L.A., I'm sure people will compare them, but I had never looked upon them as a spinoff of the Go-Gos, I took them for what they were."

When Copeland offered to manage the band, Vicki was skeptical. "I was immediately defensive - oh, he's going to try and turn us into the poor man's Go-Gos, and I'm just not interested in anything to do with this," she said.

At their first meeting, which Vicki tape-recorded in case Copeland tried to pull a fast one, "he said all the right things: Do things slowly - record an EP at a cheap studio to use as a calling card." They laughed a lot, especially when Vicki discovered her recorder's batteries were dead.

Copeland also won the Bangs' trust by treating them as equals.

He hired the Ramones' Craig Leon to produce a 12-inch EP, with five original songs. Just before the record's release, a New Jersey band called The Bangs got wind of it and demanded $40,000 for use of their (copyrighted) moniker.

So the self-titled record became *Bangles*.

"We were really heartsick about it, because I really liked the name," said Vicki. "I liked the innuendo, and the sound of it - it was explosive, and short - so we just tried to keep the syllable in the word. Even though Bangles is a much softer image, and a much softer sound. We felt like we had already established an identity as the Bangs."

Copeland booked the Bangles on a tour opening for the ska band English Beat, an

IRS act, and began casting about for a label to take them on. He and the girls were adamant the Bangles should not be on the same label as the Go-Gos.

"We had this kind of naïve, youthful confidence," Susanna said. "It was funny, we never sort of went 'Oh, it's not happening, guess I'll go back to law school.' We just had this odd feeling that it was going to work out."

Columbia Records A&R man Peter Philbin didn't take much convincing, and Vicki liked his smooth chat about "letting an act develop over time." In 1983 the Bangles were signed to Columbia with a $125,000 budget for their first album. Not long before recording was scheduled to commence, however, Annette Zilinskas left the band by mutual consent.

"Annette wasn't a great harmony singer," Vicki recalled, "plus, she was more into rockabilly. We would learn a token rockabilly song or two, which we were not very good at, so that Annette could sing. But we started to realize that we were not in sync."

Said Susanna: "She wanted to sing some leads, on more more country-ish sounds. Bass wasn't her passion."

Zilinskas and her boyfriend formed the "cowpunk" band Blood On the Saddle.

So Annette was out, and Columbia - and Michael Steele - were in. "That," Michael said, "was nice timing after all the other bands I'd been in."

Even with all the aces turning up, Vicki still nursed a fear they might be somebody's novelty "chick band." "It was never overt, but I'm sure it was being said in the boardrooms," she said.

"You look at the band, it's obvious what it is, but I think it was also obvious that we were a band that was not created by somebody. We weren't a band that was formed after ads in *Variety*. I think our 'street cred' was intact. Our origins were well-enough known that people knew we're not talking about the Spice Girls here!"

Michael: "After the Runaways, I swore to myself that I would never do another girl band as long as I fucking lived. But the Runaways was like a fake girl band; this was a real band that happened to be women."

The Bangles became a CBS act a time when the record industry was only too happy to milk a trend for all it was worth, but also at a time when acts with genuine talent were still allowed time - and money - to develop. It would take three years before the Bangles had a hit, but Columbia, bless its corporate heart, stuck by the band the whole time.

The band was paired up with staff producer (and Columbia A&R honcho) David Kahne.

Fun, fun, fun

"*All Over the Place* was years in the making, because we played those songs a lot in the clubs," said Debbi. "I felt proud of our performance; we sounded like this great, raw rock

231

band. But sonically, at the time I didn't think the album sounded good enough. And we were tortured by David Kahne."

Kahne's less-than-deft touch always managed to find a Bangle nerve. "For example, on 'Going Down to Liverpool,' he made me cry because I had to do the first line over and over," Debbi added. "I kept thinking it was sounding great to me. And he was like 'Do it again, do it again.' It ended up being work."

Vicki: "There wasn't a joy of creation going on there. Everything was complicated. As a matter of fact, it was a phrase he was famous for. He would sit with his head in his hands on the board and go 'Damn, this is complicated.' What does that say to the artist? That says OK, this is a mess. You're basically incompetent. I'm at a loss. I'm going to have to fix it."

Kahne, all agree, was brilliant at vocal arrangements, and could always be counted on to decide who would sing what - he was usually right, too. They respected his arranging talents.

And he polished the Bangles' rough sound; the garage band that had made *Bangles* was nowhere to be found on *All Over the Place*. "We were very basic as a band, and he was hearing symphonies in his head," said Vicki. "He would have all these sort of sonic images he wanted to realize, and were we just 'Huh? Uh … OK.'

"As Susanna says, we learned a lot from David Kahne, and it took years to un–learn some of it."

Kahne, the musicians say, saw *All Over the Place* as his record, and the Bangles themselves as obstacles.

"He made us more aware of what our flaws were than the things that we were good at," Susanna said. "It has a kind of debilitating effect after a period of time. On the one hand, you want to feel inspired, you want to feel confident, but you're around someone who's very vocal about what the shortcomings of the band are. You don't want somebody who's just going to say everything you do is great, but there's a different style of working."

Some of the songs ("James," "He's Got a Secret") were from Vicki's teenage scrapbook and had been performed by The Fans, Those Girls and the others; the band also pulled out favorite covers including The Merry-Go-Round's "Live" and the Grass Roots' "Where Were You When I Needed You" (left off the album, the latter became the B–side to the band's first Columbia single, "Hero Takes a Fall").

"Going Down to Liverpool" came from their English friend Kimberly Rew of Katrina & the Waves, who also recorded it.

All Over the Place didn't produce a hit, but it sold respectably, mostly through steady airplay on college stations. Today, fans still tell the Bangles it's the best record they ever made. "We'd been out playing those songs live as a band, so there's a band cohesion on that album," said Michael, adding with her trademark dry humor: "And I think that's what people respond to ad nauseam: *All Over the Place* was a cool record, thereby saying your other two albums were shit."

The Bangles made videos for both singles ("Going Down to Liverpool," directed by Hoffs' mother, featured family friend Leonard Nimoy) and got little to no airplay on MTV. The band shrugged it off and hit the road, setting a pattern that would continue virtually nonstop for six years.

They found an audience in Europe. "You didn't have the sense of 'Oh, we don't have a Top 40 hit,'" Susanna said. "Big deal! 'We can still play to a packed house in a small club.' We would play these little clubs in England, and have these incredible shows. You get so much from the audience that it bolsters up any sense of 'Oh, it's not a hit on the radio.' We didn't really care! We just figured it would happen eventually."

Certainly, there were no other bands - female, male or otherwise - playing as rich a concoction of clever songs with Rickenbacker guitars and velvety, Beatle-smooth harmonies. "It's actually one of the easiest things for us, singing in harmony," Susanna said. "From the early days of being in a choir or something.

"We did the best that we could, and given that we couldn't hear ourselves very well, those were really about paying our dues; learning how to sing in a club where you can't hear yourself. Those were days where we got a lot of training."

The band spent the fall of 1984 as road support for Columbia's top act, Cyndi Lauper. Vicki and Susanna, along with their friend Jules Shear, turned out "I Got Nothing" as the Bangles' contribution to *The Goonies*, for which Lauper recorded the title song.

Then it was time to make the second Columbia album. A cloud rolled in. "We weren't smart enough," Vicki said, "to know that we could fire our producer."

Different Light

At a pre-production meeting, Vicki said, "Kahne acknowledged the problems with the first record, he apologized for his methodology, he promised that he was in a better place and we were going to have a very positive experience."

The Bangles went back into the studio with Kahne in summer '85 to record the follwup to *All Over the Place*. Columbia was counting on a hit.

The problems began almost immediately. Copeland had kept the group on the road so much, they'd barely had any time to write new songs. So the call went out - the Bangles were sifting through material to record.

They chose a handful of songs they liked, cut the few new originals they had … and then fate stepped in, making the Columbia brass shake and shimmy.

Vicki: "Despite all their noble gestures about 'letting this band grow,' etcetera, all of a sudden they're given a gift from the gods. And the gods are called Prince. And Prince says hey, record this song, and they see the doors open to radio.

"They see the golden light shining upon them: This is how they're gonna get this band to radio."

Kahne knew engineer David Leonard, who had worked with Prince. It seemed the Minneapolis megastar, who was at the height of his *Purple Rain* fame, had taken a shine to the "Hero Takes a Fall" video, and in particular to Susanna Hoffs, whose doe-eyed coquettishness had come across particularly well.

Susanna remembers making the drive to Sunset Sound Studios to pick up a cassette from Leonard. On it were Prince's demos of two songs, "Jealous Girl" and "Manic Monday."

The Bangles were unanimous that "Manic Monday" was the one for them. "I kept thinking, Sue and I could write a song like this," Vicki said. "This is like a pop song. It seemed a little more contrived than most of our songs; ours were usually a little more obtuse.

"But it was OK. I thought well, we can record it. But in my innocence I didn't see the grand scheme until very soon after we recorded it: 'Why is David Kahne spending two weeks mixing this one song? And 20 minutes on every other one?'"

According to Susanna, Prince never contacted any of the Bangles until their version of "Manic Monday" was in the can. "I think he very much though that we would use his track and just sing over it," she recalled. "My memory is that he was really surprised when we re-cut every single thing, because he was great at making … they weren't really demos, they were recordings. And then just giving them to other people for them to sing over. Because he was such a good producer himself."

"Manic Monday" reached No. 2 on the *Billboard* chart in April 1986. Although the songwriting was credited to "Christopher," everyone knew it was, in fact, The Purple One (who happened to be called Christopher in the movie he made that year, *Under the Cherry Moon.*)

The Bangles exploded. Or, rather, the Bangle.

"Columbia said, here we have a way into radio, and it's because of Prince's infatuation with the little one in the middle," said Vicki.

"Those things have a way of spiraling out of control. And all of a sudden you have an article on the band, but there's a photograph of Susanna. And we fought that as much as we could, not just the three of us who weren't getting photographed, but management.

"But there's only so much you can do."

The press pounced upon the Prince/Hoffs connection, and their "romance" became the stuff of rock 'n' roll gossip columns. When the Bangles performed on *The Tonight Show*, guest host Joan Rivers sat them all on the couch and blurted out "Which one of you slept with Prince?"

Susanna says flatly that there never was any backstage affair. "He was sort of hanging around," she explained. "He came to some shows and would call occasionally; I had some phone conversations with him but no, absolutely not. We were never a romantic item."

The press, of course, didn't want to hear that, so the stories continued.

Getting Out of Hand

Different Light was one of the biggest-selling albums of 1986; the third single, a novelty tune written by Liam Sternberg called "Walk Like an Egyptian," topped the American chart for four weeks at Christmastime. The ubiquitous video featured the women in midriff-baring Cleopatra garb, acting out goofy hieroglyphics. "Although it's the song that we will always, unfortunately, be known for, I was all for it," Vicki laughs.

As fun and free-wheeling as "Walk Like an Egyptian" was it, too, was hard won. "Originally I was going to sing the whole song," Debbi said. "I don't know where the change of heart came from, but there was this sudden decision to get three people to sing, one for each verse. Of course, there's only three verses, so somebody's gonna get left out."

Debbi got left out.

"I was going to sing the second verse, and I got two takes and David Kahne said 'No, Micki, why don't you go try it.' And then she ended up doing it.

"I was 'Excuse me, my voice is just warming up. I know I'm not a Bonnie Raitt and just sing perfect the minute I open my mouth, but …'"

Debbi doesn't play drums on the track, either; Kahne "took care of it."

"On *Different Light*, there were a couple of other drummers that came in, but basically that's because I couldn't quite get the part as he saw it," said Debbi. "He was very much a visionary, and saw things a certain way. And would let me play, for the most part, what I was seeing. But then at certain times it would be 'Well, that's not quite right, we've got to get so-and-so in.'"

Vicki, too, felt the wrath of Kahne. "He would bring in his ringer guitar players to do certain things," she said. "At one point, I'd had to leave the studio for an emergency, and I came back, and he had had his guy show up and do a solo. It was the backwards thing on 'September Gurls.' I hate to burst your bubble, I didn't play that.

"This is one of my nightmare, nightmare stories. I walked into the studio after I had to leave, and this was already done. And Micki's loving it - she thinks it sounds great! I looked at Kahne and I went 'Oh! OK.' And he said 'Oh … did you want to try something?' My will had pretty much been broken successfully by that point. It was really awful."

Said Susanna: "I remember thinking 'Boy, being a producer is a hard job.' And I think he made it seem really hard because he was so driven by angst, and kind of perfection-istic. He had been an artist himself and never succeeded as an artist, so I think he was always tormented by 'How would I do this if it was my record?'"

"It was," said Michael, "sort of an aural version of the casting couch where, well, if I don't do all this stuff, these songs won't be hits. He knew there were going to be some big hits on that album. That album made his career, basically. And so we were sacrificed on the altar of his career."

Michael wrote and sang "Following," a haunting acoustic track on *Different Light*. "He had totally forgotten about that song," she remembered. "He was totally freaking out about which of the 27 mixes of 'Manic Monday' was the right one. We were almost done with recording and I said 'Uhh, David, remember the song 'Following'? So it was, like, two takes."

Michael thinks Kahne might have "ignored" her because she wasn't one of the group's main songwriters or singers.

"He loved Sue's voice, and he loved the way we did harmonies, but everything else was basically shit and he felt like he had to get rid of it, or try to work around it, or do something to make it palatable," she explained.

"I don't know, maybe he ran out of money before he replaced my bass parts."

According to Debbi, Kahne picked on her in particular - and not just because of her drumming. "He said I physically couldn't sing one of the songs. Physically couldn't sing. It was one of those things where you might as well just stab me right now, just kill me. Cut my throat. Cut out my vocal cords. It was so devastating. It was hard for me to bounce back from that.

"I was actually, at one point, feeling kind of suicidal. This guy was screwing with my emotions so bad, and made me feel so shitty, that I just thought well, OK ... I should've just told him to piss off. But we were caught between a rock and a hard place."

Copeland says the Bangles only told him after the fact why they absolutely, positively would never work with Kahne again. "They'd be in the studio and he'd say 'I don't like the middle bit, so you've got to re-write it,'" he explained. "They'd go home and re-write, and he wouldn't like that one. He'd say 'I wrote one, listen to this.' They'd say they liked theirs better and he'd say 'let's drop the song, then.'"

So, of course, to keep the song, they'd do it Kahne's way.

"In their view, the reason his middle bit was 'better' is because he got a piece of the publishing," Copeland said. "And they were incredibly pissed off about that. They felt that they got raped - that was their word."

On *Different Light*, Kahne was credited as a co-writer on the tracks "Walking Down Your Street," "Standing in the Hallway" and "Not Like You."

"He wanted to make a hit record, and fuck them! That was his view," Copeland said. "And if he wrote a bit of the song, he was going to have his piece of the publishing, fuck them."

Publicly, as their fortunes rose, the Bangles' look began to turn towards an '80s, rock 'n' roll kind of "feminine." They began to appear in short skirts, with teased hair and heavy makeup. Gone were the jeans and thrift-shop clothes of "Hero Takes a Fall."

"In general, the glamorization of the Bangles happened because there were more outside people in there messing with us," said Susanna. "We didn't have enough perspective to say no. You want to look good, and you get caught up in 'Oh, let's give you bigger hair!'

"I remember how big my hair was on the 'Walk Like an Egyptian' thing and feeling like 'Oh my God! What just happened to me?'

"And you get caught up in going along with what's happening. A wardrobe person comes and says 'These are great clothes; put these on.' And you're busy on tour. You don't have time to go shop.

"You look over and the person sitting next to you has got that much makeup on, too. It's just a vicious cycle. Fashion faux paus just escalating and getting exponentially worse and worse."

Vicki: "We played around more with fashion as time went on. Part of that was because more was available to us. People were coming up to us and saying here, wear this. Which happens a lot: You're starving and nobody gives you anything, but suddenly you have a hit record and everyone wants to give you everything for free."

Still, she said, "A lot of it was in response to Susanna's ability and obsessive-ness with being a star. It was what drove her. It's what kept her up at night. It started becoming more about that, and more about celebrity status, than about some other things. That was very foreign territory to me, and I didn't understand it. It sort of exacerbated the rift that was already starting to grow."

The Lead Singer Syndrome

"It probably would have been healthier for us had we allowed each other the room to go off and do whatever it was, however silly, however ridiculous, i.e. going off for six weeks and making a movie," Susanna said. "Or making a solo record.

"But we were kind of a band which focused on everybody being committed to the band and giving all of their time just to the band, and it was part of what created the pressure cooker that ended up breaking it up."

In the little-seen 1976 film *Stony Island*, a 17-year-old Susanna had a bit part. The movie was directed by Andrew David, a friend of Tamar Hoffs' from Chicago. David would go on to make *The Fugitive* and *A Perfect Murder*, among others.

Ten years later, Susanna surprised her bandmates by spending the Bangles' much-needed break acting in the wacky college comedy *The Allnighter*, produced and directed (and co–written) by her mother.

"I think I just needed to not be on tour for six weeks, and go do something that seemed fun and different and exciting," said Susanna. "It's not the thing I'm most proud of in my life, but I'm happy I did it. It was something I got to do with my mom."

Even though the cast of *The Allnighter* included genuine actors Michael Ontkean and Joan Cusak, the film - about a group of college grads looking for excitement at year's end -

was positively dreadful. "Grotesque in the AIDS era," wrote Leonard Maltin. "Though it would be a stinker any time."

"I read the script, and I couldn't believe it was getting made," said Vicki. "But I know how these things go, and it did. And it saw release, which was also amazing to me. But I get amazed by many things that see release."

Tamar Hoffs, says Vicki, was such a believer in positive thinking that she and her daughter didn't really see how bad *The Allnighter* really was.

"That's what I was up against," she said. "I wasn't going to look her in the eye and say you know what? It's actually really, really embarrassing. The only concern of mine was that it was going to reflect on the band."

Which, of course, it did. After the 'Prince thing,' the next volley of Bangles' press reports all had to do with *The Allnighter*.

"The Go-Gos accepted the fact that Belinda Carlisle was the front person, and she was going to sing the songs, and get most of the press," said Copeland. "The Bangles were very different. They did not want to see any individual in the group step forward and become the star. You had to have four spotlight operators; each one had to be in the spotlight. There were no solo band members."

There was no convincing the public, or the press. "I guess the best way I can describe it is that it became really uncomfortable for me," Susanna admitted. "Because when people would say 'Are you the lead singer?' I would say 'No, actually I'm not.' Then I'm sort of defending the fact that I'm not. It just caused this tension with all of us.

"In some way, it's obviously flattering if someone likes what you do. But the more tense everybody got about it, the more tense I felt about it."

Ever the optimist, Vicki convinced herself that everything was OK: We still make records the same way. We all write, we all sing.

To her credit, Susanna never lorded it over the others. According to Vicki, that was one reason the Go-Go's self-destructed. "It's the lead singer syndrome. Belinda would get a suite, and the rest of the girls would find out that she had a suite, and they had single rooms. It was 'What the fuck is this?'

"And she'd say 'Well, I'm a bigger star than you are.' That kind of thing never happened with us. Susanna wasn't running around like a full-on prima donna around us. She wouldn't get away with it."

All well and good, except the press only wanted Susanna interviews, and more frequently her photo appeared in print, without the others.

"The 'we're all equal' philosophy became, in a sense, a straitjacket," Copeland mused. "Because obviously Susanna began to move forward a bit, reality-wise. It's a natural thing, a little cute girl in front is going to get more attention."

In March 1987, as *Different Light* was being certified double platinum by the RIAA, the Bangles appeared on the cover of *Rolling Stone*.

The article announced, among other things, that David Kahne had been dismissed as the group's producer. "In the long run," it said, "what they may have learned is just how much running their own show means to them."

Everything But the Girls

After months of touring behind *Different Light*, and cleaning up after *The Allnighter*, the Bangles began 1988 with another huge hit: On Feb. 6, their version of the Simon & Garfunkel song "Hazy Shade of Winter" reached No. 2 on the American charts.

The band had cut the track, an old favorite from their clubbing days, for the film *Less Than Zero*, and it was included on the Def Jam soundtrack album (on paper, Rick Rubin produced, but the women insist they did most of the production work themselves).

Three enormous hits would've made most artists ecstatic. Not the Bangles. Susanna was uncomfortable, and the others, virtually ignored by the media, were miserable. "I could tell the way the videos were going very pro-Sue," Debbi recalled. "I could see it all happening." They all started wearing heavier makeup, sexier clothes and even more outrageous hairstyles.

"I felt very resentful at the time, and I felt it wasn't a true representation of what we were all about, and what we were all working for," Debbi said.

"There we were with this feeling," Vicki explained, "and it set up this dynamic where the rest of us felt like if we were going to win at this game, all of a sudden we had to play by different rules. At least I did."

The third album was budgeted at $350,000. Success, Vicki thought, has raised the bar. "The problem," Debbi said, "was we really didn't talk about it. That was one of the reasons we broke up, because when you have a relationship with three other people, it's almost like you're married. You have to talk to these people and say what you feel. And none of us actually expressed our true feelings."

"I would try to do it, and of course my emotions would take over and it would just come out all gobbledegook and go the wrong way."

"We were burned out," Susanna said. "We needed space away from each other. We didn't quite know how to do it, but what we did was we all went off to write with other people. Just to survive emotionally, we needed a break from each other."

The foursome re-convened in late spring, and although they were glad to be back Bangling, everybody felt something was wrong. "I knew things were tense but I was just used to it," said Susanna. "We were all used to it. It was just part of the fact that we just didn't know how to talk about things when they didn't feel good. Everyone would just kind of sit there feeling weird and uncomfortable. We didn't have any way to have a group Bangle therapy session."

The first order of business was bringing in Davitt Sigerson to produce; the former engineer had recently helmed an album by David & David that everyone liked. And his easygoing manner behind the board, they thought, would be the antidote for Kahne's divide-and-conquer tactics.

"Davitt had a good mix," Vicki said. "He had humor, hyper-intelligence and a very laid-back way in the studio. I was very tense about doing any guitar playing in the studio because of my bad experiences in the past with Kahne. I just felt like I couldn't play, and I was inept."

Vicki wrote a song, "Make a Play For Her Now," with former Kiss guitarist Vinnie Vincent, who turned out to be a major Bangles fan. The others found collaborators, too, and when the recording date arrived, there was a pile of new and exciting songs from which to choose.

Michael contributed three songs to *Everything*. Her "Glitter Years" was a scorching rocker that looked back fondly on the early '70s, complete with a unique David Bowie impersonation on the last verse.

"A songwriter said to me once 'You know, if that song had been about something normal, it could have been a hit,'" she laughed. "'Eh … you mean like 'love/dove'? I always thought that songs that are about something 'other' were kind of interesting."

Debbi's upbeat "Some Dreams Come True" was one of her best songs ever, and she co-wrote "Bell Jar" with her sister. Vicki turned in "Crash and Burn" and, co-written with Susanna, the crunching "Watching the Sky."

Susanna's songs, written with Billy Steinberg and Tom Kelly, were the most blatantly commercial of the lot. And "In Your Room," the first *Everything* single, was the most overtly sexual track the band had ever done.

The label was ecstatic when they heard the album, and predicted big things. "By taking more chances, the Bangles sound more comfortable than they have since their 1982 EP," raved *Rolling Stone*.

The band, however, didn't see it as taking chances.

Michael: "When Sue was covered as far as all the singles, everybody else sort of grabbed the crumbs as they could. We knew it kind of sucked. It was now 'Paul Revere and the Raiders Featuring Mark Lindsay.' I always hated what they did to that band."

Vicki knew something was off, but she couldn't put her finger on it. "All of a sudden it felt like I could be playing in anybody's band right now," she recalled. "And that feeling never really went away.

"It's like 'Eternal Flame.' It's a beautiful song, Whitney Houston would've had a huge hit with it. Anyone could've had a hit with it. It was not a Bangles song. To me. It was a really well-written pop song. There's nothing wrong with that, but I felt completely emotionally divorced from a lot of the music that was happening."

Your basic '80s "power ballad," Susanna's "Eternal Flame" would be the album's second single - and the band's second chart-topper. It's almost a solo performance.

"Everybody else loved it," Vicki said. "So I was outvoted. Everybody else thought it was fucking genius. And because of the sort of creative thinking world, it was presented to me as, 'No, but we're going to do it like a Patsy Cline record.' And I went ok, well, OK, I don't know what you mean but that sounds great.

"If you ask Susanna, she still thinks it sounds like a Patsy Cline record. In the imaginary world of Susanna Hoffs, her references were always completely amazing to me. And they still are! She has a very creative little mind, and she lives in a world that doesn't always jibe with mine. I now find it kind of funny."

"Like it or don't like it, you know?" Susanna says of *Everything*, released in November 1988. "That's where we were at the time. That's what eight years of touring brought us to, the making of that album."

For her part, Michael was glad to have Kahne out of the picture. "It proves that you don't have to be fucking suicidal to make a worthy album," she said.

And in the end …

"All the people who loved me wanted to blame everything on Sue," Vicki said. "And it was not all Sue's fault, I say this to this day. Which is why I'm able to play in a band with her, because I don't believe that she was … she was neither a victim, nor was she a perpetrator of this crime. It was partially both. Nothing is that black and white."

As the *Everything* tour approached, the four Bangles began to anticipate that old feeling of dread - the travel, the hours, the press. Their removal of Kahne had been a success, so they started scribbling pink slips.

"They were looking for somebody to blame," Copeland said. "They made me fire my partner Mike Gormley, then they made me fire my brother as the agent, so I was being forced to use people that weren't really my choices, one by one."

"The reality was that the group was having such internal troubles, it was very hard to keep going."

Copeland, who had annoyed the Bangles by giving what they saw as more attention to Sting, his other major client, was himself dropped in favor of the California management team Arnold Stiefel and Randy Phillips.

They hit the road with a strong album - and immediately found themselves once again playing 'Susanna Hoffs and the Bangles.' Susanna, Vicki recalled, "was physically ill. She was painfully aware of the fact that we were all resenting the direction that things were going, and she couldn't handle that."

The tour was ugly.

"Towards the end of it, we were just sort of going through the motions, I think," Debbi said. "A lot of us were. I think Vicki still felt like 'This can be saved.' Bless her heart, she was very idealistic about it. But I kept telling her it was going in the wrong direction. I think in her heart she knew that, too.

"The last tour, we all had such bad stomachaches. We thought we were getting ulcers. Michael was sleeping a lot because she was so depressed. We were not doing well."

Said Michael: "Part of it was just exhaustion, because we worked, and were worked, very hard. I remember falling asleep in one of those plastic chairs that they have in convention rooms. And I remember for the first time thinking 'I'm hating playing music.'

"And that was when I knew the end was near, at least for me. Because I always thought 'I'll do it until it's no fun any more.'"

Debbi, who married the tour's production manager Steve Botting during a break in June, dreaded going to work. "The whole thing was just too painful," she said. "It had already gone beyond the direction I thought it should have gone. It was such focus on little sex kitten Susanna Hoffs, and to me that's what we weren't all about. We're a band, we're musicians, we're performers, we're not trying to be little sex girls. But that's what everybody expects."

In mid-April, "Eternal Flame" hit No. 1 in America, and the tour dragged on. "I thought if we had one big single with somebody else doing the lead vocal, it would help balance out the perception, and we'd be OK," Vicki said. So Debbi's "Be With You" went out as the third single - the video, Debbi said with a sigh, was poorly shot, in a single afternoon - and when it stalled at No. 30, everyone felt a big shakeup was coming.

"At that point," Vicki explained, "the label was saying they don't want a single unless it's a Sue vocal. And as soon as I heard those words - and I heard it inadvertently - I said OK, now the illness is terminal."

The final wedge, all the Bangles agree, was driven by Stiefel/Phillips. "They were trying to kill the album so they could take Sue for their own," Debbi said. "I'm not saying anything against Sue at all, I think that definitely was a management ploy. And of course if they'd said that to me, it's hard not to go with that. You're tempted by that."

"We weren't operating like a group, we were operating like four individuals trying to protect their territory," Susanna said. "And managers come along who could care less about protecting the group and just ride out the tour for the last record, and are ready to manage different people in the band."

Susanna said she was getting whispers in both ears: You don't need these other girls.

"I though yeah, this is hard. I don't want to be in a room with people who are angry and upset and hostile. Their argument to me was why do you want to be in a room with people who are mad and frustrated?"

A solo career started sounding pretty good to Susanna. "Basically I thought my God, I'll be out of the pressure cooker," she said. "Wouldn't that be nice. I was very, very stressed out from the tour. I was like a basket case emotionally, physically. I was riddled with anxiety."

Ironically, it was Michael who first suggested breaking up the Bangles. Stiffel/Phillips was talking her up, making vague promises about a solo deal with Columbia, once she was feeling better.

"I'd hit a point where I was starting to have some scary physical symptoms," she said. "I was like, 'Fuckin' A. The Bangles thing is actually making me physically ill.' I basically called Sue up and said I can't do this any more. And she was overjoyed, of course, because she wanted to go do her solo thing.

"Nobody was in anybody's camp at that point. It was really just that I had to stop. If the band had been united, then maybe they would have gone on without me. But that wasn't the way it was.

"The other strange thing about it was that the Petersons didn't see this coming at all. It's like this train wreck or something."

The band was booked to visit Australia for the first time in October. A labor strike, however, forced cancellation of the trip, and a meeting was called at Stiefel's home on the beach - to discuss, it was explained, "the next move."

"I show up and there gathered in the room are all the Bangles, our manager, his partner, his press agent, our lawyer and our business manager," Vicki said. "And Micki won't look me in the eye. I'm like, '..W—what's going on?'

"And very soon after that, our manager cajoled out of Susanna the words 'I don't think I can make this next Bangles record. And actually, I don't think I want to do a Bangles record again.'

"It was sort of like your husband invites you to a fancy restaurant for a nice dinner, and you think you're going to celebrate your anniversary or something. And you show up and he's got his best friend and his lawyer there at the table with him, and he announces to you that he doesn't want to be married to you any more."

Vicki and Debbi - who had arrived with her husband - were dumbfounded, but tried to rally the troops. "I think our evil manager knew that," Vicki said, "and so in order to ward off any Bangles records which might be competing with his Susanna Hoffs record, he made sure he had Michael Steele on his team, too. Micki was desperately unhappy as well, for many reasons. He completely fucked with her, and there's just no other way of putting it. She'll be the first one to tell you that he told her he was going to look after her, and get her a solo deal and all this stuff, and as soon as the band was dissolved he didn't return her phone calls."

Michael: "I had to get out, and the whole CBS 'We're going to get you a deal' thing was kind of nice, but it didn't happen, basically because they dropped the ball.

"I probably couldn't have even dealt with that, I was so stressed out."

Always the most emotional Bangle, Debbi took a few precisely-aimed hits at this meeting. "Management actually blamed me and my husband by calling it the 'Debbi & Steve Show.' They were trying to pinpoint me trying to get all this attention because I had blonde hair, and I was up on the drum riser! And when the spotlight did go on me, which wasn't very often, the fans would get confused about who the singer was. Then my head turned into a lightbulb. In fact, I've seen video of me having a 'lightbulb head' because my hair was so bright and I was up close to the lights.

"They started pinpointing this fantasy about me trying to be a big star. I still don't even understand it, to this day. If anything, I was just trying to stand up for myself because I didn't feel a lot of support from anybody else. Look at the videos: Hello?!

"They were definitely dividing and conquering between Vicki and I and Micki and Sue. That was their little plan to break the Bangles up so they could get their Susanna."

Vicki tried to argue about giving one another the freedom to do solo projects and still keeping the band together, but it was too little, too late.

"It was very final, and it was like nothing you could say could change it," Debbi said. "We all got in our cars and drove off. And that was it, we had broken up."

After the Bangles

Susanna Hoffs' solo career was launched with the dissolution of the Bangles, and although she and her managers predicted she'd inherit the group's success, it didn't exactly work out that way.

For her debut, Susanna chose an unlikely producer: David Kahne, who'd humiliated the Bangles for so long in the studio. "I was so terrified by the whole thing that was going on, I didn't know what was up and what was down," Susanna said. "Somewhere deep down in my intuition I knew I couldn't really trust what was going on."

Kahne, she thought the time, was the devil that you know as opposed to the devil you don't. "Maybe he's a difficult guy to work with, but at least we made good records together."

Produced by Kahne, *When You're a Boy* (the title comes from David Bowie's "Boys Keep Swinging," which closed the album) was released in the early weeks of 1991. Susanna's single "My Side of the Bed" made it to No. 30, due in no small part to the sexually-charged video (it's difficult to misinterpret a beautiful, scantily clad woman singing the line "You can get yours on my side of the bed").

The album, however, stalled at No. 83, and critics derided its generic pop sound and cloying, come-hither lyrics. "When I didn't have Vicki and Micki and Debbi there to fight the fight, Kahne went out of control pop, out of control production, out of control keyboards," Susanna says.

"It just was a mistake. I've heard other artists speak of records they've made that way - Tori Amos, Alanis Morrisette, people have made first records that they consider to be nothing to do with them."

No longer involved with Stiefel and Phillips, Susanna began making overtures to the other ex-Bangles about re-forming the band. "Immediately after the fiasco of making the David Kahne solo record, I thought 'What am I doing? This is ridiculous.' And I was trying to re-connect with them, but they really weren't ready. Had no interest. Zero."

Vicki had cut her hair down to an inch, gone back to school and learned sign language. For a while, she was lost. "You've been spending not just the last nine years of your life, which was in Bangledom, but basically it went back to when I was in high school and playing with my best friends in a band. It never had stopped for me. I had been doing this my entire adult life, even my adolescent life had been wrapped up in this dream.

"So now, all of a sudden, it's gone. So now who am I? Am I ex–Bangle Vicki Peterson? Am I an artist in my own right? Do I even want to do this any more?"

She found a soulmate in Susan Cowsill, the one–time "cute little kid sister" of the singing Cowsill family. They started writing songs together. Vicki played guitar during a Cowsills reunion tour - "It was like being onstage with the Beatles" - and she and Susan performed a string of acoustic dates in their nightgowns. They billed themselves as the Psycho Sisters.

The Psycho Sisters soon gravitated towards a group of old friends who regularly jammed on the stage of an old rehearsal hall; Vicki knew bassist Mark Walton from the Dream Syndicate, one of the old Paisley Underground bands.

The group became the Continental Drifters. Susan Cowsill married guitarist Peter Holsapple, a Drifters guitarist, and by the mid '90s all the musicians had drifted to New Orleans, where today they are a frequent and favorite live attraction.

To date, the band has made two albums- 1999's *Vermilion,* on Razor & Tie, was critically acclaimed - and Vicki says she's never been happier. She's balancing the new Bangles project with her Drifters obligations.

Debbi began the '90s frightened and bitter. "I didn't speak to Susanna for a long time - we're talking years," she says. "We just had to heal some wounds, and we all had to do our own thing."

At Miles Copeland's urging, Debbi began to write with former Go–Go's drummer Gina Schock. Calling their band Smashbox, they cut five tracks with producer Humberto Garcia in 1992.

But Schock, she says, "got weird" and the project was never completed. Just as Debbi was wondering about throwing all the songs out, she was approached by singer Siobhan Maher, whose band, River City People, had just broken up. They had briefly discussed working together; how about now?

Dubbed Kindred Spirit, the pair toured England as Joan Armatrading's opening act in 1992. Two and a half years later, the *Kindred Spirit* album was released on IRS.

It's an atmospheric album that keeps its focus on the women's harmony vocals—and the songwriting is strong and interesting. Only one of the Schock tracks, "Here in My Eyes," made it to the finished album.

In 1994 Susanna married film director M. Jay Roach, whom she'd met on a blind date. Their son Jackson was born in 1995, son Sam three years later.

In between children, Susanna released a self–titled solo album on London (a terrific, almost underproduced set) and appeared in Roach's film *Austin Powers: International Man of Mystery*, as the guitar-playing go-go girl in Austin's band Ming Tea.

She also sang the Bacharach classic "The Look of Love" in the movie.

In 1998, Susanna and Debbi were both pregnant, and the Bangle wall started to crumble. "You can't hold a grudge forever," said Debbi. "Life's too short. And once you have a kid, your perspective changes."

Sam Roach and Brian Botting were born around the same time, and their mothers found themselves on the phone constantly, sharing parenting tips, and soon they were in a room, writing songs together. "It was fun again," Debbi said. "Just like the old days."

"Until Debbi had her son, we just couldn't connect on a human level," said Susanna. "Forget all this music stuff.

"Frankly, Vicki and I could always connect on that level. We were always friends. We could always talk to each other and just have a nice conversation, person to person.

"Which meant a lot to me. I didn't ever want to feel like I couldn't be friends with them. It was a little harder with Micki, because it was such a horrible thing that happened with the management. I didn't know about it. And I didn't know how devastating it was. She had to pick up the pieces, emotionally, from how that whole fiasco left her."

Michael moved to Northern California, among the redwoods, and lived with "a bunch of animals and no television." Both of Michael's parents died during this period; living alone, she wrote songs and played a little music with friends, only when the mood struck. She and Vicki spoke often.

"I got into a different rhythm," she explained. "I didn't have that kind of burning ambition thing any more, which was probably good. Because I think that's partially what caused the health problem."

Meanwhile Vicki, who "took a lot of convincing," came to Los Angeles and helped the twosome finish off "Get the Girl," a song for the second *Austin Powers* movie. She, too, realized things were different -everyone seemed to have the right priorities - and she convinced Michael to play bass and sing on the session. "It was a way of seeing if we can all be in the same room together," Vicki said.

Before that, "Micki never talked to Sue. Susanna just started reaching out to these people and having nice long conversations with them, and healing some of the wounds. She did all the work. She had to do all the work; it was her work to do."

The Bangles in 2000 are different people. "We handle things differently," said Vicki. "We're a little less afraid to say the scary stuff."

John Moran (1974)

19. Bo Diddley
'The day is coming, and that's a guarantee'

Bo lived in the country, not far from the Gainesville city limits. I first met him in the early '80s, and over the years, I'd check in with him to write this or that story for the newspaper. He was always surrounded by family, but I always had the feeling that he was lonely, like the neighbor kid who'd beg you to stay and play just a little bit longer. He loved to show off his electronic equipment out in the barn — he was usually hot-wiring some amplifier, soldering a guitar body or overdubbing a rhythm track with an old tape machine. He'd say "Check this out," and grab a handy microphone, hit the playback button and rap over the track. Live. Smiling the whole time. He was always demonstrating something new.

I did this career-spanning story for Goldmine *in 2003. I wanted to cover it all, for posterity, and as it turned out, this was the last time I ever spoke with him.*

At age 74, Bo Diddley may not be a spring chicken, exactly, but he's hardly courting the rocking chair. Although Bo and his wife Sylvia live a relatively quiet life on 80 acres in Central Florida, six nights a month you'll find the rock 'n' roll pioneer on a stage somewhere in America, wailing on his rectangular guitar, pounding out the most intoxicating of primitive rhythms, and singing with all the energy and fervor of a man half his age.

Bo Diddley, he's a man. Spelled M-A-N.

He'd rather be retired, casting for bass or tinkering with an old car engine, but this is how he makes his living. He receives no publishing royalties, having sold his great songs many years ago to clear up some debts. The terms of the record contracts he signed in the 1950s afford him very little money - if he didn't perform today, he says, he wouldn't have any steady income.

He's been an entertainer all his life, though, and nothing gives him more pleasure than making an audience happy.

And those audiences, they know who he is. He likes that.

"I was first, man," Diddley said. "Wasn't nobody doing nothin' until I thought of it. I was about a year and a half before Elvis Presley. And I don't like it when they jump up and say Elvis started rock 'n' roll. That's a lie. He didn't do it. He was really good, a fantastic entertainer, but he didn't do it."

Bo Diddley's great contribution to rock 'n' roll was as an innovator. He did things with rhythms that nobody in blues or country & western music had thought of. He figured out how to snake in and out of the breathy rhythm of a tremelo guitar. He introduced a toughness, a pride, into rock 'n' roll during its infancy, stitching in the naked, howling urgency of urban blues. Songs spoke volumes with just one chord. The rest - swagger, humor, lust and cool - was all Bo Diddley.

He likes to refer to himself as The Originator. "I think all the time," Diddley explained. "I'm always sitting somewhere trying to put something together that somebody else ain't did." In his 70s, he's still as sharp and straightforward as that skinny, nearsighted cat in the checkered jacket and bow tie, crowing about a stripper named Mona, trading musical jibes with a rubber-faced dude named Jerome, or asking a woman named Arline, flat out, who do you love? "I'm just 23 and I don't mind dyin'," he boasted.

He still writes music, although he doesn't realistically expect Snoop Dogg or Eminem to call him for advice. "They're not breaking down any doors to get cats my age," Diddley said. "They think that I'm finished. And I'm a tricky son of a bitch. I'm not finished, I just learned what to do."

He was born Ellas Bates on Dec. 30, 1928, a black Creole, in the southern Mississippi delta land between McComb and Magnolia. Just about everyone in the extended family picked cotton for a living. His teenaged mother wasn't able to raise a child in that impoverished climate, so at age eight months Ellas went to live with his mother's first cousin, Gussie McDaniel, and her husband, Robert.

"That's the way things was in those days," Diddley recalled. "Everybody raised everybody else's kids. I knew it as uncles and cousins and all that kind of stuff. There was quite a few of us. We shared everything.

"It ain't like it is today. If your parents were next door and you didn't happen to be a relative, if your parents had run out of some cornmeal or flour or bacon or whatever, if your mother was trying to cook, all she had to do was go across the field and ask Miss So-and-So could she borrow something? No problem."

Robert McDaniel's death in 1934 meant Gussie had to look for better work; she decided to join the flood of emigrants heading north.

So at age 7, Ellas relocated, with Gussie and her own kids, to the South Side of Chicago. His name became, legally, Ellas Bates McDaniel. They rented a house at 4746 Langley Avenue and joined the congregation at Ebenezer Baptist Church.

He loved the urbanity of his new digs and he fit right in. In Chicago, "treatment of black people was better. In the South, things were really screwed up. It didn't have to be that way, but I guess that's the way it was."

It was here, in grammar school, he got his lifelong nickname. "The kids there started calling me Bo Diddley," he said. "I still don't know what the hell it means … but I know what it means in German!" (It's a vulgarity.)

Initially, the kids had called him "Mac," because of his surname.

Young Ellas announced he wanted to learn to play violin with the Ebenezer Sunday School Band. "I wanted to do what I'd seen some dudes doing, with a stick draggin' across some strings and makin' music," Diddley said. "The church took up a collection, and the violin cost $29 at that time. And they bought me one. The lessons was like 50 cents a lesson. Are you ready for that? You can't even talk to nobody on the phone for that today."

He took lessons from Rev. O.W. Frederick - squinting at the dots on the page through his Coke-bottle glasses - and was soon proficient enough to play his instrument in church. He also sang in the choir.

One December five years later, Ellas was out shopping with his sister (technically, his first cousin) Lucille. "We went to this music store to buy some candy," he recalled. "And they had the ol' raggedy guitar hangin' up in there. And I looked at it, and I told my sister 'I want one of them.'

"I remember her saying 'You want everything you see.' I'm the same way today, man, if I see something that looks weird, I want to try that dude out.

"She bought it for me. It cost $29 or $30, almost the same thing with the violin. It was a old Kay guitar with two strings on it."

Frustrated at trying to play blues and jive music on his violin - he never got it to sound quite right - Ellas was immediately comfortable around the guitar. "When I liked what I heard John Lee Hooker doing, I said if this cat can play guitar, I know I can learn," he said.

"I tried to play 'When the Saints Go Marching In' running up and down them two strings. And I finally got enough pop bottle money. Strings were like 12 cents apiece. You'd buy one string at a time, until you got all of 'em."

Bo Diddley never learned how to properly tune the guitar; to this day, he still doesn't know the names of the strings or their proper pitch.

"I tuned it by accident," he said. "I liked what I heard. I tuned the thing, didn't know what the hell I was doing. It was said that Lonnie Johnson used to tune his guitar that way. I said 'Who in the heck is Lonnie Johnson?'

"This was before my time. I was a kid, a youngster, dealing with the same things that kids are dealing with today."

In 1940s Chicago, you had to learn how to fight. "We had a little neighborhood thing; we called ourselves the Golden Gloves," Diddley recalled. "We beat up on each other, you know? But I wasn't really what you'd call a boxer. I was what I would call a slugger, something like Mike Tyson.

"Mike'll hurt you, if he ever gets ahold of you. So the smart thing is to stay away from him. Because the cat is so powerful, he could break something on you real easy. And that's the way I was. As long as I kept you away from my head, I had it made."

Briefly, he considered training to become a professional boxer. "I didn't want to get into it," he said. "That was just to protect myself from gangs and all the stuff I grew up with. I never ran with a gang. I think a gang of boys jumpin' on one person is a very cowardly action."

Around the neighborhood, Ellas was known as the Fix-It Kid, because he could take virtually anything apart and put it back together again, good as new. He attended a vocational school and briefly thought about a career as an auto mechanic.

Music, however, was in his blood. "I started doing this and everybody thought I was the misfit in the family," he said. "There isn't anybody else doing it. I'm the only one that's got any musical background.

"My brother started in the ministry, but he could have played in some big-name baseball teams. They were after him. And he also has a talent for spreading the gospel." (Bo's half-brother is Reverend Kenneth Haynes of Biloxi, Miss.)

Ellas was constantly told that music - especially the "Devil's music" that he so enjoyed - would lead him down a path of destruction.

"I had to find out what I wanted to do," he said. "I had no idea I was gonna end up Bo Diddley."

Along with guitarist Jody Wilson, harmonica player Billy Boy Arnold and school chum Roosevelt Jackson - playing a washboard bass that Ellas himself constructed - he started playing the three or four songs he knew on street corners, the way blues musicians did, to get coins out of passers-by. They played them over and over again, and made new songs out of schoolyard rhymes.

At first they were called the Hipsters, then the Langley Avenue Jive Cats. "We did that and passed the hat," Diddley said. "I was too chickenshit to steal.

"I did it because my mother didn't have nothing. And everything that I wanted as I was growing up … it meant 'let me work so I can earn some money, so I can buy a pair of shoes, buy a pair of socks. A handkerchief to go in my shirt.'"

The origin of the famous Bo Diddley beat has been in contention for years; it incorporates elements of the old "shave and a haircut" rhythm, the early '50s shuck-and-jive hit "Hambone," Chicago blues and the open-tuning, hard-hitting guitar chords of Bo himself - heavy on the tremelo, once Bo got off streetcorners and went electric. "They didn't have no electric guitars down there," Diddley said. "I made my first electric guitar. I built the first tremelo - I actually did it. I built it with some points out of an old Plymouth distributor, and a big wind–up clock. I sat down and I put it all together to make the music go whop/whop/whop/whop/whop. Because every time they made contact, you'd get a sound. "I figured out how to do this, and a company was building one at the same time. I never went to Toledo, Ohio in my life, but somebody there was doin' one."

Then, as now, he was always tinkering. "I used to play by tapping into the audio tube in the back of a big radio. Got shocked a few times before I figured out which of the plugs on the back was the one."

By the time Ellas was 15, he and the guys were playing 20 street corners every Friday night, after school let out. "People would say 'There's them three dudes again,'" he recalled.

"We did something worthwhile, man; we didn't go out robbing people and all that. The police would sometimes take our little tip money, because they said it was illegal for us to try and make a living to buy bread."

Ellas left home, and school, at 16 and briefly went to vocational college. He married and divorced a young girl named Louise inside of a year. "She wanted to juke me around," he recalled. "All she wanted to do was get away from home."

Eventually the group came to include Jerome Green on maracas and vocals. Jerome would become Bo's onstage foil during the hit years, and an important part of the sound. "I met Jerome when I was with my second wife, Ethel Smith," Diddley said. "I met Jerome when I used to go over to her house to see her. He came up the back stairs with a tuba wrapped around his head, from school. They let him bring it home.

"I talked him into going with us on the street corners. He said 'Man, I ain't goin' out there,' and I said, 'Come on man, we're gonna pay you the same. We're gonna split up the money.'

"I stole my mother's cake bowl, and went out there and filled it up (with money). We came back with $15 apiece, for three of us. And the next weekend, Jerome was looking for me: 'Hey man, are we goin' back on the corner again?'"

Once the boys had turned 18, they left the street and getting booked into clubs. The next step was to get on record.

"I had an old Webco recorder," Diddley recalled. "And we made a dub, and I took it to Vee-Jay Records first. They looked at me and said 'What kind of crap is that?' I said I don't know, I just play it.

"They said 'Well, we don't know what to do with it,' because they was strictly into blues. John Lee Hooker and Jimmy Reed and all that kind of stuff.

"Nobody inspired me. I just wanted to be me. That's what I wanted to do, me."

"I figured I had something good enough to make a record. 'Cause the people on the streetcorner, they was jumpin' and clappin' their hands. I said 'Hey …. I'm making 'em jump.' So I figured this must be it."

In early 1955, Bo Diddley was signed by Leonard and Phil Chess, owners of Chicago's Chess Records (Bo was to record for the subsidiary label, Checker).

The idea of being on the same label as Willie Dixon, Muddy Waters and the rest of his heroes from the Chicago club scene "didn't excite me. It's just that I knew I was different from the rest of 'em. I was different from the other bands that I heard.

"I played a different type of music, and people were trying to figure out what the hell was I doing? Because I sounded like 10 people, rather than just three."

Momma Gussie and the others did not approve. "They said that I was playing for the Devil," Diddley remembered. "My aunts and uncles, everybody said 'Why don't you put that talent of yours to good use and play in the church? I said well, why do you all tell me to do that, and then you tell me I'm God-gifted?

"I said, you all can't pay me the money that I make in clubs, for playing in the church, no. I'm not gonna do it. I'm just doing it to try and make a living. I'm not hanging in clubs, getting drunk and fighting and cutting up people and cussing. I don't do no drugs, never have, never will. I'm scared of what the doctor gives me. I have no idea what the hell it is. I'm just what you call chickenshit."

"Bo Diddley/I'm a Man" was released in the spring and reached the top spot on the national R&B charts. The A side introduced the Bo Diddley beat to the world, syncopated in a blustery onslaught with Jerome's maracas and tribal tom-toms from drummer Clifton James.

Diddley's original version of the song went "Uncle John's got corn ain't never been shucked/Uncle John's got daughters ain't never been … to school."

At Leonard Chess' suggestion, he re-wrote the lyrics as a song about himself … about this character he'd created. Bo Diddley. Bo's legend would become a recurring theme.

"I'm a Man" was another ballgame altogether. Here, Diddley dealt a straight hand of Chicago blues, punctuated by Billy Boy's wailing harmonica.

"Muddy Waters came up with 'I'm a Rolling Stone,' or 'I'm a King Bee,' one of those songs, saying 'when I was 26 years old,'" Diddley recalls. "And I said well, if you're a rolling stone, I'm a man. You understand? Willie Dixon wrote those - and I thought if he's that bad, I'm a man."

Not long after, "Muddy copied it and wrote 'Mannish Boy.' There's only one word in 'Mannish Boy' that I never understood. He uses the line 'woe be.' I ain't never figured out what 'woe be' means."

The record was like nothing heard before. There were no complex changes, just gut-busting emotion on "I'm a Man" and shuffling energy on "Bo Diddley."

The success of the single meant live appearances, and Diddley's group hit the road, getting farther from Chicago with every performance. On Aug. 20, he played the legendary Apollo Theatre in New York City. "And destroyed it," he recalled. "People was trying to figure out, how is three dudes makin' all that noise?"

In those days, Diddley said, the national speed limit was 45 MPH. "I mostly drove with my band. I had a 1941 DeSoto station wagon; they called it a Stagecoach. It had a rack on the top, and we used to tie all our stuff up on top of it. And away we went."

In November, the band returned to New York to appear on Ed Sullivan's TV show. This story has become an integral part of the Bo Diddley legend; this is the artist's own version: "Ed Sullivan heard us in the dressing room practicing 'Sixteen Tons,' Tennessee Ernie's song. He said 'Can you guys play that on the show?' and I said 'Yeah, we can play it our way.' But I was there to do 'Bo Diddley' by Bo Diddley. So I did two songs, and he got pissed.

"But it was their mistake, the way that they had the program written up. I did it the way that the program said: Bo Diddley and 'Sixteen Tons.' As far as I'm concerned, that's the name of the song - and, 'Sixteen Tons.'

"Ed Sullivan said I was the first colored boy that ever double-crossed him on a song, or something. And I started to get on him, just to tell this old man the truth, right in his fuckin' face. Because I hadn't ever been said nothin' to like that, and I didn't double cross him. They made the mistake, and I lived with it for a lot of years.

"He said I would never work again. And I got 48 years of rock 'n' roll. I'm not happy that he's dead, you know, but I had something that I perfected. And I did my best. And I think that's the reason why I'm still here."

History always seems to contrast Diddley with his Chess labelmate Chuck Berry - the two even issued a patched-together duet album in the early '60s - but Bo Diddley sees this as an apples-and-oranges thing. "We were writing different," he said. "He was writing about school days and stuff like that, which was very interesting. And I wrote comical-type tunes. He couldn't be funny; I could. I could make you laugh."

Berry also crossed over to a white audience in those heavily segregated days, something Diddley never really managed. Although he made a respectable showing on the R&B charts, only one of his singles, 1959's "Say Man," made a dent on the pop side.

"Say Man" was a series of good-natured back and forth insults between Bo and Jerome, what they used to call "signifying" back on the streets in Chicago.

He considers "Who Do You Love," first released in the summer of 1956, a "funny" song. "Well, it was serious and funny at the same time," he said. For the record, there never was a woman named Arlene in his life. He just made it up.

As his fortunes faded in the United States, as Presley, Berry, Holly and so many others brought rock 'n' roll to an insatiable audience, Bo Diddley struggled. "Say Man," "Crackin' Up" and "Road Runner" were major hits, but by the early '60s, it just wasn't happening.

The live show continued to generate excitement. Guitarist Norma Jean Wofford joined his band in 1961 (following a short stint by another woman stringbender, Peggy Jones). Wofford became known as The Duchess; it was whispered that she was Bo Diddley's sister. "We told that lie so much that it started sticking," Diddley said. "But we're actually no kin. I had started adding different people to the group. It was just guys at first, and I said 'I need some glamor on the stage,' so I started putting the girls in the group."

Novelty had always been important for Diddley - his classic 1960 album, *Bo Diddley is a Gunslinger* was inspired by the movie *The Magnificent Seven* and had a Western theme - and his act had always included a little comedy, a little dancing. "Didn't none of us stand still," he recalled.

Diddley was surprised to learn, during a 1963 trip to Great Britain, that he was held in high regard by the young, rhythm 'n' blues worshiping musician crowd. The Rolling Stones, one of the tour's opening acts, dropped all Diddley covers from their set as an act of respect.

The young Stones viewed Bo Diddley with awe; Brian Jones, Diddley remembered, had an insatiable curiosity about the rhythm and the blues. And "Mick (Jagger) is like a loner; he stays by himself all the time. And you don't impose on a person like that - if that's his way, that's his way. I don't fault him for it."

Diddley's relationship with the Stones continued over time - in the '80s, Diddley and guitarist Ron Wood toured Japan together, and Bo joined the band onstage in Miami on the 1994 *Voodoo Lounge* tour.

In 1965, he appeared in the legendary *TAMI Show*, and four years later played the Toronto Rock 'n' Roll Festival, on a bill with the Plastic Ono Band. Diddley can be seen in D.A. Pennebaker's film *Sweet Toronto*.

Overall, though, the '60s were rough. Diddley continued to record and perform, but his records had little impact. The British Invasion, followed by the psychedelic and hippie movements, left little room for the pioneering rock 'n' rollers.

Diddley watched attitudes and fashions change all around him. "My generation wasn't into that shit," he laughed. "So I'm sitting outside going what the hell's going on? I'm starving in my own world, my music world. But I found out something: If you can't beat 'em, you gotta join 'em" (see the Chess albums *The Black Gladiator; Another Dimension*).

Strapped for cash because of an investment scheme gone wrong, Diddley sold his publishing in this period.

And like many artists who rode in on the first wave in the '50s, he got paid a ridiculous royalty rate. He was never a math whiz, so he signed whatever contract had been put in front of him. "The Chess Brothers were very secluded about telling an artist," he said. "It looked like to me that they were afraid somebody would step out of place and start asking for more money. I was just interested in playin' for the people. I had no idea about the business, how it worked and all this.

"They were beginning to set up little things here and there that would elude you from the right things - in other words, while you sleep, we'll figure out how we can not pay you something."

The winter of Diddley's discontent began in the glory days and has yet to blow over. He remembers precisely when he first realized he'd been short-changed:

"When I started to asking about royalty checks and all this kind of stuff, my stuff started getting played less and less," he said. "And I didn't understand. And after a while it looked like it was set before me so that I could plainly see it, that I was becoming a troublemaker because I started asking about royalty checks. This meant that I was going to cause problems. And the easiest way to shut you up was to pull your records off the airwaves. It's called blackball.

"When the people buy your stuff and make you earn the name 'So-and-so is really great.' But when your record company don't acknowledge that you got a contract with 'em, and so much revenue come in that they're supposed to give you this and that ... this didn't happen with me. Instead, they put the money in their pocket. I guess because I was a little country black boy in Chicago, I got ripped off. Because they figured I didn't know what time it was."

Then, as now, the only real money that came Bo Diddley's way was from live shows. And if somebody's making money off those classic records, it's not him. "I ain't seen shit," he said.

And so he works, flying hundreds, thousands of miles, equipped with only a guitar and a suitcase. Although he has a semi-regular group for big shows, he does most gigs with a pickup band, hired by the local promoter in each town he plays.

After Chicago, he lived in Washington, D.C. (the *Gunslinger* album was recorded on a two-track Presto machine in his basement), then Los Angeles and, ultimately, Florida (he spent a year or two in Las Lunas, N.M., too, where he was deputized and walked a sheriff's beat). He was married to Georgia native Kay Reynolds for 20 years, and bought his first Florida property from her dentist.

Every few years, some music business sharpie with a few bucks in his wallet signs him up for an album; without fail, they make little or no commercial impact.
Diddley cares very little for the 1973 *The London Bo Diddley Sessions*, which paired him with a contingent of hip young English rock players. "When you turn your back, they do whatever they feel like doing," he said. Since the end of Chess in the mid '70s, he's drifted from label to label.

In 1996, producer Mike Vernon put out the Bo Diddley album *A Man Amongst Men*, which featured "collaborations" from the likes of Keith Richards, Ronnie Wood and Richie Sambora.

Trouble was, Vernon assembled the tracks from pieces; Bo was rarely in the same room with his guest stars. "It just never occurred to them that maybe Bo doesn't want it that way, you know?" Diddley said. "So it would be my mistake if I fucked up. But they fucked up, and I still bear the cross of them messing up. And the public don't know that I had nothing to do with it."

He has a handful of bedrock songs that continue to reverberate today ("Who Do You Love," "I'm a Man," "Before You Accuse Me," "Mona"), and the "Bo Diddley Beat" is a cornerstone of rock 'n' roll (see "Not Fade Away," "I Want Candy," "She's the One").

His 1987 induction into the Rock and Roll of Fame was logical - and, perhaps not surprisingly, Bo Diddley took it with a grain of salt.

"The way I look at it, the attention is really great," he said. "But the reward in what I have done is not a plaque sitting on my wall, because I can't do anything with it. They're worth a lot of money to a collector, but to me they're not worth anything.

"It doesn't really mean anything to me. It don't pay none of my bills. Take the actors who got the Oscars and the Emmys, they don't mean nothin.' It's just that people can come to your house and see 'em and go 'Wow, you got an Oscar.' What does it mean? Is it worth a thousand dollars? $400? $200? Or worth a million dollars?

"What is it worth in dollar bills, because this is what you need to survive. Not a medal with your name on it."

Back surgery slowed him down in the '90s - he had to sit in a chair onstage for a while - and a recurring bout with high blood pressure caused him to cancel a few dates in 2002.

Otherwise, hell, he ain't slowing down.

"I figure I got 15 or 20 years, maybe longer than that," he said. "If I take care of myself. But it's winding down. I might as well face it. I don't look to kick off, but when you get to my age you start getting' scared and you start realizing that the day is coming, and that's a guarantee. We're all gonna leave out of here.

"As you get older, things become more clear to you about everyday existence. Am I going to be able to wake up in the morning? Am I going to sleep and ... you don't know that you're gone? That's the way I feel.

"That is the most scary thing in the world. You take me, traveling on the road by myself, and getting a hotel room. Go to bed, go to sleep, and I don't know if I'm gonna get up and go catch the plane in the morning. I used to not worry about that."

John Moran

20. Jethro Tull:
Living with the past

John Moran's photo, which you see on this page, was taken in Jacksonville, Florida, just before Jethro Tull took the stage on May 8, 2002. I spent the better part of 10 days following the band's Florida tour stops, talking with the witty, enigmatic and charismatic founder, leader, singer, songwriter and flautist Ian

Anderson just about every day. He is one of the most engaging interview subjects in all of rock 'n' roll. I enjoyed every minute of it, and wrote about it for Goldmine, *which printed my friend John's wonderful shot on the cover.*

Ian Anderson is sitting in the darkest possible corner of a fluorescent coffeeshop in Melbourne, Fla., the morning after a concert. From nowhere, a slightly rough-looking middle-aged woman approaches him.

"I just wanted to tell you I saw you at Woodstock," she tells Jethro Tull's 55-year-old pointman, who does a doubletake then smiles politely.

"Actually, we didn't play Woodstock," Anderson explains in his slightly upper-crusty English accent.

"Oh yes," says the woman, knowingly. "Jethro was there."

Anderson is used to comments like this. "How were we, then?" he asks, poker-faced.

He listens attentively as the woman goes off on a tangent about Woodstock - she was 7 years old, and Janis Joplin leaned down from the stage and held her hand. Anderson smiles and nods while she talks.

Satisfied, she shuffles off, and Anderson chuckles. "Oh well," he sighs. "It's easier to say 'Yeah, hi, it's me.' It's pointless to actually try to explain. People don't really hear the explanation."

The encounter - just a few days into the 10-date Florida stretch of Tull's 2002 American tour - illustrates a few of the most common misconceptions about this veteran British band. Although Ian Anderson writes and sings all the songs, is the very visible frontman and is probably the most famous flute player in rock 'n' roll - just try and think of another one as big - there is, and has never been, anyone in the band named Jethro. Anderson took the title back in 1968 - Jethro Tull was an 18th century agriculturalist - and has regretted it ever since. He calls it "the dreaded J-word."

Tull wasn't quite big enough to play Woodstock in 1969, although within a year or two they would be selling out stadiums.

These days, many people probably think the band that made *Aqualung* and *Thick as a Brick* is broken up, its members either dead or waiting tables back home.

But Ian Anderson and Jethro Tull have endured. "Other than a year in '84 when I really wrecked my voice, badly, I've never felt the urge to take a leave of absence," Anderson says. It's been 34 years so far.

The faithful are still out there - most of the shows on this theater tour have been sellouts. This despite the fact that Tull's back catalog outsells each new release with punishing regularity.

Anderson is circumspect on the subject. "You always know that the rise to success is inevitably accompanied by departure from that lofty status," he says. "And the faster you go up, the faster you come down. It's probably important to remember Jethro Tull didn't exactly struggle, but we had a fairly gentle and happily graduated rise to prominence.

"By the time we were at Madison Square Garden, we'd been kicking around for four years. We were hardly the new boys anymore."

It wasn't until the band's fourth album, 1971's *Aqualung*, that Jethro Tull - the band, the flute player or the long-dead agriculturalist, take your pick - became a household name in the States.

"It was a very gradual thing," Anderson explains. "Just as it's been gradual to slide back down again at the other end in middle age. You find the decline is inevitable for pretty much whoever you are … you don't tend to just fall off the cliff."

The Scots-born Anderson moved to Blackpool, England at the age of 12, and fell under the spell of American blues in the early-to-mid '60s. He was lead singer in an erstwhile blues/R&B group that made the pilgrimage south to London in '67; most of the band went home, broke and starving, but Anderson decided to stay and tough it out.

Along with guitarist Mick Abrahams, bassist Glenn Cornick and drummer Clive Bunker, Anderson formed Jethro Tull in the waning days of '67.

Hard to believe it now, but Anderson's dilemma at the time was what to do onstage; he wanted to add something to the group's sound, but knew he wasn't much of an electric guitarist.

One day he wandered into a London music shop. "I'm standing there with a 1960s Fender Strat in my hand, looking to swap it in, and I looked around – there was a violin, and a cello and other things in this music store – and a flute hanging on the wall," he recalls.

"I got a Shure Unidyne 3 microphone and a Selmo Gold Seal flute in exchange for my 1960s Fender Strat, which is probably worth $25,000 now."

Although Anderson would eventually adapt jazzman Roland Kirk's unique fluttery, singing-through-the-flute style, he admits his inspiration initially came from somewhere entirely different.

"My first flute lesson was from listening to Eric Clapton, when he was with John Mayall's Bluesbreakers," Anderson says. "And sitting in my bedroom, as I guess countless people have done then and through the years, running Eric Clapton at half-speed trying to learn the guitar solos."

But Anderson quickly outgrew the blues – his interest in jazz, folk and the odd harmonics of what would later be called world music, combined with his steely ambition, would drive a wedge between him and erstwhile co-leader Mick Abrahams.

Shortly after the release of *This Was* in '68, Abrahams left to form Blodwyn Pig.

"Mick wasn't happy with the stuff I was writing," Anderson says. "It was outside his comfort zone of playing. But equally, I didn't want to just do 12-bar blues covers for the rest of my life. Because I wasn't American, I wasn't black, and I knew that what they were singing about was a different set of values coming from a different place. So to imitate it, to assume some authority to sing these words and not to be black, just felt to me somehow not very natural."

Anderson claims he called the album "*This Was Jethro Tull* because it was apparent to me that the next album, if I had anything to do with it, wasn't gonna sound the way the first album did."

Released in August 1969, *Stand Up* made No. 1 in the U.K. The album was nearly a 180-degree turn from its predecessor, with unlikely shifts in tempo, wickedly incisive lyrics, and acoustic guitar flourishes in the least expected places. Most of all, Anderson's gift for odd melody and dark harmony was rapidly developing. *Stand Up* and its followup, the more pointedly electric *Benefit*, didn't sound like anything else on the English pop charts.

Guitarist Martin Barre replaced Abrahams for *Stand Up*, and he's been at Anderson's side ever since. Barre recalls botching his audition, but Anderson heard something in his playing - more free-form and less reliant on recycled blues riffs - that opened the door for him.

"Martin and I, we're complementary I suppose because we're very different people," Anderson says. "I think we value each other's contribution without it being competitive. I don't threaten his world because I'm not an electric guitar player - we have our different strengths and we're not competing with each other in any way for musical attention."

To date, more than 25 musicians have played with Ian and Martin. They've left to get married, to form new bands, for solo careers or because Ian, frankly, got fed up and fired them.

"They all own a tiny piece of Jethro Tull," Anderson explains diplomatically. "It's their family, it's their territory. Past and present members. They are a piece of Jethro Tull.

"But by the same token, I'm not gonna be too coy about it and say 'Well, I'm just another member of the band.' When we get onstage, I am a member of the band.

"But I do a whole lot more than the other guys do for the other 22 hours in the day. That's not because I'm trying to steal the thunder or whatever, it's just that I'm probably better equipped to deal with it, and to do it. The oil rises and floats on top of the water — you can mix it up again, but it'll come back up. That's the way it is with me."

On the road, Anderson is up and working by 7 or 8 every morning; if there isn't a live radio interview, he's talking to the press in Europe, where it's already mid-afternoon. There's a consistent flow of business to be taken care of with various members of his staff back in England – when he's not talking Tull, it's salmon (the Ian Anderson Companies own the largest salmon-farming concern in Scotland), or hot peppers (he raises and relishes them) or small exotic cats (he keeps many and is a conservation advocate for many more).

Anderson is also a U.K. spokesman for the early diagnosis of deep vein thrombosis (DVT), a potentially crippling condition from which he suffers. Its successful treatment has allowed him to maintain his famous one-legged onstage stance, although he strikes the pose quite a bit less now than in the glory days.

For the last few years, Anderson has also stopped shaking hands with people - promoters, fans, anyone who extends their appendage. Instead, he offers his elbow and invites the person to rub his.

He knows it puts people off and only reinforces their idea of him as an arrogant rock star. For the record, here's the deal: Anderson injured his wrist four or five tours ago, whilst jumping off a stage during soundcheck.

"It was worrying because when you're a flute player or a guitar player, you don't want problems," he says. "So it's a precaution. I go through weeks of shaking hands with people and it's not a problem. And then I get the guy - and sometimes the girl - who just does the bone-crusher. And this weakness is just so easily aggravated."

He's mounting a short solo tour in the fall, and it already has a title: "Rubbing Elbows With Ian Anderson."

TALLAHASSEE – An hour before showtime, Martin Barre is reflecting on life in Jethro Tull, 2002. "We don't make huge amounts of money, but we make a good living," says the affable guitarist. "But it's a very easygoing lifestyle; there's no bullshit. There's a lot of private time."

Barre, who's made two solo albums, says Tull - although it's Anderson's baby - is his own top priority. "I don't think I work for Ian," he explains. "I don't think anybody works for anybody. We have too much independence.

"There's a basic understanding that when there's Tull touring, we're on the phone, and that sort of machinery goes into play.

"And in between, if I want to go on a holiday I'll let Ian know, just so he knows. And if he gets a call for a gig in Buenos Aires, he knows he can't do it."

As any recording act, vintage or otherwise, will tell you, the money's in doing live shows. So Tull remains Tull by keeping the stage act fresh and exciting, as well as happily nostalgic. "The commitment to playing with Jethro Tull isn't largely a financial one," Barre says. "I would think that comes last.

"I like doing it, and I'd hate anybody else to do it, for sure, because it's my gig. And I'd be seriously pissed off if somebody else ended up doing it. It's been my gig for 34 years, and I've made the guitarist gig in Jethro Tull what it is. That's me."

The band's breakthrough and still best-selling album *Aqualung* was propelled by Anderson's alternately funny, nasty, self-deprecating and very English songs about charlatans, slatterns, old letchers and the hoary, hairy, hypocritical state of organized religion in Great Britain.

"It's nice to be sharp," Anderson believes. "It's nice to be sometimes a little cutting, but you have to be careful not to actually offend individuals. It's kind of OK to criticize generically, but not when it hones in on what people feel is a very personal thing.

"Which is why I never write songs about people I know. They're always more about the stereotype rather than specific individuals."

With *Aqualung*, Jethro Tull became an outstanding, integrated band, capable of stitching together hard rock and acoustic textures without allowing the seams to show.

The band only got better as time went on. For *Thick As a Brick* (1972), Anderson and Barre were joined by Ian's old mates from Blackpool Jeffrey Hammond (bass), Barrie Barlow (drums) and John Evans (piano).

Excess being the order of the day, they all took English rock star names: Jeffrey Hammond–Hammond, Barriemore Barlow and John *Evan*.

Did someone say excess? Anderson: "Bearing in mind that a lot of people thought *Aqualung* was a concept album - and I've always said it was just a bunch of songs - with this echo of 'concept' album ringing in my ears from the year before I thought 'OK, we'll give them the mother of all concept albums.'

"And we came up, in that slightly surrealistic English humor, in that Monty Pythonesque sort of humor, we did the album that was the spoof, the satire, the sendup of concept albums. To the point of pretending it had all been written by a 12-year-old boy and all the rest of it."

Thick as a Brick was one solid 40-minute piece of music spread out over both sides of an LP. Dark, inscrutable and counter-commercial even by Tull standards, it nevertheless became the band's first No. 1 in America.

"I was surprised that they embraced it, having taken it perhaps more literally or more seriously than it was intended," points out Anderson. "I guess I erred on the side of not being obvious enough in the case of the American audience. Because too many people took it seriously, didn't get the humor or the silliness of it."

Hailed in (some of) the world press as the next great rock 'n' roll visionary, Anderson took the band across the universe, with audiences from Jersey to Japan politely applauding the unwieldy *Brick*, played onstage in its opaque entirety. And going nuts for the songs from *Aqualung* and prior.

"We should have got off that particular merry-go-round at that point, but there was a tendency and a certain expectation and pressure that I felt - that I shouldn't have felt - that we now had to follow it up with a similar, conceptual piece," Anderson explains. "And this time it better be serious, and it better be artistically credible."

On the strength of its predecessor, *A Passion Play* spent a week at the top of the American charts. But it never - never - got played on the radio.

The critics hated the concept, the music, the lyrics. They hated the album cover and its libretto, which parodied provincial British theater. Almost overnight, Anderson and company became the poster boys for what the press - particularly in their home country - decided was pretentious, needlessly complex rock music. For the most part, they would never recover.

Today, Anderson is frank about *A Passion Play*. "It was a real stinker," he admits.

The *Passion Play* concert - which began with nothing more than an electronic pulse and a point of light, growing steadily over the course of 20 minutes - was nobody's favorite. "It was a nightmare to try and remember it," Barre recalls. "Everybody gets up their own ass from time to time. As a group, we did during that."

Still, Tull was a live act with virtually no peer. This was Anderson's moment to shine. He'd traded in the grubby overcoats and jackboots of the early days for purple tights and a codpiece. He delighted in playing the demented one-legged Pan, deftly blowing and humming through the flute while popping his eyes, grinning maniacally and flinging himself towards Hammond-Hammond, dressed head to toe in zebra stripes, or at Evan, who enjoyed wearing rabbit suits onstage.

In the summer of 1976, Jethro Tull became one of the first pop groups since the Beatles to play New York's famed Shea Stadium. They sold it out.

"If you want the sort of cruel reminders of just how fragile these things are," Anderson says, "as we were waiting to walk onstage, we were standing in this strange entranceway with vertical walls that went up 60, 70 feet, that contained the audience. Suddenly something wet, and not very nice, was running down my face, from my head. Somebody had pissed in a jar or something, and then poured it over me. And that was it - suddenly it was, 'You're on!' And I had to walk onstage that night with some other man's urine running down my head."

He laughs at the recollection ("Well, I assume it was a man") and begins to tick off the things he's been hit with: A baseball in the Adam's apple, a thorned rose in the eye.

And then there's this one: "I was playing acoustic guitar and something hit me in the chest. But it was soft, and I didn't pay too much attention. I felt something sort of sliding down inside my shirt. I couldn't see it, but it was sticky, and warm and wet.

"It was a tampon. I was singing 'Thick As a Brick' or whatever, and I remember that I managed to look down, it was bloody and awful, you know? The first thought that went through my head was 'What an extraordinary thing ... this must have been plucked from between this woman's legs during the concert ...'

"That's the weird thing to me. Either this was a demonstration of some undying sense of love and intimacy, or it was the worst thing someone could possibly do. Either way, this had been freshly removed. That's the bit that gets me."

Barre says the members of Tull were very serious about their music, even in the days of codpieces, string quartets and roadies in polar bear suits. "We looked down on (stardom) with a bit of disdain. Because we didn't want to be the rockers with the flowing hair and the tight trousers, and the drugs and the women. God, we tried.

"We weren't like that. And all the other bands that we met, God, you wanted to stick your finger down your throat. They were repulsive people."

He remembers Shea Stadium well. "We all brushed it off, played it down: 'Aw, it's just another gig.' Of course, it wasn't - it was the most amazing thing you could do in your life. And there should have been champagne, big party after the gig.

"We should have pumped it up for ourselves more than we did, but we were back in the car, back to the hotel, sandwich from the deli, TV. But maybe that was good, you know? Maybe that made us survive it."

Tull finished out the '70s with a few more great albums - including *Minstrel in the Gallery* and *Songs From the Wood* - and some spotty ones. Band members began to come and go, leaving Anderson and Barre at the forefront.

In the '90s, there were box sets and multi-disc retrospectives, a switch in labels (to Fuel 2000) and a lot of salmon up the slipstream.

TAMPA – An early–morning radio interview has gone well. Armed with a CD of home-made backing tracks, Anderson played the flute - Bach's "Bouree" first, because instrumentals are easier in the a.m. Fueled by strong Floridian coffee, he'd then done "Living in the Past," singing and playing.

The entire radio station staff, it seems - about 20 people - had crowded into the studio to watch and listen. And so, after a few photos, autographs and rubbing of elbows, he climbs into the back of a stretch limousine for the ride back his hotel on Clearwater Beach.

Question: Are you a hard taskmaster?

"As hard taskmasters will say, yes, but I'm harder on myself than everybody else," Anderson reflects. "I think you have to be prepared to be pretty ruthless with your own performance, to be self-critical. But sure, you've got to apply some kind of rules. And some people do that for themselves, some don't.

"It's the same in the band now. There's one guy who needs pushing a lot. Otherwise he just doesn't do his homework. And Martin, for instance, if I send out some notes for new arrangements a few months before a tour, when he shows up he's got it all down. He's learned it. He's done the homework."

The current lineup includes drummer Doane Perry, an American who joined the band in time for the 1984 *Under Wraps* album; keyboard player Andrew Giddings (1991's *Catfish Rising*) and relative new guy Jonathan Noyce on bass.

Talk inevitably turns, again, to the subject of living in the past. Despite putting out an album a year, more or less, for 30-odd years, the band hasn't made a ripple with the critics or on the charts in ages.

"The Rolling Stones don't sell that many records; Mick Jagger doesn't sell any," Anderson says. "The world is a different place in terms of the way the economics and the music industry are related. So you work a lot harder for the same dollar, that's for sure.

"Sixty thousand people in New York is beyond us. We're not gonna play to that many people. But we'll play to 8,000 people at Jones Beach, and collectively around that New York/New Jersey area we'll play to 20,000 people somewhere.

"So it would be reasonable to say, yes, our popularity in real terms has probably declined to something like 25, 30 percent of what it was, in numerical terms. But everybody has their peak, where you're the flavor of the month or the flavor of the year. Jethro Tull circa '72-73 was a very big band, but not necessarily for the right reasons.

"I've always had the preference to playing theaters to 2,500 or 3,000 people. That's really always been there, since we got out of the clubs. I was really happy to leave clubs behind, but I love playing the theaters."

The irony here is that some of Tull's stuff from the last decade is as musically invigorating as the famous material. Anderson realizes that his critics are comparing him with an earlier version of himself.

"If somebody's winge-ing on about the fact that I don't have any hair … age-ism and hair-ism are two favorite topics," he explains. "As if somehow you shouldn't be on the stage if you don't have proper hair any more. There's nothing I can do about that one!

"I think we've always been pretty fair game. We were then, and we still are now. I don't think we get as many bad reviews as we used to, but then I don't think we get as many reviews as we used to."

His third solo album, 2000's *The Secret Language of Birds*, contained some of the most sublime acoustic music Anderson's ever made. Every Tull album - from *Stand Up* to *Stormwatch* -included one or two delicate acoustic songs, far removed from the hard rock or the complexities of the long proggy songs with long titles.

These are gems, found happenstance by the listener as he navigates the albums. "I'm not a great guitar player," Anderson shrugs, "but I have a certain idiosyncratic style that's fun to do."

Secret Language - which, of course, was not a big seller - represented all the acoustic tunes Anderson had stockpiled for a few years.

"I get those days when I'm in the studio, and maybe the other guys haven't come in yet, or it's their lunch break, and you go in and do some quick little acoustic thing," he says. "And those songs were present on Jethro Tull records for quite a while, those ones that I just did sort of on my own.

"I stopped doing that, because there was a sense of 'We're left out of this one.' I always remember Barrie Barlow saying 'I want to play tambourine on that,' and I said 'I don't really want tambourine on that, Barrie.' And he said 'Well, in that case, if I'm not on it, then I still want paying for it.'

"I said that forcing yourself on the record just to get paid just doesn't seem like a good idea - equally, to be paid for something you're not on is a bit strange. So there was a degree of bad feeling, and understandable though it was, it was easier for me to stop doing that stuff. So by the end of the '70s, I wasn't doing that kind of stuff within Jethro Tull anymore."

Before this tour began, Anderson busied himself with the preparation of *Living With the Past*, Tull's first DVD and its accompanying album. It's a live collection, recorded last Christmas, with a set list nearly identical to the current shows.

Living With the Past, its title a tongue-in-cheek reference to the band's beloved *Living in the Past* compilation album, also includes several newly-recorded versions of acoustic Tull classics, plus a one-off reunion of the original band - Anderson, Abrahams, Bunker and Cornick.

As master of the Tull domain, Anderson is also responsible for the fairly constant flow of reissues, best-ofs and sonic improvements. He loves making the old albums sound better with each new technological advance.

"I'm not an analog freak," he says. "I'm not one of those people who say 'I only listen to music on my old vinyl pressings.' The vinyl pressings sound absolutely crap. Turntable rumble, phasing problems … I mean, the difficulty of actually getting stuff onto the vinyl was a pig.

"I personally attended and worked on every vinyl mastering session of every Jethro Tull album. I sat there and watched the wretched lacquer going 'round and 'round, attempting to squeeze another half db of level on the inner band."

In the old days, quality control often meant leaving certain songs out of your running order. "You could only stick eight or 10 tracks on a vinyl record," Anderson says. "Basically, 20 minutes a side was it. You could get 23, 24 minutes a side, but only at the penalty of even further reducing the overall signal level on vinyl, and by reducing the band width. So the compromises were unacceptable.

"Which meant that there were lots of songs recorded that never made it onto the records because of time constraints. They were either B-sides, or released on things like the *Living in the Past* album later on."

Some of the earliest Tull master tapes, Anderson says, had to undergo the risky "baking" process to re-adhere the oxide to the actual vinyl tape. "Once it's safely in digital-land, you can play around with the signal," he explains. "Then you put the tapes back in their box and hope you don't ever have to get them out again.

"Which is a sincere hope on my part, because these things have been with me through three house moves. I have about a metric ton and a half of tapes, with a specially reinforced floor to actually hold them all."

ORLANDO – Soundcheck. It's 5:15 in the afternoon, and Tull is onstage, running through the complex "Heavy Horses."

Suddenly, Anderson lays down his flute, jumps off the stage (taking care with that tender wrist) and begins stalking from one side of the theater to the other, sticking his head into the speaker stacks, listening from every corner of the room as the band plows on.

After a few angry words with his soundman - "All these rooms sound the fucking same!" - he sits for a moment to explain his behavior. The room-check is a part of his daily ritual.

"That's an important part of what I do," he says. "Especially the front fills, because the people sitting near the front of the stage often get the worst sound in the building. Because the PA's flying out over their heads and they don't hear a thing. They just hear the echo from behind them. I take it as a personal responsibility to make sure that it's as right as it can be."

Anderson's constant companion on this and every tour is his second wife, the former Shona Learoyd, whom he married in 1976.

Once an employee of Chrysalis, Tull's longtime record label, Shona joined the Tull organization as a runner and became one of Ian's onstage "flute handlers" during the *War Child* tour.

She helps her husband run the Tull machine. She is also co-director of their salmon-farming business (the Andersons recently bought out one of their closest competitors) and, she says with a roll of the eyes, she cleans up after the cats. They have two grown children.

Anderson's pre-concert rituals haven't changed in years. He does not eat past lunchtime, and about 90 minutes before every show he goes quietly into the dressing room and won't speak to anyone but Shona.

"The few words that for me describe the different emotions onstage are anticipation, focus and concentration," he explains. "It's really important that you have your mind cleared out of extraneous thoughts, and when you go onstage you're really tightly focused on the pace of things. You really have to have the right metabolic physicality about you, because if you're too hyped up, you play things too fast. You try and standardize the way you feel just before you go onstage."

By and large, every show on the tour is the same. "If we're playing these sort of theaters," Anderson explains, motioning, "we'll tend to stick with a slightly more esoteric set. If however we find ourselves at a festival, then we'll play a few more obvious tunes."

Anderson knows the diehard fans want to hear the obscure songs, but he realizes he's got to fulfill a lot of people's fantasy of what a Jethro Tull concert is supposed to be. "You know you're always going to have someone in the back, after a couple of beers, going 'Aqualung!' 'Locomotive Breath!' or whatever it is," he says.

"And it doesn't matter that you're standing there with an acoustic guitar in your hands, they expect somehow in their imagination, in their dreams, the whole thing's gonna light up, smoke machines are gonna go off, and cannons."

A highlight of the new show is "The Water Carrier," a *Secret Language* song with a mideastern flavor. Shona has an onstage cameo during the performance, dressed as a seductive belly dancer.

"I would risk that at a festival," Anderson chuckles. "We played it at a couple of biker festivals last year and got away with it. There was a temptation midway through to segue into 'Born to Be Wild,' but I resisted it, and we stuck to our guns. Happily the Hell's Angels stuck to theirs."

Rhino Records

21. Linda Ronstadt (2003)
'I grew up thinking I was a boy soprano'

After my initial conversation with Linda Ronstadt, for the 1996 Emmylou Harris story, I always looked forward to speaking with her. She was frank, she was funny, and she seemed to me incapable of telling a falsehood. She was never really "pushing product," it seemed to me. She just liked to talk. When she and Harris made the record Western Wall: The Tucson Sessions *in 1999, I conducted a joint interview with both of them.* Trio II *had come out by then, with Dolly Parton's original vocal tracks restored, and she and Linda had made some kind of peace.*

For this story, written for in Goldmine *in 2003, we were ostensibly on the phone to plug a new* Best Of Ronstadt *anthology Rhino Records had put out. But that didn't interest her – or me - at all. So I just turned on the recorder and off we went.*

There are many things about her career that Linda Ronstadt wishes she'd done differently. Still, the most successful female singer of the rock 'n' roll era is happily 56 years old, raising two young children, and working only when she wants to.

"All musicians, if they say they're doing it for the audience, they're probably bullshitting," Ronstadt says. "Music is a biological necessity. It's a way that we all have of processing our feelings.

"Everybody really should do music. And once in a while, when you're doing your music and you're processing your feelings, you strike a resonant chord with other people. And that's a wonderful feeling, and it can be very good in that you can make a living. Otherwise you have to get another job, and then you get to do your music in your spare time."

The doe-eyed Arizona native left Tucson for Los Angeles in 1964 with no particular goal, other than to sing. It took a few years of stumbling, bumbling and feeling her way along, but she finally fell in with the right people, finally made the connection with listeners. "Everybody has their own level of doing their music," she says. "Mine just happened to resonate over the years, in one way and another, with a significant enough number of people so that I could do it professionally."

Her career has been a series of happy accidents: She started off as a folksinger, then spent a while marrying country and rock, and for most of the 1970s everything she did - everything - hit big with the rock 'n' roll audience.

Her dissatisfaction with it all led to excursions into Broadway, grand opera, orchestrated standards, traditional Mexican music and straight-ahead country.

"Your musical soul is like facets of a jewel, and you stick out one facet at a time," she says. "I tend to work real hard on whatever it is I do, to get it up to speed, up to a professional level. I tend to bury myself in one thing for years at a time."

She is grateful for her fans, but has no qualms about letting them know she didn't like too many of her records. "There's a famous story where a fan is talking to this famous guitar player – I think Ry Cooder told this story – and the fan is saying oh, you were great tonight, this and that, and the famous guitar player turns to Ry and says 'Gosh, I was just trying not to suck.'

"That's what you do. You just try really hard not to suck. And when you record, you try to take out the stuff that's really embarrassing and just leave all that's really good, or maybe what you think you got away with, or doesn't suck."

Ronstadt's father was of Mexican-German descent, and he was the first in the family line who didn't operate a cattle ranch - he ran the Tucson hardware store. Linda and her two siblings - her brother was a boy soprano - grew up listening to Dad crooning Mexican songs. Mom preferred opera.

Linda's California sojourn began with Kenny Edwards and Bob Kimmel, as the Stone Poneys. The trio was a regular act at the Troubadour on Sunset Strip.

"I wanted to do traditional music, which would include Mexican music," Ronstadt explains. "I tried to talk them into doing certain Mexican songs. They liked it, but they didn't really understand the rhythms and how to play it.

"I kept trying to get back to traditional stuff with a lot of harmony, which is what I loved. I remember I had learned 'Different Drum' off a Greenbriar Boys record, and I knew it as a bluegrass approach. We recorded it that way, but the producer at Capitol didn't like it. "Came back the next day, and there was an orchestra there. So I recorded with an orchestra, because that's what they told me to do. I never liked it, but it was a big hit."

"Different Drum" (from *Evergreen, Vol. 2*, the second of the Poneys' albums on Capitol) was actually a minor hit, and when the trio split, Ronstadt naturally assumed the recording contract. Three solo albums for the label, all musically rambling and badly produced, garnered some attention from the hippie crowd but failed to turn a profit.

"Long Long Time," a weepy country ballad from her second solo release, was a Top 30 single in the fall of 1970, but the money wasn't exactly rolling in. "The immediate problem," says Ronstadt, "was getting onstage at the Insomniac or wherever your gig was that weekend, or that night. We got paid $300 a week, and we could live on that.

"It was always, let's try to get better. Can we get a better drummer, or get drums when we didn't have them before? Or can you find that magical bass player? Or you find some new songs, because you went to New York and you met Gary White or Jerry Jeff Walker, or somebody told you about the McGarrigle Sisters? You don't think about that other thing. As long as you're eating, you're just playing your next gig. And trying to get through it."

In 1972 David Geffen negotiated her out of the Capitol deal and signed her to his Asylum label. Ronstadt had a cult following, and it was no secret to anyone that, given the right material, the right producer and the right push, she was going to be huge.
For her, it was always about the music.

"I would have a manager that would say to me, 'You don't want to do that country shit. It's too corny.' And he also managed the Mothers. He wasn't a musician, he didn't really know anything about music. I would go to him and say 'I have this song written by Kate and Anna McGarrigle, and it's really beautiful. I'd like to record it.' It was 'Heart Like a Wheel.' He'd say 'It's too corny.' We struggled along with somebody that Capitol had, Nick Venet … we were never any of us on the same page. I was trying to do one thing, they were trying to do another."

While recording *Don't Cry Now* with producers John Boyland and (then boyfriend) J.D. Souther, Ronstadt met the person who would, very quickly, end her career water-treading and send things into overdrive. His name was Peter Asher.

"I don't think I would've got anywhere without Peter," Ronstadt recalls. "He walked into the Bitter End with his wife one night, and we were doing a lot of Cajun stuff. I don't know if my band was very good. I honestly can't remember who was in it."

At the time, Asher – a Londoner who'd had enough of fame and fortune as half of the '60s pop duo Peter and Gordon – was managing and producing James Taylor, and making quite a good wage. He was eager to expand his stable.

"Peter was very cordial, and he was interested," Ronstadt says. "When we got back to L.A., we had some various little meetings and he said he was interested in managing me – but as it turned out, he already managed Kate Taylor, James' sister."

That was, Asher explains, one female singer too many. He liked to give his artists his full attention.

"Bless Kate's heart, she decided about a year later that a career in music really wasn't for her," Ronstadt recalls. "I was with her one night, backstage at a show, and she said 'You know, you really ought to ask Peter again, because I don't really think I'm going to be doing this.'"

Asher and Ronstadt met again, and something clicked. "I loved everything Linda was doing," Asher says. "At that point, it was country rock, for lack of a better term, and I felt the songs were wonderful and she was wonderful. My main aim was to bring it to a wider audience. And to make the best possible record that I thought she could make."

He came in at the tail end of her first Asylum album *Don't Cry Now*, and to fully produce *Heart Like a Wheel*, her contract-ender with Capitol. Ronstadt: "When I sang 'Heart Like a Wheel' for him, he thought it was a wonderful song. He didn't think it was corny or stupid. So at least we were on the same page musically about more things than I ever was with anybody."

Asher didn't think much of the way Ronstadt's records had been produced. His idea was to focus them, to bring in the very best musicians available and to provide his singer with the best possible showcase for her instrument.

"It's easy to talk in terms of master plans," he says. "And of course one does have plans, but in general when you fall in love with an artist and their music, the plan is a fairly simple one. The plan is to make the whole thing as good as it can be. And get people to go and see them, and to make a record that you think properly presents their music to the public - and some of which you can get on the radio.

"I've had the good fortune to work with some terrific singers, and they tend to be the kind of singers whose voices are pretty unique, in all different ways. In each case, I've tried to have their voices be as well-recorded, as clear and as distinctive as it is in reality."

His first order of business, as her manager, was to put her in front of as many people as possible. Ronstadt was the opening act for Neil Young's *Time Fades Away* tour in early 1973. "So I went from being a club act to playing at Madison Square Garden overnight, which was pretty intimidating," she says. "But I loved Neil's music, and I watched every single show. Neil was using a lot of the same musical elements that I'd used. So it was real reinforcing for me to see somebody doing that so well.

"So I got a lot of exposure to people. Apparently they like the way I sang, because even in the coliseums they still listened. It was all completely over my head, I didn't know what I was doing. We were just making it up as we went along."

Released in the fall, *Don't Cry Now* became Ronstadt's first Top 50 album, but it wasn't much different, sonically, from its predecessors (owing, perhaps, to its multiple producers, each of whom had different ideas about how Linda should be presented).

Heart Like a Wheel, however, was all Asher's baby, and immediately after its appearance in late '74 it rolled into the Top Ten, making No. 1 in December.

Within a month or two, "You're No Good" (the old Betty Everett song) and "When Will I Be Loved" (from the Everly Brothers) had risen to No. 1 and 2, respectively.

"I Can't Help It (If I'm Still in Love With You)" hit No. 2 on the country chart. A duet with Ronstadt and her new best friend Emmylou Harris, the song brought Ronstadt her first Grammy, for Best Country Vocal Performance.

Asher had taken the best things about country rock – the tight, focused harmonies – and applied them to pop songs, with precise and compelling performances from the backing musicians.

And there out in front, her voice sounding big and yet still vulnerable, was little Linda, barefoot in the middle of the stage.

"The oldies," says Ronstadt, "were because I was a club act, or I had a concert that I had to pace, and they were just things that we could do. They were songs that maybe I liked, or I had some quirky interest in, but basically I sang ballad after ballad after ballad.

"Songs that I was really passionate about were songs like 'Heart Like a Wheel,' so there I was with all these ballads. I had to have some way to structure shows. It's always been a problem for me."

Between 1975 and '80, Ronstadt placed 13 songs in the American Top 40, seven of them in the Top 10. Several of her biggest singles were oldies – from Roy Orbison ("Blue Bayou") to Chuck Berry ("Back in the U.S.A") to the Vandellas ("Heat Wave") to Buddy Holly ("That'll Be the Day," "It's So Easy").

No matter that the programming on her albums was as eclectic as ever – she covered Warren Zevon, Neil Young, James Taylor, Little Feat, the McGarrigles and Randy Newman – the singles were almost uniformly old rock or R&B songs done up in the Asher style. Still, her albums went multi-platinum out of the box, she was a star of the highest magnitude, and you'd do well not to argue with success.

"When you're struggling, one is always grateful for a hit," Ronstadt says. "But I'd go 'Why that one, and why not this other one? I like this one better.' It was just that way, and I got stuck.

"Eventually I just had to turn away from a lot of those songs because I outgrew them. And they don't speak for me any more, and sometimes they just flat out bored me until I was crosseyed."

It's so easy

As she toured incessantly, as her fame grew and her bank account swelled, she began to question the validity – for her – of the songs she was putting out there. "They all have their time and their place," she explains. "I mean, if Martha Reeves were singing 'Heat Wave' tomorrow I'd listen, it's a neat piece of material. But it wasn't something that spoke for me. You have to use music to speak for you, and to speak for what your feelings are, and it just wasn't who I was after a while. A song like 'Heart Like a Wheel' isn't ever not who you are. It's a song that grows with you; it's not a song that's locked into one age.

"I just remember waxing my floor, after my boyfriend and I had broken up, and singing 'It Doesn't Matter Anymore.' I just wanted to sing that for two weeks. Or when I learned 'Willing,' you know, when Lowell George taught me how to play it, I just wanted to play it and play it. I just loved it."

Concurrent with the mega-success was a gnawing distaste for public performing, of the sports stadiums with their awful acoustics, and of the superstar grind, with its inherent lack of privacy.

On the road, Ronstadt was literally the only woman in a dysfunctional traveling circus full of men – her manager, her band, her crew. And although she sometimes got involved romantically with one of the boys, she was a reluctant center of attention. "It felt uncomfortable and awkward and unbalanced," she recalls. "My first cousin Alisa was in the first female class they admitted to Yale, and I used to think about her a lot. I thought it was very comparable what she and I went through.

"The pressure, of course, is to adopt their swagger and their speech mannerisms, which I did. I just swore like a sailor. I adopted all the slang and everything, which you do. And it was very, very hard to clean up my language, especially when I have children in the house."

And then … "I gotta tell you about drugs. I'm not gonna say I didn't inhale, because I inhaled, I snorted, I this, I that. I didn't inject. But I have some kind of a liver that just doesn't metabolize drugs. It just won't. I mean, I can't take prescription drugs or drink coffee.

"So I have to say I tried most everything and didn't like much of anything. But it was so much a part of the scene. I can't drink at all; I never drank. Some people drink and say 'I got a great buzz going, I feel really good' and they get really mellow. I just throw up. And I have to go to bed for a long time. It's like getting a bad case of the flu.

"I felt the same way about smoking pot. I just didn't like it. After 20 minutes I'd feel like I wanted to peel my skin off with a knife."

Her private life, too, was the subject of public scrutiny. After Souther, Ronstadt lived with writer/actor Albert Brooks, and was involved later with California governor Jerry Brown and *Star Wars* wizard George Lucas.

Reading about herself on the band bus, Ronstadt laughed all the time. "It was just so made up," she says. "First of all, most of us didn't have lives. We were on the road all the time. In the beginning of the book *Heart of Darkness*, he talks about how provincial sailors are. And we were just incredibly provincial.

"We'd get into these tight group dynamics. There's some kind of a neuro-transmitter that's released in your brain that's incredibly pleasurable when you're experiencing shared labor or shared endeavors. It really is fun and great. So we'd get into this tight little thing and it would kind of be 'us against them.' It increased paranoia and gave you this sort of strange fish-in-a-barrel mentality, and I don't think it's very healthy."

In the 1970s, Ronstadt's image was just as famous as her music. She was not only a great singer, she was a *hot chick*, and her album covers drove home the point again and again. "I photographed OK from one angle," she shrugs. "Those photographs are culled from thousands."

Ronstadt offers no apologies. "Am I going to say I didn't like it when someone thought I was cute? I was never beautiful, I was cute, and for some reason men liked me. I didn't have a great figure and I didn't have whatever you had to have to be like a model.

"People believe what they want to believe. When you're trying to sell records, and the record company says 'this picture doesn't really look like you, but it will sell records,' you say sure. Put a picture of a fire engine on the cover if you think it'll sell records.

"Do I think it's unfortunate that this culture forces that on women? Yes. We are taught that that's what will sell. We aim to please. And I think it's a shame."

She drew the line when *Rolling Stone* photographer Annie Liebowitz "tricked" her into posing in nothing more than a skimpy red slip. Liebowitz, Ronstadt said, had shot her against red wallpaper – and the slip photo, depicting the singer lying submissively on a bed, her red underpants exposed – was taken during a break.

A week later, Liebowitz returned to Ronstadt's home. "She brought the projector over and very politely showed us the pictures," Ronstadt said. "We said 'oh, we can't use those,' and she said 'I didn't say that you could choose them, I just said I could let you see them.' At which point Peter unceremoniously threw her out of the house."

So much for *Rolling Stone*. "I never had any respect for the magazine," Ronstadt said. "I just thought I could respect her work."

For her 1980 release, *Mad Love*, Ronstadt recorded a selection of edgy songs from Mark Goldenberg of the Cretones, and Elvis Costello. Less a conscious move into trendy "new wave" music than a reflection of the contemporary material she and the band were listening to on their long bus rides, *Mad Love* nevertheless sold considerably less than its predecessors.

"It's just that she likes good music," Asher points out. "And recognized how good punk was. And that isn't the same thing as trying to jump on a bandwagon. I think it's a genuine question of her excellent musical taste."

The combination of boredom with her career and the desire to avoid repeating herself came to a head when Ronstadt accepted an invitation from producer Joseph Papp to co-star in Gilbert and Sullivan's operetta *The Pirates of Penzance* on Broadway in 1981.

"When I was a little child, I knew all of the Gilbert and Sullivan songs," she says. "And I really wanted to play only in a theater, only as a concert artist. I didn't want to play in sporting arenas. They were clearly inappropriate places for music. And anybody that thinks otherwise is a fool.

"Those settings changed the music so profoundly, because all you can hear are those high, arching, ringing guitar solos. You don't have a chance for subtlety. You're not working with anything that's real. You're hearing echoes of echoes and ghosts of ghosts."

She loved the 14-hour days of constant rehearsal, staying in one place and ordering out for lunch. It was so very different from what she'd been doing for 10 years.

"I grew up thinking I was a boy soprano, so I wanted to use my high voice. I never really got to it early enough. It's a shame in a way, because had I over-developed the bottom part of my voice so much that it was really hard to get into that other voice."

She followed the *Pirates* production with a film version, which she despises, and a "return to form" album called *Get Closer* – which, aside from its title song being turned into a toothpaste commercial, was not a success. Which was fine with Linda Ronstadt.

It Doesn't Matter Anymore

In the old days, Ronstadt and Souther used to sit up late at night, after she'd returned home from her Troubadour gigs, and put on the Frank Sinatra album *Only the Lonely*. A collection of intimate and heartbreaking popular songs from the 1940s and '50s, it was (and still is) considered the vocal record by which all vocal records are measured. Nelson Riddle's aching orchestral arrangements were constructed around Sinatra's impeccable phrasing.

Once *Get Closer* and the *Pirates* movie tanked, Ronstadt started thinking about what to do next. "After I went to Broadway, I was really dying to not have to sing rock 'n' roll," she says. "What I wanted to do was work on my phrasing, and to get my musicianship cranked up a couple more notches.

"So I did what I always do – I go 'What was before this? What's this built on? Whose shoulders is this standing on?'" Her search led her back to Nelson Riddle, George and Ira Gershwin and Cole Porter. "There were people that I knew but I hadn't really studied. So I started to study them, and the songs are so sophisticated, they're complex.

"It's like a Brian Wilson song - if you can sing it, you can really sing it. Because it's written for a singer. So even though they're kind of quote-unquote hard, if you can do it they're easier than singing something that has a two-note range. Because you can get more out of it."

She wouldn't be the first rock singer to attempt the old standards, nor would she be the last. Still, she was determined to give it a try, and the first step, she knew, was to get Nelson Riddle in her corner.

"I think he was just dying to work," Ronstadt remembers. "He didn't particularly know who I was. I think he may have heard of me vaguely, but he didn't know my work – nor much care, I don't think. He liked some rock 'n' roll, but not very much of it. He wasn't against it. To go from as complex an art form as he practiced to as simple an art form as that … he was a musician, so he liked and appreciated good music."

Riddle pored over the enthusiastic Ronstadt's suggested song titles, putting aside the ones he didn't think she – or the orchestra – was capable of. "When he met me and heard me sing, he knew that I could sing," Ronstadt says. "And he told me so. I didn't create these songs in their original settings like Billie Holiday did, or Ella Fitzgerald, but I felt like they were really open to me for my interpretations, from my time, to tell my story. Which resonates with a lot of other people's stories."

Recorded with full orchestra, *What's New* was released in November 1983, and its resonance was heard all across America: The album reached No. 2 in *Billboard*, sold multi–platinum and spawned two nearly-as-successful sequels. Ronstadt had re-invented herself once more.

Peter Asher, being practical as ever, had wondered aloud about making a standards album, let alone three. He considered the likes of Gershwin and Porter "elevator music, a lot of old boring songs from shows."

Still he provided immaculate production on *What's New, Lush Life* and *For Sentimental Reasons*. "I was on the side of the people going 'This is a big mistake; it probably won't sell,'" Asher recalls. "Which isn't the same thing as saying 'Don't do it.'

"I did say that I thought the record company were right in their pessimistic view of whether anyone would buy it. And of course I and the record company were 100 percent completely and absolutely wrong."

In the winter of 1984, Ronstadt appeared as Mimi in Puccini's *La Boheme*, the grandest of Grand Operas, at New York's Public Theatre. "I was just following music that I loved," she says. "I was just chasing the things that I heard when I was little.

"I could've made a different choice when I was 14. I could've made a choice to become an opera singer, and then I would've only sung things like *Boheme.* I don't know whether I would've become successful as an opera singer, although I have a big voice and a big range, and I'm musical so I suppose I would've had as good a shot as anybody going into that."

Ronstadt, Harris and chum Dolly Parton had tried in the '70s to make an acoustic country record based around their three-part fireside harmonies; *Trio* appeared in 1987, put three singles into the Country Top Five and climbed to No. 6 on the album charts.

The union was short-lived, however, and *Trio II* (1997) would have a long gestation period – due essentially to a falling out between Ronstadt and Parton.

For Sentimental Reasons was originally to have been a double album, but Nelson Riddle's death in 1985 cut things short. Ronstadt and Riddle had planned to record in Brazil and Cuba with the maestro's old friend Antonio Carlos Jobim (the Afro-Caribbean sound would permeate *Frenesi*, her third Spanish language album, in 1992).

With the success of the Riddle and *Trio* records, Ronstadt realized she never had to sing "Heat Wave" again if she didn't want to. And she really, really didn't want to.

"People think you're sitting back thinking 'well, what direction do I put my career next?' And it really isn't like that at all. It's 'I kind of like this song.' It's just like following lights in the swamp – I go 'Ohhhhh. That.'"

Canciones De Mi Padre, a collection of traditional Mexican songs she'd learned at her father's knee back in Arizona, appeared in 1988. "The Mexican stuff, I wanted to do from the beginning," Ronstadt says. "But in the '60s and '70s, when I said 'I want to make a Mexican record,' they'd say well, Joan Baez cut a Spanish record and it didn't sell.' Oh. I got dead silence.

"So I'd cut a few songs in Spanish, but they weren't the songs I wanted to do. I wanted to do traditional Mexican music. And you can't just do one of those and put it on a pop record, because it just doesn't fit."

She says she knew the time was right "as soon as I got a chance to meet the guys that could play it really right, really authentic Mexican musicians … which I never had the chance to because they never went out of Mexico! And I was always on the road, playing in a hockey rink in Cleveland or something."

Canciones De Mi Padre and its followup, *Mas Canciones* (1991) did not tear up the charts the way the Riddle records had, but Ronstadt didn't care a whit. She had enough fame and enough money, thank you, and was pursuing whatever musical direction she felt like.

In 1989, following a performance in New Orleans, she and some friends went out to hear the Neville Brothers in a club, and Aaron Neville invited her onto the stage. They sang "Ave Maria" – it was the only song they seemed to know in common - and a friendship developed.

Less than a year later, the Ronstadt/Neville duet "Don't Know Much" reached No. 2 on the pop charts. Her *Cry Like a Rainstorm – Howl Like the Wind* album, featuring four duets with Neville, made it into the Top 10.

With no interest in "momentum" after so many years, Ronstadt next turned out *Mas Canciones* and *Frenesi*. In 1993, she co–produced (with George Massenburg) Jimmy Webb's album *Suspending Disbelief*.

She's made a few more pop albums since, and in 1999 collaborated with Harris on

Western Wall: The Tucson Sessions.

Her friendship with Harris, Ronstadt said, had been partially responsible for her shift away from country rock in the mid '70s. "She was chasing what I was trying to do, and she was doing it so well. I'm not saying that it made me record differently, but I surrendered a little bit more willingly to going more toward rock 'n' roll.

"But it doesn't matter, you know? Because to me, that was a profound moment, because it made me aware of the kinds of informed choices I was going to make for the rest of my life. It made me know that a certain amount of my values, and the things that I was trained and brought up with, were firm in me. And one of them was that if you see something you admire, you can destroy your own admiration of it by feeling jealous or competitive, or you can just love it. And I made that choice. And I have continued to do so."

She's sung with Pavarotti, Jagger and Kermit the Frog. She sang with Sinatra. On an early '70s TV variety show, she even sang with Neil Diamond (Ronstadt does not remember this, but the author saw it).

Her children, ages 8 and 11, are her favorite collaborators these days. Ronstadt performs when she wants to – she does orchestra shows and Mexican shows, for the most part – but at the end of the day, she's only seeking approval from two people.

"My son got hold of this new *Best Of* CD that came out," she said. "They'd sent me a box of them, and they were in the basement.

He came running upstairs and said 'Mommy, you sing oldies!' And I said 'Get that out of there!' It just ruins my day if I have to listen to it. I just can't bear it."

Photo by Bill DeYoung

(Something extra)
A conversation with Robert Duvall

A passionate horseman, actor Robert Duvall was at the end of a five-week visit to an equestrian training center in Newberry, Florida, where he was learning the fine art of jumping.

You'll recognize several movies in this rambling conversation, movies that would come to pass within a few years, including The Apostle, The Man Who Captured Eichmann, Assassination Tango *and even* Schindler's List.

We talked mostly about Lonesome Dove, *which had been adapted from Larry McMurtry's Pulitzer Prize-winning novel into an eight-hour TV miniseries. It had first aired in 1989, and was fresh on the interviewer's mind – and Duvall's as well.*

I have to tell you, I'm the biggest Lonesome Dove *fan in the world.*

Well, that's my favorite part I've ever played. I could have retired after that. The English can play Hamlet and King Lear, I'll play that part. I loved that part.

I had read the script first, and then I read the book. I read it in like 10 days. The script was well-written, so it was pretty parallel to the book.

What attracted you to the part of Gus McCrae?

Oh God, that's a great part. What happened was, I had played parts like that on the stage, more outgoing than the other part, Woodrow F. Call. *That's* the kind of part I get offered in films. They offered me that part.

Even McMurtry said "You're perfect for Gus."

So I told my agent, "I know they're considering your other client, James Garner, for Gus. See if he'll switch parts, and that way I'll do the project." He must have called me back in about three hours and he said "James Garner has passed – because of his bad back, he can't go 16 weeks on an intense location. Maybe a movie, but not a miniseries for 16 weeks." Like people wouldn't do *Apocalypse Now*, because they didn't want to be there for a year. So then I said "submit my name for Gus."

The script just drew you along. I did some research, but you didn't have to. You just followed the thing, it was so well written.

Did you get lost in that part? Did you become the character?

You really don't become the character. It's always acting. It's just, you turn in a different way doing it. It's always fun. When it goes well, it's fun. When it goes well, then you can drop it and say "OK, let's go eat, let's play, let's play ball, let's ride horses."

I'll never forget watching your face during the scene where you've just hanged Jake Spoon ...

Oh, I'll tell you what happened. I'll tell you exactly what happened there. Old Waylon Jennings is a good friend of mine. He said "How'd you do that, hoss? I never saw anything like that."

Sometimes I don't get along with directors. We had our problems, but ... I had done it, and he said "Do you want to go for another take?" And they don't always say that, but I'm glad he did. I said "Why not?" They had two cameras.

When it happened - boom - it happened, and it was as good a moment as I've ever done in my life, professionally. Thank God they sent me the tape first, because it was not in the final print. I don't know if it was spite they didn't put it in there … whatever it was, it was stupidity.

I wasn't on particularly great terms with the director at that point, so we called the producer. This guy had a lot of control. I said "Please, this is not in there, it's got to be in there, if you never put anything back in there …" I don't know, the editor must have been a moron.

That was a great moment.

Yeah … it was like life. And when you see Westerns, you never see the vulnerability in men like that. But when I was doing a little research on the Texas Rangers, they were macho killers. But in between, they would put on plays, they would paint. They were interesting guys as warriors. And when one of their leaders was shot along the Rio Grande, all the men just burst out in tears. They wept, openly, because their leader was killed right in front of them.

So this kind of moment just took over. I don't know where it came from, but it came. And I probably couldn't have repeated it. If it was a play, every night, I couldn't have repeated it.

I said to the guy "When you cut away to Call, you have got to come back to me and you've got to linger on that moment. You've got to linger as long as screen time will permit before you cut to me walking away."

A lot times with emotional things like that, when you get news that your mother died, your father died, sometimes there's a delayed reaction, an hour later. But the way this happened, also happens in life – boom, a sledgehammer.

Had I never seen that thing, and they hadn't put it in there, I would've never forgiven them. (laughs)

The guy was a TV editor. He was all right, but ultimately, maybe those guys were hacks, because they're thinking "TV." They don't look for moments. They don't even know what a moment is.

Gus wasn't afraid to show vulnerability …

Yeah, those guys … or when he was talking about Lorie, by the creek, they had a moment … those things happened to those guys. And I know as an actor, I can do those things. And I think that's sometimes what critics and other people miss. Usually the other actors are the ones who can see if an actor can do that. I know of actors that are famous – I won't say their names – and I've seen them try for it in movies. Talented guys. They back up and miss. A guy like Brando can do it. Sometimes De Niro can do it. But other actors I've seen, they go for the money but they can't make it.

You can't plan it, necessarily. So when that happened, I said "That's one of the greatest moments I've ever had in my life." And this jerk, the editor … I don't know if they did it out of spite because we had a little falling out at the end, or if they left it out on purpose. I don't know.

And I appreciate your bringing it up, because it was as good a moment as I've ever had.

The script guided me and drew me along. But I love traveling around and looking for something that'll help me with a part. We got in a car and drove way out in West Texas, in the middle of nowhere. We looked up old Sammy Baugh, the old quarterback for the Washington Redskins, a great, great talent. But he's a cowboy. He was a professional football player, and then he retired. I just read about him. And the way he talked with his hands caught me. He was 70, with white hair, and still like a champion. To this day, I don't think he knows who we were! He came in and talked to us for about two hours. But he gave me that extra thing I needed, the gestures. And I'd get those things in the part, you see?

You know what I say? I say if the mafia guys had crossed the Red River, they'd have been hung by their nuts from a tree. Those Texas Rangers are rough dudes. And there are a hundred of them left. They have to be as mean as the people they're pursuing.

One of the toughest things about watching Lonesome Dove was that you died at the end!

I'm always dying lately! Like in *Colors*, a lot of actors liked my death scene. They told me about it. They said "That's the definitive death scene." I improvised it from stuff in my life, very personal stuff, and it worked. That's what it's all about, if you can incorporate it. Without looking like "OK, now I'm stopping to gather something."

And I figured a guy that was dying, at that point, who would he call, his mother? He would lose his macho and he would ask for his wife. He'd say "Please call my wife."

The emotional line of the character is the most rewarding thing to get. And you gotta be loose and relaxed to get it. And it's something you can't plan.

The emotional moment, if you try to sit on it – like when Jake's hung, swinging – if you try to sit on it, in any given documentary, it's more moving. When you see a guy talking about his son he lost in a flood, and he's trying to sit on it. It's like Sandy Meisner used to say in acting class, sitting there with his cigarette holder, "If crying meant great acting, my Aunt Tilly could be another Eleonora Duse!" If the emotion is there and it shoots out, and you try to fight it and let it come out this way – put a lid on it – then it's more effective because it's become like life. Life is like that. So why try to force it, and then if it happens, it happens.

It's like in *The Godfather*, when I have to tell Brando that Sonny's dead. We'd done four takes, and usually that's it for me. And there, Coppola said "You want to go for one more?" I said well, why not. And the moment was difficult, emotionally, to tell Brando's character that Sonny, Jimmy Caan, had died. So that worked. The other takes were OK, but this became a special moment.

People say "bigger than life." That's such a trap. Nothing is bigger than life. If you make selections from life, then they're seen as bigger than life. But nothing is bigger or more enriching than life.

Couldn't you have overplayed Gus? Hammed it up?

Oh, yeah. But I think the thing is, once again, to be specific with the emotional line. And therefore, if it needs to be big, then your bigness is justifiable.

At first, before I got deep into Lonesome Dove, I thought Gus was very similar to Mac Sledge from Tender Mercies …

Well, Mac was a little bit more like Woodrow Call, very stoic …

… then I understood that he was a huge progression from Mac.

One of the first things I did, my first film, *To Kill a Mockingbird,* was with Horton Foote. Then we did a Faulkner short story called *Tomorrow,* and I played Jackson Fentry, who was really an introvert. And that's why I didn't want to do a guy like Call. I wanted to go the other way, which I knew I could do.

And we've just done another Horton Foote project, which is a little different. It's more like my uncles and my Dad from Virginia. Interesting piece called *Convicts,* which is one of his favorite things. In a way, he's my guy, Horton, and yet Horton loved *Lonesome Dove.*

I love doing rural guys. There are other things I want to do, too, but it's hard to get 'em off the ground. I've written a script where I play more of an urban guy, in this tango thing I've written. Connecting the two cities, New York and Buenos Aires, two middle-aged guys through social dancing. I know a guy in New York, an actor named Frankie Gio. He's from South Bronx. He says "I got two gifts in my life – fighting and dancing!" He used to be a bouncer at Roseland. He said "Italians could jitterbug, the Jews could mambo!" (laughing) So we used to go up to the Palladium in New York and all that stuff. I've kind of written the script, and Ulu Grosbard who did *True Confessions* – he's a good friend of mine – wants to do it.

Another thing I've developed is where I play a Pentecostal preacher. For years I've wanted to play one of these guys. It's called *The Apostle E. F. Hart,* which was my mother's name. But I can't use the name Hart, because there are six preachers in Texas with that name, and I'll be sued. So we're just calling it *The Apostle* for now.

Once again, the guy has an outgoing side to him. But you know how those guys are, you see 'em on television. I've been to churches all over America, black churches in downtown Brooklyn, churches in the hills of Georgia, in downtown L.A. Great preachers I've seen.

That would be a great challenge, I would think.

Oh, yeah. I dug up old J. Charles Jessup, who I used to listen to – he'd be on the radio from Del Rio, Texas years ago – that was their version of television, the evangelists. They were radio preachers. I always thought he was black, but he was white. And he was put in jail.

And you can't read 'em when you meet 'em. You can't read 'em as much as you can a gypsy. Gypsies are gypsies, but preachers are preachers. You don't know, you know? I saw what happened to Swaggart, and so forth.

I think some of the guys, when they're right and a little bit honest, they're pretty interesting. And talented! They can preach for three hours with no text. Unbelievable. Unbelievably talented. They say the only truly American art form is the American preacher. Some of the music, maybe. Jazz and country music.

You were going to make a record after Tender Mercies, weren't you?

I made an album but it never came out, because the guy that produced it is a very strange guy. Chips Moman. He's a very talented songwriter, and there were a couple of interesting songs. But it was six years ago. Maybe it'll come out, I don't know.

Are you sorry it didn't?

Well, yeah, but the sorrow's subsided because it's been six years. It's ridiculous. I mean, you make something, you come out with it. I don't know what that's about. Even if only three people hear it.

How much like Santini was your father?

Not a lot. My dad was quieter, and more of a brooder. He had a temper, but it was more of a brooding thing. My mother was more like Santini! I've met a lot of people who said their fathers were like Santini. They say this, or that, or what an ogre, but a lot of people had fathers like that, who they loved. At least he voiced things. He wasn't so passive that he never voiced opinions ... at least there was a care there.

Are there things in your career that you wish you hadn't done?

I'm sure. I'm sure. I don't think about it too hard. If I did, I'm sure I'd come up with a few! You do things for money sometimes. To pay the rent, you know?

Anything you believe you could have done better?

I have a superstition that once I've done 'em, I see 'em once or twice, then after three or four years I don't want to see 'em again. Then maybe if I'll see something, I'll watch and think well, if I don't embarrass myself I figure I'm on the right track. I figure if I watched everything I could pick out what I'd want to do again.

You were offered The Silence of the Lambs, but chose to do Days of Thunder instead. Why?

First they offered me one part, and then the other, and I said "I'd rather work with Tom Cruise than wait around for these people to make up their minds." First, I had lunch with the guy to play the Anthony Hopkins part. And he calls me 20 minutes later and says "I think I'd rather have you play the FBI, and have Anthony Hopkins play this." Which was a strange move for a director to do. So I'm just as glad I did the Cruise thing.

I think that *Silence of the Lambs* is a well-made film. I don't think it's a great film; I don't think there's one great performance in it. I think that the guy's very effective in the part; I think it's very, very talented clichés. There's nothing really fresh about it, because it's like made-up material in a way – a guy eatin' a liver, and this and that. But it was well-made. A little hammered-home with the close-ups.

It held your attention. But it was nothing near as well-made as my favorite film in many, many years, *My Life As a Dog*. I love stuff with kids. To me, *My Life As a Dog* was a perfect, perfect film.

Do you read your critics?

No. The last Broadway play I did, Mamet's *American Buffalo*, that and *Lonesome Dove* were the greatest reviews I've ever gotten. It was like I wrote 'em myself. But I get superstitious, even though they were good. I don't collect 'em, good or bad.

Let me just say this. I would be in trouble if all these critics liked me, or other fellow actors didn't like me. When Steve Hill tells me I'm his favorite actor, that's the greatest criticism. There was Steve Hill and Marlon Brando at the Actor's Studio years ago, and Steve Hill was Strasberg's favorite.

But he's a maniac. He's a Hassidic Jew that won't work on Friday nights. But he's very gifted. He was in a Horton Foote movie called *Valentine's Day*, played the craziest part. Wonderful.

So when he gives me a gives me a review that's positive … or when Waylon Jennings wants to meet me because of *Tender Mercies* … he told me what I did was absolutely impossible. And that's play a Texan. So if I get a review from him like that, or from Steve Hill, then really that's more valid than something that's in the newspaper. If somebody likes me or doesn't.

Like when Brando and these guys went to New York, he studied with Stella Adler, certain people studied with Uta Hagen. Nobody went to a workshop by Pauline Kael.

Can you still learn things from other actors?

You mean about my profession? Yeah, I learn more from other people, or documentaries, than necessarily other actors. I think Brando used to watch *Candid Camera* when he was a young actor, which makes a lot of sense.

Why didn't you do Godfather III?

Well, it was money. Coppola went on the Larry King show and said "Bobby Duvall wanted loads of money." But see, he twists it a little bit. The truth is that I said "It's unacceptable that Al Pacino gets paid five times what I get paid." Two, two and a half times, I would consider it. It wouldn't be ideal, but I would accept that. But they didn't even extend that as an offer.

So I figure, the only reason anybody's doing *Godfather III*, I'm sorry, Coppola included, is the money. He's about to go bankrupt, lose his house in Belize. He already lost his house in San Francisco, and they're trying to foreclose on his beautiful estate in Napa Valley. So he needs money badly. Why wait 15 years to do a third one? It was for money. And if it wasn't going to be proportionate, the correct amount at least as far as I was concerned, then I didn't want to do it.

I wondered if you felt that Tom Hagen was part of you and your history – that, God forbid, they might re-cast the role with another actor?

It's ironic, they had my ex-brother-in-law, John Savage, play my son. I was married to his sister, Gail Young. Not just my character, but I felt one of the weaknesses maybe in the film was that they didn't have those fringe characters like Frankie Pantangelo and Paulie Gatto from the first one. There wasn't enough of that to enrich it, really.

You saw it, then?

Yeah. It was OK. It wasn't nearly as good as the first two. I turned on *Godfather II* about a month ago – I didn't know it was on, and it was about an eighth into it. I said "That's *Godfather II*, let me watch it for a minute before I go on to some sports …" And I could not change channels until it was over. It was that well-made, I thought.

He's not the same filmmaker now, Coppola. The stuff he's done lately – teenage movies in Oklahoma, he's just not the same guy. And I think it's because he directs some trailers, and he's into the technical aspect and the futuristic thing of everything.

What's next for you?

Well, we're working on several projects. Everything's a little elusive right now. We're trying to get the rights to *Eichmann in My Hands*, the guy that actually, physically made the kidnapping of Eichmann in Argentina. We've contacted the guy in Israel. I want to play Eichmann. So we're working on that and a few other things. Sometimes it's slow, especially when you have personal projects, it's very hard to raise money.

Are there things that you would like to play that haven't been offered to you?

Oh yeah! I'd love to play *Schindler's List*. You know the book? He was an industrial German, a Catholic Christian who saved 1,200 Jews? Ah, what a character! Man. It's by a leading Australian novelist – I forget the guy's name - who wrote this true story, but in kind of novel form. It's one of the most moving books you'll ever read. And it's great - a true story!

I know that first Spielberg was gonna do it, then Scorsese, and now I think Peter Weir's gonna do it. I've worked twice with those Australian directors and haven't gotten along – so maybe the word's out!

But I really feel I could do that part. It's a great, great part. Strange, complex guy. They don't know why he saved these Jews. Even though he would court the SS, gamble with them, give them caviar and food. To kind of help his position, and help the Jews at the same time.

I would like to do that. I want to do my preacher project, I want to do my tango project. Most of the things that I do have come to me. I don't have readers. We develop projects. I've been fortunate that the things that have come to me have been great. 'Cause when I've tried to generate something, like the preacher project, it's tough. It's tough to get money. I'm not good at it.

About a year after you won the Oscar, you said "It hasn't brought in any other work yet."

(laughs) It only helped to get a little more recognition at airports! That's where you get recognized anyway. But no, nothing really happened.

The next film was The Natural.

Yeah, but I didn't even want to do that. Redford asked me to do it, and he wouldn't even give percentage points. My wife talked me into it. I don't know, it was something to do. It was a fun project; I like working in Buffalo. It's near Canada. I like Canada. Good Chinese restaurants.

Were you mad you didn't win an Emmy for Lonesome Dove?

Let me put it this way: I was a little surprised. And I will never go back for another one. Never will I go back. Because it's decided by committee, not by other actors. It's almost like, when you keep saying something's great, they go the other way. It didn't win anything! If I ever won an award, it should have been for that. Even more than the Oscar. I mean, that was my performance. What can you say?

Universal Pictures

(Something extra)
A conversation with Gregory Peck

I conducted this phone interview with the great Gregory Peck on Dec. 12, 1995. The actor was gearing up for his cross-country show, An Evening With Gregory Peck, *in which he'd screen a half-hour of film clips and then, as he told me, "spin yarns." Peck got the idea from his pal Cary Grant, who'd done something similar and told his fellow Hollywood legend how much he'd enjoyed the experience, getting out and meeting the public.*

I spoke with Peck for just under an hour. The tape had never been fully transcribed; the original newspaper story used perhaps five percent of the things he says in this amazingly candid interview.

You have to read it in his voice. Trust me on this.

After such a long career, do you feel like you've got nothing left to prove as an actor?

I guess you could say I'm on the sidelines now. The last thing I did was a nice little television movie with Lauren Bacall and my daughter Cecilia, called *Portrait*. That was early in '93. Then I did a thing which didn't come off too well, called *Other People's Money*. And then before that it was *Old Gringo*. So I haven't been working all that much lately, but then I didn't expect to after 50 years! It's like 'Fifty years already, whaddaya want?'

Can you sit back in your chair and say "I just don't need to do this any more"?

That's an interesting question, because I got so used to using my energy in a special way, as a kind of specialist. I'm a storyteller on film, is what I am. I think my main interest was usually – I think always – directed toward the story as a whole. Beginning, middle, end. And how I would fit into it, and further it. And hold the audience's attention.

That was my craft, and I did it for a long time. Do I miss it? No, I have a lot of things to do, a lot of things that interest me. What would interest me would be to make another outstanding film, another very, very good film. I don't say a work of art, but a very, very good film. That would be a challenge, and that would be fun.

So many films ... can you remember something about every one of them, or is it all kind of a blur? If I said, for example, Only the Valiant.

That one is on the negative side. That's probably the worst film I ever made. Although it's negative, I think it's sort of funny at the same time ... so I will tell it to you. At that time, I had some commitments with David O. Selznick. I was never under exclusive contract to anybody; I sort of parceled myself out here and there. I was a freelance.

David had a commitment for a picture, and the contract said he was to pay me $65,000. It sounds like small potatoes today; people who are in one or two hits are suddenly getting seven million. But those were different times.

Suddenly I got a call from his number one aide-de-camp, a fellow named Danny O'Shea, who said "Greg, you're to report to Warner Brothers next Tuesday for costume fittings for a Western they're making there." And I said "What do you mean, Danny, I haven't read it. I have to read this. This is very sudden."

He said "Look Greg, David is a little short on cash. He has sold you to Warners for $150,000." I said "David Selznick is that short on cash?" He said "I'm giving it to you straight, kid." I called my lawyer, he said "Well, you've got a contract ..."

Everybody was surprised. David avoided me. And I went and made the damn thing. And the crowning insult was, when I went to the wardrobe fittings, I was a cavalry man. It was an Indian-fighting picture. They had pants and a shirt and a hat, boots, ready for me. And as I was pulling on the pants, I saw somebody's name inside. And it was "Rod Cameron." He was an old-time leading man, sort of a Western type. Big tall guy. Mostly he played tough guys, and he played in Westerns.

So I wore a second-hand wardrobe. And well, that's enough about the negative!

How did you manage to avoid becoming a studio player? You did move around quite a bit. You remained a free agent.

Well, I was. It started because I was on Broadway. I had three shows on Broadway, and once I calculated about 30 shows, either summer stock or road companies before that. And so they began to come backstage, during my first Broadway show. It was called *The Morning Star* by Emlyn Williams. And it was a big-time production. It didn't last very long, just a couple of months, but it was a top-notch Broadway production.

So I began to get movie offers, and they were all for exclusive, seven-year deals. Well, a fella came back whose name was Casey Robinson. He was breaking away from Warner Brothers to go on his own. I told him my philosophy of remaining my own boss, so to speak, and having time to come back to the theater. And he said "I'll make a one-picture deal with you." And we did. So I ran out one summer, I think it was '43 or '44, and made that picture in 10 weeks. And went back and did another play. Then there were more offers.

I had a famous agent named Leland Hayward. And I said "no exclusive contracts." He brought me in, at his expense, and we made the rounds of the studios. The story that I've told before – sorry if you've already heard it – is that he took me to L.B. Mayer. We went to L.B. Mayer's office, which was the absolute prototype of a mogul's office: It was all white, and it was immense. White carpet, and a huge desk, and there was the great man. And he said "I want to put you in my family of stars. And I want you to rise to the very top. I can see you as the brightest star of MGM!"

Well, that was a mouthful, because they had Clark Gable, and Robert Taylor and Spencer Tracy, and Greer Garson and Walter Pidgeon, they had a whole bunch of people under contract there.

And I thought that was a little bit of an overkill. I said "Mr. Mayer, I would certainly like to make some pictures here. It would be an honor. But I want to go back to the theater from time to time, and I don't want to be tied up exclusively."

He went again into his pitch. He would look after me and select my roles, and guide my publicity, and nurture me. He really laid it on thick, like for 15 minutes! He boasted about MGM's great history, and roster of stars, he talked about Judy Garland and Mickey Rooney and all the glory of MGM. And I said "I'm just terribly impressed, Mr. Mayer, but I'm determined not to sign a long-term exclusive contract."

And, believe or not he started to cry. I couldn't believe my eyes! Tears came down his face, and he said "Please think it over. Think carefully. You may be making a terrible mistake." The tears were dropping off his chin. Really a comic but strange, bizarre scene. So I said "Mr. Mayer, thank you very much, I hope you'll ask me over to make a picture sometime."

And with that, he mopped his face, he picked up his phone and called his secretary and started talking business to her, and he ignored us. So Leland Hayward and I, we sorta backed out of the room. And when we got outside the door I said to Leland "Boy oh boy, that was something, to see a man like that cry."

He said "Oh, he does that all the time."

You were a tremendous success almost right out of the gate, without signing up.

Well, it was it was a streak of independence, I guess. I was a little bit of a maverick at that time. But it didn't do me any harm. I may have missed out on some good pictures, on the other hand I may have been in some that I wouldn't have been in, had I been tied up to MGM.

They must have been waving money at you the whole time.

In those days? Well, they were waving money, but it wasn't very big money. In those days, nobody got very big money. Clark Gable never got more than $3,500 a week. And I think he had a contract for 48 weeks a year, which was a month's vacation. They didn't pay him for four weeks! Pictures cost less to make, and they went out and grossed less at the box office. And the net profit to the studio was less. It was all in the neighborhood of a million dollars, or a little bit less or a little bit more, except for a few exceptions, like *Gone With the Wind* I think was four million. Nowadays, they spend four million on publicity for a big movie.

So everything was on a more common sense, reasonable level. Including the salaries of the biggest stars in the business. And they weren't rich. They were comfortable. They were well off. But by today's standards, you wouldn't consider people like Gable, Bogart, Cagney, you wouldn't consider them rich at all.

When did you move, permanently, back to California?

In '44. I had done *Days of Glory*, then I went back to New York and did another play after that. I grabbed the $10,000, which is what they paid me – seemed like a lot of money to me – and I went back to New York and did a play of Irwin Shaw, which was called *Sons and Soldiers*. With a wonderful actress, Geraldine Fitzgerald. And Karl Malden was in it.

And after that I got an offer from Darryl Zanuck to do *The Keys of the Kingdom*, and I couldn't resist it. So I came back out, and pretty much settled down here ever since, although we've done an enormous amount of traveling, and picture-making just about all over the world.

How did you develop your style of acting? There's so much of what we out here perceive as you in your characters. Are all these guys just different facets of you?

Well, in my mind they are. Maybe other people wouldn't agree, but I feel I've been fairly versatile in the things that I've done. And played different types. Because of my stage training, that was my ambition, not to be a movie star but to be an actor.

So yes, I think there's a great deal of difference between let's say some of the Westerns I made … I'll tell you something funny about that. I was elected the "Cowboy Star of the Year" in 1950. I had made several, *Duel in the Sun, Yellow Sky, The Gunfighter* and so on. And I bumped into John Wayne. He kind of growled at me and said "Ah, for Christ's sake. You? The Cowboy Star of the Year? Oh, for Christ's Sake, who elected you to that?" I said well, those guys in Reno that give the Silver Spurs Award every year. "Oh, Christ – you, the Cowboy Star of the

Year."

I said "Listen, Marian, you can't win it every year."

Did you all watch what the others were doing? Would you call Jimmy Stewart and congratulate him?

Absolutely. I never felt any of that intense rivalry, ever. I admired Hank Fonda and Jimmy Stewart, and Duke Wayne for what he did. No, there was room for all of us. I think that kind of thing, that dog-eat-dog rivalry among actors, is a myth. I think it's largely invented by the press. I'm sure there have been a few people who were envious, who wished each other bad luck! But I never ran into it, and I never felt it.

How about Roman Holiday? Is that a happy film for you to remember?

Probably the happiest time making a film that I can think of. Six months in Rome, 1952, working with Audrey and a wonderful director, William Wyler. It was exciting to be there. We were the first international film after the war. The Italian neo-realists, I think they used to call them, had been filming all over Rome, and Rossellini and De Sica were making some pretty great Italian films, but we were the first American company to come in with a major film. So there was excitement.

We filmed all over the streets, and we always had a big, big crowd. There's a scene on the Piazza di Spagna – I think Audrey is eating an ice cream cone, and I come down on purpose by accident, I find her there. I know she's the princess, but she doesn't know I know. And we had about 10,000 people at the bottom of the stairs watching us. It was like we were playing in an amphitheater.

But they knew "silencio," because of these Italian films all over the streets of Rome. They knew what "silencio" and "azione" meant. So they would be silent while we were speaking our lines. They could hear us. And Willy Wyler would say "cut," then he'd say "let's do it again," and if they liked it they'd say "No, no, no, no, va beni!" Or if he liked it and said "That's good, print that," they might say "no, no, no, encore una volta!" Let's do it again. So you can imagine what fun it was, and romantic and exciting and funny. Funny all the time.

You went from there right into Moby Dick. It isn't a perfect film.

I'd say that film is a little bit like John Huston's career: In and out. He was an in-and-outer. He made some great films and he made some bad films. And I think that film was in and out. It had great moments, but as a whole it's not one of my favorites. Although there are some scenes and some moments in there that I'm certainly not embarrassed by. But as a whole, the thing did not come off, and it showed at the box office.

It's hard to translate something like that into film, I think.

Well, you're exactly right. Incidentally, we looked at the two that were made before, both with John Barrymore. One was called *The Sea Beast*, and I think the other one may have been called *Moby Dick*. One was silent, and one was an early talkie, I think. And they gave Captain Ahab a love story! With a beautiful woman named Dolores Costello, who was waiting for

Captain Ahab to return from the sea. They're both pretty silly.

If it could be done, if it were ever to be done and I could in any way be connected with it, I would say "Do it a la John Ford. Make it an action picture, and let the philosophy come through between the cracks. Don't stand there on the deck and talk for five minutes, about Melville's philosophy about if there is a god, he must be a malevolent god." I think we talked too much. I think it should have been one long chase with moments – moments – of Melville's philosophy seeping through.

I have to ask the logical question here: What's your favorite? What's the best? I think I already know the answer.

Well, it has to be *To Kill a Mockingbird*. It's the one that has had the most longevity, you might say. In that it's still being played all over the country in schools, for schoolkids around the ages of 13, 14, 15. In their civics class. Or their American history class. They tie it in with the Civil Rights movement of the '60s, and the kids write essays. Mostly, though, they don't write about the civil rights, they write about father and kids. They write about the family relationship.

Bob Mulligan and Alan Pakula had acquired the rights to Harper's book – they were in great demand because it was a Pulitzer Prize winner – and I think Harper let them have the rights on instinct, on her own judgment, having met them. They were a young producer and a young director. They had made a picture, which I liked, called *Fear Strikes Out*, about the baseball player Jim Piersall, who had mental problems, and a domineering father, and was carrying a lot of baggage from his childhood which followed him. And he kind of went crazy on the field a few times. And had to have psychiatric counseling.

They'd made a very sensitive, good film with Tony Perkins. I liked that film. I'd never met these two.

They called me and they've said "We've got a book and we think you're exactly right for it. Will you read it?" I said "Send it over." I sat up most of the night; I finished it at 2 or 3 in the morning.

So you were reading it and thinking of yourself as Atticus the whole time?

Sure, sure. And I called them at 8 o'clock in the morning and said "Absolutely, I want to do it." There was no script. So at that time, I had a tie-up with Universal – I had an office bungalow, and I had produced a couple of pictures there. *Mirage* was one of them; I think one called *Pork Chop Hill*, and *Cape Fear*, the original with Bob Mitchum. So I had a kind of association with them where they would get first look at any property than I wanted to do. They call it a first-look arrangement.

So I said to Mulligan and Pakula, I think we can make a deal at Universal. And they said "Well, we want to have the final cut." Mostly, you cannot get that at a major studio. In those days, at least. I said "Let me see what I can do." Like Harper, I had an instinctive trust in these two young guys.

So I went over there with my agent, and at first they said "Oh, no, no, these are young guys, we have an expert editorial staff here, blah blah blah." I said "Well, then the book's gonna go somewhere else, and me with it." Then they began to think it over, because here they had a Pulitzer Prize winner, and they had a star. And they had a promising young director and producer. So they must've had a meeting of the suits, up in the black tower, because they came back and the answer was "OK. We'll finance it, and we'll give the final cut to Mulligan and Pakula."

In a way, they were taking in a risk, but in a way they were not. It was obvious that this was a wonderful book, and that these were very talented young guys, and everybody thought I was right for Atticus, so they weren't taking much of a risk. They would have been extremely dumb to have passed up that deal.

What was it about Atticus Finch that, when you read it, you knew you could get under his skin?

I just knew it. It was instinct. I felt it, I felt the emotions of the piece. Of course I liked what it had to say about racial bigotry, and I liked the relationship with the kids.

I liked the man. I liked what he had to say, what kind of a man he was. I felt I could be him on the screen. They say sometimes the hair goes up on the back of your neck. I just felt it. And I did all the way through. When we got started, we were like on a rail where we couldn't get sidetracked. We were in a kind of a state of pretending that this was all really happening, and feeling the emotions those characters felt, and speaking as the character.

And yet, it was me. It was me, but I guess it's a side of me that I was glad to be able to put to work in that part.

That sense of being with a singleness of purpose – cast, crew and everyone – had that ever happened before, or since? Was that something you were used to on a really good project?

I think we felt that on *Roman Holiday*. Maybe it was more intense on *To Kill a Mockingbird* than any other film. But to a degree, on *Roman Holiday* and on a little picture that I like very much, *The Gunfighter*. And from time to time on others.

By the same token, do you know when you're in the middle of a dog? You said there were some you'd like to forget.

(laughing). You're swimming upstream, and you swim all the harder. You pull out every trick in the book to try to cover up a bum script. You delude yourself. You don't allow yourself to think that way. You know it, in the back of your head, that this is liable to turn out to be a bummer! But you come to work every morning determined to make it look as good as you possibly can.

And also, there's a matter of self-preservation involved. You try not to be in a bummer. So it's the old "silk purse out of a cow's ear" – and there are times when you actually sort of get away with it. You call on something that you can bring to it, some experience you can draw on, something you've learned about life. And you kinda inject that into a scene, to give it some solid footing, some reality and truth behind it. Even though it's not a very well-written scene.

And sometimes you manage to make a badly-written scene look better. You can't make it look great, but you can make it look better. And in those cases, that's your job. That's what they're paying you for, to make it look as good as you can make it look.

The Omen *was – I was surprised to learn – your highest grossing film. I was in high school when it came out. What's your feeling on that one?*

Well, it was a commercial film, and it was a scare picture. I kind of felt like it would be a hit, and I liked the director, Dick Donner, and Lee Remick was a favorite of mine. And I said well, hell, I'll make a scare picture. And it turned out that way, and it made me a packet of money! So I have no regrets. I sort of enjoyed doing it.

You were one of the founders of the American Film Institute in '67. Why is that sort of thing important to you? A lot of actors never get involved in anything political, or anything other than their craft. Was the film restoration thing especially important to you? Or were you a figurehead for them?

No, no, I was a working chairman. Founding chairman. No, I worked at it. I gave quite a lot of time, maybe more than I should have in the middle of my career, to a year of research with the Stanford Research Group on what an American Film Institute ought to be. And what the whole, let's say constituency of people interested in film, all the way from avant-garde to documentary to educational to entertainment film, what they expected from an American Film Institute. Endless, endless, countless meetings. And a certain amount of travel, going around to talk to colleges and independent filmmakers.

We didn't have a large staff at the beginning. The National Arts Endowment commissioned an American Film Institute, and in fact LBJ said when he signed the bill to create an Arts Endowment, he said "There will be an American Film Institute, which will encourage young artists to express themselves in film, and elevate the quality," so forth, so on. And I was on the board of the National Endowment. It was called the National Council on the Arts. And LBJ blurted this out, and the people who were involved in film who were on the council at the time, we looked at each other and said "What the hell is this?" Somebody put that into LBJ's speech.

I wonder if he knew that he said it.

Oh, he knew all right. He and I talked about it many times.

So anyway, there it was, and it was a mandate for the National Council on the Arts. So it was largely George Stevens Sr., and William Parrera and I, we organized a few more people, Sidney Poitier, George Stevens. Jr. who was head of the USIA at that time. We got a committee together and Jack Valenti sat in. We decided on the Stanford Research Institute. It was just too much legwork for any of us to do.

Although I did some. I stayed in New York a couple of weeks one time looking at avant-garde film. The most far-out, the better. I wanted to see everything. I remember going in the Village to see a guy by the name of Jonas Mekas, an avant-garde filmmaker. He had a little studio in the Village. I made an appointment, I went in there … he looked at me suspiciously. To him, I was a Hollywood star, and what the hell was I doing calling on him? And I explained about the Film Institute, that we meant to be of service to every kind of film. All kinds of people interested in film as a career. I explained all this, and the Stanford Research, and that it was beginning to be clear that a big part of our interest should be restoration. That there may well be an institute for young filmmakers. And that we would be interested in grants to promising filmmakers from across the board, including the avant-garde.

He listened to me for about 10 minutes, and I said "Well, what do you think?" He said "That's a lot of bullshit."

I said "Well, thanks for your time." And I took off. I don't know whether he ever got a grant from the AFI, but I wouldn't have stood in his way if he did. I could understand how we represented establishment. And some of the other people said "Oh, hell, it's just gonna be a farm school for the Hollywood industry." They were very cynical about it.

Over the years, I still think that restoration has been their greatest accomplishment. Not only the money that they've been able to give, themselves, through the Library of Congress, but in coordinating the various efforts at the Museum of Modern Art, out at the Pacific Archives in Berkeley, at Eastman House in Rochester, coordinating the whole effort. And also making a grant each year to the Library of Congress for preservation, restoration, cataloguing. That may be the most important thing they've done.

What about the state of the art today? What's your general feeling on it?

You know, I'm not about to knock my friends and knock the industry. In print. I have private opinions but I'm not a crusader, and I don't want to deplore the state of the art. I would rather put it this way, that there are films that are being made that are purely commercial, you could say conglomerate-type films. They're product. And sometimes, because that sort of thing has been big at the box office, they will ratchet up the violence and the sex a little more each time. I don't particularly like that kind of machine-made film. My own taste runs to things that are a little different, and a little bit more offbeat.

I like some Hollywood product. I thought *The Fugitive* was a wonderful film, for example. I liked very much a year ago an Irish film, *In the Name of the Father*.

The Fugitive *is the kind of film you would have made.*

(chuckles) That's right, in my day and age I would have played Harrison Ford's role.

Did you like Schindler's List*?*

Yes, I did, I liked it very much. And I liked certain offbeat films, like *Like Water For Chocolate* and that sort of odd film which is completely original, and takes you by surprise. There's no formula stuff in there.

So I guess I do tend to like the independent, offbeat films, but at the same time I enjoy a good, well-made commercial film.

I'll close with essentially the same question I started with. Are you finished? Do you feel like you're on top of the hill, looking backwards?

I'd rather sit on the side of the road and watch the parade go by, than sit on the hill and look backwards. But there is, now and then, a hankering to jump back in the parade. But it has a little proviso attached: I wouldn't do it unless I thought the script had a great, great chance of being very, very good.

I don't do weekly TV. I'm not pining to go to work so much that I'll do any old thing. So if I do another one, it'll be something that I think has a very, very good chance of being terrific.

If it doesn't turn out that way, well, blame it on me. It'll be, my judgment wasn't quite right.

Thank you so much for giving me all this time.

I gotta finish with a tiny anecdote. We talked about *Only the Valiant*, that was my worst film. One time, Ruth Gordon read an interview with me, where someone asked me about the films I liked the least, and damned if I didn't tell them! They wrote a whole interview about it.

She said "Gregory ... never, never, never talk about your failures. They were failures because nobody went to see them, and nobody went to see them because they were failures. So why should you remind people?"

A lesson that I took to heart. So *Only the Valiant* is the only one I'm gonna knock.

Cover photo by Jim Swallow (Tom Petty insert by John Siebenthaler; Merle Haggard insert by Bill DeYoung). Cover design by Pablo Guidi.

Made in the
USA
Columbia, SC